SACRED
MODERN

PAMELA G. SMART

SACRED
MODERN

Faith, Activism, and Aesthetics
in the Menil Collection

University of Texas Press ⤳ Austin

Copyright © 2010 by the University of Texas Press
All rights reserved
Printed in the United States of America
First edition, 2010

Requests for permission to reproduce material from this work should be sent to:
Permissions
University of Texas Press
P.O. Box 7819
Austin, TX 78713-7819
www.utexas.edu/utpress/about/bpermission.html

♾ The paper used in this book meets the minimum requirements of ANSI/NISO Z39.48-1992 (R1997) (Permanence of Paper).

LIBRARY OF CONGRESS CATALOGING-IN-PUBLICATION DATA

Smart, Pamela G.
    Sacred Modern: Faith, activism, and aesthetics in the Menil collection / Pamela G. Smart.
        p.   cm.
    Includes bibliographical references and index.
    ISBN 978-0-292-73758-7
    1. Menil Collection (Houston, Tex.)   2. Art and anthropology—Texas—Houston.
3. Art and religion—Texas—Houston.   4. Visual anthropology—Texas—Houston.
5. Menil, John de—Art collections.   6. Menil, John de—Religion.   7. Menil, Dominique de—Art collections.   8. Menil, Dominique de—Religion.   I. Title.
    N576.H68S63   2011
    306.4'7097641411—dc22
                                                                            2010026706

For Eli

Contents

ACKNOWLEDGMENTS ix

1 SEVEN LAYERS OF BLUE 1

2 FAITH 21

3 NEW WORLD 46

4 COLLECTING AS A VOCATION 67

5 "WITHOUT SERVITUDE TO THE PAST, NOR RECKLESSNESS" 87

6 TOWARD A MUSEUM 107

7 INTIMACIES OF POSSESSION 125

8 CARE 148

9 INSTITUTIONALIZATION OF AN AESTHETIC 175

10 FOR AESTHETICS 216

NOTES 227

REFERENCE LIST 251

INDEX 269

Acknowledgments

D ominique de Menil took a considerable leap of faith in granting me access to the facilities of the Menil Collection, consenting to a series of conversations, and inviting me to observe her in the practice of the art of installation. Given the extraordinary care that the Menil Collection has taken in crafting the manner in which it is presented and understood, I am acutely aware of the generosity that was extended to me in enabling me to proceed with my project. Bertrand Davezac was generous in his enthusiasm for my project from the outset, and I am indebted to him for his assistance in introducing me to Dominique de Menil and to the Menil Collection. I am grateful also for his rich insights into the museum and for his interpretations of the particularly French underpinnings of the Menil project. I am most grateful for his kindness toward me. I could not have pursued this research without Paul Winkler's willingness to accommodate my extended presence at the Collection and to entertain my questions. Walter Hopps offered characteristically fulsome insights during our telephone conversations. Other members of the old guard (only a few of whom remain at the Menil), Buck Bakke, Julie Bakke, Susan Davidson, Phil Heagy, Mary Kadish, Jesse Lopez, Liz Lunning, Carol Mancusi-Ungaro, Anthony Martinez, Steve McConathy, Bear Parnam, John Peters, William Steen, and Larry Young, generously tolerated my curiosity and fundamentally informed my sense of the texture of the Menil's relationship to the materiality of its objects, the practices of care that animate that relationship, and the contradictions that were inherent in their work.

Deborah Velders generously shared her office with me for what must have seemed, to her, an interminable period while I worked my way through the richly documented exhibitions files. Deborah's rigorous interpretation of her work and of the Collection has been, like her friendship, invaluable. In the early period of my research, the exhibitions files were the only documents available to me. The establishment of the Menil Archives in 2001, under the direction of Geraldine Aramanda, has afforded me access to a wealth of data along with most of the images reproduced in the pages that follow. She has been the source of deep institutional knowledge, and unfailing in her support and friendship. My long summer in the archive was augmented, and made all the more pleasurable, by extended conversations with Marta Galicki and Kristina Van Dyke, both of whom were, like the Menil project itself, embarked on the off-modern project of recuperating the past while pursuing a critical, future-oriented engagement with the present. So too was Josef Helfenstein as he worked to define the Menil legacy. I am grateful for the hospitality he extended to me that summer and for his ongoing support of my work. As I drew this manuscript to a close, I also had the benefit of the kind assistance of Laureen Schipsi, Amy Chien, and Brooke Stroud.

Stephen Fox could not have been more helpful throughout. His scholarship on the de Menils, his formidable knowledge of the architectural and institutional circumstances they worked within and upon, and his acuity as a reader of the manuscript have been invaluable to me. Bruce Grant, Laura Helper-Ferris, Ivan Karp, Corinne Kratz, and Peter Wissoker, along with an anonymous reader, have all given generous readings of the manuscript. The book is significantly better for their comments, and I am richer for their kindness and encouragement. I am indebted to Allison Faust, my editor at the University of Texas Press, for embracing this project with such enthusiasm and moving it through the process so expertly. Susanna Hill and Lynne Chapman were invaluable in their help with bringing this to a close.

My teacher and friend James Faubion has been a constant intellectual presence throughout this project, the source of excellent advice, extraordinary forbearance, and, over the years, many wonderful dinners. Also at Rice University, George Marcus crafted a milieu that was intellectually thrilling and that showed how anthropology could be made to engage meaningfully with contemporary phenomena. I am indebted to George and to Jim beyond measure. Julie Taylor, Patricia Seed, Michael Fischer, and Sharon Traweek were wonderful teachers and contributed to my thinking in significant ways. Carole Speranza has been relentlessly encouraging for years. My early mentor Peter Wilson laid the groundwork for this. I miss him dearly.

Beyond Rice, and beyond the Menil Collection, Amy Blakemore, Chip Briscoe, W. R. Dull, Cameron Armstrong, and Terrel James made Houston the most lovable of cities.

In Binghamton, Nancy Um and Robert Ku have been the best of colleagues and the loveliest of friends. They have allowed me to stretch the limits of reciprocity well beyond anything that might reasonably be hoped for, as has my constant, though distant, friend Margaret-Ellen Pipe. She has made this book possible in countless ways.

My parents, Jean and Graham Smart, have been incredibly patient during the course of this endeavor and generous with their love. I wish I hadn't kept them waiting so long.

Doug Holmes was willing to listen to endless readings of this material and has enriched my project, and all else, immeasurably. This book would not have been written without him. Eli Holmes, my darling son, knows more about this manuscript than seems entirely fair for a child, though I love that he is interested. I dedicate this book to him. I hope it makes him proud.

This project was generously supported by research grants from the University of Otago, New Zealand. A dean's leave from the Harpur College of Arts and Sciences at the State University of New York at Binghamton, as well as a Dr. Nuala McGann Drescher Fellowship, helped immensely in bringing the project to a close. Financial support for the reproduction of photographs was provided in the form of an Individual Development Award from the United University Professions of New York.

SACRED
MODERN

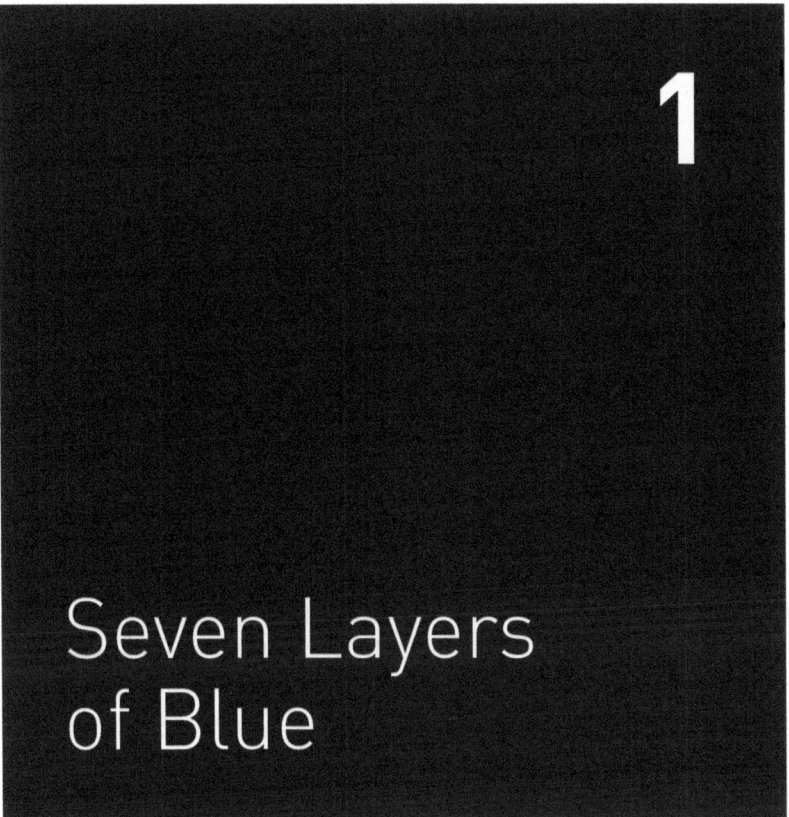

Seven Layers
of Blue

T he small windowless East Temporary Gallery was drenched in blue.
Before an empty expanse of wall sat Dominique de Menil, framed by
Paul Winkler, then the director of the Menil Collection, standing at
one shoulder and Susan Davidson, then associate curator, at the other. A pair
of preparators held Paul Klee's *Blick der Stille* (Gaze of Silence), adjusting it
slightly, half an inch this way and that, repeatedly measuring the distance from
the floor and the corners of the wall. Larry Young, the electrical technician,
prepared lights, spots and floods of various wattages assembled on the bed of
the hydraulic lift he deftly maneuvered amid artworks and people.

The walls, painted a thoroughly saturated, intense blue matte, had now
received their seventh coat, each a slightly different formulation of the same
deep marine. But the painters continued to struggle with streaking and marking. The kind of saturated matte that Dominique de Menil favored had become
difficult to achieve. Increasingly strict regulations governing the toxicity of

paint, Winkler explained to me, resulted in base formulas that do not give adequate stability to the pigment. They would proceed with the hanging and lighting of the show, then take the works down, leaving the fittings in place, in order to give the gallery one final coat to cover any marks made in the course of the installation.

The color was evidently Dominique de Menil's concern, as indeed were all of the details of the installation. Ready for her arrival, all the works had been brought into the single room in which the show was to be hung, where they were placed on pads leaning against the wall, ordered and spaced in accordance with an installation plan developed by the show's curator, Susan Davidson. Titled "A Piece of the Moon World: Paul Klee in Texas Collections," the exhibition of thirty-five works (five paintings and thirty works on paper) selected from among the sixty or so Klees collected in Texas, had initially been conceived by Dominique de Menil some years earlier and had now been revived and materialized by Davidson. Klee had only once before had a solo show in Texas, mounted some twenty years after his death by the Museum of Fine Arts, Houston (MFAH) in 1960. That show had been spearheaded by Dominique also, in the days when she and her late husband, John de Menil, were very actively engaged in the operations of that institution.

John and Dominique de Menil had begun collecting Klee's work in the mid-1950s, though the noted Houston philanthropist Ima Hogg had bought two paintings and a lithograph by Klee as early as the 1930s, works she subsequently gave to the MFAH. Twenty of the thirty-five works included in the show belong to the Menil Collection. Davidson describes the exhibition as "an investigation into how Klee was collected in Texas." Further, she writes, "the selection provides poignant and witty combinations and, it is hoped, establishes a cohesion which only an artist of Klee's intelligence and imagination could achieve."[1] This interest in the generative potential of juxtaposition notwithstanding, the works were arranged in preparation for hanging in the largely chronological schema that has become the art historical convention for structuring single-artist exhibitions.

With *Blick der Stille* positioned to Dominique de Menil's satisfaction, it was hung, and Larry proceeded to light it, instructed by Dominique de Menil on the type and intensity of bulb as well as on how the light should fall on its surface. The lighting of the work was transformative, enriching the image and imbuing the space with depth and intimacy. Attention was then turned

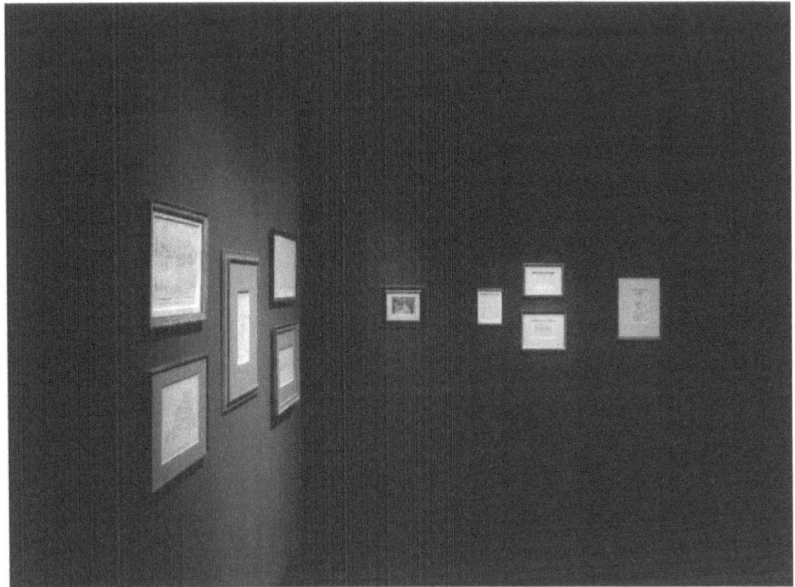

Installation of "A Piece of the Moon World: Paul Klee in Texas Collections," The Menil Collection, Houston, 1994. Photo: Paul Hester. The Menil Collection, Houston.

to the remaining works to be hung on that wall, their respective positions arrived at in relation to the central piece and the adjacent corner of the room. Dominique apparently did not feel bound to conform to the chronological ordering prescribed.

The frame of one of the works to be hung in an ensemble of pieces clustered together was, in the view of Dominique de Menil, inappropriate. The framer, William Steen, was called for and asked to select from among the many accumulated frames at his disposal some suitable alternatives. Attention meanwhile was turned to hanging another wall. Before long, Dominique invited me to accompany her to the framing studio, just as she had invited me to observe the process of installation that day; the year was 1994, at the outset of my research at the museum, then only seven years old but already among the most distinguished donor-built museums in the United States. She very quickly decided upon an elderly wooden frame from among the several that Steen had selected, one that she had bought some years before, Steen believed, and was able to confirm right away by consulting his records corresponding to the registration number on the frame. Individuated like the artworks in the collection, many of the frames carried with them distinctive provenances that the framer was quick to recount. He proceeded to offer suggestions as to suitable mats. Dominique seemed a little less assured at making this selection until she was shown a piece of silk with a peach blush that she recognized immediately as the right one—indeed, it seemed obvious to all three of us. So Steen went off to buy more silk, agreeing to have the piece reframed and ready for hanging early in the afternoon.

As the installation proceeded, the initial arrangement was substantially disrupted. Dominique worked intuitively, by trial and error, and this was as it should be, she explained to me, since installation was all about how things looked in relation to one another and to the space they inhabited. Her method of trial and error notwithstanding, she demonstrated an extraordinary command of what would work and how to achieve it. I had heard over the years of the extent to which she maintained an active interest in the minutiae of museum activities and had imagined this to be the interfering of a somewhat overbearing patron. I had clearly been wrong. Dominique was herself a curator and clearly a very skilled one.

In 1959, Dominique and John de Menil established a program in art and art history at the University of St. Thomas, a small Catholic liberal arts college in Houston, Texas. They provided resources for an art library, an art collection for teaching purposes, and an exhibitions budget; most crucially, they supported the hiring of Jermayne MacAgy as the director of the program—indeed, the project was formulated specifically for her. MacAgy was recognized for her extraordinary facility in curating and installing exhibitions and for her formidable energy. Dominique de Menil describes herself as having become a student of MacAgy's, learning from her not so much the organizational details of mounting an exhibition as how to conceive of it spatially and visually. When MacAgy died suddenly in 1964, Dominique took over her position at St. Thomas: "That was when I was led to my career, the installation of shows" (Browning 1983, 198).

Throughout the installation, Dominique repeatedly stressed the importance of lighting, framing, and the specific juxtaposition of works. The works would "sing" only under appropriate circumstances. The point of the show was not to make some art historical argument, nor was it to convey a certain reading of Klee's work, but rather, I was told, to "make the paintings look good"—paintings of which Dominique was particularly fond.

The hanging proceeded, one wall at a time, as key pieces were put in place and others were positioned around them. In this way, too, the lighting was done. Once everything had been hung and the lighting completed, all the works were taken down and removed from the gallery so that the final layer of blue could be applied.

Labels were not attached to the walls. As a matter of policy, the Menil Collection uses spare labeling, typically giving only the title, date, and the name of the artist. It is said that Walter Hopps, the inaugural director of the Collection who subsequently served as the museum's consulting curator until his death, in 2004, would have preferred that the museum eschew labeling altogether, offering instead informational pamphlets for those who particularly wanted such material and relieving others of the distraction. And this is the procedure that Dominique proposed for this show when, as the completing touches were being made to the installation, she discovered that the card on which the labels had been printed did not exactly match the final shade of the wall. The suggestion that the card simply be painted was dismissed, since doing so would not allow for the laser printing of the text. Dominique instructed the exhibitions department to produce handheld texts that could be picked up in the gallery. Each work would be identified only by a number printed on a transparent adhesive label. This swift decision, which entailed the writing and printing of a brochure at the eleventh hour, was presented not merely as a necessary solution to the problem of the mismatched card stock, but also as something that was, in any event, preferable. Labels were distracting, and anyway, as Dominique declared with implicit reference to installations MacAgy and later she herself had put together at the University of St. Thomas, this was how it used to be done.

SACRED MODERN

Formerly the private collection of Dominique and John de Menil, the Menil Collection has been open to the public since 1987 in the form of a purpose-built museum designed by Renzo Piano and located in Houston, Texas. Considered a very important collection of New York school paintings and among the most significant surrealist collections internationally, its holdings number something in excess of sixteen thousand objects, and include pieces from an array of cultural and historical traditions—antiquities, Byzantine icons, Oceanic and African art, colonial art from the New World, and the European moderns, including Henri Matisse, Pablo Picasso, Georges Braque, Fernand Léger, Joan Miró, and Paul Klee. From the outset, the Menil Collection was recognized by critics as a remarkable exemplar of a donor-built museum, in part because of the quality of the collection, but also because of its architectural form and exhibitionary effects. The notoriously acerbic art critic Robert Hughes wrote glowingly of the newly opened museum:

> Between them, Dominique de Menil, Hopps and the architect Renzo Piano have got it exactly right: this building, and the thinking behind it, comes as close to the musée imaginaire of one's hopes as one has any right to expect in America today. As a privately funded museum it is free to avoid the cliches of its bigger brethren. No boutiques, no blockbusters, no sense of competition with other museums. No sense of the sealed-off art bunker, either, with overlighted objects caught like startled animals in the glare of spotlights. Above all, none of the grandiosity and architectural euphuism of the American "signature" museum. (1987, 48)

In 1995, the Collection opened a freestanding gallery solely for the permanent exhibition of the work of Cy Twombly, and in 1997 construction was completed on a chapel built to house thirteenth-century frescoes that had been bought and restored by the Menil Foundation. While the Byzantine Fresco Chapel operates as a separate entity, with a board distinct from that of the Menil Foundation, which governs the Menil Collection, its location on the same campus as the museum gives the impression of continuity between them. Since November 1998, Richmond Hall has been open to the public; it houses three site-specific works by Dan Flavin, which were Dominique de Menil's final commissions before her death, at the close of 1997. Each of these initiatives furthers an intricate moral, political, religious, and aesthetic agenda that Dominique and John de Menil gave expression to early in their endeavors in their commissioning of the Rothko Chapel in 1964—the Philip Johnson–designed nondenominational chapel named for Mark Rothko, whose paintings they commissioned for it.[2] Together, occupying several neighborhood blocks, visually cool and lush with lawns stretching out from under the shade of live oaks in Houston's relentless heat, each of these buildings participates in the production of the seamless aesthetic that characterizes Menil projects.

Alfred Gell, in his essay "The Technology of Enchantment," addresses the way in which art objects can participate in "securing the acquiescence of individuals in the network of intentionalities in which they are enmeshed" (1992, 43). Here he draws attention to art's agency. As Nicholas Thomas points out, Gell's project responds to the failure of the anthropology of art "to dissociate itself from projects of aesthetic appreciation that do for art what theology does for religion" (Thomas 2001, 2). This failure can be read overwhelmingly in the body of anthropological literature on indigenous art that takes the tone of connoisseurship. The familiar critical response to this kind of connoisseurship has been the sociological project of demystification, in which art is revealed as being really a sign of something else—most notably of distinction and of power. While attention to the ways in which art is called upon to serve the interests of power has offered important insights, this approach overlooks both the specificity of art objects and, as Thomas and Gell recognize, their particular efficacy. It has entailed a flattening of anthropology's analysis both of art and of the institutional and social processes with which it is entwined. Current work in the anthropology of art has, as Fred Myers points out, begun to respond to this, to consider the particular work done by art objects "as indices of agency and effective in mediating social relationships" (Myers 2004, 204).

Gell's frustration with anthropology's projects of aesthetic appreciation has led him, however, to eschew attention to aesthetics altogether, as if to take it seriously would be to succumb to its mystifications. My own project shares Gell's insistence on recognizing art as an agent in social processes, but it sees the production of aesthetic domains and all the density of experience that they afford as being central to art's efficacy.[3] At the Menil Collection, the aesthetic that has been so attentively crafted is intended to produce an affecting engagement between persons and objects. This affect is not simply directed toward aesthetic appreciation, though the ability to discern aesthetic value is certainly considered a matter of considerable virtue at the Menil. Rather, the character of the engagement and its ongoing effects upon the viewer are central elements of Dominique de Menil's project of moral activism—of spiritual and political redemption in the pursuit of an alternative project of modernity.

In this light, the Menil Collection can be understood as the materialization of the collector's critique of much that has come to characterize the condition of modernity, broadly, what Max Weber terms its "disenchantments." Not only does the Collection operate as an expression of that critique, but it is also intended to serve as an agent of remediation. That their critique of modernity was pursued in concert with their progressivist enthusiasms, however, distinguishes their project from the kind of nostalgic antimodern tendencies that Georg Lukács described as "romantic anti-capitalism" (1962, 19). The de Menils, like Lukács's romantic anticapitalists, regretted the loss of the personal and immediate character of communally organized social relations. This was expressed, as we shall see, in their analyses of contemporary estrangement and alienation, which were informed by Jacques Maritain's "integral humanism" and Emmanuel Mounier's "personalism." They, like Maritain and Mounier, did not, however, long nostalgically for a return to a premodern society. Rather, they imagined modernism itself as a means of rehabilitating the modern.

Dominique's project, which she pursued in concert with her husband, John, until his untimely death in 1973, sought to recuperate sensibilities they attributed to the premodern while it was at the same time infused with an energetic commitment to the contemporary, to innovation and experimentation. Much of their activity was directed toward achieving some kind of rapprochement between these apparently divergent trajectories and, more fundamentally, between the sacred and the profane, the transcendental and the secular world.

The notion of art as a medium of redemption is of course not new, but recognition of that role, in itself, does not offer much analytically. As Weber points out, "Redemption attained a specific significance only where it expressed a systematic . . . 'image of the world' and represented a stand in the face of the world. For the meaning as well as the intended and actual psychological quality of redemption has depended upon such a world image and such a stand . . . 'From what' and 'for what' one wishes to be redeemed, and, let us not forget, 'could be' redeemed, depended on one's image of the world" (1958a, 280).

For John and Dominique, this redemptive imperative had its intellectual roots in the *renouveau catholique*, the French Catholic revivalism of the interwar years that, as Stephen Schloesser demonstrates, refused Pope Pius

IX's explicit definition of Catholicism as being "over and against modernity" (2005, 4)—a view that had been widely held among clergy and laity alike—and recast Catholic tradition as the avant-garde.[4]

While an eclipsing of the mythical and the sacred in favor of science, the exercise of reason over faith, and confidence in the idea of progress over tradition are widely considered to be defining features of the modern period, John and Dominique de Menil, like the French Catholic intellectuals in whose circles they began to move in Paris in the 1930s, sought to reclaim space for faith and for the mystical without turning their backs on science and innovation. In doing so, they resisted what Thomas Ferraro characterizes as the modern tendency to "quarantine the sacred" (1997, 9), to render it peripheral, irrelevant to the mainstream of social life, but they also positioned themselves against the Church hierarchy, insofar as it dedicated itself to convention, tradition, and an enduring past.

John and Dominique sought to recuperate spirituality while at the same time exercising a commitment to a social activism oriented to the future rather than the past, pursuing a critical project of modernity that would bind the sacred and the modern. Their specific challenge was to create conditions in which faith would have relevance, not as a regressive refusal of modernity, but as a source of meaning that was both resonant and absolute, that would sustain ongoing humanistic innovation across multiple fields and endeavors. This pursuit of a "sacred modern" resonates powerfully with Schloesser's compelling characterization of the "off-modern" commitments adopted by many French intellectuals in the interwar years: "anti-modernist in their adhesion to tradition and ultra-modernist in their embrace of time's forward motion" (2005, 14).[5] The challenge for the Menil Collection now is to institutionalize the spirit of a project that cannot be pinned down, that is "fundamentally an ambivalent synthesis of past and present," as Schloesser characterizes "off-modern" projects (2005, 13).

THE LEGACY

In 2005, I received a letter from Josef Helfenstein, the director of the Menil Collection since May 2004, asking me to participate, along with others, in the process of thinking about the future of the museum. This was followed by a call from the museum consultant who had been retained to assist the Menil Collection in producing a strategic plan. This is a task that she and other museum consultants commonly perform on behalf of museums seeking accreditation from the American Association of Museums (AAM): accreditation requires an institution to have a strategic plan that sets the terms against which performance can be evaluated. For Helfenstein, the imperative was not, however, to fulfill the requirements of the AAM, but to forge some kind of consensus that would guide the museum as it looked to the future under his direction. It was also therapeutic in its intent to draw back into the fold people who had come to feel estranged from the Menil over the years since Dominique de Menil's death.

I was flattered. In the early period of my fieldwork in and around the museum, my status had been, at best, awkward. Several things had occurred in the intervening years to effect a different kind of relationship with the Menil. First, my dissertation was completed, so I was no longer a graduate student. Moreover, my dissertation had, on the whole, resonated well with Menil personnel, and was now routinely given to new staff members as a means of familiarizing them with what the museum was about. It was also easier to conduct research at the museum: although I still needed to be escorted from one office to another, there was now an archive, where I had a desk to sit at and ready access to a wealth of documents; earlier, the archive had not been established, and Dominique de Menil, who had consented to my project only ambivalently, had elected not to make unpublished documents available to me. But the key difference was that Dominique was no longer alive. Nobody seemed to feel as intensely protective of the Menil and its representation as they had earlier, when every element of the institution seemed to resonate in deeply personalized terms. While people had been surprised that I had managed to gain consent to pursue my research, this hardly conferred immunity from suspicion and anxiety. It was rare for anyone to talk with me with anything less than guarded care. In part, this caution was an expression of loyalty to Dominique, but it was also an artifact of the economy of information that had prevailed at the Menil.

While people routinely explained to me the attenuated mode in which information circulated within the organization, and recounted instances in which other staff members had not been made privy to information that they believed was needed to effectively carry out their responsibilities, my informants also harbored beliefs about their own exclusion. They worried that they specifically had been cut out of the loop, that they had been deemed unworthy of inclusion. But, in fact, there was no model by which plans, policies, and decisions should properly be disseminated through the organization. So people routinely operated with fragmentary knowledge, and in any particular instance it could have been due to oversight or design. One never knew for sure, no matter how much one agonized over it.

Complicity in this ran deep. Information one had been made privy to tended to be held very closely—not, apparently, simply because it was a scarce resource to be expended judiciously, but because one had to show oneself worthy, by virtue of one's discretion, of this honor of bestowal. In the absence of departmental budgets, or formal hierarchies of authority, stature was reckoned in no small measure in terms of inclusion in the dissemination of information, opportunities to travel on behalf of the Collection, and inclusion as guests at functions associated with the Collection or the foundation. What was at stake was not so much one's relative position in a hierarchy, though that was not entirely insignificant of course, but the halo of insider status.

The pervasive anxiety about exclusion and position in an organization in which one's circumstances were contingent upon the patronage of the founder, was compounded by a closely guarded sense of privilege to be working for the Menil Collection, sharing in its reputation for excellence, and appreciating the pleasures and possibilities of working with such a fine collection and with a degree of flexibility unusual in other major museums. But there was something more, a sense that they were part of something special and important, and that afforded them domains of experience that could not be had elsewhere.

That I struggled with a lack of information was exacerbated by the character of my own positioning in relation to the Menil. I was studying an aesthetic project suffused with impeccable decorum and directed toward a rehabilitation of degraded sensibilities. I felt compelled, if I was to be taken seriously, to demonstrate that I too was in the possession of exquisitely calibrated sensibilities. But in truth, this motivation was not entirely pragmatic. I too wished to be considered worthy, but in the museum's thrall, it wasn't just recognition I sought: I wanted to *be* worthy.

While this was analytically less than ideal in some respects, it did have the virtue of emphatically posing the question of how to understand the Menil aesthetic, the techniques by which it was produced and operationalized, and the investment that many staff and members of its public clearly had in its perpetuation.

There have been a number of extremely rich analyses of museums over the past couple of decades. We have learned much about how museums as institutions have served projects of nation building, of identity formation, of surveillance and discipline, of distinction, of commoditization, of knowledge and power, and so on. While many art museums seem to have surprisingly little interest in aesthetics, their attention focused instead on art as history, there is nevertheless a striking absence of analytic attention to aesthetic registers of practice and experience.[6] Ivan Karp and Steven Lavine, in their groundbreaking collection *Exhibiting Cultures: The Poetics and Politics of Museums* (1991), attempted to redress this oversight by drawing attention to poetic aspects of museums. But what came to the fore, and was exemplified in Steven Greenblatt's contribution to the volume, his now famous essay "Resonance and Wonder," was a sense of poetics belonging to some longed-for past, a lost possibility, a sense that museums had foresworn poetics in favor of instruction or entertainment. In this sense, these academic responses came very close to Dominique de Menil's own position, her own understanding of the general state of art museums, though in her analysis we see a more reflexive elaboration of this sense of loss and one that seeks to lay out a resolutely future-oriented remedy, and one that is informed by moral rather than merely sentimental commitments.[7]

So when, a decade later, the museum consultant who had been retained by the Menil Collection asked me what I considered to be critical to the museum's mission, and whether new acquisitions to the collection ought to extend to work produced beyond the temporal purview of the founder, and what initiatives I thought the museum should pursue in the future, and so on, I was startled to find the extent to which my responses mirrored not the prospective orientation of Dominique de Menil but the nostalgic, preservationist turn of many of my interlocutors both within the museum and among its devotees beyond its employ. I knew my response to be wrongheaded in many ways, but there it was: sentimental, conservative, and absent critical reflection.

This was the provocation for what follows, which is, at its core, an exegesis on the problem of the Menil legacy and why it matters.

EXPERIMENTALISTS

Unlike the founders of the Barnes Collection or the Isabella Stewart Gardner Museum or many other once-private collections, Dominique de Menil did not leave a restrictive set of directives for the future of the art collection and its management. Noted for her energetic engagement with the administration of the museum at every level and a high degree of certitude as to how things should be done, one might have expected the collector to stipulate a regime of practice that would continue after her passing. Instead, to the chagrin of many of her closest collaborators, she focused throughout the last decade of her long life on ensuring the financial viability of the Menil Foundation, and thereby of the Collection, at the expense, many feared, of the spirit of her project. This anxiety concerning the endurance of the Menil Collection's distinctive character, recognized especially in the founder's preoccupation with establishing an engagement with artworks that is acutely aesthetic rather than pedagogical in character, eschewing the usual rendering of art as history, was not unfounded.

The task of creating a space where "poetry would be allowed to prevail over pedagogy"[8] and where visitors could engage with artworks not as an act of admiration, nor of the passive consumption of high culture, but as interlocutors actively participating with the artwork in what she called a process of "mutual interrogation" had been pursued through every detail of the museum's conceptualization and realization.[9] In the architecture of the museum, through the installation of exhibitions, and throughout the organizational structure and institutional practices of the museum, the Menil Collection has sought to produce an affecting engagement between the museum's visitors and its artworks that would create the conditions of possibility for a personal, resonant encounter that would rehabilitate our sensibilities—a resolutely aesthetic experience that would overcome the flattening and distancing of the experience of modernity.

Among museums, this flattening can be observed in the cumulative effects of conformity to institutionalized professional codes, submission to criteria of funding agencies, routinized procedures for showing art, and bureaucratized management practices. In short, conformity to "best practices," which are codified institutionally by such organizations as the American Association of Museums, diminishes the differentiation across the field of museums. In consequence, each museum comes to feel like every other one, and indeed like the experience of many other public institutions, in a general flattening of the experiential terrain. "Distancing," refers here, in relation to museums, to the kind of relationship between viewers and artworks that museums tend to foster; whether experts assimilating artworks to their knowledge of art history, or "outsiders" looking upon artworks in admiration or bafflement, there is a notable sense of estrangement between the museum's public and its artworks, absent the active "mutual interrogation" that Dominique de Menil sought to recuperate.

Failure to sustain all that had gone into the attentive crafting of what has come to be known as the "Menil aesthetic" would, it was feared, seriously compromise its affective promise. Or rather, since no one seriously worried that this would happen as long as the museum continued to be imbued with Dominique's charismatic authority, the real source of concern was that Dominique's own efforts to ensure the financial viability of the museum might be taken up by others after her passing in a manner that would surely entail the dissolution of the aesthetic that made the Menil Collection so distinctive. There continues to be, more than a decade after Dominique's death, considerable anxiety concerning the maintenance of past practices, articulated as an index of the extent to which the legacy of the founder and patron is being honored.

There is, however, another element of the legacy of Dominique de Menil that is perhaps not quite so evident within the cool elegance of the Menil Collection: a spirit of experimentalism, namely, an experimentalism oriented toward the future and not defined by nostalgia for the past. In refraining from imposing a set of covenants that would constrain the Menil Foundation, under whose aegis the Menil Collection is funded and managed, to preserve the museum as the fulfillment of her project, Dominique instead created a context for ongoing experimentation, entrusting the legatees to interpret her sacred modern vision anew. Indeed, this discomfort with the strictures of the past characterized the radical project of patronage that Dominique and John embarked upon together soon after they and their children left Europe in 1941, taking up residence in Houston.

When occupying forces entered France, John was in Romania on business for Schlumberger, the oil-services company founded by Dominique de Menil's father, Conrad Schlumberger, and uncle, Marcel Schlumberger, who together developed the oil detection technology, the electrical resistance log, that had been key to making drilling for oil profitable. In Romania, John contributed to the efforts of the resistance, disrupting oil shipments from Romania to the occupying forces, before making his way to the United States, where Schlumberger had begun to establish a base of operations unconstrained by the exigencies of occupation. His wife and their two small children, Christophe and Adelaide, fled to southern France, where she gave birth to their third child, Georges, before making their way via Spain to the New World, where they and John de Menil were reunited. In Houston, John initially served as the head of Schlumberger operations in South America, and was centrally involved in the restructuring of Schlumberger, whose headquarters had been in Paris. By 1969, when he retired, he was president of Schlumberger Overseas and chairman of the board of Schlumberger, Ltd.; he is widely held to have been a major force in the emergence of Schlumberger in the 1970s as one of the world's largest corporations.[10]

Some find it difficult to reconcile the politically leftist convictions of John and Dominique de Menil and their efforts on behalf of these convictions, with the source of the wealth that underwrote them. The oil industry is inevitably tainted with the international politics of oil extraction and commerce, but during the decades when John worked so assiduously to further Schlumberger's reach (from the 1940s to his retirement at the close of the 1960s), he was able to share his father-in-law's sincere belief that Schlumberger's ability to help others find oil was a natural extension of his political commitments. Georges de Menil, who is an economist, characterized his father's view this way: "You were bringing to human frontiers technology that helped people. . . . During the war it contributed something crucial to the war effort. After the war, it contributed something crucial to the growth of the world economy" (quoted in Auletta 1983a, 69). The stories that are recounted of Schlumberger and the wealth it generated are characteristic of the narratives that tend to be told of first-generation oil-industry ventures. They tell of the spirit and character of its founders, of their commitment to invention and discovery, and, by omission, distance themselves from the operations of the industry itself. Schlumberger is distinctive in this regard, perhaps, only insofar as its protagonists, at least through the second and third generations, self-consciously sought to do things differently, to sustain a pioneering spirit of experimentation and innovation that was not vested in the standard hierarchies of authority and reward (Auletta 1983a, 1983b; Bowker 1994).

There is no doubt that John's noted acumen in the oil industry and, of course, the couple's Frenchness and their glamour lent weight to their projects among Houston society, who might otherwise have dismissed them as mere mavericks.

A COUNTERMODEL

As I have observed, much of the critical scholarship on museums over the past decade or two has focused on the various ways in which the interests of power and distinction are served by these "high" cultural forms. This kind of approach has meant to demystify museums, to reveal the otherwise veiled or simply unrecognized dimensions of their privilege and symbolic authority, which are effaced in the familiar rhetorics of cultural enrichment, aesthetic autonomy, and taste. Much of this interpretive labor has been directed toward the particular narratives that have been contrived within the exhibitionary spaces of the museum and, more broadly, toward museums as sites of exclusion or, perhaps, as public institutions working to forge a citizenry appropriately deferential to civic authority.

This form of analytical engagement with museums, characterized by what Paul Ricoeur (1970) referred to as a hermeneutics of suspicion, has done much to alert us to how deeply these institutions and the representational practices they pursue are implicated in the maintenance of extant hierarchies of value in relation both to objects and to persons. The hermeneuticist of suspicion, however, convinced that "high" cultural domains, and the elites whose aspirations and resources underwrite them, fundamentally serve bourgeois class interests, is inclined, indeed obliged, to regard actors' own characterizations of their intentions as merely justifications or rationalizations for the exercise of what are, in reality, very different commitments. As James Faubion has observed, with reference to an elite interlocutor's explanation of the obligation of "service" that is the ethical rationale for his Portuguese nobility: "The hermeneuticist of suspicion is likely—and has every right—to read such a justification of standing as a rationalization or méprisement, a witting or unwitting apologia for privilege and advantage alike. The hermeneuticist of suspicion is, however, free and even compelled to read *any* ethical self-justification in precisely the same terms, thus offering an interpretation that may well be true (or not), but of no sociologically discriminatory power" (Faubion n.d., 188; italics added).

Faubion alerts us to the key issue: for all that the hermeneutics of suspicion has done to draw our attention to the operation of power in hitherto thoroughly mystified domains, its great shortcoming lies in its inability to observe meaningful differences among the many and varied projects taken up by elites and their institutional proxies, since they are all rendered equally and seamlessly self-serving. In the case of museums, analyses of particular institutions have foregrounded processes and representations that maintain existing power relations and further the interests of domination, but at the expense of observing that museums might also be understood as sites of creativity and critical experimentation.

This is far from the only account that recognizes the critical, future-oriented experimentation with which many museums are engaged. Some have addressed efforts to change the narrative content of exhibitions (Sherman 2007), others focus on attempts to effect more collaborative relationships with local communities (Clifford 1997), while yet others have acknowledged the propensity for some museums to host within their walls performative interventions by artists critical of the museum's own collecting and curatorial practices or of the complicity of the museum in compromising political economies (Welchman 2006). There are more comprehensive studies that have focused on museums that are centrally directed toward a reconsideration of the very form and function of the museum itself. Sharon MacDonald's account (2002) of the Science Museum, London, is a close-grained study of the conceptualization and mounting of a "permanent" exhibition in the context of a fundamental reorientation of the museum that was meant, among other things, to establish it as a vital presence in contemporary public culture. Others have addressed institutional and representational experimentation at museums that have more profoundly called into question the character of the museum as a social form and its potential as an agent in contemporary politics. Steven Dubin's investigation (2006) of the transformation of museums in postapartheid South Africa, Kylie Message's attention (2007) to the energetically self-reflexive character of many contemporary museums, and Andrea Witcomb's analysis (2003) of a range of self-consciously future-oriented institutions, along with the compendium of studies brought together in Ivan Karp, Corinne Kratz, Lynn Szwaja, and Tomás Ybarra-Fausto's collected volume (2006), together evidence the vitality of the kind of careful, empirically informed analysis of museums that had been all but eclipsed under the sway of the hermeneutics of suspicion. These kinds of studies are marked by their attention to the complex and often crosscutting exigencies in which museums are enmeshed, both internally and in relation to external imperatives, in contrast to what has been a tendency to render them as monolithic both in intent and in effect. They are also distinctive in their focus on museums not solely as representational economies but as institutions populated by people who are themselves engaged in critical analysis of their own practices, procedures, and institutional trajectories.

Among these examples, the museums under scrutiny range in their purviews from science and technology to ethnography and history. That there has been little work of this sort on art museums might seem odd, given that critical experimentation has hardly been absent in their precincts. And, moreover, in the case of contemporary art museums, their orientation to the future is inevitably a matter of ongoing critical reflection. The pervasive perception of art museums as being closely identified with elite interests, however, is such that anything short of profound skepticism on the part of analysts appears simply as bad politics. The recently published collection of essays (Cuno 2003) by current and former directors of a number of major art museums (Glenn Lowry, Museum of Modern Art; Neil MacGregor, British Museum; Philippe de Montebello, Metropolitan Museum of Art; John Walsh, Jr., J. Paul Getty Museum; and James Wood, Art Institute of Chicago) seems only to intensify this suspicion. While not all of its contributors equally subscribe to this view, the volume conveys a fundamental commitment to the idea of the art museum as a place of respite that should be preserved in all its patrician dignity.

Given this deep conservatism that is attributed to art museums, and that some museums evidently claim for themselves, along with the recent oppositional dominance of a hermeneutics of suspicion, an ethnographic analysis such as that offered here, which is concerned with understanding the museum from the perspectives of its founders, personnel, and those members of the public to which the museum presents itself, may seem disconcertingly sympathetic, precisely because it takes seriously the aspirations and investments of its protagonists on their own terms. And this effect is intensified by the fact that the de Menils' projects were inseparable from a modern tradition of critical experimentation, with which they were thoroughly preoccupied. I recount their efforts to formulate and redefine their projects in relation to a series of critical activist agendas, including the civil rights movement in Houston, Texas, and the ecumenical commitments of Vatican II, not because I wish to show them in a flattering light, but because examination of their projects can illuminate a modality of modernity that otherwise is obscured. In other words, the context in which this ethnography unfolds is itself a critical field in which cultural authority is being contested. That said, the de Menils and their interlocutors were, as I will show, never reticent about asserting their convictions in a manner that was itself fully imbued with a cultural authority that they scrupulously cultivated.[11]

In characterizing the Menil Collection and its protagonists as engaged in a complex critical project, I do so not out of admiration, naïve about the problematic political economy that underwrites high cultural forms, but rather in order to be able to make analytic distinctions that a hermeneutics of suspicion cannot make, to show that the authority of the museum can be mobilized in the service of diverse interests, seeking to foster moral and political sensibilities in their publics that cannot properly be reduced to the subjection of audiences to dominant hierarchies of value and social propriety.

In what follows, I offer an account of the Menil Collection that regards the museum as a countermodel to the contemporary orthodoxies of museums as institutions. It has explicitly refused much that has come to characterize the professional and representational practices of contemporary museums. It doesn't, for example, direct its operations toward increasing its audience, and its exhibitions do not purport either to educate or to entertain. Yet, at the same time, perhaps the most significant project with which museums have been engaged throughout their modern history, the definition and elaboration of contemporary relationships between subjects and objects, is self-consciously at the forefront of the Menil Collection's program. In this sense, the Menil should not be seen as an eccentric case that is therefore of limited analytic value, but rather as an exemplar of imperatives that are pervasive, but elsewhere often misidentified.

While the literature on private (as opposed to institutional) collecting overwhelmingly focuses on the collection as an agent in the collector's practices of self-formation, there has been little or no attention paid to the ways in which a formerly private collection opened to the public might, intentionally or not, become engaged in the constitution of other selves—of those who care for the collection and those who come to constitute its public. At the Menil Collection, this has always been a central preoccupation that has informed every aspect of the museum.

Attention to this crafting of relations between artworks, those who are entrusted with their care, and their publics has, in turn, provoked an analysis that recognizes the critical commitments that the Menil Collection is called upon to advance and the manner in which they are pursued across the presentational, operational, and performative domains that constitute the museum. The elegance and refinement that the Menil Collection exudes belie its radical character, which is underpinned by imperatives that in important ways run counter to dominant interests, albeit pursued in a manner that reinvests privileged high cultural forms with suasive force.

The defining register in which the museum pursues its critical project is aesthetic, the very modality that we have become inclined to associate with a defense of the status quo. It is the character of this aesthetic, the processes by which it has been created and materialized, the sensibilities that it is meant to generate, and the way it operates as an agent in broader domains of social and political life that are the central concerns of this ethnographic study. My analysis examines the ways in which throughout the architecture, exhibitions, and managerial structure—and, indeed, in all aspects of its operation—"the Menil aesthetic," as it has come to be known, has been actively crafted.

What follows then, is not an ethnography of the Menil Collection as a place or of Dominique de Menil as a collector, but of an aesthetic—specifically, of the processes by which an aesthetic is created, is materialized, and participates in broader domains of practice.

2

Faith

I n her address at the dedication of the Rothko Chapel in February 1971, Dominique recalled two events whose influence had been decisive for her and her husband.

In January 1936 Father Congar delivered eight lectures on ecumenicism which marked the beginning of his ecumenical career. I had the privilege to hear him and it marked me for life.

In the summer of 1952 we visited with Father Couturier, another Domini-can, the church where Léger and Matisse, two towering artists of their time, had contributed their greatest work. We visited also the site where Le Corbusier was going to build his famous Chapel at Ronchamp. We saw what a master can do for a religious building when he is given a free hand. He can exalt and uplift as no one else.

The influence of those events was lasting. If we played a part in the birth of this chapel, which indeed we did, it stems from the orientation we received those early days, through those two men.

But this chapel has deeper roots than our own involvement. . . . It is rooted in the growing hope that communities who worship God should find in their common aspiration the possibility to dialogue with one another in a spirit of respect and love. This hope, this nostalgia, explains the Chapel, as it explains many spontaneous initiatives of brotherhood coming up all over the world today among religious people.

The rest is good will and circumstances. (Menil 1971)

Though Dominique de Menil described her aspiration for genuine respect and dialogue among people of all faiths as nostalgic, her project was clearly not fed by the kind of nostalgia that sustained the activities of Catholic traditionalists for whom Catholicism stood, by definition, "over and against modernity" (Schloesser 2005, 4). Pius IX's *Syllabus of Errors* (1864) was a condemnation of modernity that explicitly defined the timeless, eternal values of Catholicism in opposition to modern temporality, rationalism, liberalism, and the doctrine of religious toleration. And later, Pius X, repositioning the papacy in the wake of Leo XIII's more conciliatory approach in the intervening years, required in 1910 that all priests having pastoral charge sign the "Oath Against Modernism" (Schloesser 2005, 56).[1] French Catholics, marginalized by republicanism, increasingly looked to the past, to an imagined medievalism, for the conditions in which faith might flourish.

Both Marie-Alain Couturier and Yves Congar, in their efforts to reconcile the Church with contemporary society, saw the future of the Church in its ability to reorient itself to contemporary conditions rather than in the attempt to reclaim some past historical moment. Couturier's work was to focus primarily on freeing liturgical art from the confines of academicism, reinvigorating its affective force through the use of contemporary artistic forms. Congar, engaged with questions of theology and ecclesiology, argued for a historicized theology that would afford "greater attention to the experiencing subject, whose needs and concerns shift with the contours of history itself" (Nichols 1990, 250). Dominique and John de Menil found the projects of both men compelling and shared their conviction that insofar as faith had come to seem irrelevant to modern life, it was in large measure because of the Church's insistent refusal to engage with present circumstances. While Dominique and Congar both deeply felt a nostalgic longing for the reunification of the Church, East and West, they have sought it not through a return to orthodoxy but through a set of contemporary reconfigurations.[2] The de Menils' enthusiastic support of John XXIII was perhaps the most direct expression of their commitment to a rapprochement between the Church and contemporary life, but it can be observed throughout the fabric of their endeavors.

The respective preoccupations of Couturier and Congar were developed within the context of the *renouveau catholique*, a Catholic revivalism that emerged in the interwar years in opposition to both the Gallican Church, fiercely nationalist and antirepublican, and the peripheral, though vital, Ultramontanist Catholicism, which "both imagined itself and was imagined by others as the antithesis of the dominant 'modern' cultural and intellectual ideologies: Liberalism in politics, science (i.e., positivism) and historicism in thought, Realism and Naturalism in art" (Schloesser 2005, 5).[3] But the conditions that supported the considerable reinvigoration of Catholicism in France and had a profound effect on a generation of French intellectuals in the years following the carnage of the First World War lay beyond doctrinal struggles in a distinctively modern search for meaning.

"Two revisionist contexts," Schloesser persuasively argues, provided the necessary opening for the *renouveau catholique*:

> First, seeing the postwar epoch as a time of bereavement in need of creative synthesis of both tradition and present; and second, rethinking the "modern" as ambivalently *off-modern* in its nostalgic futurism. Catholic revivalism became a salient influence in postwar France because it was an act of memorialization, an attempt to restore meaning and self-identity to a traumatized culture. Its actors accomplished this through a creative recasting of traditional Catholic tropes as the ultimate expression of postwar modernity. They self-consciously considered themselves to be off-modern: anti-modernist in their adhesion to tradition and ultra-modernist in their embrace of time's forward motion. (Schloesser 2005, 14)[4]

This temporal ambivalence, as we will see, took root in Dominique and John de Menil's sensibilities, and was expressed throughout their projects.

CULTURAL CATHOLICISM

John and Dominique's friends Raïssa and Jacques Maritain were central to this effort to come to terms with the contemporary.[5] They, like many of their circle, returned to the Church or converted to it, to a faith that offered a meaningful alternative to the rationalism of the Enlightenment, which had ceased to seem plausible in the devastation of the war. Indeed, in the immediate aftermath of the war, "Maritain was the voice of anti-modernity. He spoke of five centuries of Western civilization since the Renaissance as if they were in error, and he left no doubt that he was a defender of a past order of civilization. Yet, by 1930 . . . Maritain began to exhort fellow Catholics to prepare the way for a new civilization" (Amato 1975, 55).[6] Maritain's perspective underwent a critical temporal shift from a longing for the integralism of medieval times to a future-oriented project that expressed decidedly off-modern convictions. The doctrinal problem that the Maritains, along with many other French intellectuals, faced was to reconcile the traditional Church, committed as it was to the absolutism of eternal truths, with the constantly changing character of the contemporary.[7]

Schloesser's compelling analysis shows how the *renouveau catholique* had come to position Catholic intellectual and cultural discourse at the very center of elite French life through the articulation of a cultural Catholicism that sustained the emergence of a Catholic avant-garde in art, music, and literature.[8] Instead of the perception of religion and culture as two irrevocably opposed forces, Catholic revivalists, Schloesser argues, reconceptualized both the "eternal" and the "modern," drawing, significantly, on "three traditional Catholic ideas: hylomorphism, sacramentalism, and transubstantiation" (2005, 6).[9] Each of these tropes exemplifies "a vision of the world as a dialectical composite of two interpenetrating planes of reality: seen and unseen, created and uncreated, natural and supernatural. As such, they offer an alternative way of imagining relationships. Two entities—God and world, divinity and reality, even . . . Catholicism and culture—need not be seen as extended bodies in competition with one another. . . . Dialectical images suggest other possible modes of interrelating: one thing can point to, participate in, bear within, carry, actualize, perfect, translate, transpose, transform—or even become—something else" (6–7).

Key here, then, were questions of what constitutes reality and how it might be accessed: "Was the truly real 'natural' or was it 'eternal'? Changing or unchanging? Of nature or through grace? Rational or revealed?" (Schloesser 2005, 56). The challenge for those seeking to reconcile the Church with contemporary culture was, as Schloesser observes, to establish a dialectical relationship between the naturalism and positivism of cultural realism and the eternalists' notion of unchanging reality residing behind mutable forms. The Maritains worked to elaborate a theologically defensible argument on behalf of this off-modern rapprochement through a creative reworking of Thomas Aquinas, arguing, in short, that contemporary reality, and specifically modern art, far from standing irreconcilably in opposition to eternalism, might serve as a vehicle by which the ineffable could be reached:

> The modern world had excluded religious belief; Catholicism had excluded the modern world. However, by recovering and recasting its dialectical tradition—in other words, through using the Church's own heritage—Catholic revivalists could re-imagine the relationship between religion and culture. Catholicism and "modern civilization"—eternal and avant-garde, grace and grotesque, mystical and dissonant—could now be seen in categories other than simple competition: form actualizing matter, grace perfecting nature, substance underlying surface. (Schloesser 2005, 7)

While Maritain framed his ongoing elaboration of this dialectic throughout his career in Thomist terms, his elevation of modern art, poetry, and aesthetic experience over positivist science and naturalism in art, as privileged means by which reality might be accessed, was informed by his early intellectual mentor, Henri Bergson.[10] "Bergson's fundamental notion of 'intuition' providing unfiltered access to reality would remain a constant in the Maritains' thought for the next half century" (Schloesser 2005, 64), notwithstanding the fact that Maritain was to become a trenchant critic of Bergson.[11] And, as we will see, this privileging of intuition, which takes on a moral inflection insofar as the exercise of intuition is also conceived as an exercise of freedom—a refusal to accept mere appearances—was particularly evident in the rhetoric and the practice of Dominique de Menil.

In her foreword to *Sacred Art*, a collection of excerpts from the writings

of Marie-Alain Couturier, selected by Dominique de Menil and Pie Duployé, archivist of the de Menil–sponsored Couturier Archive, Dominique
wrote: "The texts we present here constitute, as it were, a rigorous, coherent
discourse. But analytical reasoning in no way belies the spark of immediate
perception. Art, he tells us, when it is approached through the intuition
of the senses, perpetuates and makes the spirit present. Thus it joins truth
to itself" (Menil 1989a, 9). I recount this comment in part because it gives
voice to Couturier's, and Dominique's, understanding of the significance of
intuition in the apprehension of art and, thereby, of the ineffable. We will see
presently an elaboration of the entailments of this view for Couturier within
the pages of the Catholic journal *L'Art Sacré*, which he coedited with Père
Pie-Raymond Régamey from 1937 to 1954, except during his exile in North
America during the war, as well as in the chapel projects he was instrumental
in commissioning. More significantly for our purposes, we will see them pursued in the terms of apprehension that Dominique sought to conjure for art
across a variety of institutional settings. But what is particularly notable in this
passage is an articulation of what was, in fact, Dominique and John de Menil's
own method of disciplined experimentalism—not the experimentation of
positivist science, but a "rigorous, coherent" analysis that was, at its core, an
act of faith, informed by intuition and directed toward the restoration of the
spirit. It was an inevitably unstable off-modern effort to restore meaning and
sensibility and, thereby, to make faith plausible in contemporary life.

SOCIAL THEORY

Central to this endeavor was their perception of modernity, which was shared
by many young European middle-class intellectuals who, brought up in the
aftermath of the First World War, were destined to experience the cultural
disillusion of the 1920s, the social and political disintegration of the 1930s,
the devastation of the Second World War, and the threat of further world
war in the late 1940s. In the face of what one observer has characterized as
"the advancing avalanche of contemporary calamity not for France alone
but for all of Europe during the 1930s" (Salomone 1975, xvi), they shared the
conviction that the world was in absolute crisis, a crisis that had been centuries in the making, and that a reordering of the world could not be achieved

without the integration of the spirit throughout all domains of life. This was the conviction expressed in Maritain's "integral humanism" and in the "personalism" formulated by Emmanuel Mounier, the founding editor of the Catholic journal *Esprit*, who would become a central figure in the *renouveau catholique* and for whom Maritain had been a key early mentor.[12]

Notwithstanding differences between them and their eventual parting of company, Maritain and Mounier occupied considerable common ground in religious, philosophical, and political spheres. Maritain, like Mounier, articulated his philosophy in opposition to the two competing ideologies of individualism and collectivism. Both men elaborated a social theory in which the person, rather than society, the state, or a systematic ideology, was understood as the foundation of political philosophy; as opposed to the atomistic "individual," the "person" implies intersubjectivity, community. And similarly, the personal relationships constituting "community" are distinguished from the crushing rationalism and bureaucratization of "society." Individualism was understood to be the destructive essence of modern secular culture, rendering it vulnerable equally to bourgeois complacency and to various forms of collectivism, among them fascism and communism; as Amato puts it: "Having only his individual subjectivity and his own particular traditions for his defense, modern man was unable to resist the emerging collectivizing forces of money, society, state and ideology" (1975, 63).

Thus, for Maritain and for Mounier, individualism and collectivism were two sides of the same coin. But it is not only the atomism of bourgeois individualism but also its relentless antagonism toward recognition of the spirit that so impoverishes it, according to this view.

Committed to the primacy of the person as a free and spiritual being, Personalism denies all attempts to reduce the human person to any immanent order of society, politics, and history. Committed to the person as an embodied and communal being, Personalism equally denies all doctrines that deny man's temporality and his historicity in the name of a transcendent order. In its metaphysical impulse, Personalism thus aspires to be a new realism by recognizing equally man's spiritual and material nature. In its spiritual inspiration, Personalism affirms that man's freedom is fundamental, but that it is realized only amidst other men in their social and historical conditions. In its ethical and political aspirations, Personalism seeks to affirm the existing unities between thought and action, person and community, community and historical situation. (Amato 1975, 13)

Commentators have quite rightly observed that the integral humanism and personalism of Maritain and Mounier, rather than offering an empirically rigorous analysis of the contemporary crisis that could sustain a new historical order, are most compelling as expressions of the defining anxieties and aspirations of their milieu. Indeed, increasingly when such totalizing worldviews came to seem even to their authors in the wake of the Second World War to be entirely inadequate to the political complexities that prevailed, Maritain's and Mounier's theoretical formulations "passed more and more from being total philosophies of man and society, and more became interior dispositions toward modern man and his conditions" (Amato 1975, 162). Indeed, writing in defense of personalism in 1948, Mounier observed that its critics made the error of conceiving of it as an overarching system, "whereas personalism is perspective, method, exigency" (Mounier 1951, 193). And fundamental to this approach was the notion that it is not sufficient to merely reinterpret the world: one must change it by binding understanding to action.

This imperative to link contemplation to action was the theme of the first Rothko Chapel colloquium, "Traditional Modes of Contemplation and Action," held July 22–30, 1973. Convened some two years after the dedication of the nondenominational chapel, the colloquium was the first of what were to be many such ecumenical events that John and Dominique planned for its future. Arrangements for the nineteen religious scholars—described as being from "the Far East, the Middle East, Africa, Europe, and North America, including Hindus, Buddhists, Muslims, Jews, Christians, an interpreter of Native American Indian religion, and a representative of African traditional religions"—were being finalized when, just three weeks before their arrival, John de Menil died.[13] Indexing the seriousness of their commitment to this, Dominique was adamant that the colloquium should proceed as scheduled, for this had very much been her husband's project too, despite his worsening health as the event took form. The colloquium addressed concerns that were dear to them both, and it would proceed as a tribute to John.

This event, like the Rothko Chapel itself, can also be seen as a tribute to the Second Vatican Council and its sponsor, Pope John XXIII. The de Menils' deep concordance with Vatican II was evident in Dominique's significant contributions, from 1981 through 2001, via the Menil Foundation, to the Instituto per le Scienze Religiose of Bologna, whose founding mission was to ensure that the legacy of John XXIII would be properly appreciated and disseminated.[14] With the foundation's assistance, the institute, under the directorship of Giuseppe Alberigo, established a papal archive and research facility and has produced a significant body of scholarship, including the multivolume *History of Vatican II* (Alberigo and Komonchak 1995–2006). The Rothko Chapel embodies the ecumenicism so powerfully endorsed by Vatican II, though its position on ecumenicism is more far-reaching than that of most other ecumenical Catholic formulations: not merely nonde-nominational, advocating the unification of Christian churches, but pursuing instead a more universalizing interfaith approach to matters of spirituality. The charter of the Rothko Chapel, which operates under the governance of the freestanding Rothko Chapel Foundation in order to ensure that it can pursue its mission robustly, without the pressure of competing claims upon Menil Foundation resources, identifies its program thus: "to provide a place of worship, a place of meditation and prayer for people to gather and explore spiritual bonds common to all, to discuss human problems of worldwide interest, and also share a spiritual experience, each loyal to his belief, each respectful of the beliefs of others" (Barnes 1989, 108). The Rothko Chapel became, as Susan Barnes reports, "the world's first broadly ecumenical center, a holy place open to all religions and belonging to none" (108).

Indeed, in this commitment to pluralism and in the projects of social justice for which the Rothko Chapel Foundation serves as an institutional hearth, Dominique and John pursued through the chapel a project of spiritual and political activism that is fundamentally informed by sensibilities shaped by the *renouveau catholique*, most particularly by Maritain's integral humanism and Mounier's personalism, and by the contentious work of two Dominicans, Yves Congar's ecumenicism, and Marie-Alain Couturier's efforts to renew sacred art.[15] Each of these figures was engaged in a project of the "desecularization of the world," each grappling in an off-modern manner with the intractable dissonance between Church tradition and the possibilities of the new, drawing on modernity itself to try "to recover the wondrous—the 'mystical'—that it had once eclipsed" (Schloesser 2005, 16–17).

FOSTERING FAITH

It was Couturier's view, in fact, that what he observed as the contemporary malaise of the spirit was not solely the result of the disenchantments of modernity and its attendant flattening of experience, but was occasioned also by the experiential poverty of Catholic contemplation and worship, specifically by the architecture of churches and the sacred art within them. In *L'Art Sacré*, Couturier characterized the problem in this way:

> It was an unbroken tradition: century after century it was to the foremost masters of Western art, diverse and revolutionary as they might be, that popes and bishops and abbots entrusted the greatest monuments of Christendom, at times in defiance of all opposition. From Cimabue and Giotto to Piero, from Masaccio to Michelangelo and Raphael, from Tintoretto and Rubens to Tiepolo, that tradition of courage and mutual confidence was kept alive. The most powerful currents of Western art had never been diverted from the Church.
>
> With the nineteenth century all this began to change. One after another the great men were bypassed in favor of secondary talents, then of third-raters, then of quacks, then of hucksters. Thereafter the biggest monuments were also the worst (Lourdes, Fourvière, Lisieux, etc.). Within the broad range of the work done for the *Chantiers du cardinal* one hundred and twenty churches could be built around Paris without even consulting a single one of the great French architects. (Couturier 1989, 34)[16]

The Church's adherence to styles in which "there no longer is any sap" or "any seed of genuine rebirth" compromised the vitality of the Church (Couturier 1989, 52). Or, more emphatically, Couturier is reported to have told his Dominican superiors: "Our church art is in complete decay. . . . It is dead, dusty, academic—imitations of imitations . . . with no power to speak to modern man. Outside the Church the great modern masters have walked—Manet, Cézanne, Renoir, Van Gogh, Matisse, Picasso, Braque. The Church has not reached out, as once it would have, to bring them in. And here we have men who speak directly to the people with the same simple power of the great artists of the Middle Ages. . . . These moderns are greater than the sensual men of the Renaissance" (*Time* 1949).

Pie-Raymond Régamey, coeditor (with Couturier) of *L'Art Sacré*, makes clear the significance of the context of worship in sustaining a robust congregation: "Our faith needs to be aroused, supported, and guided; it must be given a favorable atmosphere" (Régamey 1963, 18). The architectural and decorative character of churches is significant not only for the labor they might perform in creating an environment conducive to faith; church art and architecture, in the view of Couturier, and of his fellow Dominicans who formed the nucleus of the sacred art movement, are themselves distinctively resonant instruments of faith, offering privileged access to the ineffable—or at least that would be so were they not so seriously compromised by a bloodless, derivative academicism. "The fact is," Couturier wrote, "that aside from exceedingly rare exceptions, nothing good comes out of the Academy. Probably the source itself is bad and the Academy should be closed. . . . What we really ought to save for the heart and the imagination is non-knowing, ingenuousness, the candor of modesty. . . . What is wrong with the Academy is that it does away with all mystery, takes precautions against the miraculous—or, alas, organizes it (Couturier 1989, 124).

The elaboration of this understanding of sacred art, formulated within the context of the *renouveau catholique* and drawing substantially on the philosophical formulations of Maritain, was the central preoccupation of *L'Art Sacré*, a monthly publication directed primarily to a readership of clergy in the hope that they might be persuaded to participate in the rehabilitation of church art. *L'Art Sacré* gave voice to a sustained critique of academicism and of the Church's endorsement of the academic ideal, codified by the Council of Trent (1545–1563), which signaled the decadence of sacred art and the defeat of the poetic (Rubin 1961, 65–68). William Rubin argues that this academic style became increasingly "sterile" in the wake of the French Revolution and the subsequent crystallization of bourgeois values and religious taste. Motivated by a desire for legitimacy and a sense of continuity with the aristocracy it had replaced, the upper middle class not only embraced academicism but also put it in the service of sentimentality and pietism that brought about the absolute nadir of sacred art (Rubin 1961, 8).

What emerges here is a sense of profound compromise, specifically of sacred art, but more fundamentally of the spirit. It was Couturier's project, through *L'Art Sacré*, to "restore the sensitivity of the eye," since in the rehabilitation of sensibilities, the "reform of ideas" is not sufficient: "In matters of

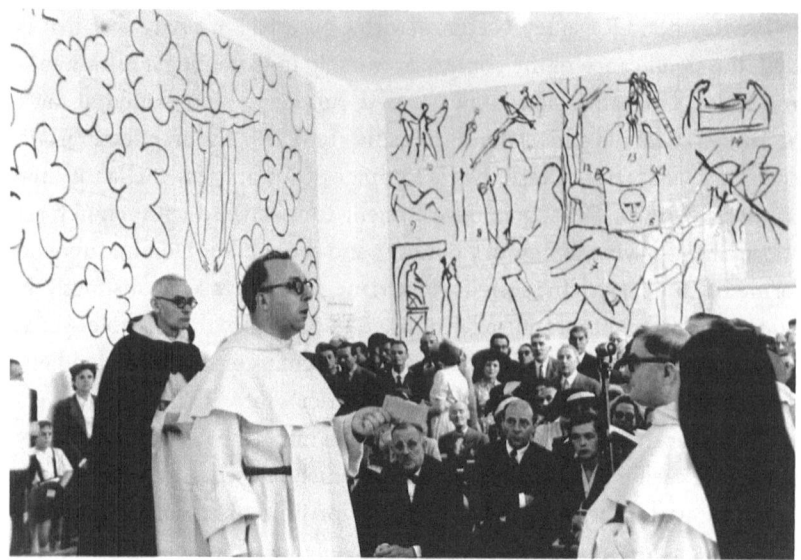

Father Couturier (far left) at the consecration of La Chapelle du Rosaire at Vence, France, June 25, 1951. Photo: Henri Cartier-Bresson. Courtesy Menil Archives, the Menil Collection, Houston.

art one judges not by what one thinks but by what one feels. In other words, by what one is" (Couturier 1989, 14).

This not only underscores his insistence on, let us say, a poetic experience of art, but also draws attention to his notion that one's aesthetic judgments are a reflection of one's soul: "What we like judges us. Secretly at first. Then, on one fine day, for all the world to see" (Couturier 1989, 61). For Couturier, this was most painfully demonstrated in what he describes as the public taste for sentimental devotional art—referred to as *l'art de Saint-Sulpice* or *bondieuserie*—and ornamental buildings of worship. The pervasiveness of these forms was an indictment, as Robert Schwartzwald points out, of "the Church's inability to respond convincingly to the spiritual needs of modern society" (1990, 134). Its popularity, however, was evidence more broadly, for Couturier, of a profound malaise afflicting Catholic sensibility, both clerical and lay: "To begin with, there is the painful fact that Christian people have indeed become a 'public' for their art—passive or distrustful onlookers in the presence of these sacred works" (1989, 61).

But the modern art introduced by some dioceses in an effort to assert the Church's contemporary relevance hardly resolved the matter. Indeed,

in the view of Couturier and Régamey, this "modernistic" painting, a derivative "faux-moderne" version of the challenging experimental art of the
early decades of the century, far from making a laudable effort in the right
direction, was all the more insidious in its assertion of a "healthy modernity
equidistant from banality and outrage" (Régamey, quoted in Rubin 1961, 19).
This idea that virtue lay in a tempered, diluted version of the contemporary
was deeply at odds with the spirit and the aesthetic of the sacred art movement. As Philip Nord described the intent of the movement's founders:
"The innovators' agenda was clear. They wanted to shake off the dead hand
of the past in favor of '*l'art vivant*.' They wanted a setting for prayer and
contemplation that would be austere and direct, addressing itself without
sentimentality or excess of anecdote to the intuition of worshipers. And they
wanted structures that in their monumentality and rigor would express the
total life of the community. . . . A new Church, it was hoped, would make for
a new piety, no more the affected "rosewater piety" of old but a spirituality
more rigorous" (Nord 2003, 8).

Couturier pursued his argument for the restoration of faith through the
renewal of sacred art not only in the pages of *L'Art Sacré* but also in his col-
laborations in the design of the churches of Assy (1950) and Audincourt
(1951), and of the chapels of Vence (1951) and Ronchamp (1955), and in
his negotiation of highly controversial commissions for artworks for these
sanctuaries from leading modernist artists, among them Matisse, Léger,
Lipchitz, Georges Rouault, Marc Chagall, and Pierre Bonnard.[17] Writing of
La Chapelle du Rosaire in Vence, the chapel that Matisse described as his
"crowning achievement" and that is now commonly known as the Matisse
Chapel, Couturier notes: "It was not to be a place where stained-glass windows and paintings would describe and teach complex things that people
already knew anyway, but a place which by its beauty would change their
hearts—a place where souls would be purified by the purity of its forms"
(1989, 94).

These Dominican projects were sufficiently controversial to provoke a
response from Rome. What offended the Church was not so much the look
of the modern works that Couturier commissioned, though that was indeed
a fraught issue, but the fact that with the exception of Rouault, none of the
major artists were Catholics; indeed, among them were atheists like Léger,
and the Jewish Lipchitz.[18] Couturier admitted that this was not ideal, but

that under the circumstances, it "would be safer to turn to geniuses without faith than to believers without talent" (1951, 269).[19] "We knew very well," Couturier noted in a December 1947 interview in *Harper's Bazaar*, "that some of these artists were not strictly practicing Christians; that some were separated from us by serious divergences of a political as well as of an intellectual order. Trusting in Providence, we told ourselves that a great artist is always a great spiritual being, each in his own manner" (quoted in Schwartzwald 2004, 140).[20] By contrast, modest talents, in the "deplorable" conditions of the day, "create, as it were, a slope on which everything goes down hill, inexorably, turns to mediocrity" (Couturier 1989, 119).[21] Couturier was then, as Schwartzwald (n.d.) so astutely characterized him, "resolutely democratic on issues of *access* to the means of artistic creation and especially art appreciation," but "aristocratic" when it came to hierarchy of artistic quality—and both John and Dominique de Menil shared this disposition.

They also shared Couturier's profound respect for distinguished artists and architects. Couturier, himself an artist who worked on a number of Dominican commissions, enjoyed a rich intellectual rapport and deep friendship with leading contemporary artists and architects—among them Picasso, Matisse, and Le Corbusier—and a deserved reputation both within the Dominican Order and beyond it as an "erudite, urbane scholar of modern philosophy, arts and letters" (Langdon 1988, 547).

The first of Couturier's projects to create modern places of worship in collaboration with contemporary artists was the church of Notre-Dame de Toute Grâce of Assy, in the Haute Savoie. The church was begun in 1937, but because its progress was interrupted by the war and Couturier's consequent long exile in North America, it was not completed until 1950. Rouault, a devout Catholic, was commissioned in 1939 to create scenes from the Passion and the book of Isaiah and to depict St. Veronica in stained glass, his first ecclesiastical commissions despite his already advanced years. Bonnard, also a Catholic, was asked to paint St. Francis de Sales with the sick for the south transept in 1943. But it was in 1945, after Couturier's radical reevaluation of his early conviction that sacred art could be created only by pious artists, that Couturier persuaded Léger, then a communist, to create the façade mosaic *The Litanies of the Virgin,* and Jean Lurçat, also a communist, to produce the *Apocalypse* tapestry for the apse.[22] Several additional commissions were agreed upon in 1947: Lipchitz was asked to make a statue of the Virgin, and Chagall, Jewish like Lipchitz, was engaged to decorate the baptistery. Braque agreed to make the bronze door of the tabernacle. In 1948, Matisse, of no religious affiliation, was commissioned to make a ceramic mural depicting St. Dominic, for which he used Couturier as the model. About a dozen more commissions went to artists of lesser stature, and Couturier himself made some of the stained-glass windows.

What the chapel lacked in stylistic coherence, many commentators have observed, it overcame in its evocation of a spiritual unity. The Reverend Richard Douaire, noting his initial fear that the chapel might seem less a place of devotion than a museum of religious art, wrote: "To place the work of so many artists of such individuality in juxtaposition seemed in theory to threaten the artistic unity and spiritual purpose of the edifice. Yet it is in the very quality of the works themselves that unity is established and maintained. Notre-Dame de Toute-Grâce is not a museum!" (Douaire 1951, 29). And certainly it lacked nothing in its audaciousness, putting an end, Couturier observed, "by means of direct achievement, the absurd divorce which for the past century has separated the Church from living art"; it did so by appealing "to the greatest of independent artists, no matter what might be their personal convictions" (Couturier 1951b, 31).

In the small Sacré-Coeur of Audincourt, begun in 1949 and consecrated in 1951, a church for a parish of Peugeot workers, Couturier's conviction that nonfigurative iconography could sustain a more affecting experience than the naturalism prescribed by Rome was realized more resolutely with Léger's continuous, seventy-meter band of stained-glass windows, the *Instruments of the Passion*, which encircle the building and provide the sole interior decorative element.[23] Jean Bazaine made a large mosaic for the exterior. Couturier would soon begin to work with Le Corbusier in the planning of the Chapelle de Notre-Dame-du-Haut, in Ronchamp, and Sainte Marie de La Tourette, a Dominican convent near Lyon.[24] Neither of these projects was completed before Couturier's death in 1954. But perhaps the most compelling, and certainly best known, of his projects is La Chapelle du Rosaire, in Vence, for which Matisse took on not only all of the internal elaboration, right down to the design of the vestments, but also worked with the Dominican follower of Couturier, Louis-Bertrand Rayssiguier, on the architectural form of the chapel.

ARCHITECTURAL COMMISSIONS

When Dominique and John traveled with Couturier in the summer of 1952 to the churches of Assy and Audincourt, to the chapel at Vence, and to the site at Ronchamp where Le Corbusier was preparing to build his chapel, they experienced places of worship that were genuinely contemporary, not reproductions of established Church architecture and decoration, but sacred spaces that seemed to them to be as alive as they were affecting.

It would not be long before their own parish priest in Houston announced that the construction of a new church was planned. In a conversation with her daughter Adelaide, Dominique de Menil recounted:

> Jean went to the parish priest and said, "If you have to build, I will help you with the plans, paying for the plans, and the architect's fee if you choose a great architect." We put him in touch with Philip Johnson who is a charmer, and the parish priest was charmed and delighted, and Philip went ahead and made plans for a church. . . . The plans were presented to the bishop, who equated anything modern with communism. And I tell you [the plans] were almost pseudo-gothic, very traditional, without anything aggressively modern at all. But the bishop turned it down and the plans were abandoned completely.[25]

John's position on church architecture is stated emphatically in a letter that he wrote to the Reverend Father Cemon in relation to another project proposed by St. Michael's Church:

> When Father Roach called me some time ago to serve on the board that was going to raise funds for the new seminary, I told him I would be glad to accept if the seminary that was to be built is contemporary and good architecture. But otherwise I could not.
>
> It is a principle from which I cannot depart, to contribute only to such religious or educational buildings that are in keeping with our time. In the twelfth century, Catholics did not build Greek Basilicas, nor did they build medieval cathedrals in the eighteenth. At all times, except since the last century, have Catholics promoted the best of their time. It was the best architects and the best painters who erected and decorated the churches.

The split that now exists between church and creative art is of concern to many. It is also a challenge. Ever since Father Couturier made it clear to me, I have promised myself to encourage, within my means and reach, any attempt made to keep up the great tradition of the Church. This positive attitude, unfortunately, has a negative counterpart.

If I cannot take my share of the erection of the buildings, it does not mean that I am not interested in the seminary as such. As evidence of this, I should be extremely happy to contribute to the intellectual life of the seminary by offering lectures from great Catholic scholars and thinkers as Jacques Maritain and others, and I do hope to help, somehow, along that line.[26]

It was not long after hearing of the bishop's rejection of the Johnson plans for St. Michael's that Father Sullivan, the president of the University of St. Thomas, a small Catholic university founded in Houston in 1947 by the Basilian Fathers, went to John with a proposal that he and his wife commission plans for an entire academic campus. With the assurance that the project would not require the approval of the bishop, since the Basilian superiors were in Toronto, Dominique de Menil explained, John and Dominique agreed to go ahead as long as they could specify the architect: Philip Johnson, the (at that time) modernist disciple of Ludwig Mies van der Rohe. The Basilians welcomed the proposal, and Johnson produced a plan that would allow the campus to be built in increments; several buildings were completed in the late 1950s.[27] There was also talk of building a chapel in the spirit of the projects of Couturier, though in deference to more pressing projects, this was not pursued with any seriousness until 1960.

The University of St. Thomas presented an opportunity to the de Menils to pursue not only their interest in architecture and their abiding motivation to support the work of talented exponents of modernism, but also their commitment to fostering a critical, though forward-looking, intellectual engagement with the contemporary world, a commitment that had crystallized for them within the off-modern milieu of the *renouveau catholique*. Throughout the 1950s and 1960s, the de Menils stewarded the development of the school. They bought land around the single-building campus, which they donated to the school; established and funded an art history department, installing at its head the charismatic Jermayne MacAgy; contributed to the salaries of professors in art history, economics, and theology; and funded in large measure the development of a teaching collection of art and artifacts, a significant art library, and an extremely well-regarded exhibition program.

ROTHKO CHAPEL

Macmity, who had become Dominique de Menil's very close friend and her mentor in the domain of curating and installing exhibitions, died unexpectedly in 1964. It was, for Dominique de Menil, "as if the floor had opened up under my feet."[28] It is such moments, she told me, that call for an act of faith. Dominique and John's resolve to build the chapel that they had been thinking of for some time was such an act. They had very much wanted to emulate the kinds of chapels that Couturier had commissioned in France. With the Matisse Chapel in their minds, the de Menils proposed to the president of the University of St. Thomas that they proceed with the chapel that the Basilian Fathers had wanted to build on the campus. This proposal specified that Philip Johnson, whose design for the development of the university campus was already partially completed, would be asked to design the structure, and Mark Rothko would be asked to make a series of paintings for the interior.[29] The cost would be borne by Dominique and John de Menil. Not only had Rothko been a friend of MacAgy (who had curated a show of his work for the Contemporary Art Association in Houston in 1957), but Dominique and John were familiar with his work also; indeed, they already owned three of his paintings. But in thinking of Rothko for the chapel, they particularly had in mind the series of murals he had painted for Ludwig Mies van der Rohe and Philip Johnson's Seagram Building.[30] Peter Selz wrote of these paintings: "Like much of Rothko's work they really seem to ask for a place apart, a kind of sanctuary where they may perform what is essentially a sacramental function. . . . Perhaps, like medieval altarpieces, [they] can properly be seen only in an ambiance created in total keeping with their mood" (Selz, quoted in Barnes 1989, 43).

John and Dominique de Menil shared this perception. So, just eight weeks after MacAgy's death, Dominique visited Rothko and asked him to consider making paintings for the planned Catholic chapel.[31] He readily accepted the commission, and soon after began an extended process of consultation and

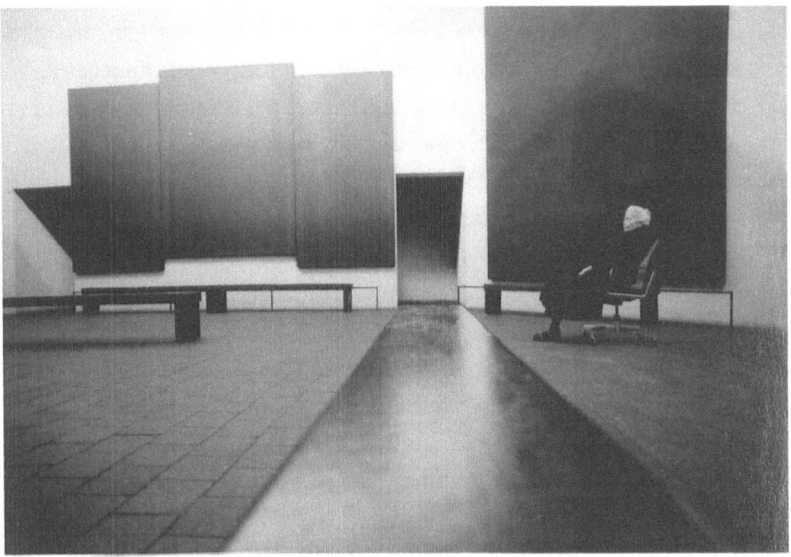

Dominique de Menil in the Rothko Chapel, 1997. Photo: A. de Menil. Courtesy Menil Archives, Menil Collection, Houston.

collaboration with Philip Johnson. Johnson and Rothko agreed early to an octagonal plan, and specifications for the interior dimensions were set in place almost from the outset, and remained unchanged throughout.[32] This plan owes much, it is said, to Rothko's experience of the octagonal, late twelfth-century Byzantine Cathedral of Santa Maria Assunta, in Torcello, Italy, and the pair of mosaics that he found so moving therein. No doubt Dominique would have taken pleasure in the notion that what was to become an iconic articulation of modernist art and architecture was meant to evoke just the same experience as had been conjured in a Byzantine church.

Considerable difficulty between the artist and the architect emerged, however, over two issues: the height of the building and the manner in which it was to receive light (Barnes 1989, 81).[33] Differences between Rothko and Johnson over these matters became intractable, leading Johnson finally to withdraw from the project, leaving it in the hands of Howard Barnstone and Eugene Aubry, who had worked as supervising architects on a number of Johnson projects in Texas and had done considerable work for the de Menils. It was their task, in accordance with Dominique and John's wishes, to complete the building as Rothko conceived of it. All the plans, including the specifications of the materials to be used, were subject to Rothko's approval. Construction had begun when Rothko died in February 1970, and was completed as he had planned it. Johnson agreed to design the chapel's main entrance and to orient the chapel on the site. He had also, together with the artist, designed the reflecting pool for Barnett Newman's *Broken Obelisk*, which stands on an axis with the main entrance to the chapel, on a site selected by Newman.[34]

Though aspects of the design were subject to important revisions as the project developed, these modifications were minor, perhaps, compared to the institutional shifts that it underwent. When the de Menils moved their art department from St. Thomas to Rice University in 1969, they assumed that the chapel project for the University of St. Thomas would proceed unaffected. However, just as the Basilians had finally found the de Menils' presence intolerably overbearing in other university affairs, so they anticipated it would be with the chapel also. The de Menils then looked to the Institute for Religion and Human Development, in Houston, on whose board John de Menil already served. The institute (now the Institute for Religion and Health) is an ecumenical institution located within Houston's Texas Medical Center. With its acceptance of the offer, the institute and the de Menils set about determining a site for the chapel, for which the paintings had been complete since 1967. It was decided to build the chapel on its present site, which the de Menils already owned: a lot adjacent to the University of St. Thomas yet not impossibly distant from the medical center. Thus, it could be used readily by both constituencies.

Although this formal association with the institute lasted only from 1969 until late in 1972, it had a profound effect on the conceptualization of the chapel as an ecumenical place of worship. This conceptual shift was no doubt also informed by the pronouncements of Vatican II, which so powerfully endorsed ecumenicism, but its roots, for John and Dominique de Menil, lay in the ecumenical teaching of Congar. The chapel operates as a space of contemplation, but, with the de Menils' conviction that contemplation should lay the foundation for action, it also serves as the institutional hearth for those projects pursued by John and Dominique that came together under the rubrics of social justice, world peace, and spirituality, albeit initiated with an iconic aesthetic and architectural statement.

CONTEMPLATION AND ACTION

The injunction to take others faiths seriously was derived, for the de Menils, from Congar's ecumenicism. It also underpins the integral humanism that informed the de Menils' own commitments to human rights and the pursuit of social justice, which they expressed personally and through the operations of the Rothko Chapel.

Dominique and John heard Yves Congar speak in 1936, in a series of sermons delivered at the basilica of Montmartre, in which he laid out a theological argument for an ecumenical Church.[35] "It wasn't any particular thing he said," Dominique recounted. "It was like a little seed deposited. There was some receptivity. The seed grew like the mustard seed mentioned in the Bible" (quoted in A. Holmes 1991, 228). From Congar, she and her husband had learned that, as Dominique put it:

> If you want to want to love and create common bonds you have to understand what makes the other person tick, what his faith is all about. You don't merely respect his religion, but you have a curiosity about it—an awareness.
>
> It makes no sense for everybody to try to convert others to their own beliefs. Religion is part of a culture. People should not lose their culture which came to them from their ancestors and is very precious (quoted in Johnston 1977, 8).[36]

One imagines that as appealing as Congar's ecumenicism was for Dominique and John de Menil, so too was his enthusiasm for reform, and more particularly for reform that did not turn its back on the present. His teaching and writing anticipated by some thirty years the papal focus on ecumenicism that was to find expression in the Second Vatican Council. Indeed, in the intervening years prior to the election of John XXIII in 1959, Congar's views were to draw sharp rebuke from Rome. Engaged with issues of theology and ecclesiology, Congar had for several years in the 1920s regularly attended Maritain's weekly meetings at Meudon, participating in an exegesis of the writings of St. Thomas Aquinas that would establish a philosophical underpinning for the contemporary transfiguration of faith. But for all of Maritain's off-modern attention to temporality, his commitment to Aquinas was essentially ahistorical. Congar's hermeneutics called for a different approach to St. Thomas, an approach that focused less on the interpretation of Thomist scholarship and required instead a return to the source, and in a manner that considered the historical context within which Aquinas wrote, "in order to put his thought in a period, since everything is historical—absolutely everything, including the Bible and Jesus" (Congar 1988, 73). Attention to the particularity of the historical moment of Aquinas's writing, for Congar as for other Dominicans trained at Le Saulchoir, mitigated against an essentializing reading of Aquinas and drew attention to the orientation of St. Thomas toward the contemporary lives to which he addressed his theology. This pastoral orientation can be observed also in Congar's call for the Church to attend more closely to the historically contingent experiences and concerns of parishioners. Rome feared, however, as Congar's biographer relates it, that the sort of emphasis he was placing on historical context "would end up by turning theology into cultural anthropology, deprived of any real hold on its divine subject-matter, revelation" (Nichols 1990, 251).

Congar's program for the renewal of the Church was wide ranging. In his teaching and writing, Congar argued that "the separated churches which had been born from particular theologies, might complement each other" (O'Meara 1997, 183). This ecumenism, Rome made clear, risked being "construed as indifference to specifically Catholic doctrines" (Nichols 1990, 252). His theological pluralism, along with his criticism of the exercise of Rome's authority, only intensified the Vatican's suspicions: "The division of theology into closed camps, neo-Thomism as a monopoly, the isolation of Rome from Eastern Orthodoxy, the rejection of new approaches for parishes, the narrow confines of a pyramidal ecclesiology—all of this was not the defense but the impoverishment of Catholicism" (O'Meara 1997, 183–184).[37] After a career of constraints imposed periodically by the Holy See, exile from France, removal from teaching, and close censorship of his publishing, Congar was dramatically rehabilitated by Pope John XXIII, who personally insisted that he be called upon as a central participant in the Second Vatican Council, and indeed Congar is now regarded as one of the key architects of Vatican II.[38]

Congar's ecumenism is woven into the fabric of the Rothko Chapel. According to Dominique de Menil, such ecumenism, however, did not imply that the chapel should be a neutral space: "Neutrality is admirable ... but it is standoffish. I see the vocation of the Rothko Chapel as active" (Menil 1974, 4). With its colloquia, the chapel has brought together people of various faiths from around the world, but it has also brought into conversation intellectuals from a range of perspectives, and it has taken a number of initiatives to recognize and support the work of human-rights activists. Dominique described the motivation for these events:

> Churches and synagogues are too much like clubs, and as we all know clubs are meant to keep people out. Maybe that is why so many of the young are staying away. [...] They know that we are threatened by economic collapses, police states, atomic warfare. They try to do something about it, but they don't know how and what. Their helplessness has reduced them to disorderly acts which lead nowhere.
>
> The Rothko Chapel could give them hope and courage. [...] I see there a series of great encounters which would bring together brains and hearts—fresh brains and experienced brains, young hearts and hearts enlarged by life. (5)

This attitude was exemplified by the second and third colloquia planned by the chapel: "Human Rights/Human Reality," held in December 1973, commemorated the twenty-fifth anniversary of the United Nations Declaration of Human Rights and brought together "three scientists and two men of faith," along with a broader public, for what was formally described as "an exchange on the fateful connection between human rights and social and economic reality, and to provoke, in public discussion, reflections toward new attitudes"; and "Toward a New Strategy for Development," held in February 1977, approached "concretely the problem of the growing gap between rich and poor nations throughout the world" by inviting "ten papers ... from distinguished development economists and social scientists, some from developing countries (Bangladesh, Brazil, India) and others from the industrialized world."[39]

In response to the question, "Isn't this getting away from the ecumenical vocation of the Chapel, from its artistic and religious functions?" Dominique de Menil responded, in a manner that resonates strongly with the conviction of the *renouveau catholique* and, more specifically, with its integral humanist social theory:

> The mere fact of assembling in the Chapel gives a spiritual orientation to the debates. It means that man's reality implies transcendence. This may look to many a marginal circumstance—to me it is central. [...] If society in its orga-

nizing effort suppresses the deepest aspirations of man—his transcendental component—we will have large communities where man will indeed be reduced to the condition of an insect. [...] I hope the Rothko Chapel will be a place ... where people will become aware of man's total reality and will be moved to improve the world. (Menil 1974, 6–7)

In the planning of the first Rothko Chapel colloquium, "Traditional Modes of Contemplation and Action," Dominique and John insisted that after their initial work to establish contacts with appropriate scholars, the colloquium be substantively organized by someone who was not a Catholic, indeed, not a Christian. In so doing, they ensured that a serious commitment was made to disrupting conventional hierarchies of authority. Here, people of other faiths would not be treated merely as guests who must defer, even if only out of politeness, to the defining preoccupations of the host. This was, then, very self-consciously, not merely an exercise in toleration. Subsequent colloquia and symposia included "Islam: Spiritual Message and Quest for Justice" (1981), "Religions of Asia" (1988), "Self, State, and Society in Buddhism and Confucianism" (1990), and "Christianity and Churches on the Eve of Vatican II" (1991).

The Rothko Chapel has pursued its activist project also in giving formal recognition to selected protagonists engaged in the struggle for social justice and human rights, in the form of monetary awards that serve to support further work and that, more importantly perhaps, draw public attention to the political struggles in which the recipients are enmeshed. A brief description of the awards gives some indication of the character and scope of the foundation's commitments in this area. The Rothko Chapel Awards, of $10,000 each, are given to five people every five years in recognition of their commitment to truth and freedom. Recipients have included two workers in the Federation of South African Women, and the Palestinian cofounders of Law in the Service of Man. The Oscar Romero Award ($20,000), named after the archbishop assassinated as he said Mass in San Salvador in 1980, is bestowed every other year. Recipients have included a bishop from Ecuador, a cardinal from São Paulo, a Lutheran bishop, and a Catholic activist in San Salvador—"people who put their heads on the line," as Dominique de Menil put it (quoted in A. Holmes 1991, 228). The Carter-Menil Human Rights Peace Prize ($100,000) is presented every year. Dominique de Menil was approached by Jimmy Carter to establish this award jointly. "She accepted, welcoming the greater media attention the former President would be able to generate" (228), since perhaps the most important aspect of awards of this sort is to signal to the recipients and their adversaries alike that people are paying attention to the struggle.

While the Menil Foundation has come to serve as the organizational hearth for Dominique de Menil's many art world interests, the Rothko Chapel Foundation now serves that function for those projects that come together under the rubrics of human rights, world peace, and spirituality.[40] The projects of these two foundations might be distinct, but their underpinnings bear a remarkable unity—indeed, they functioned effectively as a single entity for many years—an aspect of which Dominique de Menil expressed in her characterization of Rothko's work on the chapel project. As he worked, she recounted, "his colors became darker and darker, as if he were bringing us on the threshold of transcendence; the mystery of the cosmos, the tragic mystery of our perishable condition. The silence of God, the unbearable silence of God" (de Menil 1971).

PROSPECTION

The foregoing extended engagement with the theology and social theory of the *renouveau catholique*, focused particularly on those protagonists who became defining friends and advisers to Dominique and John de Menil, lays the foundation for the analysis of the Menil Collection that follows. While the particular projects they became involved with had much to do with un-anticipated felicities of circumstance, the sensibilities of the de Menils, along with their analysis of what kind of labor these projects might perform and the manner in which they should be pursued, were deeply informed by the intellectual formulations of the *renouveau catholique*. Most fundamentally, the de Menils derived from this their methodology—the critical, off-modern experimentalism deployed in the service of their sacred modern project.

3

New World

In his essay "New York in 1941," Claude Lévi-Strauss characterized the sense of possibility that this New World city presented: "New York (and this is the source of its charm and peculiar fascination) was then a city where anything seemed possible. Like the urban fabric, the social and cultural fabric was riddled with holes. All you had to do was pick one and slip through it if, like Alice, you wanted to get to the other side of the looking glass and find worlds so enchanting that they seemed unreal" (1985, 258–267). John and Dominique de Menil, by all accounts, also found it beguiling, traveling there often from the home they had established in Houston, where Schlumberger's New World operations were based.[1]

But Houston—which Dominique had reached in 1941, having had to take a circuitous route through Spain and Cuba with her two young daughters and newborn son to reunite with her husband, who had traveled there via Asia—was another matter. Couturier visited them in Houston after the war, staying with them in their modest first house, which Philip Johnson would later refer to as "a tract house" (quoted in Welch 2000, 42), and wrote, on his return to Paris: "Naturally, when I was in Houston I had to admit that you were right about being there, but from here, when I think of your little patch of green grass and the impossibly proportioned rooms that are privileged to house you, I wonder at the degree of absurdity to which our world has come that people like you are reduced to living in such circumstances, so removed from all civilization."[2] Dominique expressed this sense of being cast adrift from Europe in a talk she gave some years later: "In Europe the poorest person can enjoy the most beautiful works of art without having to spend a cent—art is everywhere—there is not a village that doesn't have a lovely old church, an impressive castle. In Paris there is Notre Dame and the Louvre available for everybody. Art is . . . just like the air one breathes. We become conscious of it when we lack it. I became conscious of art and particularly of beautiful architecture when we made our home in Houston."[3]

In his analysis of Philip Johnson's unlikely significance in the architectural history of Texas, *Philip Johnson and Texas*, Frank Welch records Johnson's reflection on his early visits to the city in the 1940s: "There just wasn't much to Houston. . . . I couldn't understand how anyone lived there, but that was before the personality of the place came through to me: I found out those people weren't afraid to try *anything*! There was a yearning there for a new start" (quoted in Welch 2000, 42).

It was precisely this aspect of Houston that so suited John's sensibilities, and "when a New York friend remarked that Houston was a cultural desert, John de Menil replied, 'It's in the desert that miracles happen'" (Colacello 1996, 181). Indeed, more than one of his associates recounted his observation, made without irony, that there was no reason why Houston, built on a marsh like Venice, couldn't become the Venice of the New World. John de Menil, who formally anglicized his name when he and Dominique were granted United States citizenship in 1962, is fondly remembered for his enthusiasms. In his obituary for John, Morton Feldman recalled: "He had a gentle radar for the unusual. A crazy idea, a beautiful idea, an irreverent or a religious idea, as long as it had some 'guts and personality' behind it, it got immediate attention and, many times, immediate support (Feldman 1973, 82).[4] In New York in the 1960s, he listened to the Velvet Underground and enjoyed the company of artists and filmmakers. And in Houston, he and Dominique were renowned for their dinners and parties, to which they invited artists, poets, intellectuals, oil millionaires, architects, priests, and political activists. The architect Anderson Todd, recalling these events in the 1950s, to which he was invited as a young member of the Rice University School of Architecture faculty, observed that it was at the de Menils' that he first saw an African American being entertained socially by whites in Houston (Welch 2000, 58).

These Houston occasions were not merely social amusements—they served in the development of a critical mass of people who could be called upon in the defense of various progressive agendas, whether in art, politics, or religion. They also served in the construction of the de Menils' singular public profile. To their disruptive cultural and social agendas, most notably, perhaps, their championing of modern art and civil rights, they brought the authority of European culture and wealth. This authority was no doubt furthered by John's notable acumen in the oil business, Houston's premier industry— acumen that was underpinned by his intelligence and energy as much as by his "unbending willpower and tenacity concealed beneath an exterior of tact, human respect, and personal charm" (Allaud and Martin 1977, 214).

Years earlier, in 1924, John had been the recipient of a Polignac Foundation Fellowship, awarded on the completion of a degree at l'École des Sciences Politiques, where he studied as a night school student, having taken a low-level position at the Banque de l'Union Parisienne. Born in Paris to a titled Catholic family whose fortune had been lost, John left school at seventeen, determined to work to recover the estate of his family. The fellowship afforded him a round-the-world trip. On his return, he wrote a report in which he described "in detail the wool and sugar markets of the Pacific and the West Indies"; the report brought him to the attention of bank officials and, as his son Georges recounts it, "marked the beginning of what then became a meteoric career."[5]

In 1931, when he and Dominique were married, he was in charge of investment services at one of the largest French banks, and under considerable pressure from Conrad and Marcel Schlumberger to join the family company.[6] For Marcel, he outlined his reluctance this way:

> There are also—and I think this is what matters to me—the 600 people I have under me. What a wonderful adventure it would be if I succeeded in establishing friendly relations with them, breaking through their distrust and

resentment. The feeling of being one of the rare ones who approach this job with a new heart. Desire to have a part, there or elsewhere, in the quest for a harmony cruelly absent from the life of these great anthills. Now you will understand, I am sure, that if Prospection [as Schlumberger was then called] proposed purely a financial and fiscal post to me, I would be very reluctant to accept it. (quoted in Schlumberger 1982, 120)

Here we get a sense not only of John's youthful frustrations with the confinements of conventional, depersonalized management practices, but also of his desire to make his mark. But in light of what John and Dominique together achieved in Houston, the ambitions expressed here are strikingly modest. Houston, by contrast, allowed an unusual degree of proximity of action to ideas, an observation reflected in Dominique's recollection of the city that she came to love as her husband loved it: "I always felt a sort of energy in Houston. . . . I always felt that what didn't exist would happen within a couple of years. I always felt things were possible" (quoted in Verhovek 1998, 2).

In Houston, they radicalized the French intellectual discourse with which they had become engaged in Paris and subsequently in New York, pursuing their intellectual and religious commitments through projects across a range of domains: social justice, spirituality, education, and the arts. And notwithstanding their internationalist commitments and their enduring distaste for parochialism, they became tireless champions of Houston's development as a modern, vibrant city. In Paris or New York, Dominique and John might have quietly carved out a domain for themselves and their projects, but in Houston they had a more or less empty canvas to work on, and they energetically pursued the opportunity this afforded them to play a thoroughly defining role. This was no doubt in the interest of making Houston less alien to their sensibilities, as is suggested in Dominique's early assessment of the city: "I would never have started collecting so much art if I had not moved to Houston. . . . Houston was a provincial, dormant place, much like Strasbourg, Basel, Alsace. There were no galleries to speak of, no dealers worth the name, and the museum—that is why I started buying; that is why I developed the physical need to acquire" (quoted in Browning 1983, 192).

But while John and Dominique de Menil might, through their efforts, have effected a transformation of Houston that was congenial to their own tastes, they did so also with a strong sense of civic duty. Dominique, commenting on the extent and style of their engagements with Houston's cultural and social development, characterized it this way: "Yes, it is a fantastic amount of time and money and energy we spend. But Houston is becoming a great city and we must do all we can, as it grows, to help in its design, its art, and awareness. We came here, we became involved, and now we are prisoners of our own very great interests" (quoted in A. Holmes 1970, 35). Indeed, their patronage took the form of a vocation—both a duty and a compelling desire.

INSTITUTIONAL LANDSCAPE

Notwithstanding the extraordinary sense of possibility that Houston afforded, Dominique and John de Menil were far from the only players on the scene, and their energetic pursuit of their ambitions was not universally welcomed. Resistance to their efforts had much to do with the substance of what they were trying to achieve, but it was also a response to what was perceived as their high-handed style.

In the late 1940s and the 1950s, the Houston art world was in a state of upheaval. Aline Louchheim, an art critic for the *New York Times*, described the situation in 1953:

> In Houston, a three-cornered situation keeps the artworld at a heated pitch.
> 1. There is the museum, controlled by a board whose membership . . . is primarily of persons of power and prestige, which had for a long time shown little interest in modern art.
> 2. The splinter group, the Contemporary Art Association, an ardent group of laymen, artists, and architects and designers, aggressively democratic. With the benefit of donated services . . . they built their own building and they put on their own ambitious and often ingenious shows (which are, in fact, usually the best shows of modern art originated in the region).
> 3. The schism within the CAA based on many factors: Personality clashes, fear of domination by an individual, differing philosophies of professionalism versus cooperative endeavor, European versus American art. (Louchheim 1953)

Louchheim identified John de Menil as the leader of the "minority group" in the CAA, promoting professionalism and internationalization in an institution that was conceived of by some as a venue for the promotion of local artists. Since its founding in 1948 in response to the Museum of Fine Arts's lack of interest in contemporary art, the CAA had been run by committee decision, and its exhibitions were organized by volunteer board members, among them John de Menil. With Dominique's assistance, he produced a show of Van Gogh drawings and paintings for the CAA in 1950, works that at the time had been shown only in New York, Chicago, and Paris.[7] He also initiated exhibitions of work by Max Ernst, Joan Miró, and Alexander Calder. Not only did they bring to Houston modern art of a stature that had not previously been shown there, but they brought also a full-time director to an organization that had formerly been sustained by the voluntary activities of a rather small circle of modern-art enthusiasts.

Resisting the protests of several board members, who resigned over the issue, and after agreeing to underwrite her salary, the de Menils engineered the hiring of Jermayne MacAgy from the California Palace of the Legion of Honor, where she had had the distinction of being the youngest museum director in the country and had become known for her highly theatrical installations.[8] When she took up her position with the CAA in 1955, she did much to further this reputation. On the very small budget of $20,000 a year, she created twenty-nine shows during her four years as director, many of which drew national attention (Browning 1983, 194–196).

While MacAgy's shows received national critical attention as well as considerable local enthusiasm, her exhibitions were considered expensive (even though the de Menils largely underwrote them) and controversial. MacAgy was, according to Ann Holmes, the fine-arts editor of the *Houston Chronicle*, "brilliant, visionary, but impatient with slow progress and a then prevailing amateurism" (1970, 35). This tension and the controversial character of her shows, along with some board members' resentments over authority on the board, made it difficult to secure enough funding to meet the operating costs of the museum. In 1959, her contract was not renewed. Holmes (1959a) reported that it was understood that her advocates on the board tolerated this outcome only because MacAgy was being positioned by the Modern Art Committee of the Museum of Fine Arts, Houston (MFAH) for a job at that institution. Indeed, Holmes suggests, that was the primary impetus for

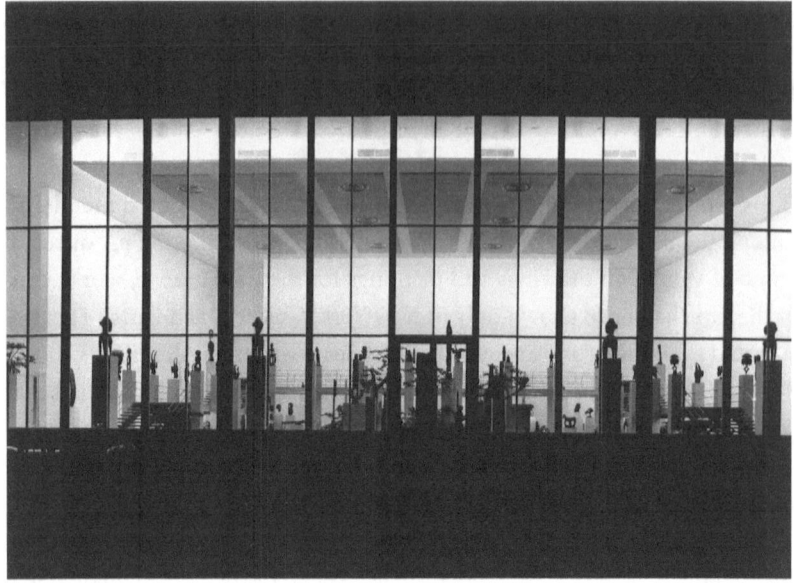

Museum of Fine Arts, Houston during the opening of "Totems Not Taboo," 1958. Photo: Hickey-Robertson. Courtesy Menil Archives, Menil Collection, Houston.

the formation of that committee, on which Dominique de Menil and her close associate, the architect Howard Barnstone, served. Formed in 1959, it sponsored just two exhibitions, "Paul Klee" and "From Gauguin to Gorky," both of which were curated and installed by Jermayne MacAgy.

MacAgy did not confine herself to curating contemporary shows. In February 1959, the MFAH was host to a MacAgy show that the de Menils, "as her angels," had sponsored (A. Holmes 1970, 35). Designed as the inaugural exhibition for Cullinan Hall, the new, Mies van der Rohe–designed addition to the museum, "Totems Not Taboo" (1959) was an exhibition of 240 pieces of "primitive art," though it included 5 contemporary pieces also.[9] "Efforts are made," Ann Holmes reports, "to relate these [primitive] pieces to contemporary art, though in the most unobtrusive way, showing their common simplicity, use of geometric form and their ability to powerfully convey emotions and ideas" (1959b). The kinds of objections that might today be provoked by an exhibition seeking to show affinities between "primitive" and modern art had not been formulated mid-century.[10] The critical issue regarding "primitive" art in 1959 was not how to value it without reference to its continuities with abstract modernism—the argument that coalesced around the Museum of Modern Art's "'Primitivism' in 20th Century Art: Affinity of the Tribal and the Modern" (1984)—but, rather, whether it was worthy of the art museum at all, in response to which MacAgy's show took an emphatic position.[11] Doran Ross points out that "ever since the first publication of Robert Goldwater's *Primitivism in Modern Art* (1938), the subject of African art's influence on early-twentieth-century European art has been used as a point of access to the arts of Africa, if not as an explicit rationalization for showing these arts in the major art museums of the United States" (2003, 37). In any event, it was widely considered to be the most spectacular show ever seen in Houston (Beauchamp 1983, 21). Beyond its enthusiastic local reception, it also attracted national attention. René d'Harnoncourt, the director of the Museum of Modern Art, hailed it as "one of the three most exceptional exhibitions he had ever seen" (quoted in Tomkins 1998, 58).

The year 1959 was also the year in which, after five years, the contract of the Museum of Fine Arts's first professional director, Lee Malone, was not renewed. With the hiring of Malone, the MFAH, like the CAA, had entered a more professional era, after twenty-five years of shows from local or regional sources and commercial galleries.[12] Malone mounted several large exhibitions and made a point of cultivating patrons for support. John and Dominique de Menil became quite actively involved with the museum during this period, refocusing their energies as relations with the CAA became increasingly fraught. Their increasing participation in the operations of the MFAH indicated a significant softening of the board toward modern art. John de Menil's old friend Aaron Farfel recalled that their early overtures to the MFAH had been repeatedly rebuffed: "I remember John's going to the Museum of Fine Arts and begging, pleading with them to let him hang some modern art. He would have taken space anywhere; he begged them to let him have the basement even, but he was refused every single time" (quoted in Browning 1983, 194). During Malone's tenure, the de Menils worked particularly on two shows— "Seventy-five Years of Sculpture" (including works by Brancusi, Calder, Lipchitz, Aristide Maillol, Henry Moore, Picasso, and Auguste Rodin), and "Paul Gauguin: His Place in the Meeting of East and West" (Beauchamp 1983, 20)—mobilizing the loan of works from Europe and from within the United States of a significance that no Houston institution would hitherto have contemplated.

Thus, 1959 began with the directorships of both the MFAH and the CAA unfilled. It was reported that, unofficially, MacAgy was being made available for the position at the MFAH (A. Holmes 1959a). MacAgy would be relieved of being the central focus of the divisive politics of the CAA, politics informed largely by the question of whether the museum should position itself as a distinctively local or regional institution, or as a professional operation participating in an international art world. By no means incidental to this polarization was the figure of John de Menil, who was deeply identified with MacAgy and with the project of internationalization, and characterized by a willfulness that many found compelling, others galling.

The struggle at the CAA had serious implications for the viability of the institution. While John and Dominique de Menil funded the director's salary and the exhibitions, many former or potential donors became unwilling, in the midst of such controversy, to make the contributions necessary to sustain the basic operating expenses of the museum.

The board of the MFAH seemed disinclined to risk a similar controversy. MacAgy was not hired, and a three-person search committee was established: S. I. Morris, the president of the board; Nina Cullinan, who in 1954 had given $250,000 to fund the Mies van der Rohe addition; and John de Menil. All three had an interest in contemporary art. According to a later account: "One year later, in June 1960, Ann Holmes, Fine Arts Editor of the Houston Chronicle, saw the wire service announcement of [James Johnson] Sweeney's resignation [from the position of director of the Solomon R. Guggenheim Museum] and immediately called John de Menil, who called Sweeney to offer him the directorship" (Beauchamp 1983, 24). Sweeney's reputation as an advocate of the avant-garde suited the committee well. He was one of Peggy Guggenheim's close advisers, and Dore Ashton described him as a powerful figure "well-connected with the international art world" (40).[13] While director of the Guggenheim, he had instituted the now common practice of circulating exhibitions drawn from the permanent collection to museums nationwide and overseas, and in so doing gained significant international recognition for the museum. Also during his tenure at the Guggenheim he had had to develop ways of hanging exhibitions in the notoriously difficult space of the newly designed Frank Lloyd Wright building. This experience would stand him in good stead for the challenge of installing shows in Cullinan Hall.[14] Indeed, S. I. Morris recalled that Sweeney seemed like "an answer to a prayer"

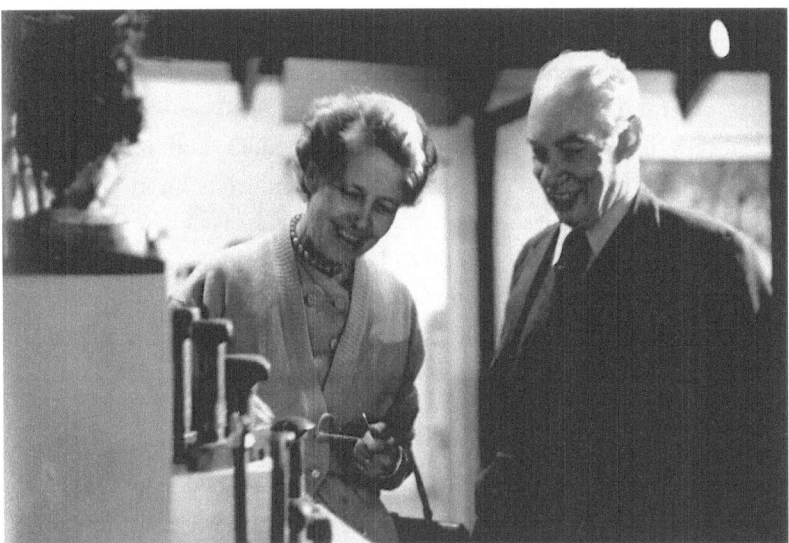

Dominique de Menil with James Johnson Sweeney at "Trojan Horse: The Art of the Machine," curated by Jermayne MacAgy, at the Contemporary Arts Association, Houston, 1958. Photo: Eve Arnold. Courtesy Menil Archives, Menil Collection, Houston.

(quoted on 40). Announcing Sweeney's appointment in January 1961, Morris declared: "'The appointment of James Johnson Sweeney as director of the museum is the first step of an ambitious and energetic plan to establish Houston as a national center of the arts on an international plane . . . an art center of world reputation" (quoted in *Houston Press* 1961).

Sweeney was willing to come to Houston because of his friendship with John and Dominique de Menil, and with Mies van der Rohe, and because of the opportunity to mold the image of the museum, as he had done during his tenure at the Guggenheim.[15] John and Dominique's offer to contribute to his salary, said to have been the highest among U.S. museum directors at the time, was, by all accounts, also quite significant (Tomkins 1991). He was to be paid $30,000 a year (though it was rumored to have risen as high as $50,000), along with a $10,000 travel allowance, and to be provided with an apartment with an excellent address. (By comparison, just two years before, MacAgy had earned $10,000 as the director of the CAA.) So, in the months after John de Menil's approach to Sweeney, the board of the MFAH was quietly engaged in a campaign to raise the funds required to hire him, since in addition to his compensation package, Sweeney required sufficient funds for acquisitions (including $10,000 annually expressly for the purchase of works by living artists) and for mounting exhibitions (Beauchamp 1983, 86–87).[16]

Sweeney may have had a reputation for big spending both professionally and personally, but he was perhaps even better known for his installation of exhibitions. It had likewise been MacAgy's particular facility for exhibition design that had brought her to John and Dominique de Menil's attention for the CAA, and later it would be the same quality that would particularly draw Dominique to Walter Hopps for the directorship of the Menil Collection.

In a 1958 address to the Northeastern Museums Conference, Sweeney outlined his approach to exhibitions:

> The future of the art museum lies perhaps in the area of the *bistro* which serves a connoisseur's choice, rather than in that of the more democratic approach which attempts to give the greatest relative satisfaction to the greatest number.
>
> How else can we hope to raise the public taste, which is our primary duty as museum directors and educators? . . .
>
> The education of the public taste in art should be undertaken through the stimulation of interest by the quality of a work of art, rather than by information about a work of art. To do this, concentration was necessary. One fine painting thoroughly appreciated, like one great book well read, would have more cultural effect than a world of digests or surveys. To focus the observer's attention on quality, a small museum, or an exhibition of limited scale, was most effective. (quoted in Beauchamp 1983, 93)

This characterization, awkward now for its unselfconscious or unapologetic elitism, is strikingly similar to Dominique de Menil's own renderings, though perhaps absent the redemptive underpinnings of such an endeavor.

Sweeney was, as Edward Mayo, the registrar of the museum, put it, anxious to move the MFAH "out of the provincial ranks," and during his tenure, he brought in works by Picasso, Calder, Miró, Léger, Piet Mondrian, Braque, and Jean Tinguely, much of the funding for which was provided by John and Dominique de Menil. Sweeney's correspondence throughout his directorship indicates that the de Menils were very closely engaged with the MFAH's dealings.[17]

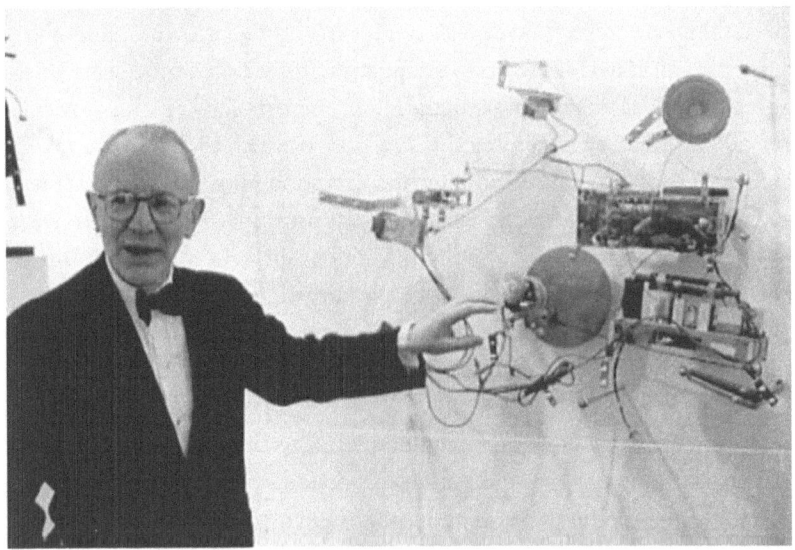

John de Menil at the Jean Tinguely exhibition, Alexander Iolas Gallery, New York, 1962. Photo A. de Menil. Courtesy Menil Archives, Menil Collection, Houston.

The Tinguely acquisitions were perhaps the most controversial ones made under Sweeney's directorship. The MFAH accessioned thirteen Tinguely sculptures: ten were bought from the Alexander Iolas Gallery, Paris, with funds provided by the de Menils; Iolas and the de Menils each gave an additional piece; and Tinguely would later give a thirteenth one (Beauchamp 1983, 114–115). The story of the acquisition of the Tinguely sculptures circulates widely, at times as illustrative of John de Menil's charismatic enthusiasm and certitude, at others as a narrative of rather cavalier extravagance. Accounts vary, but Sweeney sets the scene this way: "In Paris last winter, I was taxiing down the Boulevard St. Germain when throngs pouring into a gallery blocked our way. I hopped out and inched my way in to find the reason for such excitement. It was Tinguely. The show had a unity. It represented 10 years of the artist's explorations, a cross-section of his work—not just a single expression. It was the sort of selection a museum should offer to represent a sculptor's efforts and achievements" (quoted in Geeslin 1965). Apparently, Sweeney cabled John de Menil, whose cabled response, it is said, read: "Buy whole show!"

This extraordinary acquisition of an entire exhibition of mechanical sculptures was met in Houston with a very mixed response. Not only did it do nothing to convince Sweeney's opponents of the virtue of modern art, but it also alienated some of his supporters. Indeed, this purchase, which now circulates as a central story in the Houston mythology of John de Menil, crystallized unease concerning the direction in which Sweeney was taking the MFAH. Because of its exhibition and accession program, the MFAH had become "a place embattled": "The accessions program . . . has brought what some feel are 'so many crazy modern paintings into the collection.' Others move right past the modern works, unperturbed, but flinch at the sight of the . . . great masks and ritual sculptures from the primitive South Sea islands or from Africa. Still others snort with derision at the pre-Columbian things" (A. Holmes 1968a, 23).

Sweeney's stewardship of the museum came to an end after twelve years. The final straw for a board that was deeply divided over his program for the museum was his refusal to accept the gift of a Fragonard from Sarah Campbell Blaffer, one of Houston's leading patrons and the mother of MFAH board member John Blaffer: Sweeney asserted that it was a fake. This was merely the climax of what had become an impossibly tense relationship between Sweeney and the majority of the board (and influential donors). He was thought to spend too much time in New York and Paris and to spend too extravagantly. Sweeney and his wife, Laura, "would later be labeled 'snobs' for their critical remarks about Houston. Their unwillingness to make Houston their permanent home was taken as criticism by those who were actively promoting the city—an additional indication of 'disloyalty'" (Beauchamp 1983, 76).

In 1960, Houston was the seventh-largest city in the United States, with a population of 938,000. The following year, its population exceeded 1,000,000, buoyed by the strong, oil-based economy. In 1963, ten new buildings opened in the downtown area, increasing office space by 41 percent. But luxury hotels and restaurants didn't open until after the legalization of the sale of liquor by the glass in 1971, since these sales provided the profit margin on which such businesses relied (Beauchamp 1983, 77). Sweeney, it was said, would send his shirts to New York to be laundered. But perhaps the most serious objection to him was due to his being too strongly identified with the ambitions of the de Menils.[18]

While the appointment of Sweeney's successor, Philippe de Montebello, represented a continuation of the drive to professionalize and internationalize the MFAH, it ran counter to the de Menils' ambitions. Indeed, this shift marked a powerful tension between, on the one hand, the bureaucratization that tends to be a corollary of professionalization and, on the other, the potency of professional "expert" care in the production of the auratic quality of art objects. The sensibilities of de Montebello tended sharply toward the bureaucratic, while the de Menils were committed to a more impassioned relationship to works of art.

The CAA and the MFAH, both prior to and since active involvement by the de Menils, had notably differing conceptions of their commitments to Houston. The CAA, while concerned to bring modern art to Houston audiences, saw itself as having an important role in encouraging local artists, offering opportunities for them to show their work. The MFAH saw its local obligations as being not to artists but to donors, offering a theater for their largesse. And in the end, both institutions found the de Menils' interests to be at odds with their own, and their participation to be intolerably overbearing. As Jane Blaffer Owen, daughter of the aggrieved Sarah Campbell Blaffer, put it, "Well, if they thought *they* were going to teach *us* about art..." (quoted in Browning 1983, 194).

"MY CAREER, THE INSTALLATION OF EXHIBITIONS"

When MacAgy's contract at the CAA was not renewed in 1959 and it had become apparent that she would not be hired at the MFAH, John and Dominique saw the opportunity to establish a position for her as the chair of art history at the University of St. Thomas. In addition to teaching art history, MacAgy curated, installed, and produced a catalogue for a show each semester, and in conjunction with John and Dominique (who subsidized her salary along with the salaries of several other professors in theology, economics, and art history, each of whom they had a hand in recruiting), she worked on putting together what became known as the Young Teaching Collection, which numbered some five hundred objects by 1968.[19]

MacAgy's legendary facility for the conceptualization and installation of exhibitions—her ability to produce enthrallment—along with her verve and charisma, defined her tenure at St. Thomas and was at the heart of the strong affinity that she and Dominique shared.

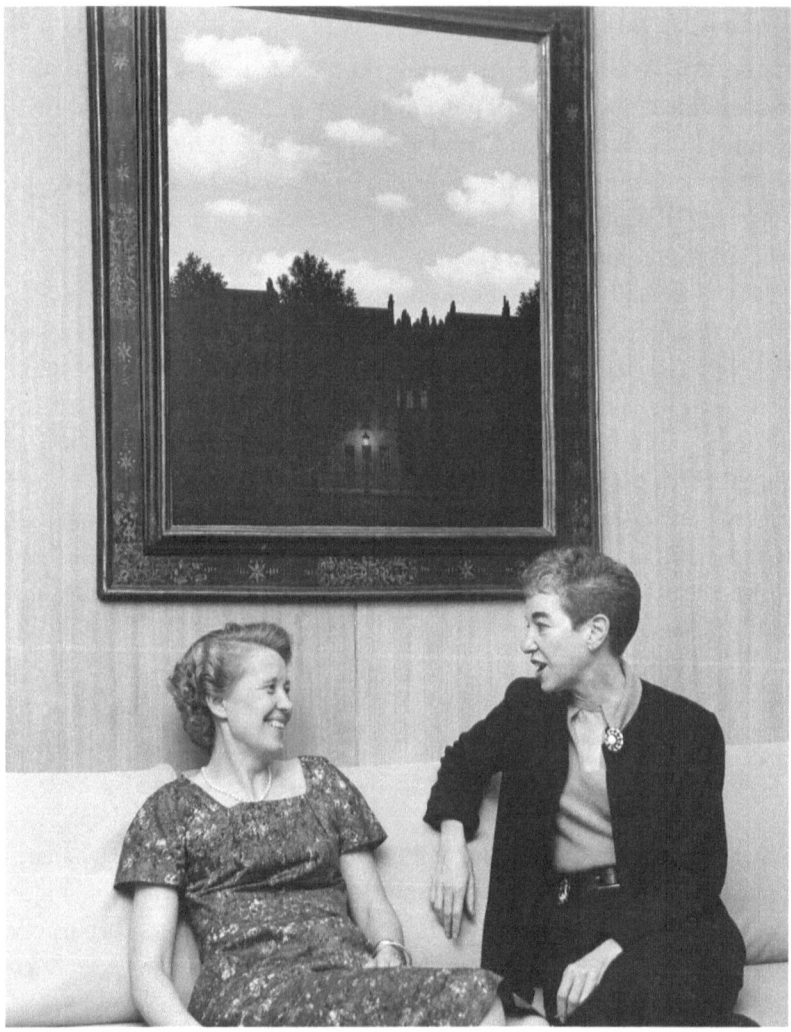

Dominique de Menil and Jermayne MacAgy at the Menil residence with L'empire des lumières, *by René Magritte (1952), ca. 1960. Photo: Maurice Miller. Courtesy Menil Archives, the Menil Collection, Houston.*

In a comment that is remarkably resonant with Couturier's observation that churches needed to create an environment conducive to faith if people were to be drawn to them, Dominique de Menil wrote of the alchemy that MacAgy's installations achieved:

No one could be expected to love art, unless seduced. Jermayne MacAgy was a master at seduction. She could cast a spell on practically anything. If she decided an object should be raised to the dignity of an art object, an art object it became. Nothing was too humble, too banal or too corny to be excluded from her phantasmagorias. . . . Her exhibitions seemed to prove Marcel Duchamp right. The spectator completes the creation. Without his cooperation, there is no work of art. Her talent insured that cooperation. Each of her installations produced an atmospheric miracle which set the work of art in such a light that it would shine and talk to anyone who would care to look and listen. (Menil 1968b, 10)

It was a huge loss to Dominique when MacAgy died suddenly in 1964. It was also a great loss to her students and associates, and to Houston's increasingly energetic art scene, which she, along with her patrons, had been profoundly instrumental in fostering. "Whoever accepted her leadership," Dominique wrote, "became a new and talented person" (1968b, 12), and so it was that Dominique herself took over as head of the art department: "I finished her shows and tried to keep things going, and that was when I was led to my career, the installation of shows" (Menil, quoted in Browning, 1983, 198).

While it may have appeared at the time that Dominique simply adopted the incantatory modes of MacAgy, it soon became clear that while they bore strong resonances of MacAgy, these newly acquired skills had been recast to serve a very distinctive Catholic aesthetic and moral temperament. In addition to producing an ambitious schedule of exhibitions and guest speakers, Dominique continued to build the teaching collection, both through her own donations of works and through contributions coaxed from other collectors and from artists and dealers.[20] It was not unusual for Dominique and John to buy works to fulfill the needs of particular exhibitions. As Dominique put it: "When we are doing a Monster show, we buy monsters. Or when we are doing art with facets, we buy faceted things" (quoted in A. Holmes 1968a, 23). And some pieces, particularly antiquities and "primitive" objects, were collected to enhance the learning experience of students.

In the foreword to the catalogue for "A Young Teaching Collection," an exhibition of 252 works from the collection, which was shown at the MFAH

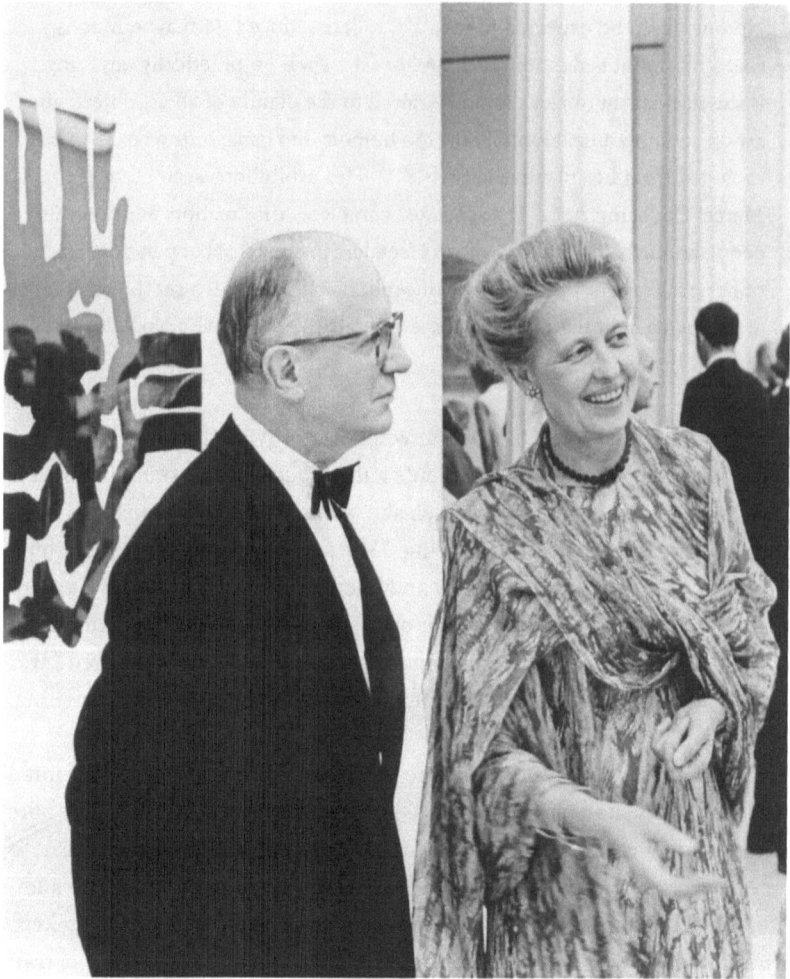

John and Dominique de Menil at the opening of "A Young Teaching Collection" (1968–1969), an exhibition organized by the University of St. Thomas and held at the Museum of Fine Arts, Houston. Photo: Hickey-Robertson. The Menil Collection, Houston.

in 1968 to mark ten years of the St. Thomas Art Department, Dominique invoked Couturier to explain the importance of such a collection:

"When you love a painting you want to touch it," once wrote Marie-Alain Couturier. . . . He believed a work of art needs intimacy to be understood and loved. It is precisely this intimacy that a teaching collection provides. The student can look at a painting day after day; he can observe a sculpture from all angles, feel its weight, smell it, caress it. A work of art has invaded its territory and demands a response.

This challenge is never offered by slides and photographs. They are superb tools, indispensable tools, but they are only tools. They are remote from the original and this very remoteness leaves us emotionally distant. Scholarly judgments can be passed without involvement. (Menil 1968a, 10)

The shows that Dominique de Menil mounted were, like MacAgy's, thematic; they did not attempt to give an art historical narrative, but put together often rather unlikely objects in such a way that they would command a fresh attention. This was achieved partly through the juxtaposition of objects and partly by the construction of space, both concretely and through the effects of color and lighting. What Dominique sought in her installations were "incantations," as she put it, provoking a visceral response that would exceed, and perhaps subvert, intellectual readings. In so doing, Dominique began experimenting with the religious, philosophical, and aesthetic elements of the off-modern. It marked the beginning of her career of aesthetic activism.

Throughout Dominique's various articulations of this insistence on a poetic experience of art can be read not only the voice of MacAgy, but of Couturier also. Writing to his coeditor of L'Art Sacré, Father Régamey, Couturier stated his position emphatically: "I insist on the primacy I will give, as far as I possibly can, to 'poetry' over pedagogy. You tell me that the two are reconcilable; but you know perfectly well that concretely that is not so: poetry is always sacrificed to pedagogy... For once it is going to be the other way round: pedagogy will be sacrificed to poetry" (Couturier 1989, 10–11). Dominique de Menil rigorously pursued this injunction and worked assiduously to produce conditions in which visitors would engage with artworks not as mere admirers, nor as passive consumers of high culture, but as interlocutors actively participating with the artwork in what she called a process of "mutual interrogation."

PROMOTING AN ART SCENE

Recognizing that a vibrant art scene relies not only on exhibitions, but also on a substantial audience for those shows and on an art market that sustains dealers and artists, the de Menils worked energetically in the husbandry of a taste in Houston for contemporary art. In 1964, with the University of St. Thomas providing a physical platform for their public programs, they established Art Investments Ltd., "an experiment ... [whereby] investor-collectors could gain greater confidence in their judgment and greater enthusiasm for collecting," but without personal risk, since purchases would be made by managing partners John and Dominique de Menil (*Business Week* 1964, 30). While such groups became commonplace in the 1980s, this was a sufficiently unusual phenomenon in 1964 for its inauguration to warrant a story in the nationally circulated *Business Week*. The de Menils' aim in establishing such a group was, as *Business Week* reported it, "to widen the base of interest in art, and open up for it the capital resources available to other investment areas" (31). Among the works purchased were a Magritte, two paintings by Max Ernst, and a pastel by Odilon Redon.

They also instituted Art Associates, with an initial membership in 1965 of 270. It was to serve as a vehicle through which members might by encouraged in their interest in modern art. Under its auspices, speakers of international stature were brought to Houston for lectures and symposia, and a newsletter focusing particularly on events generated by the University of St. Thomas Art Department was circulated. Among the guests were Buckminster Fuller, Andy Warhol, Leo Steinberg, Philip Johnson, Marcel Duchamp, René Magritte, and Jean-Luc Godard. And the Print Club, with membership dues of just five dollars, offered members, at cost, eighteenth- and nineteenth-century prints as well as posters, lithographs, and etchings by contemporary artists. The Print Library, through which prints could be borrowed, allowed for remarkably easy access to original works of art selected by Dominique de Menil and Bill Camfield, the first of several young art historians that she brought to St. Thomas, and his wife, Ginny, the club's director. As Bill Camfield described it: "Once or twice a year my wife Ginny ... would go to New York or Paris. I was going back and forth for a while to do research in Paris and [we would] come back with these wonderful prints—major 20th-century and 19th-century figures. Then there would be a big sale of these and everybody came out. It was a big social event, and people could acquire a Rouen print or a Picasso etching, or what—you name it—a contemporary piece by some European or whoever" (quoted in Reynolds 2008, 22).[21]

While these initiatives served importantly in the development of Houston's art scene locally, the de Menils set their sights on generating a considerably more far-flung audience for art in Houston. When the annual convention of the American Federation of the Arts (AFA) was held in Houston in 1957, hosted by the MFAH, John de Menil was determined that the opportunity to promote Houston as a cultural center of significance would not be lost. He chartered a private jet and subsidized the hotel expenses for more than seventeen New York–based publishers, editors, and critics. Instead of the anticipated attendance of 200, the convention attracted 1,400 people and, in order to cater to them in a manner that would reflect well on Houston, racked up a considerable deficit. John's note to James Schramm, the president of the AFA, indicates the degree of his identification with the convention and of his generosity in relation to projects to which he was committed: "Do not let the matter of cost bother you. . . . There is a small group here who will be prepared to take care of the deficit as it comes out after accounts here have been cleared."[22] The de Menils also covered 50 percent of the cost of a special insert on the AFA convention in Houston that was included in the fiftieth-anniversary edition of *Life* magazine.

This interest in gaining a wider audience for Houston's achievements was pursued in other print media too. Having read the story "Metropolis USA" in an in-flight magazine on Swiss Air, John de Menil wrote to the *Swiss Air Gazette* to point out lacunae in their treatment of Houston. The article omitted mention of the Space Center, he noted, and of the developing importance of Houston's chemical industry. But most centrally, he drew attention to the author's neglect of Houston's "remarkable cultural development." He mentioned the high caliber of the symphony and the theater, but focused on the visual arts, with which he was most involved.[23] He singled out the MFAH, with its Mies van der Rohe–designed addition, and its director, James Johnson Sweeney, "one of the most famous museum directors, nationally and internationally." And he also highlighted the University of St. Thomas campus being built by Philip Johnson, with an art history department headed by Jermayne MacAgy, whose attributes he went on to extol. "Such a two as Sweeney and MacAgy is quite exceptional and I do not believe that many cities have the like of it" (the letter is in Sweeney 1962b). A letter written just two weeks earlier to *Houston Town and Country* voiced similar concerns, again noting the particular distinction of Sweeney and MacAgy: "What city in this country can boast to that equivalent?" (the letter is in Sweeney 1962a).

What is striking in this is the degree to which John established himself as an "ambassador for Houston," but equally noteworthy is his habit of asserting the distinction of the city in terms of the excellence of the people it can attract, albeit people who, like Sweeney and MacAgy, had essentially been brought to Houston by the de Menils.

Without question, it was the creative energies of people like these, for whom the de Menils served as patrons, and the strikingly ambitious and compelling exhibitions they mounted that were responsible for Houston's emergence as an art world destination of international stature. The collection itself was to become an equally compelling component of this.

4

Collecting
as a Vocation

T
he catalogue *The Menil Collection: A Selection from the Paleolithic to the Modern Era* (1987) reproduces in pride of place on its frontispiece Max Ernst's *Portrait of Dominique*, commissioned by John and Dominique de Menil in 1934. This was the painting they had left behind, wrapped in brown paper, on top of an armoire when they left Paris during the war, not liking it sufficiently to ship it to their new home in Houston or to leave it in the care of friends. The narrative of the rejection and subsequent rehabilitation of *Portrait of Dominique* has become the story that is told repeatedly to conjure the extent to which the sensibilities of the de Menils were transformed.[1] It is presented specifically as the story of Dominique and John's aesthetic conversion, but more broadly it offers an account of the redemptive character of art. Describing Jacques Maritain's conversion to Catholicism, Amato observes that it meant that "religious concerns came to occupy the center of his attention and to form the habitual center of his energy" (Amato 1975, 52).[2] This

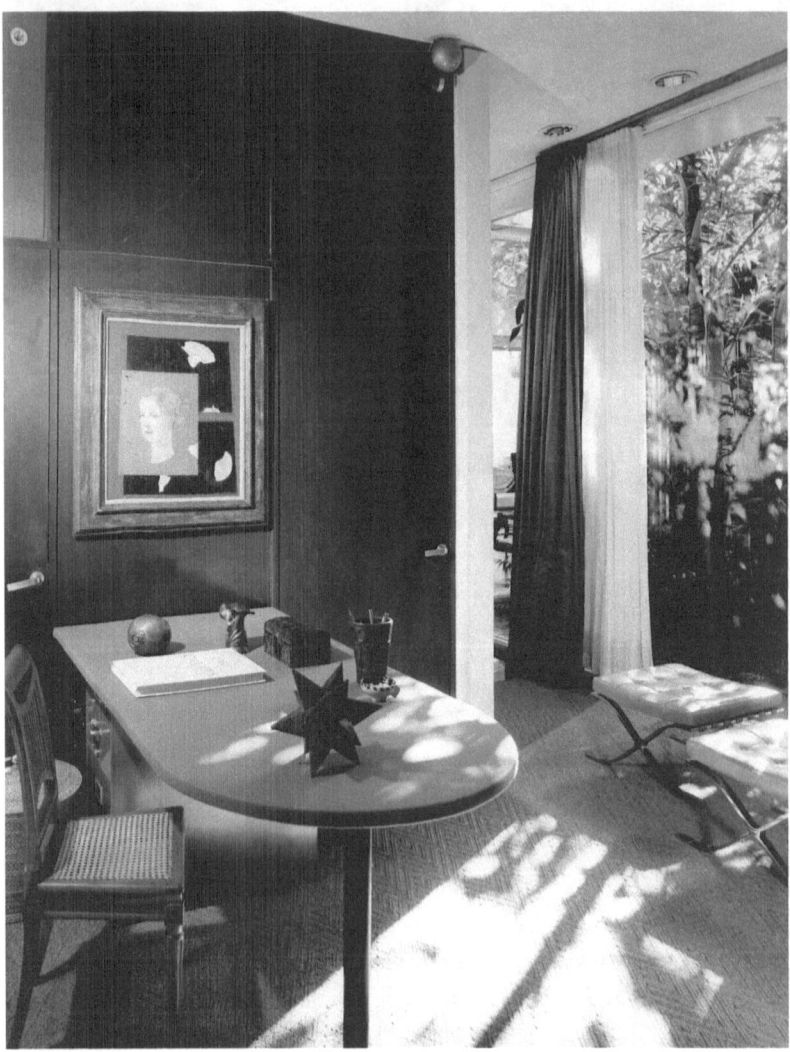

Study, Menil residence, with Portrait of Dominique, *by Max Ernst (1934), 1964. Photo: Balthazar Korab. Courtesy Menil Archives, the Menil Collection, Houston.*

was as true of Dominique's religious conversion as it was of her aesthetic one. The idea of the efficacy of art, specifically in the rehabilitation of modern sensibility, became central to the project of the Menil Collection.

Dominique and John de Menil had come to commission the painting because a mutual friend had told them that Ernst was in need of money. "Well, sure," Dominique recounts their response, "we'd love to commission him. But what could he do?" They pursued with their friend the idea that Ernst would paint something for the dining room, with birds, since this is what Ernst suggested:

> I immediately had a vision of something looking like a Renaissance fresco, with foliage and birds. Then I was shown a picture of Max Ernst's, of birds, and I was totally distressed, because in those days I just couldn't stomach that. We told our common friend to tell Max Ernst that we liked birds that looked like birds.
>
> We knew, nevertheless, that he needed the money and we wanted to help him and John had an idea. We had seen the portrait he made of his wife Marie-Berthe, so John asked if he would make my portrait. John sent him a check right away and I sat a few times with Max Ernst and that was the first time I met him and I enjoyed it. He painted my portrait and here it is. Now, we never liked it very much . . . At the time we thought that there really was not very much background and the face was not much of a resemblance. Nevertheless, there it was. (Menil and Menil 1964)

Not only had the painting been abandoned for the duration of the war, but it had earlier also languished for more than a year at the frame shop, since no one had cared to collect it and Ernst's wife had left no delivery address when she had left it for framing. It was not until the framer finally put the painting in his store window that a neighborhood priest recognized the image to be of Dominique, and the portrait was claimed (Menil and Menil 1964). Long since redeemed from its neglect, the painting now resides at the heart of what has become internationally one of the most significant collections of the work of Max Ernst, which itself forms a part of the 16,000-piece Menil collection.

The discussion that follows examines the content of the collection, the collectors' practices of collecting, and the manner in which their collecting was informed by, and operated in the service of, Dominique and John de Menil's sacred modern commitments. The off-modern character of these imperatives (at once nostalgic and open-enddedly future oriented, conservative and critically experimental) renders their collecting at odds with much of the scholarship on such practices of acquisition, insofar as collecting is construed as being resolutely governed by the teleology of unity and closure.

COLLECTORS WITHOUT REMORSE

In 1945, John de Menil returned to Houston from a business trip to New York with a Cézanne watercolor, *Montagne* (ca. 1895). This, Dominique de Menil recounted, marked the beginning of their collecting, although at the time she thought the cost of the painting a ludicrous amount to pay for an artwork that was simply "a few blotches of color on white paper" (quoted in Swan 1985, 66).

Unlike many collectors who characterize themselves as having always had a special appreciation for art, Dominique described herself as having been awakened to it under the guidance of Couturier, who, she repeated in a variety of ways, "opened her eyes" and "taught her to see." Couturier's aesthetic judgments were inevitably infused with moral adjudications, and this was by no means incidental to their seductive force. "The fervor of [Couturier's] words," Dominique de Menil observed, "borne by the gravity of what he had to say, transcends the ephemeral and touches us like the mark of the absolute" (Menil 1989a, 9).

On their frequent trips to New York, where they established a secondary residence, they moved among exiled French intellectuals, artists, and dealers, furthering their friendship with Jacques and Raïssa Maritain, and developing their particularly close friendship with Couturier. Couturier had traveled to New York late in 1939 to give a series of Lenten sermons, and, unable to return to France because of the war, he subsequently stayed on for some five years, circulating among exiled artists and working on the intellectual refinement of his own project concerned with the spiritual restoration of French liturgical art.[3]

Couturier not only fostered Dominique de Menil's ability to "see" art, but also encouraged her to buy it:

> He cured me completely of my puritanical block against collecting. He sort of made it a moral duty to buy good paintings. . . . I remember one summer [during a brief stay] in Paris, he was visiting us, and my mother was there. We had been offered a lovely Rouault and we were not going to buy it because the day before we had bought with Father Couturier a superb Japanese sculpture.[4] So at least we hesitated and he said, "Well, you must buy it. If you can afford it, just

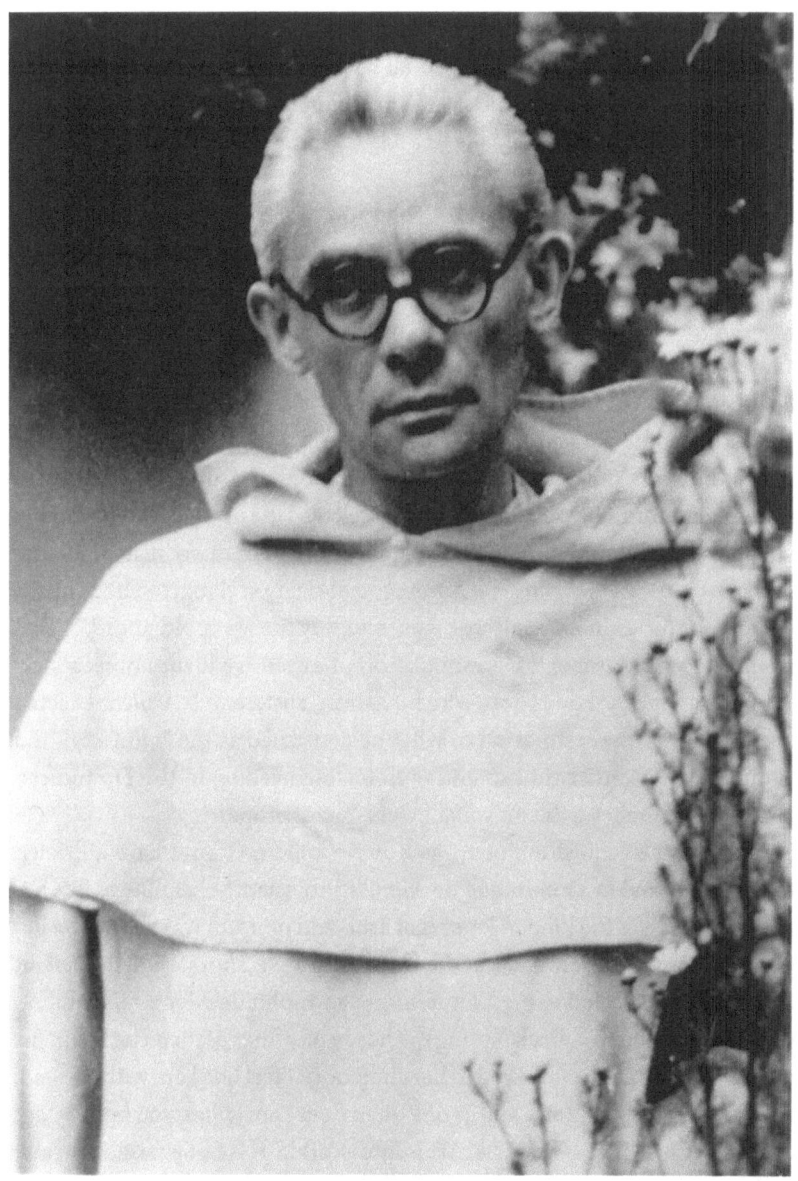

Father Couturier, Houston, 1967. Courtesy Menil Archives, the Menil Collection, Houston.

buy it." I remember my mother interfering and saying, "But Father, if they keep buying art they will have nothing to eat but crumbs." And then, completely undisturbed, he said, "Madame, let them eat crumbs and hang good paintings on their walls." So we bought the Rouault. (Menil and Menil 1964)

On their frequent business trips to New York, John and Dominique would accompany Couturier on tours to dealers Paul Rosenberg, Valentine Dudensing, Kurt Valentine, and Pierre Matisse (Menil 1983, 36). Dominique, however, was not immediately seduced by the work she was being shown, and was anyway initially uncomfortable with the idea of spending significant sums on the purchase of art, but her husband had no such reservations and quickly embraced Couturier's advice.

Dominique's reticence was informed in large measure by her Alsatian Protestant upbringing. "Father Couturier relieved me of my *latent Puritanism* I had inherited as a tradition," Dominique wrote. "For many years I felt that purchasing art was a *slightly bad* action, too pleasure seeking, too hedonistic. Father Couturier made it almost a duty to buy art we could afford."[5] That Couturier would impel the accumulation of expensive luxury objects may seem to have been at odds both with his ascetic, austere style, which reflected his longing for the restoration of what he construed as the "modesty" and "simplicity" of earlier times,[6] and with his own calling to the Dominican order, which eschews the personal ownership of property.

Treating the acquisition of art as a duty would no doubt have appealed to what endured of Dominique de Menil's Protestant sensibilities. But her understanding of the kind of labor that art could perform was shaped by her Catholic convictions. In a talk at the University of St. Thomas titled "Delight and Dilemma of Collecting," Dominique and John de Menil reflected on their compulsion to collect. Noting the heady pleasures of their engagements with art, Dominique confessed to her audience, "I feel like I am with a friend, trading fond recollections, and as one often does I am telling you how we got drunk. Because that's what it is. Art is intoxicating. It is not a rarified nicety; it's hard liquor" (Menil and Menil 1964). But this indulgence, she observed, is followed by "a remorse of some sort":

How can one drink and enjoy it when there is the war in Vietnam.
When people are hungry in the world.

When there is the ugly reaction to the moderate move of the school board. When there are people around us, police and others, who treat the blacks as I wouldn't treat a stray dog. And this is the time when the blacks have revealed their greatness by producing some of the best writers and poets in the country.

But apparent decadence here is redeemed by recognition of the distinctive efficacy of art in offering access to "eternal truths":

Well man does not live by bread alone and there is redeeming value in art. Look at great artists. They can be difficult, dissolute but they are never base and in their quest for perfection they come closer to eternal truths than pious goody goodies.
So we are collectors without remorse.

Under the sway of Couturier's moral authority and enthusiasm, Dominique came to see that their shared convictions concerning the significance of art could be served through its acquisition and subsequent exhibition, and she joined her husband in actively acquiring works, continuing to do so passionately throughout the years following her husband's death in 1973. "We try not to stop collecting," she commented. "Once we stop we belong to history" (quoted in A. Holmes 1968a, 23).

Their collecting was unsystematic, informed, Dominique insisted, not by policy but by "instinct" and "love": "There is no special theme for the permanent collection because you don't buy with ideas in your head" (quoted in *Houston Post* 1968, 7). This is not to say that their acquisitions were ill informed, far from it, but rather that the objects that constitute the collection should not be made to submit to an overarching logic of the whole. This sense of the sovereignty of the artworks in the collection (a theme pursued more systematically in the following chapter) and of her love for them is expressed in the parental idiom Dominique used to characterize their collecting, written in her foreword to the collection's catalogue: "However well parenthood is planned, children are what *they* are, not what parents decide. Like children, treasures of a collection are what *they* are" (Menil 1987, 7). In the same text, we get a stronger intimation of the methodology of their acquisitions: "Complex sets of circumstances brought these treasures into the family: a chance

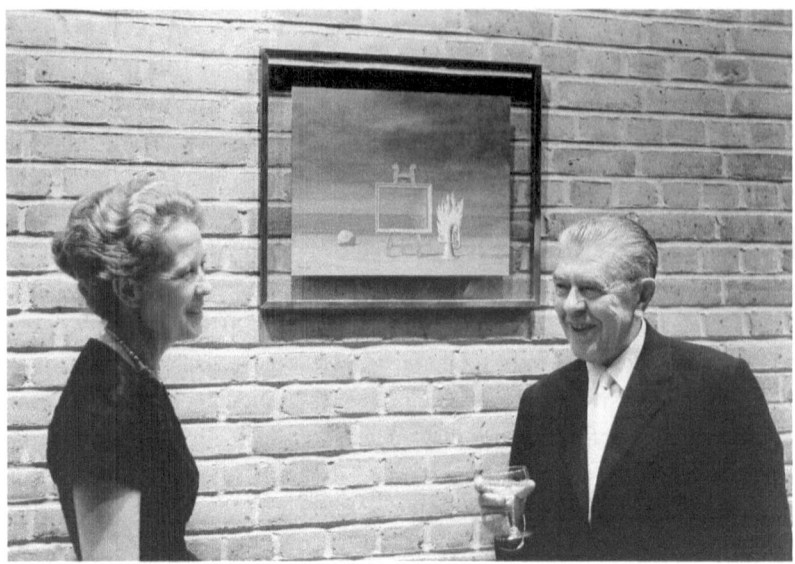

Dominique de Menil with René Magritte, University of St. Thomas, Houston, 1965. Photo: Hickey-Robertson. Courtesy Menil Archives, the Menil Collection, Houston.

encounter, a visit to an artist or dealer, a glance at an auction catalogue, a successful bidding, and, of course, a favorable moment for collecting. Nothing was excluded from consideration, yet deep inclinations existed. Constraints, too: price and availability" (7).

Like many modern collectors, including, for example, Louise and Walter Arensberg, and Peggy Guggenheim, who were guided in their acquisitions by Marcel Duchamp, the de Menils' collecting was strongly affected by personal relations with artists, notable among them Duchamp, Max Ernst, René Magritte, and Jim Love, and more latterly Robert Rauschenberg and Cy Twombly.[7] "The collection developed on its own," Dominique explained, "like a garden where some things grow and others do not. When artists are your friends, you sometimes can't resist." Victor Brauner, for example, "had great intelligence and sensitivity. I loved his color, his folkloric verve. We bought from him once a year. This helped him to live, and for us it was such a pleasure. Many things happened this way, without preconceived notions" (quoted in Swan 1985, 66).

EXPERTS

It was Duchamp who introduced the de Menils to the work of Magritte. But it was the famously flamboyant dealer Alexander Iolas who cultivated their interest in surrealism and guided their acquisition of the work of Magritte and other surrealists, among them, Victor Brauner, Giorgio de Chirico, Marcel Duchamp, Max Ernst, Roberto Matta, Joan Miró, Francis Picabia, and Yves Tanguy, along with the work of the surrealist-inspired Americans Man Ray and Joseph Cornell. "I was very lucky," Dominique de Menil commented as we discussed her practices of collecting, "because I learned also from a great dealer, Alexander Iolas, who was a Greek from Alexandria, and he, like Jerry MacAgy, he had a great eye—and I would trust his judgment. I had to learn. When he told me, 'Take it, you have to have it,' like the "Metaphysical," by de Chirico, he just told me to take it and I trusted his eye—his judgment. Every year, he would always keep the best piece that he had, the best painting for us."[8]

It was, no doubt, not only the quality of Iolas's judgment that exerted its suasive force on the de Menils, but also the character of his engagement with the business of selling art. The former principal dancer with the Monte Carlo ballet once commented, "For me, each exhibition is like a ballet premiere [...] I do not regard the gallery as a commercial profession. It is an ... artistic profession. ... I am not an art dealer just to sell paintings. The collectors are friends of mine who," he concluded with characteristic flourish, "fall in love with everything I do or see" (quoted in Papanikolas 2006a, 67).

Dominique de Menil identified Iolas, along with Couturier and MacAgy, as the most influential to the acquisitions that she and her husband made. When asked whether her initial purchases of surrealists were due to what she saw at Iolas's gallery, Dominique was quick to acknowledge his importance: "Yes, to a large extent. At first I resisted Surrealism; it was such a strange world. I felt outside of it. But Iolas kept showing us great works. He was so convincing; he was himself so convinced of the importance of what he was showing. I remember my skepticism in front of our de Chirico, *Hector and Andromache*. I was not taken in; I bought it on his word, on faith" (Brown and Johnson 1983, 38).

Iolas was famously compelling in his adjudications. When he died on June 12, 1987, the same week that the Menil Collection was opened to the public, his

New York Times obituary noted his charismatic persuasiveness: "In promoting work that initially found few to favor it, he was able to reassure the potential client by his hierophantic manner, his often sensational mode of dress and his mischievous and sometimes irresistible charm" (*New York Times* 1987). While the work that he was showing her may have seemed initially beyond Dominique de Menil's purview, it now forms a central element of the Menil Collection. Indeed, it is the work of surrealists that the de Menils collected with the most intense concentration. The collection includes more than one hundred works by Ernst, fifty-four by Magritte, and as many by Brauner. Rare surrealist publications by André Breton, Paul Eduard, and Julien Levy are also part of the collection. Moreover, surrealism, in light of Dominique and John's off-modern commitments, can be seen to embody preoccupations central to their aesthetic. Not only was its subject, as James Clifford points out, "an international and elemental humanity 'anthropological' in scope" (Clifford 1988, 243), but the surrealists shared the de Menils' interest in the generative tensions between the old and the new, the material and the transcendental, the banal and the mystical. Hal Foster notes this in relation to de Chirico, who "works to depict the world as 'an immense museum of strangeness,' to reveal the 'mystery' in insignificant things. His is an aesthetic of enigma" (Foster 1993, 62). In "What is Surrealism?" Max Ernst gives voice to an understanding of what was centrally at stake in surrealism, a statement that would no doubt have been appealing to the de Menils, as much for its substance as for the grandeur of its pronouncement: "The fundamental opposition between meditation and action (according to Classical philosophy)," Ernst writes, "coincides with the fundamental separation between the outer and the inner worlds. Here lies the universal significance of Surrealism, that no part of life is closed to it" (quoted in Schmied 1973, 23).

The de Menils were willing to act on faith, but they routinely solicited the judgments of experts. "Duchamp sparked the de Menils' interest in Magritte and legitimized it with his own high regard for the artist; Iolas, who both catalyzed and cultivated the de Menils' fascination with surrealism, guided them in collecting Magritte's work;" but it was the critic and curator David Sylvester who "ensured that their purchases were shrewd ones" (Papanikolas 2006b, 88).

Duchamp, Magritte, Ernst, Iolas, and Sylvester all belonged to the coterie of people known in de Menil circles as "remarkable" and who, in return for their virtuosity, were the recipients of de Menils' patronage in various forms. They supported artists not only through the purchase of artwork, collecting in depth rather than across a wide range of artists, but also through the production of noteworthy exhibitions and catalogues that attracted international attention. Iolas received their sustained business, selling them more than 300 works over the years, and benefited from the attention generated by the exhibitions they mounted. His first gallery in New York, the Hugo Gallery, with its blue velvet walls showcasing European art of the interwar years, was established with the de Menils' financial backing (Papanikolas 2006a). In 1967, John and Dominique de Menil commissioned Sylvester to produce the catalogue raisonné of Magritte's work. After twenty-five years of de Menil support, what had initially been a four-year, one-volume contract culminated in a five-volume catalogue, a critical biography, and a major exhibition.[9] The de Menils also sponsored what evolved into Werner Spies's seven-volume catalogue raisonné of the work of Max Ernst.[10]

Just as there was a network of experts provoking and guiding the de Menils' acquisition of surrealist works, so too in other domains of their collecting. In the late 1950s John and Dominique became interested in African, Oceanic, and Northwest Coast objects, their attention piqued, no doubt, by their encounters with surrealists. Recalling visits to Julius Carlebach's gallery in New York, Dominique de Menil observed: "It was the time when Carlebach was selling Northwest Coast art acquired from the Heye Foundation. He had been selling them to Max Ernst, Breton, and others. But even apart from Carlebach's early little store, one could make discoveries, and that was one of my favorite pastimes in New York in the fifties and early sixties" (quoted in Browning 1983, 35). But it was John Klejman who did much to shape their tastes in African as well as Oceanic objects, serving as dealer and adviser: "John Klejman . . . made buying African art very tempting. He lived just a couple blocks from us in New York, and he had fabulous African and Pacific Island pieces. We started slowly, but every year added a few more primitive works" (Dominique de Menil, quoted in Browning 1983, 37). The de Menils bought more than two hundred African objects from Klejman's New York gallery, and a further three hundred pieces, among them Oceanic objects and antiquities (Van Dyke 2007).

Kristina Van Dyke, associate curator for collections at the Menil Collection and a specialist in Malian visuality, notes:

> There is an undeniable Surrealist sensibility to the African collection, some-
> times revealing itself in a strong resemblance between African and Surrealist
> works in the collection.... There are also objects that simply appear surrealist
> in their form, such as the ivory Lega spoon that merges a utilitarian object
> with the human body.
>
> Klejman was himself attuned to this resonance in describing the object
> for his clients on the invoice: "A very fine carving in ivory of a human figure
> conceived surrealistically." (Van Dyke 2007, 39)

The Menil Collection's object files reveal the extent to which expert knowledge was sought on these objects as on all others. Nicolas de Kun, a Belgian
engineer who worked in the Congo and was the source of ten of the thirty-one
Lega pieces that the de Menils bought from Klejman, supplied descriptions
and assessments of the works along with the names of the villages from which
they were acquired. "In addition," Van Dyke points out, the files "include correspondence between the de Menils and de Kun as well as reports he prepared
about the Lega works he collected at the request of the couple, attesting to
their desire to know more about them and anticipating the careful research
that would define their patronage for years to come" (39).

John de Menil's energetic correspondence with artists, dealers, scholars,
critics, and curators was routinely remarked upon by the people I talked with
who had been in his orbit during the two decades of intensive acquisition that
he and his wife engaged in until his death. Employees of the Menil Foundation, working before the opening of the Menil Collection out of offices in the
various spare bedrooms and converted garages at the de Menil residence on
San Felipe, assisted in cataloguing the collection, but the detailed substance
of the object files, until 1973, was largely the labor of John.

The sustained effort that was invested in the acquisition of knowledge
about the objects in their collection might appear, at first glance, to be at odds
with the collectors' insistence that artworks should properly be engaged with
viscerally, aesthetically, and not as objects of art history. But this would be to
misunderstand the thrust of this activity. On one level, expertise is key to a
collector's ability to make sound investments, ensuring the authenticity and
legality of an acquisition through the tracing of provenance. In addition, the
authorities with whom John and Dominique developed close friendships
were, among other things, instrumental in establishing access to works as

they came onto the market; they "enriched their collection and enhanced their expertise by operating varyingly as mentors, advisors, go-betweens, and spies" (Papanikolas 2006b, 93). But their assiduous labors in relation to the objects in the collection were directed not only toward their acquisition but also toward their proper care once in the collection. To know an object, to devote oneself to understanding it in its many aspects, is to enliven it and care for it, to elaborate the density of the relationship, to use Annette Weiner's term, between the collector and the collected. Moreover, insofar as aesthetic engagement was, for Dominique and John, a matter of ethics—a task to which one should apply oneself in the training of one's sensibilities—effort was called for, and the acquisition of expertise was just one of a range of modalities in which this cultivation of an aesthetic disposition was pursued.

PREMODERN IMAGINARY

Notwithstanding Dominique de Menil's insistence that the selection of works for the collection should be more a matter of intuition than reason, their acquisitions were informed by "deep inclinations" and came to articulate a remarkably unified expression of their off-modern intellectual and aesthetic commitments. The Menil Collection identified four primary areas within the collection: "antiquities, Byzantine art, the arts of tribal cultures, and twentieth-century art" (Hopps 1987, 9).[11] The antiquities, Byzantine, and "tribal" art, particularly from Africa and Oceania and the Pacific Northwest coast of North America, were understood by the de Menils, however naïvely, as "pure" expressions of tradition and humanity, innocent of the secular rationalism and naturalism ushered in by the Enlightenment; they embodied a longing for the integralism of an imagined premodern past. In the introduction to the catalogue for the exhibition "The John and Dominique de Menil Collection" at the Museum of Primitive Art (New York, 1962), Dominique wrote of the particular allure of "primitive" art:

> Wave after wave has brought to our shores beautiful and mysterious treasures from unknown worlds: figurines, animals, fetishes, masks, ceremonial or useful objects.
>
> They are often called primitive for want of a better name.

They are the most sincere and most unself-conscious art that ever was and ever will be. They are what remains of the childhood of humanity. They are plunges into the depths of the unconscious. However great the artist of today or tomorrow, he will never be as innocent as the primitive artist—strangely involved and detached at the same time.

What could never have been written is there, all the dreams and anguishes of man. The hunger for food and sex and security, the terrors of night and death, the thirst for life and the hope for survival. (Menil 1962, unpaginated)

The romantic nostalgia that permeates this characterization also imbues the de Menils' taste for Byzantine and medieval art—in its invocation of a humanity not yet corrupted by modern rationalism and individualism. But Byzantine art also resonated with Dominique in very personal ways. "There was," Dominique related to guests at the opening of "Spirituality in the Christian East: Greek, Slavic, and Russian Icons from the Menil Collection" in 1988, "always a love and reverence for Byzantium in my family, thanks to Gustave Schlumberger," the eminent Byzantine scholar.[12] Her interest in Byzantine art was, furthermore, an expression of her deep ecumenicism. Drawing my attention to an image of St. Peter and St. Paul, Bertrand Davezac, the Menil Collection's senior curator until his retirement in 1999, explained that it was "emblematic of [Dominique's] ideas and dreams, the rapprochement of the two churches—with St. Peter representing Rome, and Paul, Constantinople, the two pillars of the church. . . . Byzantium, for her, is the lost sheep, and her dream is for the two arms of Christianity to be reunited, and that's what having the Byzantine collection symbolizes."[13]

While the collection seems, at first glance, to be remarkably diffuse, containing pieces from disparate cultural and historical traditions, in light of the understandings generated within the context of the renouveau catholique, we can see the collection instead as a coherent materialization of sensibilities formed within that milieu.

In the tradition of critical reflection on the modern condition that we have been describing as off-modern, with its uneasy juxtaposition of anti-modern nostalgia and ultramodern enthusiasm for the possibilities of the contemporary, we can see in the premodern elements of the collection an expression of the collectors' nostalgic yearnings. The modern art they acquired reflects, of course, their embrace of the new, the contemporary;

surrealism itself manifested the dissonant, apparently incompatible elements of the off-modern. These temporal preoccupations were underpinned by the profoundly Catholic imperatives pursued within the milieu of the *renouveau catholique*, and were given form by the conviction that art offered a privileged medium by which the ineffable might be grasped and the spirit restored. The collection materialized a critical experimentalism that was imbued with faith and hope.

NATURALISM

There are three key issues at stake here in understanding the content and style of the de Menils' collecting, all of which were addressed systematically by Maritain, subsequently elaborated upon by Couturier (though not always in ways that were strictly in alignment with Maritain), and pursued by Dominique and John de Menil. First is a question about what constitutes reality and how it might be grasped, which played out in arguments between naturalism and abstraction. The second concerns the conceptualization of the relationship between the artist, the artwork itself, and the viewer. And third is an analysis of the contemporary, of its malaise and what has caused it.

The matter of the real and how it might be accessed was, as noted in Chapter 2, central to the project of the *renouveau catholique*, since this problem guided its theorists' quest for a rapprochement between the eternal and the ever-changing contemporary. The tension between naturalist and eternalist worldviews revolved around the meaning of reality. Schloesser characterizes the conflict this way: "For naturalists, reality was the material of history, subject to constant change; their realism led to agnosticism or atheism. For eternalists, reality was form behind the matter, impervious to change; their realism led to metaphysical and theological truth. Realists and eternalists thus shared a dualistic view. They imagined the world as a struggle between enormous forces set in opposition to one another" (Schloesser 2005, 35). Recognizing that this dichotomy ensured a gulf between the worldly and the sacred that rendered each irrelevant to the other, Maritain worked to articulate a theologically defensible formulation of the relationship between the material world and the ineffable, with nonnaturalistic modern art as its fulcrum. This was in stark contrast to the Church's position on sacred art, which had endured since the Council of Trent's 1563 decree that had sought to contain the affective character of art by closely prescribing both the subject matter and the style of Church art. David Freedberg characterized Tridentine thinking on art in this way: "If we must have images at all, then we must ensure not so much that they do not bring us down to the level of the senses but that they lift us to higher planes; that they assist us in proceeding from the material to the spiritual; and that they offer us mortals enwrapped in our senses the possibility of mediation—at least with the divine" (Freedberg 1989, 358–359).

Tridentine decrees on painting codified and canonized not only the subject matter of images but also the style of their presentation, their "finish." This prescribed finish, which Cézanne described derisively as "*le fini des imbéciles,*" required that the image be brought "to a plane of realistic imitation in which brushwork, drawing, and other elements of the *facture* were buried, [and] became a central standard of judgment in religious art" (Rubin 1961, 14). Modernist painting, in its preoccupation with painterliness at the expense of referentiality, opened a gulf between secular art and art of the Church. Far from ensuring pure sensibilities, Couturier argued, the Tridentine proscriptions served art and its audience poorly. Over time, they fostered decadence, with bloodless academicism its "aristocratic" form and the sentimental art of Saint-Sulpice, its "popular" counterpart (Rubin 1961, 15; Couturier 1989). It is these symptoms that served as the fulcrum for the much more extensive critique of modernity that was articulated by Couturier and his associates under the banner of what emerged as the sacred art movement.

The interplay between materiality or external appearances and unseen reality that modern art fostered rendered it particularly efficacious in bridging the divide between the contemporary and the eternal, the worldly and the otherworldly. At least, this was the argument that Maritain elaborated, drawing on and recasting familiar Catholic tropes.

Just as traditionalist French Catholics focused on the Renaissance as marking the beginning of religious art's decline into sensual representation, so, too, Catholic modernists condemned the Renaissance for ushering in the "five centuries of error" that had brought Europe to its parlous circumstances. Maritain, as Schloesser argues, appropriated this conservative aesthetic, but put it to radically different use: "By discrediting realism he could closely link medieval and contemporary non-representational art with one another" (2005, 154). In his essay "Notes on Saint Thomas and the Theory of Art,"

Maritain wrote: "Medieval art was naturally, instinctively, protected against naturalism . . . by the hieratic traditions which came to it from the Byzantines: it did not 'copy the materiality of nature,' nor did 'it copy immoveable super-sensible exemplars'" (quoted in Schloesser 2005, 150). Later, Schloesser points out, Maritain added this gloss: "The art of the Renaissance on the contrary allowed itself *to be gravely contaminated*" (154).[14] It wasn't just a matter of nonnaturalistic art offering access to the eternal, but also "about restoring organic integrity to a fragmented body politic" (154). The emergence of the bourgeoisie also played its part in the degeneration of religious art: "Maritain also located the Renaissance as the moment when the artisan's *métier* became corrupted into the artist's *beaux-arts*, and he concluded in a way consonant with his boyhood socialism: 'The divorce was a consequence of the changes that had taken place in the fabric of society and in particular of the rising of the bourgeois class.' The Italian Renaissance had divorced art (as Machiavelli had divorced politics) from ethical concerns, and in the nineteenth century, they had sacrificed true Art for naturalist representations, satisfying bourgeois tastes" (154). We see here intimations of the conviction, central to the understanding of art elaborated within the *renouveau catholic* and deeply held by Dominique and John de Menil, that the aesthetic qualities of artworks lie not in the character of the objects themselves but are predicated on the human virtues of those who craft these objects. The art object is a trace of humanity, just as it is a means by which that very humanity might be fostered.

Couturier saw in "native arts" a "manifestation, an almost unbearable presence, of the pagan supernatural" (Couturier 1989, 72). This was the source of its great virtue, for Couturier and for Dominique de Menil, who frequently cited him on this matter. This spirit, which, in light of their radical ecumenicism, did not need to be Catholic, or even Christian, derives from the artist, or at least is channeled by the artist, by virtue of his "atavistic instinct for the sacred and its transcendence" (92). Couturier speaks of this in a variety of ways: here, with reference to Matisse's comment "All my life, my only strength has been my sincerity": "Sincerity producing the whole strength of a life and its work, and thereby touching the secret recesses of the hearts of millions from one end of the earth to another. . . . The sincerity of one lone man, if it goes deep enough in him, reaches, for all other men, a universal substratum of truth which nothing else can penetrate" (83). The best modern artists, in Couturier's view, in their refusal of naturalism and their uncompromising commitment to their aesthetic vision, availed themselves of the same purity of spirit that is evident in "native arts," that enchants their works.[15]

Couturier's interest in "native arts" lay not only in drawing parallels with modern art, but also in elaborating what he called a "universal humanism," a humanism owing its central elements to the integral humanism of Maritain. This notion, as Couturier articulated it, served both as a critique of the idea of the salvage of "pre-contact" traditions, and as a legitimation, however questionable, for the collection of objects and their subsequent presentation in the aestheticized space of an art museum. Couturier's critique was rooted in a sober appraisal of reality: "The effort to go on forever preserving and protecting will be in vain: the world is too small. No barrier can hold" (Couturier 1989, 83). The project of preserving the distinctive styles of different peoples was not only bound to fail by virtue of continual encroachment or contamination, but was also misguided, he argued, since it was not specific styles that were truly at stake: "In the matter of native craftsmanship, what we must save is not such and such forms, noble and pure as they may be, but the human gifts that assure this nobility and purity and that would still assure them in entirely new forms" (83).

Couturier's critique of "salvage" did not imply that objects from earlier traditions should not be preserved, rather that the attempt to preserve the traditions themselves, which denied the inevitability of transformation, was mistaken. Indeed, "what must be done," he argued, "is to save all that can be saved out of the past of peoples, and to give special care to all that is alive" (72).

While "native arts" needed to be protected "from the tawdry products of commerce and academicism," Couturier felt no compulsion to protect them from influence. Indeed, just as African art had a powerful impact on Western art, so might Western art have an equally enriching effect on African art: "True values and true greatness do not kill each other. They make each other grow, they ennoble each other by association and exchange . . . and the fruitfulness springs from the indivisible unity of human nature" (83).

For Couturier, then, the universality of aesthetic virtue lay not in the character of objects themselves, then, but in the universally human virtues of those who crafted the objects. Those virtues were what missionaries in the colonial period jeopardized, if not irrevocably overwhelmed, Couturier argued. He also claimed, rather more extravagantly perhaps, that such virtues were what "the pagan and naturalistic Italian Renaissance, by liquidating the Middle Ages, banished completely from the Western Christian world" (72).

Philip Nord characterizes this analysis in an extended passage that resonates with the integralist convictions of the *renouveau catholique*.

> Catholics did not doubt that the modern world had gone awry, tracking the initial false step to the Italian renaissance. The Renaissance's paganism and aesthetic naturalism has alienated flesh from spirit, the person from the community that nurtured him. The result was an atomistic pursuit of interest and pleasure that was at the source of all contemporary France's moral failings. . . .
>
> What was needed was a new age of faith, and there were examples in the past to look to: Golden Age Spain and the French Middle Ages. Then, faith had burned with an unparalleled intensity. Saints and knights strode the earth, but they served in obedience to a wider purpose, to the human collectivity of which they were part, to the will of God whose instruments they were.
>
> The heroes of these bygone ages had critical lessons to teach the modern-day believer, lessons of valor, risk, and adventure. (2003: 5)

The notion of risk and adventure, with all its masculinist associations, in contrast to the limp imitation of naturalistic painters, was conjured by Dominique de Menil in a talk she gave to Rice University alumni in 1972. For the artist himself, "art is a tough exploration, a tough venture where the risks are enormous." While virtuosity can be acquired by labor, great painters struggle for something beyond that, "a grace which descends only upon those who work ceaselessly and risk everything" (quoted in A. Holmes 1972). This risk taking, underpinned by strong convictions and sustained effort, characterized not only the artists that the de Menils championed, but also all those people who were among the "remarkables" whose counsel they sought and whose projects they, in turn, supported. It also suffused their own dispositions.

The notion of the artist as someone with special gifts of insight is far from confined to the *renouveau catholique*. It has its roots in romanticism, and is explicit in the work of Charles Baudelaire, which Maritain drew on heavily, and persists in various forms today, despite having been the subject of significant critique.[16] There is, as Charles Taylor observes, "a kind of piety which still surrounds art and artists in our time, which comes from the sense that what they reveal has great moral and spiritual significance; that in it lies the key to a certain depth, or fullness, or seriousness, or intensity of life, or to a certain wholeness" (1989, 422). Indeed, raising a subject that will be pursued in Chapter 10, "for many of our contemporaries," Taylor continues, "art has taken something like the place of religion" (422).

But for Dominique de Menil, it was not just the disposition of the artist, and its trace in the work of art, that was at stake in the production of aesthetic experience. In contrast to high-modernist formulations that would have the artwork speak for itself, she insisted that without an active interlocutor, the object was essentially mute. Producing the conditions that this kind of engagement with art might flourish in, that would foster between artworks and their viewers a relationship of "mutual interrogation," as Dominique was wont to describe it, was central to the de Menils' exhibitionary projects.[17] This acutely aesthetic experience is directed not so much toward aesthetic appreciation or connoisseurship, but toward an affecting engagement between persons and objects that would overcome the flattening and distancing of the experience of modernity. The character of this engagement and its ongoing effects upon the viewer were central elements of the collectors' project of patronage that, consistent with the political philosophy of Maritain and Mounier, pursued social reform through a reform of personal sensibilities.

"Without Servitude to the Past, nor Recklessness"

I n 1976, Dominique de Menil wrote a memo to board members of the Menil Foundation a memo; in 1989, she circulated it again to board members, with a note explaining that she had happened upon the original, "which appears to me a bit naïve. . . . Yet, the ideas expressed remain pertinent":

> We are often asked what . . . are the basic ideas behind our projects, which cover such a wide range of activities? Jean used to say: "We do what others don't do." This is not just a provocative remark. It is a whole program.
>
> Of course we could join hands with others who do excellent work, but somehow the vocation of this foundation is elsewhere. We are in a position to be more creative and more daring. We should try to discern the men that are the greatest, and hopefully at an early stage in their career when it is not yet obvious that they are great, and when a small help can be crucial, and we should try to do what is not yet perceived as important, but will be.

This policy of independence of mind involves higher risks than conformity to established programs, and it obligates us to surround ourselves with people of great discernment, people who have an instinct, a natural taste for the highest quality.

We face a world in chaos. The problem is both a moral failure and a failure of intelligence—morality and intelligence being the two sides of the coin. It would be exhilarating if within the limited means of this foundation we would encourage ideas capable of making a breakthrough, works of a redeeming quality and far reaching consequences.[1]

This gives expression to the kind of transformative revisioning that the *renouveau catholique* called for, which was informed by a critical disposition toward the contemporary, a nostalgic longing for an imagined lost past, and optimism for the possibilities of the new. Indeed, this formulation brings to mind Miyazaki's characterization (2004) of the "method of hope," insofar as the de Menils' patronage did not simply respond to an emergent present, but sought to shape it while remaining open to chance and the unanticipated. As discussed in the introductory chapter, they were not engaged in a utopian project, driven by the investment of hope in a particular outcome, but, rather, through their projects, they engaged in a hermeneutics and a practice that served to keep hope alive. And so in his efforts to characterize the "personality of the Foundation," John de Menil identified it in terms of "continuing historical zones of commitments without servitude to the past nor recklessness."[2]

Particularly marked, too, in Dominique's articulation is the understanding that their projects stood or fell on the qualities of particular individuals rather than institutions. This artifact of the "personalist" social theory they adopted from Maritain and Mounier had a defining effect on both the style and the substance of their patronage. Their personalist approach could also be observed in the extent to which their projects of patronage were directed toward dispositional outcomes—the reform of sensibility rather than social structure. This was clearly the case with aesthetic effects, but the de Menils sought to transform affect across a range of social domains, most notably in the fields of social justice, education, and architecture as well as art, though under their auspices, all these were inevitably intertwined, and inflected with the exigencies of making faith plausible.

These other types of projects pursued by the Menil Foundation, or by the de Menils themselves, which are the subject of this chapter, have often been remarked upon, sometimes as a prehistory of the Menil Collection, but mostly, perhaps, as a testament to the virtue of the patrons. Whatever skepticism one might harbor concerning the motives of art world benefactors—and under the ascendancy of the hermeneutics of suspicion, as I have argued, this is considerable—might be relieved, or at least softened, when presented with evidence of righteousness, especially in the form of political action on behalf of social justice. These endeavors—school-board politics, the support of civil rights activists, and so on—work powerfully as testaments to virtue not just because the cause seems unequivocally just, but also because the effort looks like real politics. In addressing not just the content but also the style of their patronage, I seek to develop an understanding of John and Dominique de Menil's method of activism, a method they pursued in every domain of their engagement. This method, their mode of engaging with the world, was essentially the substance of their endeavors, since it was a politics of practice—the practice of ethical citizenship imbued with the spirit, with faith—rather than material outcomes that they pursued. This was the case no less in their art world activities than in their endeavors in social justice or education.

This discussion of their patronage beyond museum making, serves in part to lay the foundation for an understanding of their activism, which was extended into the institutional form and exhibitionary practices of the Menil Collection. It also establishes the broad purview of their interests, which might put pressure on the tendency to view the Menil Collection as the culmination of their work, as the fulfillment of their commitments. The museum is, of course, the most substantial of the projects undertaken by the Menil Foundation, and the sheer cost of maintaining it curtailed myriad other enterprises that might have been pursued, so it certainly did become the overwhelming focus of the foundation and of Dominique de Menil. And, moreover, the opening of the museum just as Dominique was entering the final decade of her life only intensifies the sense of the museum being the climax or pinnacle of the de Menils' endeavors. But to see the museum itself as their legacy—as the materialization of their commitments and a means of temporal transcendence—is to misunderstand the character of their investment in it. Had the museum opened earlier, it is not obvious that Dominique would have been content to oversee the maintenance of an institution whose internal imperatives are in constant tension with the practices and effects that

she sought to facilitate. There were many indications of her growing frustration with the ever-increasing financial demands of the museum, and with her
consequent inability to be responsive to new initiatives. As one staff member
put it, in an apt but unpretty locution, "the baby had swallowed its mother."

DELUXE

Concerns with social justice—in the particular form of U.S. racial politics—
education, and art came together emphatically in relation to the figure of
Mickey Leland. John de Menil had taken a particular interest in the young
activist who had recently dropped out of college to run the campaign of a
black minister, D. Leon Everett, for the all-white Houston school board when
they met in the mid-1960s. "I went to breakfast, lunch, and dinner at their
house," Leland recalled, "and met every important person they knew. I spent
hours talking with John about world politics and philosophy. He wanted me
to be exposed to every aspect of their life that would give me the chance to
do things for my community. They helped make a black militant who hated
white people in to a humanitarian" (quoted in Glueck 1986, 45). Having
been groomed by John for a career in politics, Leland served Houston as
a state representative until 1979, when he was elected to Congress, serving
until his untimely death in a plane crash while on a humanitarian mission
to Ethiopia in 1989.

Ann Holmes gives an account of the significance of this association
between John de Menil and Leland: "Knowing that one person can spark a
reform, he gave Mickey the encouragement and financial help necessary to
get his education. Racial tensions were running high at the time, remembers
Richard Murray, a political scientist at the University of Houston: 'Mickey
Leland was considered the most dangerous political leader. But John taught
Mickey, and Mickey was like his son. That frightened some people who
thought the de Menils limousine liberals'" (1991, 230).

Leland did invaluable labor for the de Menils and gained important political insight in negotiating the complex political terrain of "The DeLuxe Show,"
the 1971 exhibition initiated and sponsored by the Menil Foundation and
mounted in a long-defunct cinema (the De Luxe) in the Fifth Ward, a poor
black inner-city neighborhood in Houston.[3] African American community

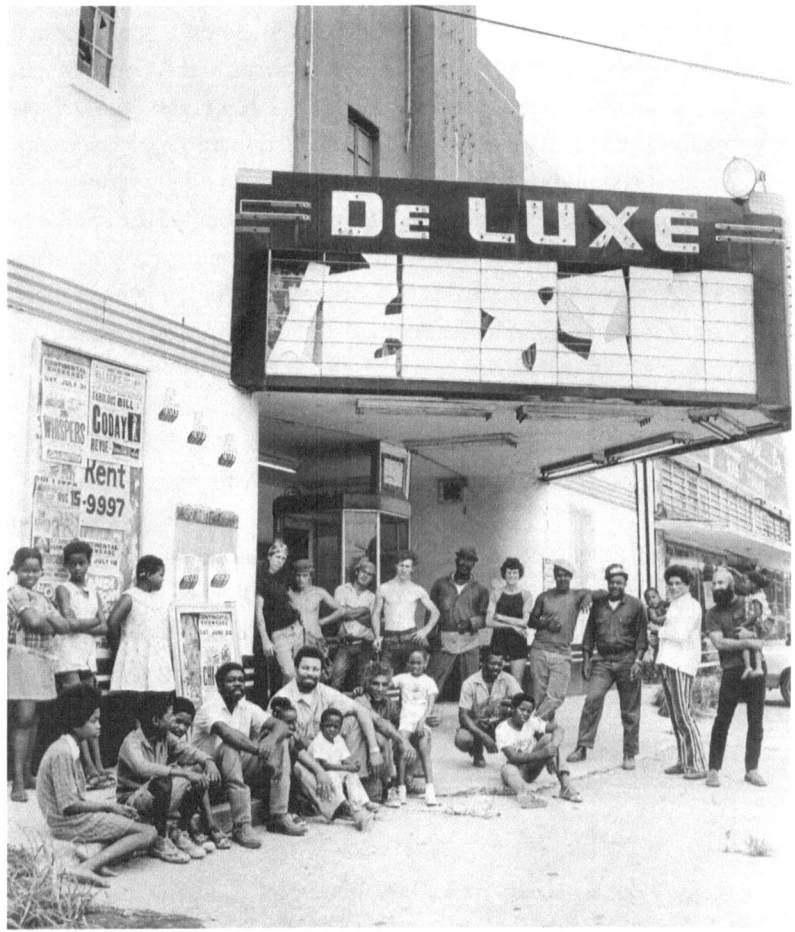

The De Luxe cinema during construction for "The DeLuxe Show," 1971. Second from right, Mickey Leland. Photo: Hickey-Robertson. Courtesy Menil Archives, the Menil Collection, Houston.

activists in the neighborhood were, at least initially, deeply suspicious of wealthy white liberals coming into a black neighborhood with an exhibition that, far from responding to local input, insisted from the outset on elite curatorial standards of object selection and exhibition design. To ameliorate the perception of privileged imposition, while no doubt taking pleasure in the provocative character of the gesture to their social cohort, John de Menil contracted with the local chapter of the Black Panthers to provide security for the exhibition and to serve breakfasts daily to neighborhood children.[4]

Curated by the New York artist Peter Bradley, the show was one of the first racially integrated exhibitions of contemporary artists in the United States. Bradley, in an interview published in the show's catalogue, notes: "The DeLuxe show marks the very first time that good black artists share the attention with good white artists. The black artists look good with them simply because they *are* good" (*The DeLuxe Show* 1971, 67). The show was mounted in response to a nationwide controversy over barriers to black artists and, more proximally perhaps, in response to criticism that the de Menils' exhibition "Some American History" (Rice University Museum, February–April 1971), examining slavery and black life in America, had focused primarily on the work of white artist Larry Rivers.[5] People in the de Menils' circle had floated the idea that they do a show of African American artists in a black neighborhood, and in his usual style, John had sought advice on the idea. Peter Bradley recounts:

> That's when I said that no black artist of any worth will allow his work to be shown in an all black situation, even in a black neighborhood. Some artists were upset by the 1971 Whitney show of black art, from which many withdrew (I refused to be in it) on the principle that we don't want to be lumped politically. We were proven to be right, at least as far as art criticism is concerned; for you'll remember that press coverage of the Whitney show concentrated on black political stances. Hardly a word was said about the art itself! (*The DeLuxe Show* 1971, 68)

John asked, "Well, what would you do?" Bradley told him, and just a couple of days later John asked whether he would be willing to put a show together (69).

As a measure of the stature of the de Menils' endeavors, Clement Greenberg came to town for the opening of the show, and in an interview published in the catalogue, he noted, with more than a hint of surprise, the "attentiveness" of its neighborhood audience (65).

Dominique and John de Menil's conviction that the exhibition was worth doing is a testament to their understanding of the recuperative potential of art. In this and other endeavors to offer African Americans access to their distinctive aesthetic heritage, which included exhibitions of African art and the work of contemporary African American artists such as Peter Bradley and

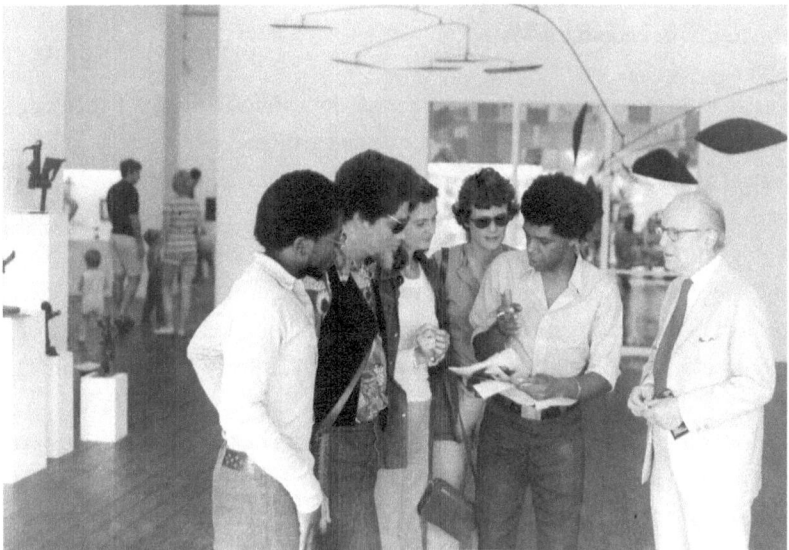

Mickey Leland (second from left), Simone Swan, Helen Winkler, Peter Bradley, and John de Menil at the opening of "For Children," Rice Museum, May 1971. The community excitement that "For Children" generated was, according to a Menil Foundation memo from July 1971, one of the motivations for "The DeLuxe Show." Photo: Hickey-Robertson. Courtesy Menil Archives, the Menil Collection, Houston.

Joe Overstreet alongside the work of other artists, they conceived of the art as a source not only of identificatory pride but also of a kind of transport of the spirit occasioned by exposure to work of excellent quality compellingly exhibited.

Following "The DeLuxe Show," works from the de Menils' collection continued to be shown in the former cinema over the next three years, though control of the venue was increasingly turned over to the Black Arts Center in recognition of the symbolic importance of the De Luxe becoming subject to neighborhood African American authority rather than their own.[6] In the end, it was not so much competing visions that drew to a close the de Menils' financial and emotional investment in the site, but rather the recognition by John de Menil, as he sought to put the Menil Foundation's affairs in order in anticipation of his death, that, in his absence, the complex and often fraught relationships involved in sustaining these highly personalized commitments would be insupportably difficult to sustain institutionally.

IMAGE OF THE BLACK

Perhaps the most enduring of their projects concerned with race is The Image of the Black in Western Art. Dominique de Menil had been shocked on her arrival to the United States to discover systematic racial segregation and had wondered "why, when great artists have seen blacks as beautiful, dignified, noble, they were not considered so here" (quoted in Glueck 1986, 46). This, she said, was the provocation for The Image of the Black in Western Art, a project of extraordinary scope, which the Menil Foundation financed from its inception in 1960 until 2000, when Harvard University assumed full responsibility for the project's archive and publications. Its objective has been to undertake a scholarly survey that traces the ways in which blacks have been represented in Western works of art. The purpose throughout, as articulated by the project, has been "to provide a richer field of experience to the ways the Occident has thought and felt about the black African" (Menil 1976, xi). Dominique said of her impetus for the project that racism relies upon a failure to recognize the humanity of others, and it was her belief that through exposure to imagery that reflects that humanity, racist sentiments would be rendered unsustainable: "With such a naive approach, a serious enterprise was started" (xi).[7]

In the face of such an abundance of material, one is faced with a great variety of people, commented Dominique de Menil:

> All cast in roles they did not choose. They are actors in plays written by whites. Though whites are invisible their presence is felt everywhere. It is their customs, their tastes, their prejudices, their phantasms, and their romanticism that have been captured in these images. . . . These voiceless blacks, these ghosts, have carried nevertheless one of the longings of mankind. They were a symbol of universality and of the equality of men before God. On twelfth-century enamels the apostles address themselves to a white man and a black man who signify humanity in all its variety. (Menil 1976, ix–xi)

Project staff initially searched out examples from a variety of forms of representation—sculptures, frescoes, illuminated manuscripts, paintings, and drawings—in archaeological sites, museums, private and public collections, churches, and libraries throughout the world. Each image was photographed, researched, and then catalogued in what has become a huge archive that has sustained a remarkably ambitious program of research and publication. The project set up an office in Paris under general editor Ladislas Bugner, with a branch in Houston, run by Karen Dalton. Published in both English and French, *The Image of the Black in Western Art* was initiated as a multivolume work in 1976; as of this writing, the final volume is in preparation.[8] On the publication of the first volume, *From the Pharaohs to the Fall of the Roman Empire*, Dominique de Menil, as a guest of Mrs. Mondale, made a formal presentation of it to the library of the vice president's house. Dominique closed her address with the observation that "by going to the root of it, by looking at the past, we can understand the present and shape the future. And all of us here belong to those who are determined to shape the future."[9]

Like other de Menil benefactions, this was not something they had charted in advance, but rather it emerged in response to the enthusiasms and expertise of a particular individual, in this case Ladislas Bugner, who was initially approached merely to curate an exhibition on this topic. An appealing idea pursued with excellence was allowed to take on a life of its own. It was characteristic of their patronage that they became involved with specific projects in response to particular individuals. Edmund Carpenter, the husband of the de Menils' daughter Adelaide, pointed this out, prompting John de Menil to write: "In fact most projects stem from one individual: the negro iconography could not have been without Bugner; the Institute of Religion would not have been worth supporting if it weren't for Tom Shannon. Our small contribution to Masters Nursery actually is Margaret Mahler, etc."[10] The de Menils lent their support to many projects for which they were not the principals, each of them in alignment with their commitments, each driven by protagonists whom they found personally compelling. Support of the therapeutic nursery at the Masters Children's Center, in New York, was due to both Margaret Mahler herself and her mission, child psychoanalysis, at a time, if such can be imagined, when its therapeutic promise had not yet caught hold in New York. The anthropologist Alan Lomax's Choreometrics project, which sought to find in the cross-cultural analysis of dance fundamental human forms, was attractive for its interest in observational film and the idea of a common humanity expressed in dance. The Children's Storefront, a school in Harlem appealed to the de Menils because of the educational opportunities it offered African American children and because of its founder, the poet Ned

O'Gorman. Ivan Illich's Centro Intercultural de Documentación (CIDOC), in Cuernavaca, Mexico, was supported for its Catholic critique of Rome's missionary practices in Central and South America, for his "retraining" of missionaries under the guise of language teaching, and for his advocacy of active critical engagement.

RACE AND EDUCATION

Another central strand of their commitment to the amelioration of the effects of racial discrimination draws attention to the significance, in their view, of access to high-quality schooling. It began with their very early, very public support of a prointegration slate of candidates for the Houston school board in the 1960s. The Menil Foundation went on to develop, in collaboration with the Houston Independent School District, a scholarship program for promising black students that would prepare them for college and support them through the completion of their academic training; the foundation independently funded a number of other black students whose merit and need had been brought to its attention.[11] The foundation gave ongoing support to SHAPE, Inc. (Self Help for African People Through Education), initially paying the rent on a couple of buildings, one for the program's general activities, the other for a school. In 1972, it was agreed that the school, with an enrollment of two hundred students, would move into a larger building to be purchased for SHAPE by the Menil Foundation.

Texas Southern University, a historically African American school in Houston, was the recipient of very focused funding for the pharmacy program, guided by Mickey Leland's assessment that if it were to develop a research program to augment its established clinical training, its graduates would be competitive with those from the University of Houston's program.

Beyond these programmatic interventions in the politics of race, John and Dominique retained lawyers to represent civil rights activists facing charges. They directed financial support to Martin Luther King, Jr., and caused disquiet among their neighbors in River Oaks, a neighborhood defined by oil-industry heavyweights and old Houston society, by their practice of welcoming African American activists, scholars, religious figures, and artists as their guests at meetings, dinners, and parties in their home. On the occasion of the American

Federation of the Arts national conference that was held in Houston in 1957, Dominique and John de Menil made a point of insisting that the conference hotel, the locally fabled Shamrock, refrain from excluding African American participants from using its conference facilities (Fox 1999). Chandler Davidson, a sociologist at Rice University, recalled responses to them in the 1950s and 1960s, and indeed through the 1970s: "The de Menils were looked on as people who broke ranks with the city's top society. To them, the de Menils may have seemed like traitors to their class" (quoted in A. Holmes 1991, 230). Dominique dismissed this observation with the remark, "A *lot* of people stood for civil rights and human causes—Oveta Hobby, the George and Herman Brown families, Nina Cullinan and many others" (quoted on 230).

Notwithstanding Dominique's downplaying of the extent and distinctiveness of their involvements, it is indicative of their willingness to engage the politics of race and the facts of segregation in Houston (and indicative, too, of their taste for symbolic gestures) that when they commissioned Philip Johnson in 1949 to design their new home in River Oaks, they had him orient its main entrance to San Felipe, a street that had hitherto been used only for rear service entrances—for the comings and goings of African American and Hispanic employees—as Stephen Fox, a noted Houston architectural historian, pointed out to me.

ST. THOMAS

The de Menils' commitments to education extended beyond the sponsorship of students to projects on an institutional scale, although these projects also were highly personalized. For example, John and Dominique were as deeply involved emotionally as they were financially in the stewardship of the University of St. Thomas, for which they had commissioned architectural plans, bought land, and funded the establishment of an art history department, along with an excellent library of slides, books, and periodicals; the nascent teaching collection; and an ambitious program of exhibitions and visiting scholars and artists, as we have seen. While the character of the program, and the buzz of enthusiasm around it, was owed principally to the charismatic drive of Jerry MacAgy, and subsequently of Dominique, students in the art history department were not taught solely by these figures. A small but

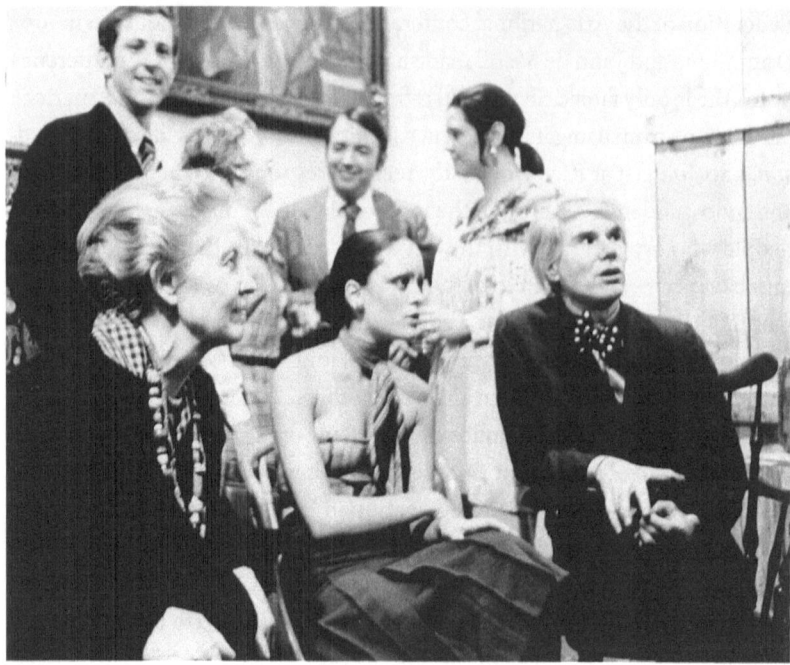

Dominique de Menil (far left) with Andy Warhol at the University of St. Thomas, May 1968. Photo: Hickey-Robertson. Courtesy Menil Archives, the Menil Collection, Houston.

well-regarded faculty was hired, among whom were people distinguished for their work in areas in which the de Menils were collecting. Mino Badner, a specialist in African art, is said to be largely responsible for the extraordinary quality of the African work that can be seen in the Menil Collection. William Camfield, hired directly from graduate school at Columbia, had a special interest in surrealism. A few years later, Walter Widrig and Philip Oliver-Smith, who specialized in antiquities, joined the faculty, along with the theorist and critic Thomas McEvilley.

The excitement that by all accounts animated the department, and indeed firmly established St. Thomas at the heart of Houston's countercultural scene of the 1960s, was fueled by a heady mix of critical discourse and experimental practice, alloyed with the luxury of first-rate resources and the overwhelming sense that one was participating in something audacious. To this small campus in a city widely imagined to be a cultural backwater came Buckminster Fuller, Andy Warhol, Leo Steinberg, Marcel Duchamp, Jean-Luc Godard, and

René Magritte, to name just a few of the guests that the de Menils brought to St. Thomas.[12] And those students who, through their abilities and their ambition, came to form the nucleus of the art department and its activities were also drawn into the de Menils' life beyond the campus. One such student, Karl Kilian, who with early assistance from Dominique and John became the owner of a Houston bookstore distinguished for its selections of art and architecture books and its knowledgeable staff, recalled: "Along with other St. Thomas students, I was often asked to the Menil house and we were entertained like adults. Fred Hughes, who later became Andy Warhol's business manager, was a St. Thomas friend and another frequent visitor at the de Menils'. When they would have New York visitors that they wanted to impress, we were sort of shown off as exhibits 'A' through 'J' to persuade the Easterners of the education quality coming out of St. Thomas" (quoted in Welch 2000, 58).[13]

In addition to Kilian and Fred Hughes, who went from his studies at the University of St. Thomas to work for the de Menils' dealer Alexander Iolas in Paris before taking up what became his life's work with Warhol, several alumni of the St. Thomas art history department who were also beneficiaries of the de Menils' mentoring went on to have distinguished art world careers. Among them were Mark Haxthausen, who became chair of the graduate program in the history of art at Williams College until his recent retirement; Helen Winkler, who worked closely with both Jerry MacAgy and Dominique de Menil and went on to collaborate with Philippa de Menil and Heiner Friedrich in establishing the Dia Foundation; and her brother Paul Winkler, who in 1980 was called from his position as assistant director of the Museum of International Folk Art in Santa Fe to serve as the Menil Collection's assistant director, with primary responsibility for overseeing the planning and construction of the museum. He went on to direct the museum from 1991 until his resignation in 1999, working in close collaboration with Walter Hopps (who had been the Collection's inaugural director but who stepped down in order to focus more on curatorial matters) and with Dominique de Menil. Until Dominique's death at the close of 1997, the three worked essentially as a management team, attending to administrative matters, formulating the exhibition schedule, curating exhibitions, and, a particular pleasure for each, installing them.

In 1966, John de Menil wrote to several other foundations in Houston, seeking financial contributions to St. Thomas (and wrote to still others explaining that he and Dominique were themselves unable to contribute to additional projects, since they were committed at St. Thomas and elsewhere "more than their whole income"): "The Art Department has a budget of $150,000, including $50,000 for exhibitions and catalogues. We personally contribute 80% of this budget. If a broader support could be gained, we would be free to help other departments in the university grow to the same high level attained by the art department. Houston at large would benefit by having a first class liberal arts college."[14] In fact, the de Menils did fund positions in economics and in theology for scholars whose approaches furthered their intellectual, political, and religious interests. And this was characteristic; they didn't endow a position in the abstract, but rather paid the salaries of specific people they wished to support.

Given their commitment to the kind of informed, disciplined, critical thinking that such a school could foster in its students, the de Menils saw access to this kind of intellectual training as a very consequential element of social reform. In 1969, however, the de Menils ended their close association with the University of St. Thomas. Father Patrick Braden, the president of the college at the time and possessing none of his predecessor's affinity for his benefactors' enthusiasms, commented: "It began to look more like de Menil University than St. Thomas. The issue was really the kind of institution St. Thomas was to be—would it maintain its Catholic identity or would it become a secular college?" (quoted in Glueck 1986, 66). John de Menil had not only insisted that the board become open to lay members, but was equally insistent that his own allies be appointed to the board—all this amid rumors that he himself had his eye on the presidency. The presence of the de Menils and their coterie was so pervasive that "it became difficult to operate without stepping on one of their toes" (Braden, quoted on 66). Philippe de Montebello's observation regarding the de Menils in the wake of Sweeney's departure from the Museum of Fine Arts, Houston might equally apply to this situation: "When they didn't control things, they stepped aside" (quoted on 46).

This is no doubt true. But it is also the case that when the MFAH board replaced Sweeney with de Montebello, it did so directly in opposition to the vision for the museum that the de Menils had worked relentlessly to realize. "They became interested in Baroque and Renaissance art, and," as Dominique de Menil explained, "we were not as interested" (quoted in Johnson 1990, 8).

It was not, by any means, that Sweeney had been pliable and they recognized that de Montebello would not be. Strong willed though they undoubtedly were, that kind of authority was never what they wanted. In their taxonomy, Sweeney was one of the "remarkables"—gifted, distinguished, a force to be reckoned with who also shared their taste for provocation and risk. A more nuanced reading of Dominique and John's tendency to focus their efforts on projects they could direct reveals it to be due in part to disappointments they had experienced with the unfolding of projects over which they weren't able to exert their influence, and in part to their strong sense that they were charting a new course. It was also dispositional. Ann Gruner Schlumberger, John's sister-in-law, writes of him:

> I do not think that I'm wrong in suggesting that he had cherished the dream of a life dedicated to serving the weak and the rejected . . . [but] he was nonetheless tainted with elitism. Jean believed in the demonstrative power of example, the duty of the "chief" to preach by example. . . . This man who wore his heart on his sleeve, this most brotherly of men, succumbed at times to what I am bound to call flashes of authority. . . . It seems to me that what unleashed these storms . . . was almost always a refusal to follow his lead on ground which he had long ago and painfully explored, and which therefore appeared to him to be the only right one. (1982, 120–121)

This kind of elitism, underpinned by the convictions of faith and a strong sense of moral authority, brings to mind Schwartzwald's characterization of Couturier, expressed in an aesthetic idiom, as someone "resolutely democratic on issues of *access* to the means of artistic creation and especially art appreciation," but "'aristocratic' when it came to hierarchy of artistic quality" (n.d., xxiv). In his own explanation of his high-handed tendencies, John observed: "I'm too attached to what I'm doing, and once I've given myself to it I want to succeed right away. This is so true that it's hard, if not impossible, to ask God to send me a failure if he thinks it's good for me" (quoted in Schlumberger 1982, 121). While Dominique's disposition was inflected with a more reserved sensibility, she shared with John an unwavering sense of the authority of their adjudications, which they both imbued with moral force through their extraordinary expenditure of personal resources—energy, attention, and money—to produce the effects they sought.

Erwin Panofsky's characterization of the Abbot Suger's twelfth-century project of rebuilding the Abbey of St. Denis, notwithstanding its temporal distance, suggests something of the kind of understanding of oneself in relation to one's projects that seems apt. Panofsky argues: "This is not the Renaissance man's thirst for fame, [rather] Suger's [was a] colossal, but in a sense, profoundly humble vanity. The great man of the Renaissance asserted his personality centripetally, so to speak; he swallowed up the world that surrounded him until his whole environment had been absorbed by his whole self. Suger asserted his personality centrifugally: he projected his ego into the world that surrounded him until his whole self had been absorbed by his environment" (1979, 29–30). Suger, in a sense, became identical with the abbey; he "divested himself, to some extent, of his existence as a private individual" (31).

Indeed, Panofsky's characterization of Suger's style of patronage resonates further with the practices of Dominique and John de Menil, practices that when not lauded have been perceived as meddling. Panofsky invokes the definition of "patron," as one who "countenances or protects or deigns to employ a person, cause or art." It is in contrast with this characterization of the distanced, disengaged patron that he portrays Suger's practices of patronage, which are notably participatory. In the process of the extraordinarily ambitious rebuilding of the abbey, Suger found himself unable to obtain some exceptionally long beams that were critical to his plan. Despite assurances that there were no such timbers to be found in any forest nearby, he set about searching for them himself, leading a party of carpenters "with the courage of . . . faith, as it were, to search through the wood," where they successfully, though not without difficulty, tracked down what they required (Suger 1979, 97). Panofsky comments:

> A man who takes his carpenters into the woods in quest of beams and personally picks the right trees, a man who sees to it that his new chevet is properly aligned with the old nave . . . is still more akin to the amateur or gentleman architect of the earlier Middle Ages—and, by the way, of colonial America— than to the great patrons of High Gothic and Renaissance periods who would appoint an architect-in-chief, pass judgment on his plans and leave all technical details to him. Devoting himself to his artistic enterprises "both with mind and body," Suger may be said to [have acted] . . . not so much in the capacity

of one who "countenances or protects or deigns to employ" as in the capacity of one who supervises or directs or conducts. . . . It would seem that very little was done without at least his active participation. (Panofsky 1979, 35–36)

This kind of involvement bears a strong resemblance to the de Menils' style of patronage, and Suger's writings certainly offer some insight into a distinctively Catholic mode of relating to the material character of objects, whereby this attention can be understood as a form of ministry—as a vocation. Although it would be foolish to make too much of the parallels between Suger and Dominique and John de Menil, it is instructive to bear in mind this formulation of the patron, which differs so markedly from the current prevailing model, and, more importantly, to recognize the complexities of the subjectivities of those who pursue these kinds of projects—subjectivities that should not be coded merely as "elitist." Such a coding has tended to foreclose the kind of detailed analysis of the particular aspirations, anxieties, and worldviews that I have sought to pursue here, in favor of sustained attention to the politics of privilege upon which such projects are predicated.

RICE

Their aspirations for St. Thomas thwarted, the de Menils resolved, with considerable regret, to transfer their programs and their modified ambitions to Rice University, taking with them students as well as academic and administrative staff, along with most of the teaching collection and the art library that they had created for St. Thomas. At Rice, they established the Institute for the Arts, which allowed them to pursue their projects—lecture series, guest speakers, exhibitions, film studies, collection management—with the participation of university faculty members and students, but without any obligation to align these activities with the requirements of accredited university programs.

Having resolved to make the move, the logistics of relocation took on some urgency because Dominique de Menil had committed to host (originally at St. Thomas) a traveling exhibition from the Museum of Modern Art, "The Machine as Seen at the End of the Mechanical Age," curated by Pontus Hulten. A temporary structure to house the Rice Museum (established by the de

Menils independently of Rice's own Sewall Art Gallery)[15] and the Rice Media Center, dedicated to film studies, was designed in December 1968 by the Houston architects Gene Aubry and Howard Barnstone and was completed in readiness for the show's opening on March 26, 1969. It was extremely well suited to that show, and it continued to prove itself with each subsequent exhibition (see Hulten 1968).

On a far-flung corner of the Rice campus, distant from the more sedate architecture and intellectual activity that then prevailed at Rice, known at that time principally as a science and engineering school, the Art Barn (as it quickly became known) and the adjoining Media Center, simple yet commanding structures clad in unpainted corrugated iron, gave architectural notice that things at Rice were about to change. Conceived as temporary structures, in part because they had to be designed and constructed in such haste and in part because the de Menils had entered into only a five-year agreement with Rice, the buildings remain on their site forty years later, still appearing architecturally distinguished and home now to the Marian and Speros Martel Continuing Education Center. The uncharacteristically cautious five-year commitment was, no doubt, in response to the institutionally rather lukewarm reception Rice gave the de Menils. At St. Thomas, their initial involvement emerged out of the opportunity to build a well-designed campus and as a solution to the "problem" of finding a position for Jerry MacAgy as she faced not being renewed by the board of the Contemporary Art Museum. But they found there an enthusiastic partner in Father Murphy, the president of the university, who was ready and willing to rise to the occasion. Their association with Rice arose out of their need to find an alternative to St. Thomas, but it faced what might most generously be described as institutional indifference. Students, however, were far from indifferent, and almost immediately "the barn" began to serve not just as the base of the Art Institute's activities, but also as a magnet for students from across the campus.

"The Machine" show was as startling as the building that housed it, featuring "strange machines that drew pictures or threw balls, machines that waved plastic hoops with all the skill of a cowboy playing with a lariat," and video art, which had only just begun to find its way into museum exhibitions (Johnston 1971, 6). The following year, the Art Barn showed no fewer than six exhibitions, three organized by Dominique de Menil and her associates, and the others organized by the Metropolitan Museum of Art, Philadelphia's

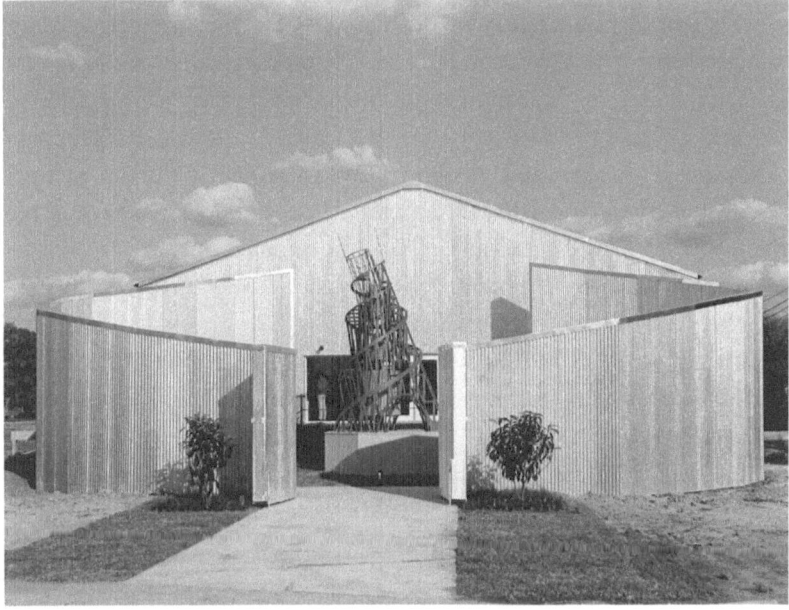

Rice Museum exterior with Vladimir Tatlin's Tower during the exhibition "The Machine as Seen at the End of the Mechanical Age," 1969. Photo: Hickey-Robertson. Courtesy Menil Archives, the Menil Collection, Houston.

Institute of Contemporary Art, and kicking off the year, the Rhode Island School of Design's "Raid the Icebox with Andy Warhol," the concept for which had been suggested to Warhol by John de Menil.

All their shows received considerable local attention, and many that they organized not only traveled internationally, but attracted national and international attention in Houston. Students and graduates hired to staff the Rice Museum worked on much of the organizational detail of putting together exhibitions, assisted in the production of exhibition catalogues, took artworks and slideshows to elementary schools, and did research on the teaching collection. And many migrated between Rice and the Menil Foundation, housed in the Menil residence on San Felipe, since the boundaries between these operations were far from distinct.

The Menil Foundation had in the 1960s given financial support to several film projects, a number of which were abandoned before completion, but at Rice the de Menils much more systematically pursued this interest, which Dominique had first taken up while studying film for a year in Berlin as a student. It never occurred to John or Dominique that their projects were not sufficiently significant to be of interest to even the most celebrated of figures, as was evidenced by the loans they sought—and very often were granted—for exhibitions. So it wasn't particularly surprising, perhaps, that John was able to persuade Roberto Rossellini, head of the Centro Sperimentale di Cinematografia, Italy's national film school, and Colin Young, head of the National Film School in London, to develop a plan for the Media Center as a center for the study of film and photography, rather than as a facility for professional training in film production.

James Blue, Mark McCarty, David MacDougall, and Gerald O'Grady formed the faculty of what was one of the first such programs in the country, and Rossellini and Young continued to make periodic contributions to the program. James Blue, the program's founding director, was already recognized as a defining figure in experimental and "socially conscious" documentary film in the 1960s, and pursued these interests at Rice and later at the Southwest Alternate Media Project, which emerged out of the Rice Media Center and was underwritten by the de Menils until 1977, when it became a freestanding nonprofit entity; it continues to function today as a critical force in documentary film. McCarty and MacDougall, who arrived straight from graduate school, were ethnographic filmmakers and theorists, moving in the same intellectual circles as Dominique and John's son-in-law Edmund Carpenter, who was also trained in anthropology and engaged in the late 1960s in defining the field of visual anthropology. O'Grady was a defining figure in the emergence of the field of media studies and went on to develop and direct the media studies program at the State University of New York at Buffalo. The Media Center continues to operate as the base for film, video, and photography students at the university, though it cannot be said to command anything like the presence that it had under the de Menils' leadership.

Dominique de Menil served as director of the Institute for the Arts until 1980, when she stepped down to focus on planning a museum that would not be vulnerable to the shifting preoccupations of a larger institution over which her projects could claim no enduring hold. Plans for the Menil Collection were publicly announced in 1981.

6

Toward a Museum

The proposed Menil Collection was not the first time that John and Dominique seriously pursued the idea of a freestanding museum. In 1972, they had approached Louis Kahn to produce plans, not for a museum exactly, but for "a gallery with open storage, a concept more reminiscent of the open stacks of a library than a traditional museum" (Loud 1989, 245). When the de Menils were first establishing their working relationship with Rice, what was to become Rice's Sewall Gallery, embedded within an academic building, was already in the planning stages. It represented a modest commitment to the exhibition of art on campus, and John had voiced his objections to the design, but there was already some momentum growing for the development of an extensive arts complex on campus. Though the initiative for this project had not been theirs, Dominique and John pledged two million dollars toward what John described as an "Art/Architecture/Music Building" to be designed by Kahn, from whom preliminary plans had already been commissioned.[1] Perhaps if Rice had moved ahead with the development of this facility, the de Menils and their collection would have stayed at Rice in an expanded Institute for the Arts. The university, it is said, was less than wholeheartedly enthusiastic about such an outcome, particularly since this venture would have required granting the de Menils a degree of autonomy that was at odds with the institutional structure of Rice.

Since Rice declined to proceed, Dominique and John turned their attention to other ways to further their mission of using their collection to "introduce students and the public to art, taken off its marble pedestal and shown as a daily companion, stimulating and refreshing."[2] As things stood, the collection remained largely in storage facilities off campus—indeed, it was dispersed in residences and in storage in Paris, New York, and Houston, and there were always elements of it traveling in exhibitions, both theirs and on loan to shows that originated elsewhere. It would not be until 1984, at the Grand Palais, in Paris, at the invitation of Pontus Hulten, that the collection itself, or a significant portion of it, was brought together and shown as a collection.[3] In fact, it was the first time that even Dominique de Menil herself had seen it in a single location. "La Rime et la Raison" was an exhibition of 678 pieces from the collection of John and Dominique, along with works from the collections of their children and of their former son-in-law (and Menil Collection trustee), Francesco Pellizi.

"The announcement by the Menil Foundation that it has commissioned Kahn to design the Rothko Chapel Plaza will make it clear to Rice," John de Menil wrote the members of the foundation's grants committee (which constituted the board's inner circle), "that we are out of their building plans on the campus."[4] What they sought from Louis Kahn in 1972 was not just exhibition and open-storage space, but something of a cultural precinct extending from the site occupied by the Rothko Chapel and Barnett Newman's *Broken Obelisk* and adjacent to the University of St. Thomas. The memos circulated among Menil Foundation board members concerning this project are oddly charming in the broad gestural sweep of the vision outlined in them, hand in hand with occasional elements of what to many would seem distracting detail. John writes, for example, of the need for a place where "decent simple food can be served to guests" within walking distance of the Rothko Chapel. "We have initiated formalities for the immigration of a highly recommended Indian cook," he continues, "and we are playing with the idea of farming out an Indian restaurant that would be popular in the neighborhood."[5] The chapel, "with over 2000 visitors a month, and growing" (just a year after its dedication), needed accommodations for its guests, and the modest bungalows occupying the several city blocks that they were in the process of purchasing could be restored to "solve the problem of low cost homes without undue subsidy."[6]

Even as plans for the neighborhood grew more elaborate—a small hotel, apartments, townhouses, houses "sprinkled over the land" (in which residents would use their "gifts on the ground floor and live upstairs; so the ground floor would have a flow of things passing through"), several city streets purchased and closed off to create a pedestrian enclave, a grove of palm trees, and roof gardens—the exhibition and storage space retained, conceptually, the modest air of a workshop, in the spirit of the Art Barn.[7] Indeed, meeting, seminar, and storage rooms were treated as no less important than gallery space. Noting that the collection was of such a size that only a small portion of it could be on display at any one time, Patricia Loud, writing comprehensively on Kahn's art museum architecture, described the design challenge posed by the collection's storage: "The whole collection was to be available to any visitor with very little effort. Even drawings that had to be protected from light were to be centrally located in cabinets with drawers clearly marked and easily accessible. Everything was to be open to anyone who had an appointment to see it. . . . It was a concept with enormous appeal to Kahn" (Loud 1989, 247). This interest in open storage is, of course, by no means novel now, and even then Kahn was already engaged with this question for the "study collection" at the Yale Center for British Art. However, Kahn considered the extensive storage facilities required for the Menil project "an expression of generosity on the part of the donors and wanted that quality to be visually expressed. His design would have institutionalized the concept of study-storage to a greater extent than had been done in New Haven. This de Menil design might therefore have materialized as a new kind of museum expanding the building type" (257).

Kahn traveled to Houston early in 1973 to meet with his clients and to see Dominique's show "Max Ernst: Inside the Sight," which traveled to sixteen museums in the United States and Europe. In October, a few months after John's death in June, Kahn completed a set of pastel drawings for the project, and it was presumably in response to these renderings that Dominique reiterated, with perhaps more vigor than earlier in their conversations, that "this project needs to be conceived of as a park, quite compact, with no monumentality," reiterating an early articulation that the project should rely heavily on "beautiful frugality."[8] When Kahn died suddenly in March 1974, the project was put aside.

It is perhaps worth noting that throughout this period of energetic and detailed planning for the future of the collection and the nettlesome "DeLuxe Show" project, as well as ongoing negotiations with Rice to establish an arrangement that would extend their relationship beyond the initial five years, John was living with the cancer, diagnosed in August 1970, that would take his life on June 1, 1973.

VISIONARY BUILDERS

One of the most striking elements of Kahn's plan is that it is not first and foremost a design for a museum, but rather a spatial conceptualization of a range of activities and interactions, only some of which were expected to occur within the exhibition and storage space. Just as important were the elements designated as meeting rooms, seminar rooms, and conference facilities. The plan conjures an image of the precinct as a place of work—in contrast to the idea of the museum as a leisure destination—and a key element of that work is the exchange of ideas.

The conviction that architecture can perform important conceptual labor was manifest in this ensemble of buildings. Further, as I discussed in relation to the Rothko Chapel and Couturier's chapel projects, the potential for architecture to produce aesthetic and spiritual effects—to move or seduce—was very much on the de Menils' minds. But Dominique and John also understood that working with architects in the vanguard of modern architecture, as was the case with artists too, drew them into social networks both within and beyond Houston that were appealing both personally and programmatically.

Though the de Menils commissioned few buildings, they are recognized as unusually significant architectural patrons. Each of their architectural projects was meant first and foremost to fulfill the requirements for which it was designed, but beyond that, each one was meant to stand as an example for others.

We have already observed their commissioning of drawings from Philip

Johnson for their parish church and, subsequently, the plans for the University of St. Thomas and the Rothko Chapel. But their first commission of Philip Johnson was not for a public project but for their own home, for a growing family that would number five children by the time the house was completed. Their choice of Johnson is instructive. Weighing whether to approach Mies van der Rohe or Johnson, they opted for the latter—less expensive than his mentor (of consequence, since in 1949, Schlumberger wealth had not yet begun to flow) and without his reputation for being unresponsive to his clients. But also, as Frank Welch reports, Johnson "was building that house in Connecticut that everyone was talking about, and he was an important fixture at the Museum of Modern Art" (Welch 2000, 41). John de Menil met Johnson at the apartment of their mutual friend Mary Callery, who was a sculptor, the owner of "more Picassos than anyone in New York," and a charismatic figure among New York's postwar avant-garde elite (22). "Charmed by his wit and worldly ways, [John] asked him to come to Houston to meet Dominique" (41).

It was not that there were no architects in Houston from whom they could have commissioned a modernist house, but the de Menils were never parochial in their ambitions, and as Welch points out, while they were "sophisticated and worldly," they, "particularly John, were not immune to big city glamour" (41). A Philip Johnson–designed house linked the de Menils to the aesthetic rigor of Mies van der Rohe while also giving them entree to the defining modern institution of the time and to elite circles of modernist collectors. And, in turn, members of the modernist elite in Houston increasingly turned to the International Style aesthetic for their own homes as a means of asserting their affiliation to the de Menils, as Fox and Welch have so persuasively argued (Fox 2005; Welch 2000). And this provocation to emulation was not entirely incidental: "They really had the thought that if they brought someone like Philip Johnson to Houston and he designed a nice house, it would lead to better architecture in the city. They definitely wanted to improve the climate even then," as the de Menils' close Houston friend Marguerite Barnes observed (quoted in Welch 2000, 43).

While Fox and Welch both maintain that the house did serve to provoke further modern architectural commissions in Houston, Johnson himself saw it as falling short of exemplary—it was never published under his auspices (Fox 2005). The explanation that I was given repeatedly over the course of my research was that Johnson had objected to his clients' insistence on an interior décor that was not consistent with the austere, high-modern Miesian style. Johnson, however, notes that he was unhappy with the architectural resolution of the building, the result of Dominique's "insistence on functional concerns" (Johnson, quoted in Fox 2005, 6). Either way, while Dominique and John de Menil might have been dazzled by Johnson, they were neither of them willing to simply defer to his authority. Dominique insisted, to Johnson's chagrin, that the front exterior wall be broken with windows so that their cook would have the pleasure of a view from the kitchen, and she called for the house's ceilings to be raised from nine feet to ten and a half, a change that necessitated a rearrangement of proportions throughout.

Both John and Dominique wanted something "more voluptuous" (Dominique de Menil, quoted in Welch 2005, 45) than the interior that Johnson had imagined for the house, and it was John who had the idea of calling on Charles James, Dominique's famously flamboyant couturier. James introduced color and texture into the interior in unorthodox juxtaposition. He used velvets and silks and felt in crimson, fuchsia, and chartreuse, covering the doors and walls of the hallway of the children's wing with crimson and fuchsia velvet. The doors of Dominique's dressing room were colored in a subtly varying palette of softly hued milk paint. The furniture was an eclectic mix of old and new, including ornately carved chairs by the Victorian cabinetmaker John Belter, Venetian settees, and curvaceous sofas and banquettes designed by James (Welch 2000; Fox 1999).[9] The willingness of John and Dominique to assert their own vision, even in the face of the dismay of their architect, whom they both admired and liked, conveys something of the characteristic certitude of their convictions as well as of the extent of their social confidence, which enabled much of what they achieved.

What was finally crafted was a mise-en-scène imbued with off-modern, experimental sensibility. It served as an instrument not merely of the clients' self-fashioning—though it certainly did serious labor in this regard—but also of the fashioning of a much more extended milieu. The architect was also well served by the house. Although his misgivings about it meant that he was unwilling to have images of it published in architectural magazines, this loss of exposure paled in light of the wealth of commissions that his work for the de Menils generated. For Schlumberger, Johnson designed an office building for what is now the Schlumberger-Doll Research Center in

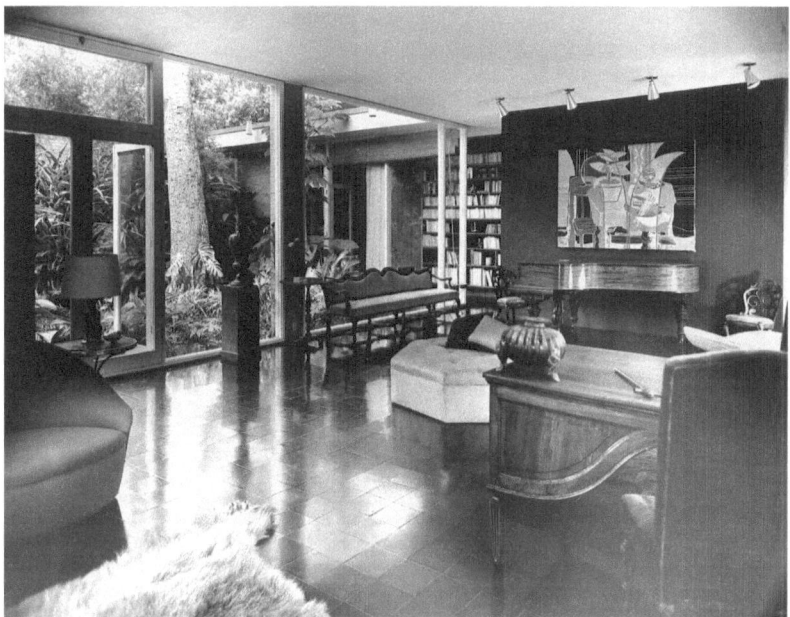

Living room, Menil residence, c. 1957. Photo: Clarence John Laughlin. Courtesy Menil Archives, the Menil Collection, Houston.

Ridgefield, Connecticut, and made plans for a number of unbuilt projects. He designed houses in Connecticut and France for Dominique de Menil's sister and brother-in-law, Sylvie Schlumberger and Eric Boissonnas. It was John de Menil who recommended Johnson as architect for the Amon Carter Museum in Fort Worth, the Art Museum of South Texas in Corpus Christi, and, as we know, the University of St. Thomas. And it was due to these commissions that Johnson's long-term association with the developer Gerald Hines was established. Their collaboration had a defining impact on Houston's skyline: the Post Oak buildings, Pennzoil Place, the Transco Tower, and Republic Bank Center are just the most visible of his projects in Houston.[10]

Dominique and John de Menil were also important patrons of Howard Barnstone, a Yale graduate who took up his position at the University of Houston School of Architecture in 1948, and of Eugene Aubry, who became his partner. John commissioned Barnstone (then partnered with Preston Bolton) to design a series of housing complexes in Venezuela, Argentina, Peru, and Trinidad for employees of Schlumberger Surenco, the corporation's

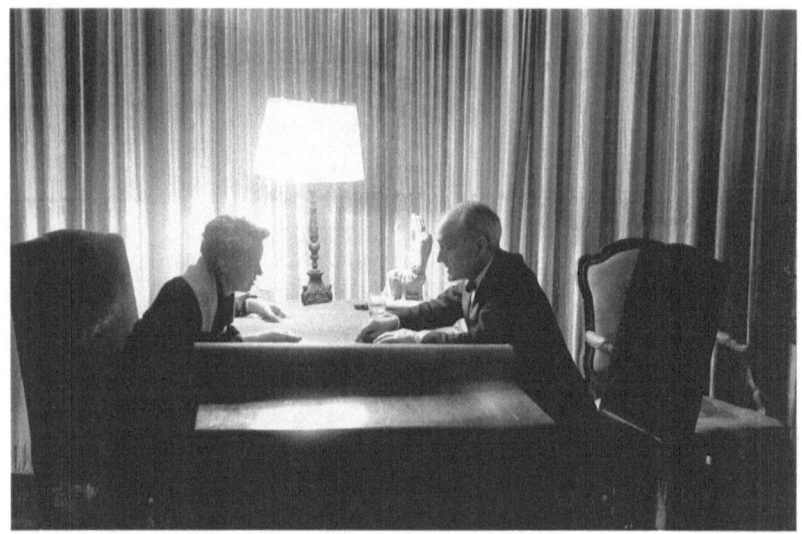

Dominique de Menil and Philip Johnson in the living room of the Menil residence, reviewing plans for the University of St. Thomas, early 1950s. Photo: Henri Cartier-Bresson. Courtesy Menil Archives, the Menil Collection, Houston.

Latin American division, which John de Menil headed (Fox 2005). When differences over how to handle light entering the chapel became intractable between Rothko and Johnson, it was Aubry and Barnstone whom the de Menils called in to bring the project to completion. The Rice Media Center and the Institute for the Arts buildings were, as I have mentioned, designed by Aubry, as were the pair of joined houses built for the art dealer Fredericka Hunter and the vice president of the Menil Foundation, Simone Swan, both financed by John de Menil (Fox 2005). These metal-clad buildings—which became the residences of the Menil Collection's inaugural director, Walter Hopps, and curator Bertrand Davezac—in what was then the blue-collar West End, laid the foundation for what was to become Houston's distinctive "tin house" movement, of which perhaps the most distinguished exponent is the architect Cameron Armstrong.

Barnstone and Aubry gained important commissions, were able to develop enviably close relationships with Johnson, and became part of the de Menil inner circle. "Life with them became a rich, dense mesh of professionalism and intimacy," Dominique Browning observed. "People who worked for them became their closest confidants, drawn inextricably into the tangle of their many projects" (1983, 207). Barnstone, at the same time that his career was taking off, became the de Menils' "house architect," patching up problems with their house. François de Menil observed, perhaps a little disingenuously, "My first understanding of an architect was as the guy who fixed the roof" (quoted in Middleton 2004, 1). The architect was also hired to design the Schlumberger in-house publication *Intercom*, and was free to assign Henri Cartier-Bresson or Eve Arnold to photograph Schlumberger operations for its pages, with no concern for expense. "But then," Browning continues, "Barnstone and Aubry were expected to help the de Menils decorate their tree and wrap presents at Christmas—and willingly they went. Each year the de Menils set out beautiful gifts and gave the young architects the pick of the lot before they started wrapping" (1983, 207).

The seduction of wealth and charisma was not, however, without its price, as Aubry recognized: "Mrs. de Menil's generosity was astonishing, and everything she did was to very high standards. The people around her were always referred to as her court, never to her face of course. Their lives were completely wrapped up in her life, and in a way, to their detriment. I think they were subtly held back. The guys who really want to get ahead do not sit around waiting for the crumbs. I saw this was coming and I got out. But still, life with her could never be awful" (quoted in Browning 1983, 208).[11]

Among those people to whom the de Menils were close, the "remarkables" were never diminished by their patrons' shadow, since their sense of themselves and their professional trajectories were by no means entirely contingent on the favor of the de Menils; because of this and their own charismatic virtuosity, they were treated as equals. But for the courtiers, to pursue Aubry's characterization, the calculus of privilege and compromise was a complicated and sometimes painful one.

EXPERIMENTAL PRACTICE

With Kahn's death following so closely on the grief of John's passing, plans for the long-term disposition of the collection seemed to be put aside. But already in June 1976, Dominique de Menil and members of her staff at Rice quietly embarked on an intensive two-week tour of nine regional U.S. museums, traveling in François de Menil's private plane. According to notes kept during the trip, they met with museum personnel at each institution, asking questions concerning exhibition practice, storage, architectural space, and so on, and making their own observations.[12] When Dominique de Menil resolved in 1979 to build a museum to house the collection, she called on Walter Hopps, then the senior curator for twentieth-century art at the National Collection of Fine Arts. Initially, Hopps was brought in as a consultant to advise on the lighting problems in the Rothko Chapel and to curate "La Rime et la Raison." When it became clear that he and Dominique could work together, he was chosen to be the director of the museum that would be built for the collection. Before the close of 1980, Renzo Piano had been retained as its architect.

Andrew McClellan characterizes Renzo Piano as the architect of choice for those who "resist the spectacular and instead pursue refined conditions for viewing and contemplation through delicate lighting, quality materials, and serene public spaces" (McClellan 2008, 93). He writes not in appreciation of the facility of the Menil Collection to "intensify the experience of art," but to dismiss it as emblematic of the "conservative backlash" against the increasingly prevalent "expressive" museum architecture exemplified by Frank Gehry's Guggenheim Museum Bilbao, completed in 1997, a decade later than the Menil Collection (93). McClellan wonders whether Piano was "atoning" for the Centre Pompidou (1977), which he designed with Richard Rogers, a museum that the author considers favorably "in radical contrast" to Piano's subsequent projects (94).[13]

The cool elegance of the Menil Collection, however, belies the spirit of experimentation and activism that resides at its core. It was because of the Pompidou, not in spite of it, that Dominique de Menil hired Piano. In 1980, Pontus Hulten, then the director of the Centre Pompidou and a close associate of Dominique, recognizing how well matched the client and the architect would be, encouraged them to meet. Hulten described his own role as follows: "I understood Mrs. de Menil's desire to build a museum for her family's collections, and also knew that she was not enchanted by the Pompidou Center. . . . It was therefore necessary to arrange for them to meet. For me, the best way to get to know someone is to make a journey together. I suggested to Mrs. de Menil that she travel with Renzo to Israel, to visit a very small museum that I am very fond of, built in the '30s [sic] by an unknown architect" (quoted in Le Thierry d'Ennequin 2001).[14]

In selecting Piano, Dominique de Menil made a notable decision against what Otto Karl Werckmeister describes as the kind of "sovereign play of creative freedom" that she afforded artists whose work she commissioned, but that she never extended to architects (1991, 77). Describing the process of deciding on an architect, Dominique spoke highly of Piano's propensity to collaborate with his clients. Also highly regarded was his problem-solving approach to architecture, whereby the form of a building is informed by a complex interleaving of art and technology.

The *Architectural Review*'s special issue "Architecture of Commitment" (1987) featured a cover story on Piano, giving special attention to the Menil Collection project. Its opening characterization of Piano mirrors the terms of Dominique's enthusiasm for him: "Renzo Piano is an architect well known— and regarded in some quarters as almost puritanical—for his continuing polemical advocacy of such notions as client participation, interdisciplinarity, the mastery and *use* of technology, and an experimental 'hands-on' approach to design. . . . For Piano these are moral issues, more important and more interesting than questions of personal style or form. . . . [It is his] commitment to *idea* above ego—that gives his built work its distinctive gentle confidence" (Farelly 1987, 32). More significant for Dominique than the form of the architecture, though this was of by no means incidental importance, was the practice of the architect—and the alignment of this practice with her commitments as his client and collaborator.

Piano and his associates—Peter Rice and Tom Barker of Ove Arup and Partners of London and the Houston architect Richard Fitzgerald—in collaboration with Dominique de Menil, Paul Winkler, and Walter Hopps, embarked on a painstaking process of design and building that took seven years. In an interview with Jason Edward Kaufman of the *Art Newspaper*, Piano identified Dominique de Menil as "a classically good client. She was very tough and stubborn, but was also very light in the sense that she would listen, but at the same time she knew what she wanted. A good client is not necessarily an easy client. A client with a strong character is normally much better" (quoted in Kaufman 2002, 1). Stephen Fox illustrates both Dominique's recognition of the absolute importance of the architecture working well and something of her approach to achieving the right outcome. He recounts that during the process of design, Dominique is reported to have said, "If the workspaces in the museum proved not to be suitable once the staff moved in, they would be demolished and reconstructed" (quoted in Fox 2005, 20).

Such an attitude shouldn't be taken to suggest anything cavalier about the process, nor to suggest a lack of confidence that the architect would get things right. But rather, as Fox points out, one can't know whether a building or some part of it is right without actually putting it to use, without working in the space. And, "if it wasn't right, the Menil ethos was to set it right" (20). The Menil Collection, and indeed Menil projects broadly, have always sought to be exemplary. But what is revealing in Fox's anecdote, as he astutely observes, is an ethic of practice that imbues the Menil Collection with much of its force: "The Menil aesthetic was founded on Dominique de Menil's ethos about working out exemplarity rather than presuming it could be ordered up and paid for. The ethos of 'working' that emerged at the Art Barn at Rice was materialized at The Menil Collection over and again in a commitment to fundamentally re-think how an art museum should operate and what its relationship to its public should be" (20).

We see a consequence of this self-consciousness about the relationship the museum establishes with its public in the resolute modesty of the building's external profile. Dominique de Menil's primary directive to Piano was that the building "should look small on the outside and be big on the inside."[15] She wanted the museum to sit comfortably in the residential neighborhood of small clapboard houses adjacent to the Rothko Chapel. The four-hundred-foot-long, horizontal building is clad with wide-board swamp cypress in a white steel frame, its cladding stained the same soft gray of the surrounding wooden bungalows.[16] Indeed, as the art critic Robert Hughes observed in his uncharacteristically laudatory review of the newly opened Menil Collection, this gray has become something of a Menil signature: "(Gray is to Dominique de Menil's cultural activities what orange is to the Hare Krishnas.) Unexpressive, inviting, distanced: the color declares a policy, or rather an ethic" (1987, 48).

At first glance, the building is self-effacing: neutral in color, nonmonumental in scale, and absent any signage or inscription to identify it. But rather than accommodating itself to its context, it is actually the centerpiece of a carefully curated environment that is as steady a rendering of the Menil signature as the museum's interior. The Rothko Chapel and Barnett Newman's *Broken Obelisk* are on the next block, separated from the Menil Collection by treed lawns dotted with sculptures by Tony Smith, Jim Love, and Mark di Suvero. Across the road is the Cy Twombly Gallery, designed by Piano exclusively

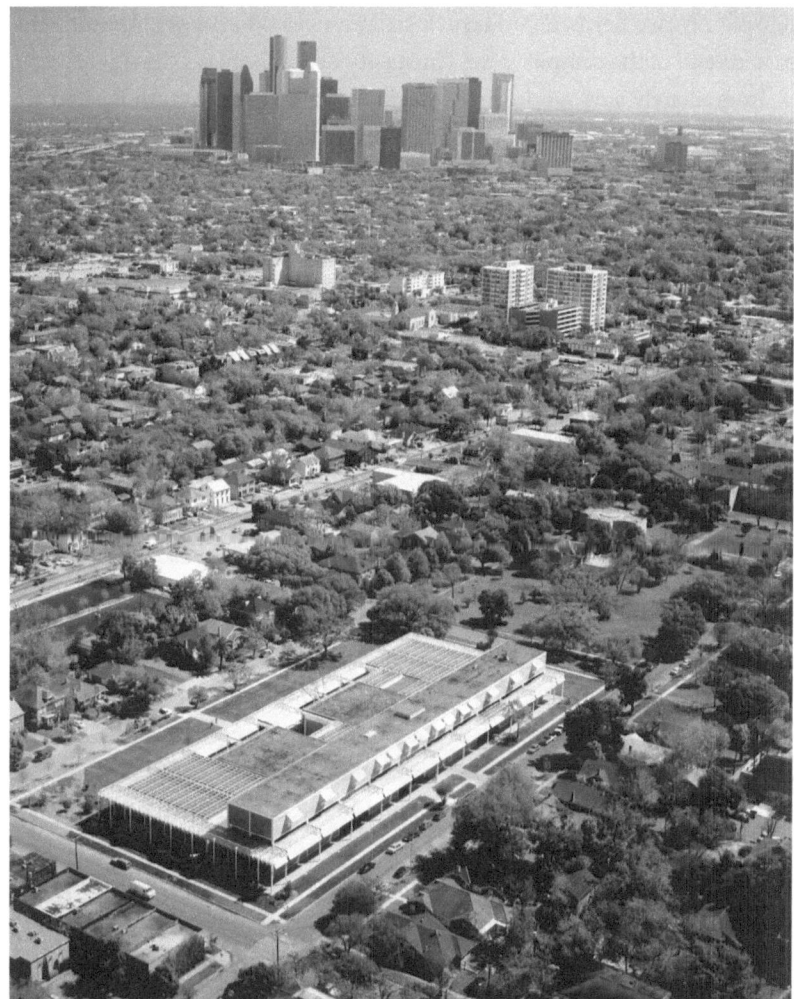

Aerial view of the Menil campus, looking northeast toward downtown Houston. Courtesy Menil Archives, the Menil Collection, Houston.

for the permanent exhibition of Twombly's work.[17] At the end of that block is the Byzantine Fresco Chapel museum (1997), designed by Dominique de Menil's architect son, François. On the southwestern edge of the campus is Richmond Hall, the only preexisting building in the Menil ensemble and the only one to face onto a busy thoroughfare. Initially used for temporary storage and the occasional exhibition, it is now the site of a Dan Flavin installation, one of only two permanent Flavin installations in the country. Abutting the eastern end of the campus is the University of St. Thomas.

Immediately surrounding the block on which the museum is sited are several blocks of 1920s wooden bungalows; all those belonging to the de Menils have been painted the same white-trimmed gray, and all their interiors were remodeled by Howard Barnstone. In late 1973, Patrice Marandel and Dominique de Menil mounted "Gray Is the Color," an exhibition of grisaille at Rice's Art Barn. This, Fox reports, was Barnstone's "point of departure" for painting all of the houses owned by Menil Properties in their distinctive hue: "This bit of magical realism introduced Houston to the possibility of a Surreal sub-urbanism with what Lars Lerup [Rice University's dean of architecture] describes as 'a situational tour de force.' The effect (and I remember when it was new) was like having René Magritte as your color consultant. The houses were all different *and* the same. It was mesmerizing, and accomplished with the simplest of means" (Fox 2005, 18). Bought up quietly by John and Dominique de Menil during their period of ambition for the University of St. Thomas, and with some vigor through the early 1970s in preparation for their earlier plan for the site, some of these houses are used by the Menil Collection, others serve as the administrative base for the Menil Foundation, and many have been turned over to various nonprofit arts organizations, notably Inprint (a distinguished literary organization), Da Camera (a presenter of ensemble musical performances at the Menil Collection and elsewhere), and SWAMP (Southwest Alternate Media Project).[18] Others are rented out. Initially, tenants were participants in the arts community, though they are now drawn from a rather broader pool of applicants. There was, while Dominique was alive, a sense in which the occupants were as carefully scrutinized and managed as the buildings and grounds.[19]

The effect of all this was summed up by Richard Ingersoll: "The context hasn't been saved but invented by reassembling existing buildings into a more coherent collection; some of the buildings that were on the site of the museum were redistributed to the surrounding lots like checkers on a newly set checker board. . . . This invented 'neighborhood' provides an uncommon physical and social homogeneity that protects the museum from the encroachment of speculative real estate and commercial activities" (1987, 43–44).

Piano clearly took seriously Dominique's insistence on maintaining a modest appearance for the Menil Collection, but despite the museum's refusal

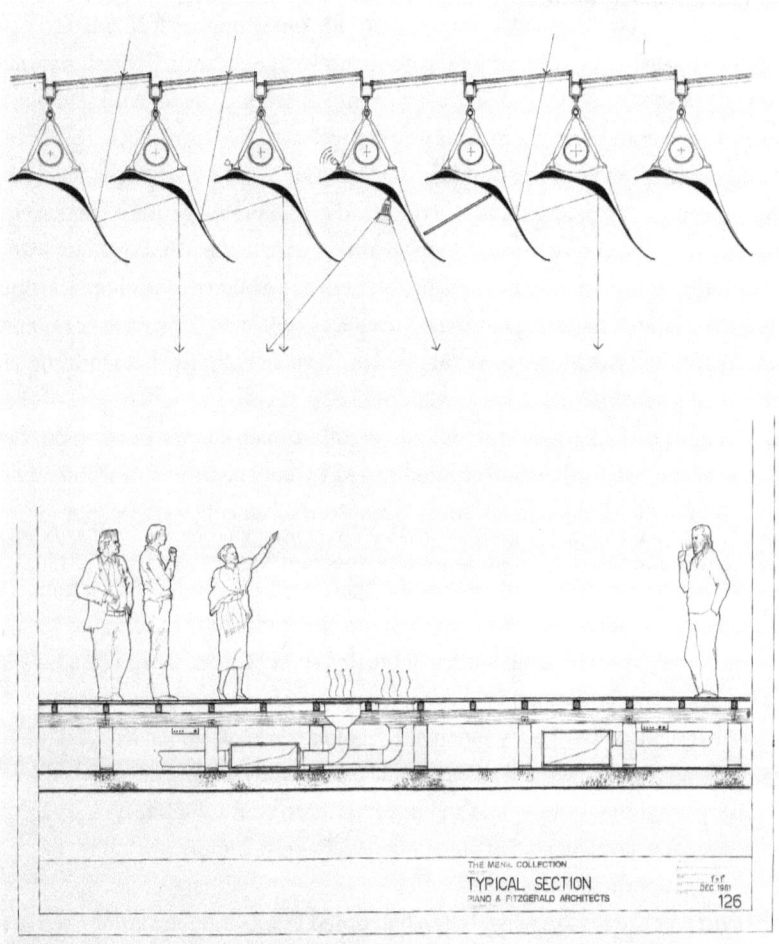

Renzo Piano, drawing of a typical section of the Menil Collection, December 1981 (showing, left to right, Walter Hopps, Paul Winkler, Dominique de Menil, and Renzo Piano). Photo: Renzo Piano Building Workshop. Courtesy Menil Archives, the Menil Collection, Houston.

of the massive authority typical of monumental buildings, it is not entirely antimonumental: "The profane aspects of the consumerist art experience have been removed and, consistent with the respect for spirituality, the building has been sited like a primitive temple in a *temeños*: it sits alone on its block, set off by a peripheral portico that rings it with a special filtered halo of light" (Ingersoll 1987, 46).

Light was the other key concern, both for Dominique de Menil and for Walter Hopps. The problem was to come up with a means by which natural light could be used in the galleries without subjecting the artworks to light levels that would harm them. This was complicated by Dominique's particular desire to allow into the building daylight that would visibly change with the time and season and weather conditions. This preoccupation was surely informed by the convictions of Mark Rothko, who had battled so adamantly with Philip Johnson over just this problem in the design of the chapel.[20] But also, the mode of handling natural lighting was central to the success of Louis Kahn's Kimbell Art Museum in Fort Worth, Texas, a building that Dominique de Menil knew and liked very well. Indeed, it was the oft-cited goal of the Kimbell "to make light the theme" (Ingersoll 1987, 46). Commenting on the virtue of the Kimbell, Michael Fried noted by contrast the conditions that prevail in the National Gallery in Washington, observing with dismay:

> In those big rooms . . . with no natural light, the work doesn't change from minute to minute, day to day, hour to hour. The works don't breathe. One of the things I've loved about looking at the *Raft of the Medusa*, especially in the old Louvre where you could get into the museum fast, was that you could be walking and look at the sky and think, *I'm going to see how the raft looks today.* And you'd run in there and a cloud would pass over the sun and the raft would change, and the waves would all but break there. And I think that's a great quality that a certain kind of museology can freeze out. (2003, 132)[21]

Light was the reason why Hulten had urged Piano and Dominique to visit the museum in Ein Harod, where light is treated in what Hulten described as "a particularly intelligent manner" (quoted in Le Thierry d'Ennequin 2001). Subject to intense solar conditions similar to those in Houston, the museum utilizes concrete structures to filter light in such a way that an extraordinary luminosity is conjured.

Piano's response to the problem of light has become the defining feature of the structure of the Menil Collection, though until his visit to Israel with Dominique, Piano had, by his own account, been quite indifferent to the question of natural lighting (Le Thierry d'Ennequin 2001).[22] Piano developed a system of baffles that would prevent direct sunlight from entering the interior spaces, but would reflect sunlight, in its changing conditions, into these spaces.

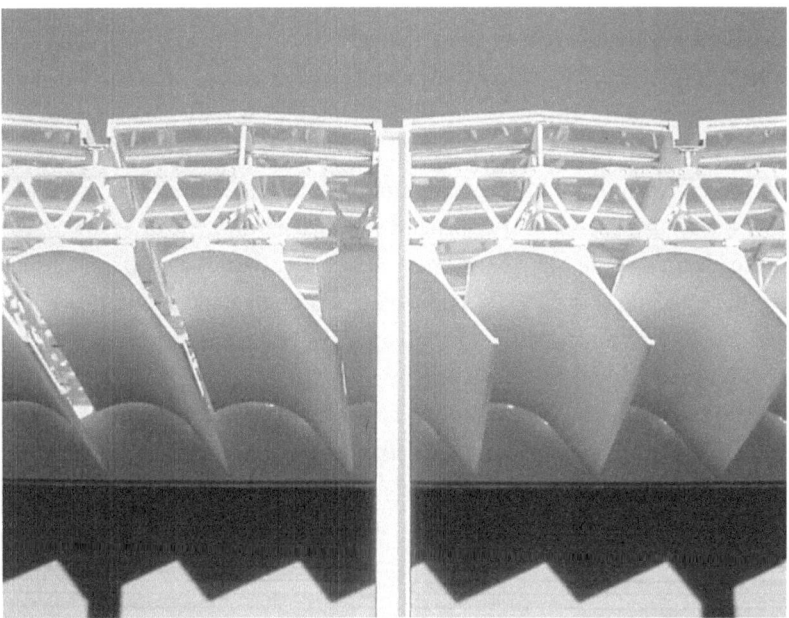

Detail of ferro-cement leaves, Menil Collection. Photo: Hickey-Robertson. The Menil Collection, Houston.

These ferro-cement baffles, or leaves, as they have come to be called, attached to ductile-iron trusses, together form the roof structure. They are the result of an exhaustive process of technical innovation and experimentation implemented to meet the specific demands of the project. The trusses also carry ducts for return air, and these ducts help remove the heat that is intensified by the ultraviolet-proof glazing that covers the roof above the truss structure. This roof system forms a unifying platform for the building, creating a section consistent with the loft tradition, which pulls together the galleries, internal gardens, and the internal and external walkways. If the Menil Collection can be said to have a logo, it is the elegant cross-section of the leaves.

The very dark stained pine floors accentuate the height of the sixteen-foot ceilings, though they are informed by other imperatives. Wooden floors allow internal walls to be moved with ease, since they can be anchored to the floor with screws. But more crucially, perhaps, they have been used to carry air into the building, through the use of intermittent sections of finely slatted boards through which treated air is pumped. What might appear as a trivial detail of design takes on some significance in the Menil Collection. The walls are rendered readily movable because they are not made to carry ducts or any other service technology, and their surfaces are thoroughly clean. This is of particular significance for a museum that hangs the very large works that are characteristic of the New York school painters—indeed it is an issue at all museums that show contemporary painting, much of which is made with the vast spaces of contemporary museum galleries in mind.[23] But at the Menil Collection, close attention to the location of potential visual distractions like air ducts and thermostats takes on a particularly marked significance, since its exemplary attention to detail, its economy of care, has come to be central in conjuring its characteristic aesthetic.

The seamlessness of the museum's appearance is complemented by the quiet that prevails in the galleries, not so much because people feel compelled to be silent, but because Dominique de Menil went to considerable expense to ensure that the air conditioning would create no noise.[24] A great deal of care was also expended on the walls themselves. Steve McConathy, the building manager, told me with notable satisfaction that the Sheetrock interior walls of the museum were "the truest walls in all of Houston."[25] In the care it takes with the walls upon which artworks are hung, the Menil Collection demonstrates its commitment to the preeminence of the art object, ensuring that one's engagement with it is not compromised by extraneous utilities. But there is also a sense in which the walls themselves have value: members of the exhibitions department routinely inspect them for marks and touch them up as necessary; guards are instructed not to lean against them; and, as was seen with the Klee show we observed at the outset, a great deal of care is taken regarding their finish in preparation for the installation of exhibitions. They have value as part of an economy of exemplary care that sustains what has come to be known as "the Menil aesthetic."

While the museum building is meant to sustain the preeminence of the object, it is by no means a neutral space. Piano argues: "The famous theory about making neutral space for museums because then the architecture does not compete with the art is a stupid idea. If you make a neutral space you kill art. . . . That is why the research we have done on the Menil is about atmosphere . . . You have to work on the immateriality of the museum—light, vibration, proportion" (quoted in J. Kaufman 2002, 2).

7

Intimacies
of Possession

On the page facing Dominique de Menil's foreword to the Menil
Collection catalogue is a painting by Domenico Veneziano, *St. John
in the Desert* (ca. 1445). It is not as a particular jewel of the Menil
Collection that this work is reproduced in such a prominent position. It is
not only not held by the Collection, but never will be. Once belonging to
Bernard Berenson, it is now in the Kress Collection of the National Gallery of
Art in Washington, D.C. In her foreword, Dominique de Menil wrote this of
the painting: "A lonely adolescent is disrobing in the solitude of mountains;
a gray landscape with brownish green bushes and a flash of dark ruby-red—
his cloak. I am so fond of this strange and miraculous little painting that I
experience it as totally mine when I stand in front of it. And I think that in
years ahead there will be those, unknown to me, who will take and 'possess'
works that I have acquired" (1987, 7).

It is the strangeness of this choice of image that I wish to pursue here, since it suggests imperatives that seem to run counter to the orthodoxies of personal collection and recasts possessive impulses as something that might be seen as instruments of virtue rather than decadence. It lays the foundation for an analysis of how the Menil Collection—beyond its architectural form—crafts conditions in which works of art might be experienced intimately, in contrast to the distancing effect produced by many museums. This production of an artifice of intimacy is, along with an economy of exemplary care, one of two key performative registers through which the Menil Collection seeks to enliven art, to produce conditions of possibility that would sustain aesthetic experience.

VICARIOUS POSSESSION

The use of this image appears at first glance to be either a particularly brazen act of appropriation or, conversely, perhaps a strangely forthright marking of humility for the collector to draw attention to the limitations of her own collection. In any event, we read, in the accompanying text, of Dominique's unabashed declaration of possessiveness, which is ameliorated, in the next turn, by her sanguine recognition that objects in her own collection will be similarly subject to such impulses. Indeed, as we shall see, Dominique de Menil did not regard such possession as simply an unavoidable by-product of others having access to the works in her collection—far from it. It is precisely this possessive relationship that she sought to foster in those who engage with the collection. Without imagining this intimacy of possession, no matter how fantasized, the museum becomes a site of alienation where objects that can never be enlivened by the possibility of ownership are paraded before us. Dominique's reference to possession here speaks of the alchemy by which we might all become collectors, albeit vicariously, rather than merely passive consumers.

This notion of possession in the absence of ownership was addressed by the nineteenth-century essayist William Hazlitt, who characterized the experience of possession as both an impulse of envy and a process for overcoming envy by recognizing the superior character of one's own engagement and appreciation. He offers by way of illustration an anecdotal account of the experience of "passing through a fine collection of pictures" and "adopting" the objects of admiration, a practice that "always end[s] in a daring project of usurpation, and a determination to expel the actual proprietor, and supply his place so much more worthily with our own identity" (Hazlitt 1991, 193).[1] While Hazlitt's somewhat snide characterization draws attention to the redemptive impulse even of this vicarious mode of possession, it also reveals, in its ambition to displace the "actual proprietor," what must be, for the collector, the disquieting aspect of this possessive relationship.

What seems so surprising about Dominique de Menil's invitation to others to engage with works in her collection in a manner imbued with the intimacy of possession is that insofar as collectors experience a high degree of identification with their collections, one imagines that others' "possession" of constituent works might be considered an affront to the integrity not only of the collection, but of the collector also. But this kind of reading is informed by the notion that the collection is, for the collector, first and foremost an instrument by which a unified, stable, and enduring self might be constituted. While the Menil Collection should quite properly be understood as an instrument of the collector's project of self-fashioning, to reduce it to merely such a self-serving motivation is to overlook the driving imperative of the Menil Collection to affect the subjectivities of those who engage with it. Opened to the public in the form of the donor museum, it is engaged in a complex set of relationships that offer redemption not only for the collector, but also for the personnel who care for it and for those who form its audience—and for its constituent objects too. Analytically, it presents a very particular organization of a relationship between objects and subjects that can offer access to alternative projects of modernity.

The literature on private (as opposed to institutional) collecting overwhelmingly focuses on the collection as an agent in the collector's practices of self-formation. As Jeremy Braddock observes, "Collecting has been understood as an almost entirely *interior practice*, what Baudrillard called 'a discourse addressed to oneself'" (2004, 48). There has been little attention given to how a formerly private collection opened to the public might, intentionally or not, become engaged in the constitution of other selves—the selves of those who care for the collection and of those who come to constitute its public. At the Menil Collection, this was always an absolutely central preoccupation, as it was for Alfred Barnes too, as Braddock observes.[2]

In what follows, I address these three registers of redemption—of the collector, of objects themselves, and of those who might vicariously possess the collection or elements of it. In addition, I show how the collection, especially as it was envisioned in the context of the museum, is employed as an agent in the pursuit not simply of a more enchanted relationship with art, but also in the restoration of sensibility that, in the view of Dominique de Menil, would lay the groundwork for social reform.

I argue that the scholarship on collecting, which characterizes the practice as one impelled toward a future moment of completion or, alternatively, as a recuperation of the past does not adequately address the kind of experimental, open-ended, and creative project that was at the heart of the de Menils' collecting.

SELF-POSSESSION

The idea that there is a defining relationship between possession and personhood has been well established in the theorization of possessive individualism (Macpherson 1962) and has been further elaborated in discussions of collecting as an intensified form of this (Handler 1987; Clifford 1988; Maleuvre 1999). In this view, the collector's urge to possess is driven by a desire to materialize the self, whether as an expression of self, as a means to shore oneself up against loss, or as a technology of self-constitution.

The collection is, as James Clifford notes, a "strategy for the deployment of the possessive self," an exercise in "making the world one's own, [gathering] things around oneself tastefully, appropriately" (Clifford 1988, 218). In this process, the collector is not simply a consumer of objects but also, as Susan Stewart notes, someone who "generates a fantasy" in which the self "becomes producer by arrangement and manipulation" (Stewart 1993, 158). While the ordering of objects within a preestablished series, as in the recreating of a Victorian parlor, say, or in the collecting of seventeenth-century Italian paintings, suggests not so much production as the reproduction of a given form, the eclectic collection bears the sign of mastery. Writing of the deployment of a collection in the arrangement of a domestic interior, Stewart observes:

Each sign is placed in relation to a chain of signifiers whose ultimate referent is not the interior of the room—in itself an empty essence—but the interior of the self.

In order to construct this narrative of interiority it is necessary to obliterate the object's context of origin. In these examples eclecticism rather than pure seriality is to be admired because, if for no other reason, it marks the heterogeneous organization of the self, a self capable of transcending the accidents and dispersions of historical reality. (1993, 158)

The Menil Collection is surely such an object: a materialization of a heterogeneous self that enables a unified expression in the form of a signature, "the Menil aesthetic," notwithstanding Dominique's insistence on the openendedness of her collecting.

According to Bertrand Davezac, the Menil Collection's long-serving curator of Byzantine and medieval art: "Museum collections build continents, this one archipelagos." The Menil Collection makes a virtue of its fragmentary character—"the object of the islands is not to fill the sea"—and hence it has no gaps, no seams; "what is not there is not missing." The collection seeks only to be "exemplary" (Davezac 1984).[3] Dominique de Menil embraced this construction of the collection enthusiastically.

In contrast, the "encyclopedic" collections of so many museums, with their aspirations of offering a comprehensive representation of the world or, in the case of museums of art, the history of art, assert a massive whole, albeit one that is inevitably incomplete.[4] Much has been made of the totalizing drive of collections, the seduction of the imagined worlds they seem to represent, and the gratifying stability of apparent coherence that they conjure.[5]

The teleological thrust of collections and the coherence that they are predicated upon are, in the ideal type delineated in the literature, considered their defining features, distinguishing them from mere accumulation. Collections are subject to an overarching logic that governs acquisition, serves to identify what is lacking from them, and thereby makes it possible to imagine them as complete wholes. It is toward the fulfillment of this logic that practices of collecting are directed, though its attainment must always be deferred, since, as Jean Baudrillard warned, the closure of completion amounts to a radical closure for the collector—to death (Baudrillard 1996).[6]

While the thrust of collecting, according to this orthodoxy, is toward the future, insofar as it is toward an end yet to be achieved, it suggests an impulse of containment, of delimitation. Rather than an embrace of the unfolding present, there is something inherently conservative about collecting under this model, something of a rearguard attempt to hold everything in place, and often, one reads in the narratives of collectors, an attempt to retrieve, or to salvage, what remains of some longed-for lost order and meaning. This rendering of collecting—characterized by the effort to achieve the completion of a predetermined whole that might function as a surrogate for the self—while imbuing collecting with the respectability of discipline, conjures an overwhelming sense of airlessness, of enclosure.

We do, however, get a sense of the efficacy of objects in the exercise of agency: "Between the world's irreversible evolution and ourselves, objects interpose a discontinuous, classifiable, reversible screen which can be reconstituted at will, a segment of the world which belongs to us, responding to our hands and minds and delivering us from anxiety" (Baudrillard 1996, 94). But instead of these practices of self-constitution being construed as a lively grasping of the world, this characterization evokes a flight from it, mere mastery over things as a surrogate for a life fully lived. Collecting has the whiff of pathology rather than appearing as an intensified form of the vital and generative relationships that we are all engaged in with the object worlds we occupy.

What I wish to propose is a countermodel: a collector whose collecting, while certainly responding to anxiety, can hardly be said to be merely psychologically compensatory or to operate as a flight from the world. Even though Dominique de Menil's off-modern Catholicism conceived of the objects of the collection as agents of religiosity, it also carried with it the conviction that contemplation is not the end in itself, but the predicate to action.

DONOR-BUILT MUSEUMS

Before we systematically address the Menil Collection as a countermodel to the regressive, claustrophobic character of the orthodox formulation of collecting and examine how Dominique de Menil deployed the collection in the context of the museum, I want to draw attention to the fact that in the form of a public museum, the collection inevitably accrues distinctive agency beyond that of the private collection.

Donor-built museums, which open once-private collections to the purview of the public, can be understood as extensions of the collectors' projects of the self, wherein the content and style of the museum become part of a rhetoric of a distinctively constituted self. While in such museums it seems that the public is called upon merely to bear witness to the creation of the collector, the members of the museum's public in fact become drawn in as agents in the process of the collector's self-authorship, as are the museum's trustees, its staff, media commentators, and others. This brings to mind Debbora Battaglia's characterization of the self as "a representational economy: a refraction continually defined by mutable entanglements with other subjects' histories, experiences, self-representations." According to this view, selfhood is "a chronically unstable productivity brought situationally—not invariably—to some form of imaginary order" (Battaglia 1995, 2). An illustration of this can be found in press coverage of the de Menils' activities. Reportage by Ann Holmes, who wrote on the arts for the *Houston Chronicle* from the late 1940s to the late 1990s, provided an evolving narration of their endeavors that served to underwrite the personal distinction of Dominique and her husband and imbued their projects with moral force: "Many a handsome dinner and garden supper was held there [at their Philip Johnson–designed home] in the past, to honor scholars and artists and to launch art projects. . . . Their massive art enterprises preoccupy this attractive couple. They are now seldom, if ever, seen at parties. They entertain hardly at all. Their home, with its glass walls, its indoor jungle garden, its changing plethora of art, is like the administrative wing of a museum. . . . Children's bedrooms now converted into business offices, curatorial dens, study areas. The garage, an airconditioned storage area for art works" (1968a, 13).

There is here, and elsewhere, a growing sense of the seriousness of their project, and of the depth of John and Dominique's devotion to it. This was emphasized in a considerably more recent portrayal of Dominique: "For one who once loved and owned gowns by Balenciaga, Dior and her favorite, Charles James, she makes no time for clothes shopping. 'What I have is what I had, or what my daughters bring in for me to wear. I don't even find time to get them adjusted—such negligence!'" (A. Holmes 1991, 230). But it is the following characterization that marks not only the extent of her preoccupation with serious concerns to the exclusion of trivial pleasures or comforts, but also the increasingly pious character of this preoccupation, that reveals something of the operation by which such distinction may be fashioned: "Perhaps the key to understanding this extraordinary woman comes with a glimpse of her bedroom.... The bed, as plain as a pallet, is covered with a blanket. Yet around it are the tomes de Menil is reading, books on profound historical and spiritual subjects. On the walls are an African crucifix and works of art—some of them complex and difficult—by artists she admires. The room's occupant clearly does not concern herself with bodily comforts. She seeks deeper truths" (228). A striking recoding is achieved here, whereby the display of art becomes a sign of piety rather than luxury in order to depict Dominique de Menil as preeminently engaged with transcendental preoccupations.

Press coverage of Dominique de Menil's considerable efforts over the last decade of her life to secure an adequate endowment for the Menil Collection did nothing to disrupt this portrait of otherworldliness. The aura of the Menil Collection had been crafted in such a way that its project was rendered transcendent and Dominique's worldly labors appeared as devotional ministrations. This characterization of Dominique as otherworldly excludes the other aspect of the dialectic that she, like the protagonists of the *renouveau catholique*, was engaged in—the eternal was always in productive tension with a grasping of the world in order to transform it. She did nothing, however, to actively disrupt this construction of the figure of Dominique de Menil. It is perhaps the case, as it seemed to many, that later in her life she did become increasingly oriented toward this aspect of her faith, but in any event, this attribution of transcendent preoccupations did seem to lend weight to her worldly efforts.

In Houston, Dominique de Menil derived distinction from a variety of sources: her preoccupation with spirituality; the moral worthiness of modesty; her finely calibrated aesthetic sensibilities; her humanitarian commitments; her Frenchness; and her wealth. These various signs of eminence were long established by press coverage of her activities, but they had their most authoritative articulation in the form of her various public projects, which together established a remarkably coherent expression of a unified self.

Not all modern exercises in self-formation, however, yield anything so coherent as a unified self; indeed, such an outcome relies not only upon a sense of one's own authority, but also upon resources adequate for its mobilization. A unified self is a luxury, fashioned out of the more or less disparate fragments of a life.[7] The self becomes the organizing principle in terms of which such fragments might be rendered sensible, in much the same way that the collection organizes the meaning of disparate objects. But these are not merely analogous operations, since a collection can serve powerfully in the constitution of a self.

Notwithstanding the "multiple agents and agencies," to use Battaglia's phrase (1995, 8), involved in the self-fashioning of the collector who opens his or her collection to the public, the donor museum—insofar as it appears to present the singular vision of the collector—has the peculiar ability to convey a sense of the collector as a self marked by autonomy and personal distinction. And, moreover, insofar as the museum bears the sign of permanence (Pomian 1990, 47), it can be seen as a technology by which a transcendent self might compellingly be articulated. The Isabella Stewart Gardner Museum, the Barnes Collection, and the Frick Collection, are like the Menil Collection in this regard, notwithstanding the fact that each institutionalized the continuing agency of its collector quite differently.

SIGNATURE

The seamlessness of the collector's signature that is written over the Menil Collection, what has come to be referred to as the Menil aesthetic, along with its particularity in posing itself in distinction to dominant tendencies in art museums, marks the Menil Collection as a notably idiosyncratic project, the product of the distinctive vision and agency of its founder. The twofold character of the signature as both symbolic and constitutive is identified by James Faubion when he notes that the hermeneutics of the relationship between "creature and creator" that is marked by the signature "would reveal in a work or a text, not merely its author's self-projections but also his, or her, exercises of self-formation" (Faubion 1993, 193).

The aesthetic coherence of this project is illustrative, perhaps, of what Pierre Bourdieu conceptualizes as the "stylization of life": "a systematic commitment which orients and organizes the most diverse practices—the choice of a vintage or a cheese or the decoration of a holiday home in the country" (Bourdieu 1984, 56).[8] For Bourdieu, such expressions of taste, and thereby of distinction, operate through the demonstration of the extent to which one is free of the constraints of necessity. Hence the bourgeois taste for "luxury." But gratuitous luxury is not the only register in which distinction operates. An expression of detachment from "ordinary urgencies" might equally take the form of contemplative asceticism. What is central to such marking of distinction is that it operates in the register of the aesthetic. Claims to authority that are asserted in the form of taste are, as Bourdieu observes, "less likely to be contested than any other, because the relation of the 'pure,' 'disinterested' disposition to the conditions which make it possible, i.e., the material conditions of existence which are rarest because most freed from economic necessity, has every chance of passing unnoticed. The most 'classifying' privilege thus has the privilege of appearing to be the most natural one" (56). The more seamlessly this stylization of life can be achieved, then, the greater its authority as a means by which distinction might be asserted. When this distinction is marked by asceticism, as we saw in the journalistic excerpts, it carries with it the additional weight of moral authority.

While Bourdieu is surely right in this, it hardly lays the matter to rest. His insights into the operation of taste in the crafting of distinction have overwhelmingly been taken to render all projects that craft aesthetic engagement as bad-faith exercises of legitimation. This has had a disconcertingly flattening effect—asserting an overwhelming singularity in the aspiration of those who wish to pursue an aesthetic disposition in relation to art. Indeed, what I wish to pursue here is precisely a countermodel—an alternate set of aspirations that arise out of deeply held commitments and anxieties.

In what follows, I sketch out a countermodel of the collector as one who is engaged in the redemption of objects, and then address the central, most important element of their collecting, which is concerned not with acquisition but with exhibition.

THE COLLECTOR'S COUNTERMODEL

To get a more acute sense of how the collection operates in the service of Dominique and John de Menil's off-modern Catholic commitments, we should note not only their practices of collecting and the content of the collection, which I drew attention to in Chapter 4, but also Dominique's disavowal of any overarching logic of the whole—her denial that any conceptual frames dominate over what should, in her view, properly be aesthetic judgments informed by intuition. And, moreover, the scholarly formulations that construe the collection as necessarily delimited in its ambitions in order to sustain a (fictive) narrative of completion thereby valorize closure rather than the kind of open-ended experimentalism to which the de Menils were committed. Furthermore, although objects in the collection are called upon to express the singular vision of the collector, Dominique maintained a sustained objection to the idea that artworks might be viewed as more or less exchangeable elements in a series, which the scholarship on collecting posits. Insisting on "love" as the sole guiding principle for the selection of objects, Dominique ratified the sovereignty of each object, a sovereignty conveyed in her rebuke when I asked whether she could identify pieces that were particularly central to the collection: "That is no question to ask! That is like asking a mother to choose among her children."

Contrary to critiques that represent the act of collecting as one in which objects are wrenched from their original circumstances and meanings and deprived of their use-value (Crimp 1993), Walter Benjamin compellingly evokes the collector's countermodel whereby the collection rescues and consecrates its constituent objects. For Benjamin, "perhaps the most hidden motive of one who collects" is the essentially redemptive impulse that underpins the collector's project of the salvage and liberation of objects (quoted in Holdengräber 1992, 112). Paul Holdengräber elaborates on Benjamin's insight here. "The great collector," he observes, sets himself a "Sisyphean task," "the utopian and doomed duel with and against dispersion. This 'struggle against dispersion,' perhaps, one of many possible responses to a world in disarray, dispersed, whereby the collector is 'moved' to take things in for repair, provide shelter, and thereby see himself as saving the destitute things of this world, cannot, he knows, last. It is the collector's hope that if he does not find immortality, his collection will, for things so patiently assembled should remain housed under the same roof" (112).

The fifty-eight-piece collection formerly owned by the London real estate magnate Eric Bradley, which forms the nucleus of the Menil Collection's Byzantine collection, was acquired at the urging of Bertrand Davezac in 1985. Its acquisition offers an illustration of Dominique's participation in this "struggle against dispersion." Davezac had heard that the collection was to be put on the market, likely to be sold piecemeal. "I thought it would almost be a catastrophe, because its beauty and worth as a whole would disintegrate into anonymity," Davezac explained. "Dominique de Menil had said there couldn't be any more acquisitions, but I urged her, persuaded her, to at least see the collection. She did, and she had a revelation. Only the Menil could really salvage it as an entity" (quoted in Johnson, 1988a, 17).[9]

The narrative of the rescue, restoration, and subsequent consecration of the thirteenth-century Cypriot frescoes for which Dominique de Menil commissioned a purpose-built chapel reveals the extent of her impulse to "save the destitute things of the world." The frescoes, or rather fragments thereof, cut out from their original housing with a chain saw into thirty-eight rectangles, were offered to the Menil Collection on the black market. Dominique described her impulse to come to the rescue: "If someone is drowning in front of you, and though you can hardly swim, you are tempted to jump into the water. A masterpiece (the dome and apse) would have disappeared, and worse, their true function of sacred images, of great icons, would be lost forever. So, we jumped" (quoted in Shkapich and Menil 2004, 45).[10] Recognizing that without her intervention the frescoes would be sold piecemeal, dispersed into irretrievable fragments, she resolved to buy all of it that could be located. Specialists were brought in to seek out and adjudicate the various national claims to the frescoes, and a conservation lab was set up in London expressly for their restoration.[11]

Having determined the legitimacy of claims for Cypriot provenance—it was established that the frescoes had been removed from the apse and the dome of the chapel of St. Themonianos in the village of Lysi in the district of Famagusta, at the time of the Turkish occupation in 1974—Dominique de Menil entered into discussions with the Church of Cyprus, offering the restored frescoes as a gift to the nation in return for an extended loan of them to the Menil Collection. A twelve-year loan was agreed upon, and Dominique proceeded with plans to build a consecrated chapel to house the frescoes, designed by her architect son, François, and sited on the grounds of the Menil Collection campus.[12] In a letter to her son, Dominique wrote of the religious rather than solely aesthetic (or acquisitive) thrust of the project: "to restore the sacred fragments to their original spiritual function." She continued, François recounts, that she felt that a museum presentation would leave out an "intangible element, difficult to weigh and express, yet very real, which

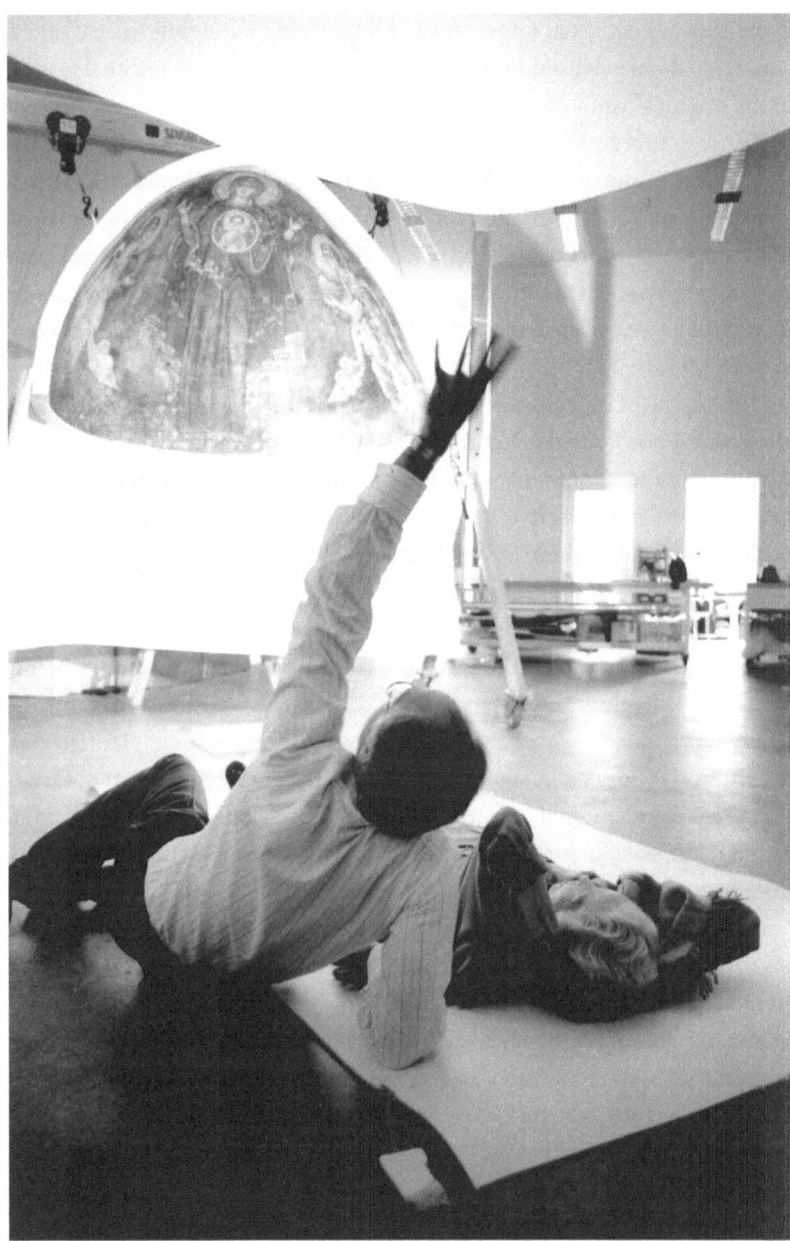

François and Dominique de Menil visualizing the dome of the Cypriot chapel as it would be installed in the new chapel designed by François, ca. 1996. Courtesy Menil Archives, the Menil Collection, Houston.

is the frescoes' spiritual importance and their original significance. Only a consecrated chapel, used for liturgical functions, would do spiritual justice to the frescoes" (quoted in Shkapich and Menil 2004, 49).

Through this endeavor, not only were the frescoes rescued from certain fragmentation and dispersal, they were, in Dominique de Menil's articulation of an often-recited legitimation for the collection of the cultural property of others, rescued from the oblivion of inattention: "Within 20 years after these frescoes are installed in this chapel here, I expect more people will have seen them than viewed them in their little chapel in Cyprus over 700 years" (quoted in Johnson 1993, 1).[13]

This rescue of objects may appear to some as more confining than liberating. But this is far from Dominique's understanding, which on this matter is very much in alignment with Benjamin's. In his essay "Unpacking My Library," Benjamin asserts: "To a book collector, you see, the true freedom of all books is somewhere on his shelves" (1982c, 60). In striking contrast to characterizations of the collector as someone exerting his or her agency on objects that can be manipulated at will, for Benjamin, as Holdengräber points out, the "absolution of objects" that the collector achieves, far from placing such objects freely at the disposal of the collector, establishes a relationship wherein the collector "accedes" to the objects, serving as their historian and interpreter (Holdengräber 1995, 196). Charles Taylor makes a similar observation in his comment that "the world is not simply an ensemble of objects for our use, but makes a further claim on us . . . of attention, of careful scrutiny, of respect for what is there" (1992, 513).

This is the kind of labor that John de Menil was engaged in, I argued, in his considerable efforts to document each of the objects that entered the collection, and it has been continued, most assiduously, by Mary Kadish, who, before the opening of the museum, worked in the Menil Foundation's offices at the de Menil residence, and has subsequently managed and augmented the collection files at the Menil Collection. We will also observe this attentiveness in the economy of care that the museum is governed by, which I will elaborate on in the following chapter.

This kind of attentive disposition toward objects stands in stark contrast to Robert Musil's biting characterization of the alienation inherent in the commodification of relationships between persons and objects: "At home these men's works [Kant, Schiller, and Goethe] were kept in the bookcase with green glass panes in Papa's study, and Torless knew this bookcase was never opened except to display its contents to a visitor. It was like the shrine of some divinity to which one does not readily draw nigh and which one venerates only because one is glad that thanks to its existence there are certain things one need no longer bother about" (Musil 1955, 115). When Benjamin asserts, by contrast, "to a book collector, you see, the true freedom of all books is somewhere on his shelves" (1982c, 60), he sees objects liberated from such perfunctory relations of acquisition, reenchanted through the engulfing intimacy of possession.

Didier Maleuvre makes a gesture toward historicizing the character of what he calls the "entanglement of subject and object found only in ownership":

> Bourgeois mentality in its early phase valued accumulation and ownership as the mark of social fulfillment. The early bourgeois subject saw the world in terms of possession and non-possession. It never occurs to Robinson Crusoe that the island on which he has just been stranded can be anything but his dominion. He relates to his objective environment first and foremost as an owner, thereby transforming it into an extension of himself as subject. That is why an attack on any part of the kingdom was construed as an attack on the king's body, that is, against the sacredness of the subject-object. By contrast, the owner in advanced capitalism is a mere plenipotentiary. From the president of a democratic nation to the private homeowner, the individual is just a manager of resources that, objectively defined, can be passed on to the next competent person. No longer to be eternally possessed . . . the object loses the glow of familiarity that ownership gave. Subject and owner are no longer bound together by sentimental ties. (1999, 97–98)

This kind of relationship to objects—marked by mere stewardship rather than the density of possession—is exemplified by the collecting of James A. Michener. The vociferous objections voiced by private collectors in response to the narration of his collecting practices at a symposium on collecting indicates a deep investment in recognizing and maintaining the kind of deeply personal, impassioned, possessive relationship that Maleuvre suggests can no longer be sustained. Michener, they averred, was no collector. For Michener had set about putting together an art collection that from the outset was intended to be given up for public edification.[14] He went about assembling the collection in a very systematic manner, a process that was designed in part to help Michener himself learn about and come to understand American art. He allocated three months in 1960 for library research and then proceeded in strict accordance with his findings, selecting each piece as a representative of a particular art historical moment.[15]

A good deal of the protest was concerned with the rationalism of his approach, which allowed of no passion and rendered the artworks mere examples rather than singular entities. He desired only, it seemed, to make up the set within the time frame and budget he had allocated, and then to donate it for the betterment of the state of Texas, in his view among the most culturally bereft of states. But also expressed was the sense that something was wrong with the trajectory of the project: this was all art in the service of history.[16]

Of course, this is precisely the circumstance of objects in most public collections, and one that readily renders the objects subject to the exercise of the credentialed expertise of the professionals who manage them. Indeed, were museum professionals or trustees to exhibit a possessive relation to objects in the collection, it likely would be considered unseemly. It is for this reason that Benjamin observes that while "public collections may be less objectionable socially and more useful academically than private collections," it is in personal collections that "the objects get their due" (Benjamin 1982c, 67). And surely Benjamin would include donor museums in this latter category insofar as they assert the singular possessive vision of the collector, in all its attentive intimacy, and convey an air of the enduring permanence of that vision.

Whereas civic collections tend to be defined by their bequests, and by the shifting agendas of their successive directors, the Menil Collection has always conveyed the impression of a supervening identity—even if it is articulable only as a certain singularity of vision. In this respect, as in others, the Menil Collection has been considerably more like a private collection than a public one. Historically, it has not been forced to accommodate the disparate interests of its trustees, unlike civic collections, which must always mollify their overseers, lest they withdraw their support or dismiss the director, as so often happens. Right up until her death, Dominique de Menil served as president of the Menil Foundation, and the board had largely been composed of family members and personal associates of long standing who had a deep understanding of her project or were at least willing to defer to it.

And while the Collection has accepted gifts of works, most notably perhaps from artists and dealers with whom they have worked over the years, as well as from others with personal associations with the de Menil family, it felt no obligation to accept gifts that it considered inappropriate or undesirable. Moreover, donors offered pieces fully cognizant, it would seem, that their contribution would be subsumed by the "Menil vision": gifts are seldom acknowledged on Menil labeling, and the names of major donors to the museum are discreetly inscribed in stone on Michael Heizer's *Charmstone* (1991), which is installed outside of the building, consistent with what Walter Hopps described as its policy of not naming donors within the museum itself.[17] With the opening of the museum in 1987, the transformation from a private to a public collection was officially complete, though Paul Winkler, the museum's director, later described it, with evident satisfaction, as still having "the identity of a private collection" (quoted in Kalil 1993, 24).

Now, more than a decade after the death of the founder, the composition of the board has changed considerably, the now institutionally persuasive planning and development department has altered the terrain of benefactions, and since Paul Winkler's resignation as director and board member in 1999, there has been a less resolute position taken in response to potential donors. Thus far, however, this shift has been modest in its apparent effects. And certainly attention to the endowment and recognition of the need to encourage donors is by no means a new phenomenon for the Menil Collection. We will return to these issues in Chapter 9 when we consider the challenges posed by the absence of the possessive intensity and charismatic authority of the founder.

INTIMATE ARTIFICE

Maleuvre points out the consequences resulting from "the decline of ownership" of art:

> With the decline of ownership comes also an increased alienation between subject and object. Something that may account for the aloofness of art in the modern gallery is the fact that it does not belong to anyone . . . No doubt the emancipation of art from ownership means that art can begin to stand on its

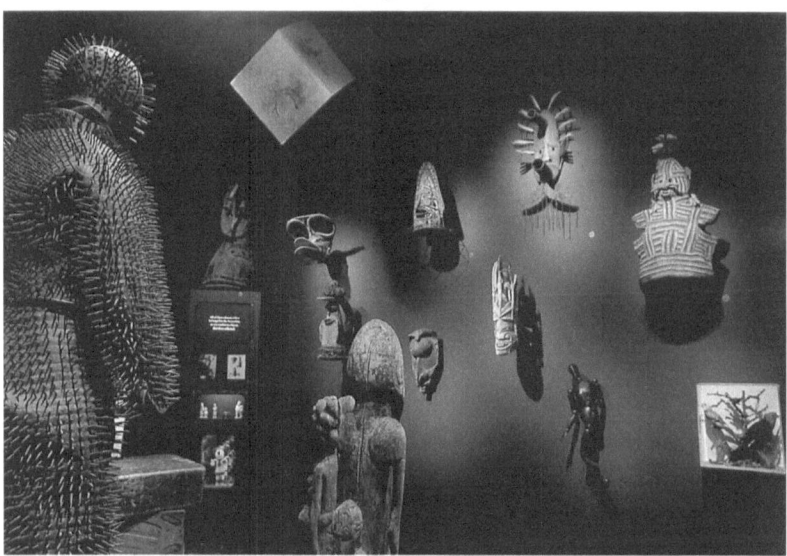

"Surrealism + Witnesses: A Surrealist Wunderkammer," works from the collection, curated and installed by Walter Hopps, 1999. Photo: Paul Hester. The Menil Collection, Houston.

own, its artistic integrity no longer overshadowed by the collector's prestige. That art is not to be "had" agrees with the emancipatory thrust of art. On the other hand, the separation of art from ownership contributed to the autonomization of art and the frigid division of subject and object. Today the subject no longer has a place in the space of art, except one that is strongly marked by exteriority. Looking at art has become synonymous with being an intruder in the realm of art. (Maleuvre 1999, 99)

It is precisely these circumstances that Dominique sought to overcome in the Menil Collection and, indeed, in all of her and her husband's exhibitionary projects. Maleuvre describes the very malaise that the protagonists of the *renouveau catholique* observed and sought to remedy, even though he perceives its source in the conditions of late capitalism, while Maritain and his cohort understood it to be, first and foremost, a consequence of the complacency and exteriority occasioned by rationalism and naturalism in the absence of faith.

The aesthetic that has been so attentively crafted at the Menil Collection is intended to overcome the alienation that museums typically generate, to produce instead an affecting engagement between persons and objects that is charged with the intimacy of possession. The density of the relationship that possession affords is extended at the Menil Collection beyond the prerogatives of ownership to the museum's visitors. In public exhibitions, in which objects cannot be handled freely, as they can in a teaching collection, the challenge is to produce the artifice of intimacy.

The entrance to the Menil Collection opens into a large, airy lobby, intersected by a long luminous central promenade. To the south of this axis are restricted-access service areas; to the north, public galleries. In the interior layout, Dominique de Menil was concerned to minimize the experience of fatigue that so often accompanies visits to museums. So instead of cavernous galleries that open one onto the next, which can engulf and overwhelm, galleries can be entered one at a time off the central passageway. In this manner, each of the four major galleries and a minor gallery are constructed as more or less discrete spaces that can be reached independently of one another.

The large open spaces of the galleries are themselves subdivided, some temporarily in response to the requirements of specific installations, others more or less permanently in order to create more modestly proportioned spaces for some of the semipermanent installations.[18] With this arrangement, Dominique and her colleagues sought intimate spaces for contemplation in which individual works were not inevitably subordinated to the whole.

In this spatial organization, the Menil Collection does not replicate the conventional arrangement of art museums, which represents art as part of the inexorable unfolding of history, a historical narrative that is inevitably recapitulated by one's progress through the galleries. Describing James Stirling's celebrated design for the addition of modern and contemporary art galleries to the Staatsgalerie in Stuttgart, Douglas Crimp observes just this tendency: Stirling reiterated the layout of the original picture galleries, even to the extent of continuing their sequential numbering, so that they "open on to each other *en filade*. . . . The idea of art as an uninterrupted historical continuum that can be laid out in a suite of connected rooms is never for a moment interrupted" (Crimp 1993, 313).

That audiences move through museums barely pausing before the exhibited objects reflects not only this conventional architectural organization of museum experience, Philip Fisher argues, but expresses the very character of these institutions: "That we walk through a museum, walk past the art, recapitulates in our act the motion of art history itself, its restlessness, its forward motion, its power to link. Far from being a fact that shows the public's ignorance of what art is about, the rapid stroll through a museum is an act in deep harmony with the nature of art, that is, art history and the museum itself (not the individual object, which the museum itself has profoundly hidden in history)" (1991, 9).

Consistent with this, the space of museum galleries is reduced, Fisher argues, to a "path" that one follows from one image to the next, and from one room to the next. "In so far as the museum becomes pure path, abandoning the dense spatial rooms of what were once *homes*, or, of course, the highly sophisticated space of the cathedral, it becomes a more perfect image of history, or rather of the single, linear motion of history preferred since Winckelmann" (1991, 9).[19] The Solomon R. Guggenheim Museum, with its inclined ramp, is the ultimate expression of this. Indeed, as Fisher continues, "in the Guggenheim . . . the absence of rooms completes the spatial truth of the museum which throughout the nineteenth century still pretended to be a princely living space . . . where, along with other things, art could be found" (9).[20]

The Menil Collection poses itself strenuously, if understatedly, in opposition to such a rendering. Exhibitions there, in the complex juxtapositions that they establish, are not conceived of in linear, art historical terms. And the architectural organization of the galleries mitigates against such an impulse also, since they do not unfold sequentially, one on to the next.

The intimate character of these spaces relies not only on their architectural form, but also on a range of more ephemeral evocations. It has been the museum's practice to pay careful attention to the effects achieved through lighting and to avoid placing physical barriers between artworks and viewers: no lines are drawn on the floor, and Plexiglas has been used sparingly, and inevitably with regret. There are no didactic wall panels, and labeling is minimal; docents and audio guides are absent. And, moreover, there are no crowds. Works are hung considerably lower than at many museums, so one is not obliged to gaze up at them in a stance of veneration. Hopps, who, like MacAgy, had an extraordinary facility for the installation of exhibitions (and who also shared with MacAgy, and with John and Dominique de Menil too, a respect for artists that is strangely muted in most art museums) characterized it this way: "Jerry [MacAgy] used to say she wanted the center of the paintings to 'hit the tits.' . . . Anyway, that's what we work with here. It's a somewhat lower hanging point than you'll see at the National Gallery or the Metropolitan. With those museums, you get heavier traffic, acoustiguides, and so forth, and you tend to hang higher, so that people can see over other people's heads. Here we can create a greater feeling of intimacy with the work hanging lower" (quoted in Tomkins 1991, 37).[21]

In many ways, Dominique wished to replicate in the museum the conditions in which she lived with art in her home, where art was not estranged from daily experience. "I want a place," she told a group of students in 1976 when she was in the midst of deciding on what kind of public facility she would create for her collection, "where people can sit down and rest—can play the piano—or write letters—relax and enjoy the painting—like I do in my home."[22] This is not to say that art should be employed merely to create a pleasing environment, but rather that she wished for others to be able to experience themselves in among art rather than looking upon it as an outsider. She expressed misgivings about museums, observing, "There are no 'places' for enchantment any more—The museums of today are tiresome and boring. They 'over' do things, give the person 'too much' to see."[23]

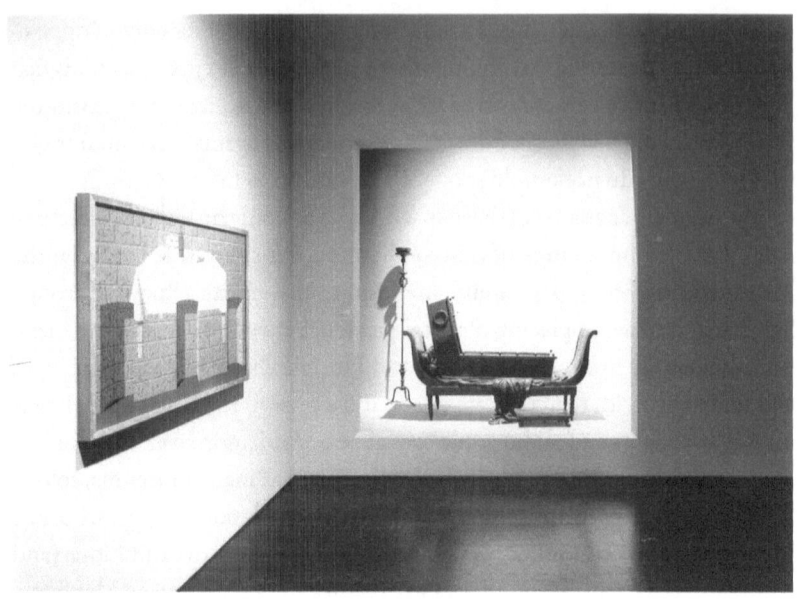

Walter Hopps's installation of René Magritte's L'aimable vérité *(1966) and* Madame Récamier de David *(1967) in the surrealist galleries. The Menil Collection, Houston.*

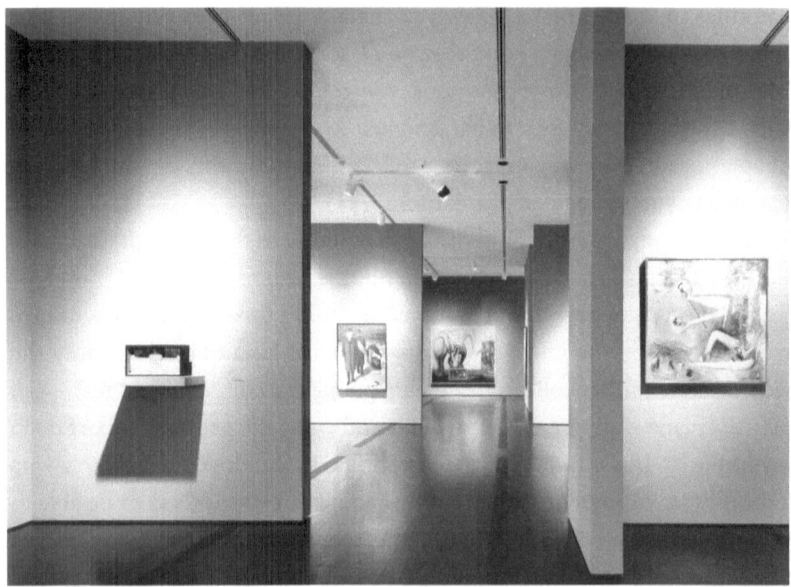

Clockwise from left: *Joseph Cornell,* Palace *(1943); René Magritte,* Le sens de la nuit *(1927); Max Ernst,* Le Surréalisme et la peinture *(1942); and Roberto Matta,* L'infidèle *(1942), in the surrealist galleries. The Menil Collection, Houston.*

In many ways, the model of the house museum, since its referent is the domestic interior, seems to be a more apt expression of Dominique's desire to conjure the artifice of intimacy than the more austere surroundings of museum galleries. But in house museums, no matter how graciously one is admitted, it is inevitably as a guest, with all the exteriority and deference that status entails. And, moreover, their contents are so heavily coded as the belongings of someone else that vicarious possession is inevitably thwarted.

What Dominique sought was to create a different kind of museum form and, thereby, a different kind of relationship between art and its audience, one imbued with an affecting density. "I'd like people to feel no awe," she told Louis Kahn, "no museum feeling, never too many things in the exhibition space. This allowing intimate contact with the work of art. Let's keep grandeur for the Pantheon."[24]

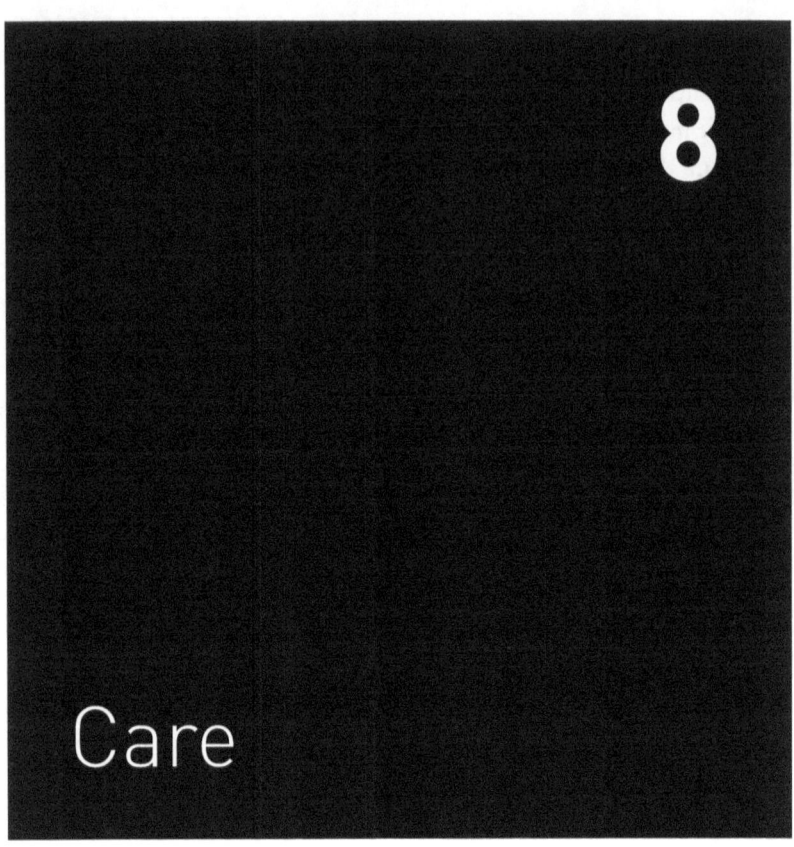

8

Care

Stored away, objects remain inert. Art of the past, like art of the present,
needs attention and love to become alive. We are all familiar by now, with
the famous statement of Rothko: "Art lives by companionship."
—DOMINIQUE DE MENIL, NOVEMBER 11, 1988

L ike most museums, the Menil Collection shows only a small proportion of its collection at one time, but Dominique de Menil, as we have
seen, was concerned to make the art in storage available for viewing.
By the time the museum was completed, it has to be said, the imagined
audience for the works in storage tended more toward the scholarly than
to the broader audience that had been talked of in the conceptualization of
the Kahn plan, presumably because by this point the operational burden of
bringing people into a secure space had become apparent. (Though it is true
that these kinds of logistical costs had not discouraged Dominique and John

from managing a widespread and informal system of loans of artworks to offices and academic institutions throughout Houston in the 1950s and 1960s.) In any event, open storage not only made the collection available to museum personnel and to scholars, but also allowed Dominique herself ready access to her collection for the first time. Before the construction of the museum, the collection, as we have noted, had never been together in one place, being dispersed primarily throughout warehouses and residences in Paris, New York, and Houston, although significant elements of it had been briefly brought together in Paris for "La Rime et la Raison." The storage areas were, in the earliest of Piano's drawings, designated as the "treasure house," a characterization attributed to Dominique and still used quite unselfconsciously by Menil personnel. Located not in the basement but elevated on the second floor, "for all to see," works are stored there in optimal environmental conditions.[1] But at least as important as the conservation virtues of the treasure house is its symbolic presence as the jewel of the building. As Richard Ingersoll notes, the treasure house and the adjacent seminar rooms, whose walls, hung with paintings, are an extension of the treasury, create "a sense of mystery and a desire to be initiated into the elite group that can ascend to the inner sanctum on the second floor" (1987, 47).

Even now, twenty years after the opening of the museum, curators visiting the Menil Collection from other museums are struck by the circumstances in which the collection is stored. Whereas in most museums works are hung in storage on racks that must be pulled out one by one, at the Menil Collection, paintings are hung on the walls, and three-dimensional objects are arranged carefully on shelves, giving the impression that everything can be seen at once. There is ample room to stand back to look at a work, or at works in relation to each other, and, what is perhaps even more unusual in museum storage, the doors and the usually tightly covered windows can be opened to admit natural light for viewing. While this is far from desirable from a strictly conservation point of view, from a curatorial perspective it offers optimum conditions for looking at works for the purposes of exhibition planning and research. It is an arrangement, as assistant curator Michelle White pointed out, "designed for the curator," as is the location of the curatorial offices adjacent to the treasure house. In most museums, curators primarily work from images on computers and seldom make what is typically a trek to distant storage rooms, where the work can be viewed only in less than favorable conditions.

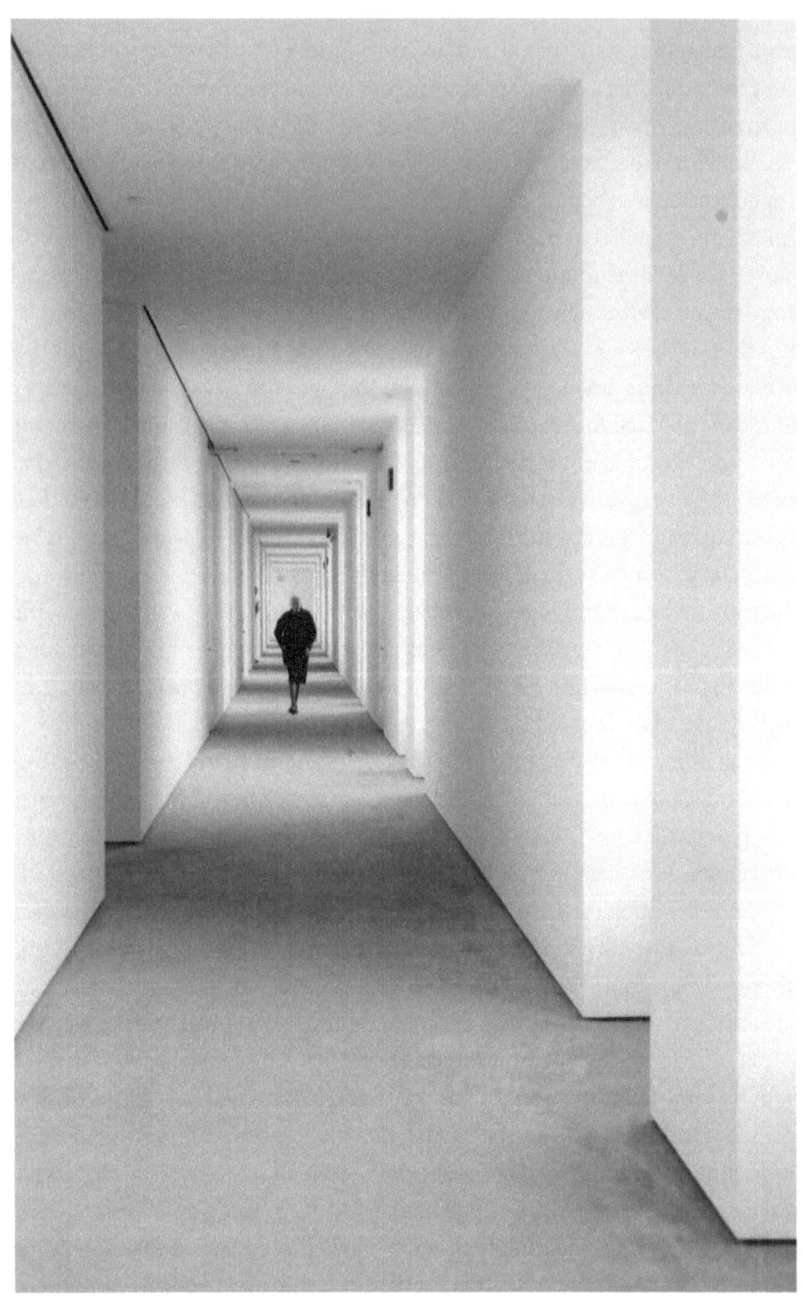

Dominique de Menil in the hallway of the second floor of the Menil Collection, adjacent to the "treasure house." Photo: A. de Menil. Courtesy Menil Archives, the Menil Collection, Houston.

The shelving system for objects in the storage rooms of the treasure house was designed, Stephen Fox notes, by the Houston architect Anthony Frederick. "Here again," Fox observes, "the institutional commitment to think about how objects of different sizes, weights, material, and conditions of fragility can best be protected yet made easily accessible to curators and scholars prompted design intervention rather than resort to a manufacturer's catalogue for equipment that the public would never see anyway" (2005, 20). This is just one instance of an acute attention to detail that is replicated throughout the museum—in work spaces just as in public areas—and that is directed, in this instance, toward the care of the object but that has the further effect of fostering a careful disposition among those who work with the collection.

This care of objects is reiterated in their daily handling and management. I observed it, for example, in the painstaking crafting of miniature replicas of pieces in the collection by a Houston artist who had been on the Menil Collection staff as a part-time preparator for years. During my period of extended research at the museum, he worked on this project almost exclusively, as he had long been doing, as was evident in the already substantial collection he had produced. The miniatures were made for use in the scale models of the galleries during installation design. Hopps would arrange the replicas in the model, then study the assemblage through a periscope-like device that produces something of the visual effect of being in the full-size gallery.

The careful installation planning, for which Walter Hopps was known, mitigated against the unnecessary handling of artworks when exhibitions were being hung: "If I don't know where every single thing is going, within three inches, I'm not happy," Hopps commented (quoted in Tomkins 1991, 35). But this pragmatic imperative does not begin to explain the considerable attention expended on the miniatures. Their creator was not the only person affronted by my asking why they didn't simply print color photographs reduced to scale, since each of the objects had already been photographed for the purposes of collection management. The question raised a suspicion, as had many of my questions over the course of my early fieldwork, that my sensibilities were not sufficiently attuned to the Menil aesthetic, or else surely I would not have needed to ask for an explanation—a suspicion that at every turn threatened to derail my entire research project. In any event, the elaborate character of each diminutive replica can be understood only as lavish care, as pure excess.

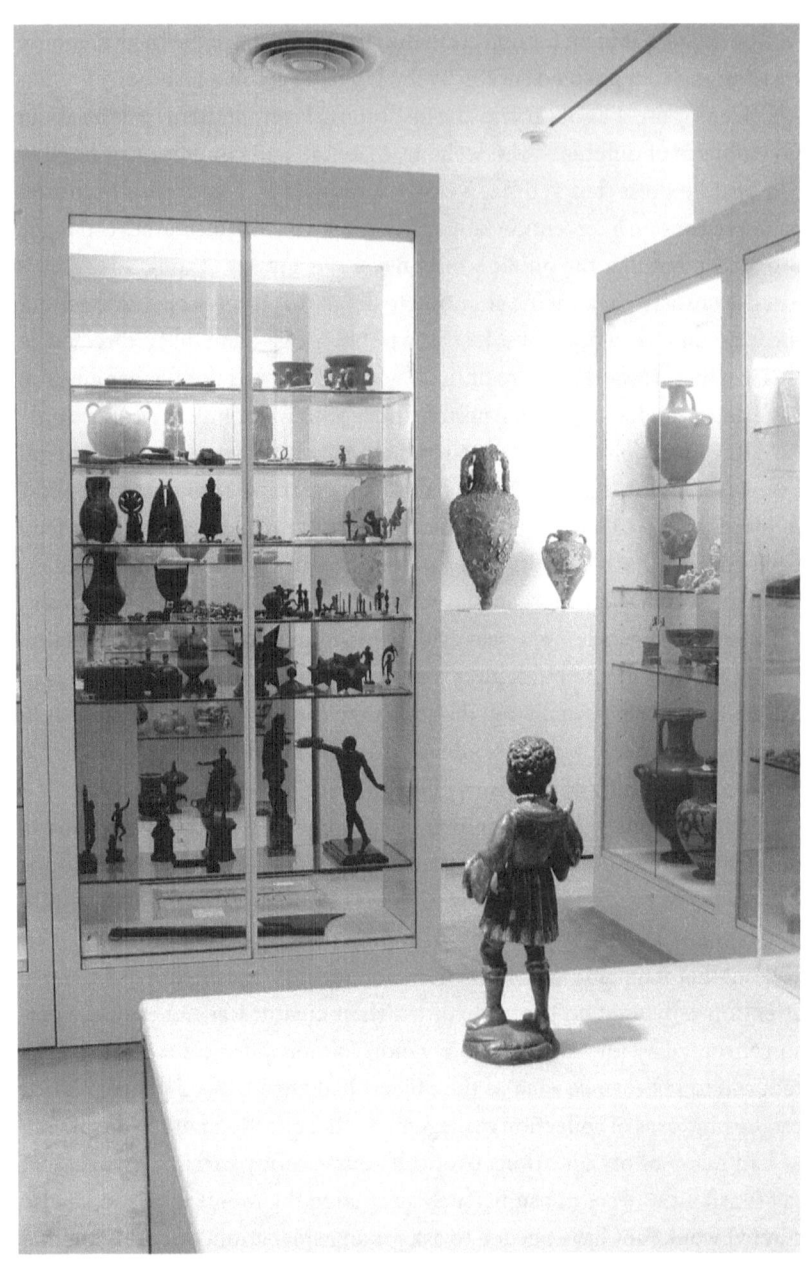

Antiquities storage, the Menil Collection, Houston. Photo: Hester + Hardaway. The Menil Collection, Houston.

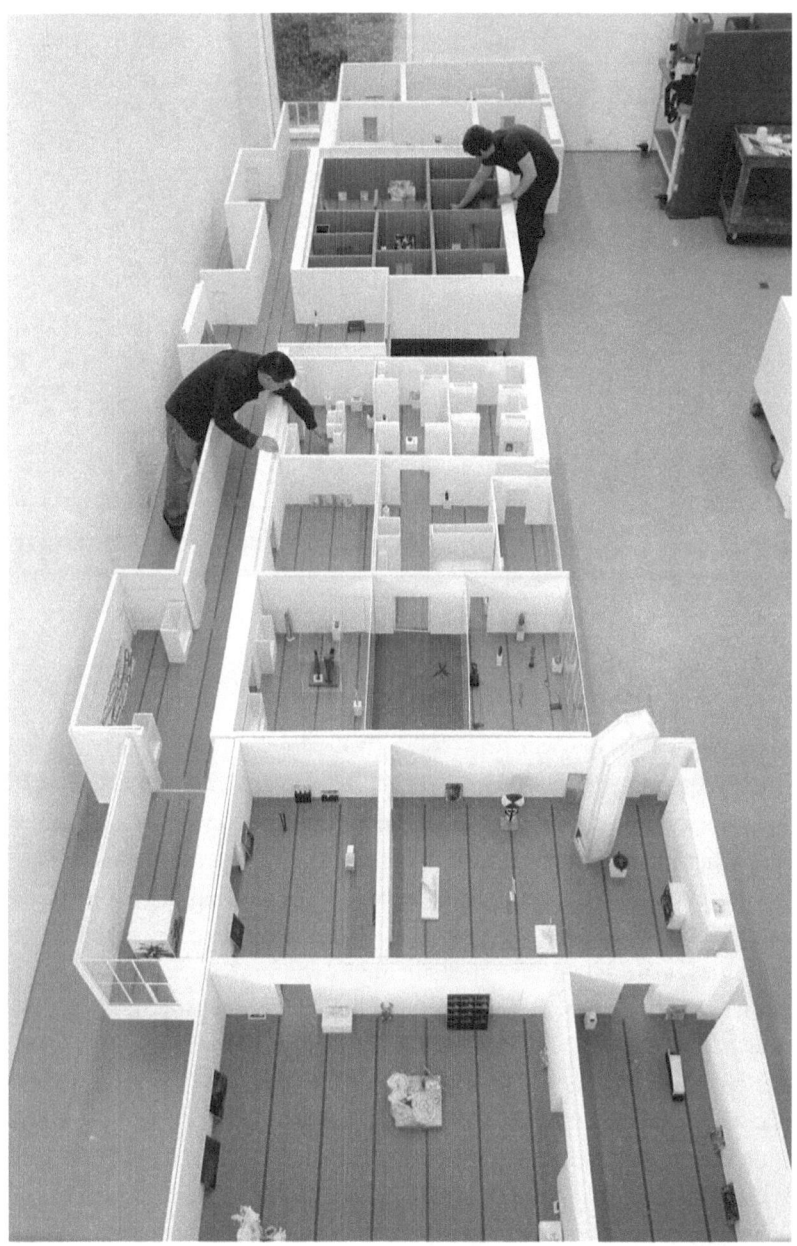

Scale model of Menil Collection galleries in the exhibitions department. Photo: George Hixson. The Menil Collection, Houston.

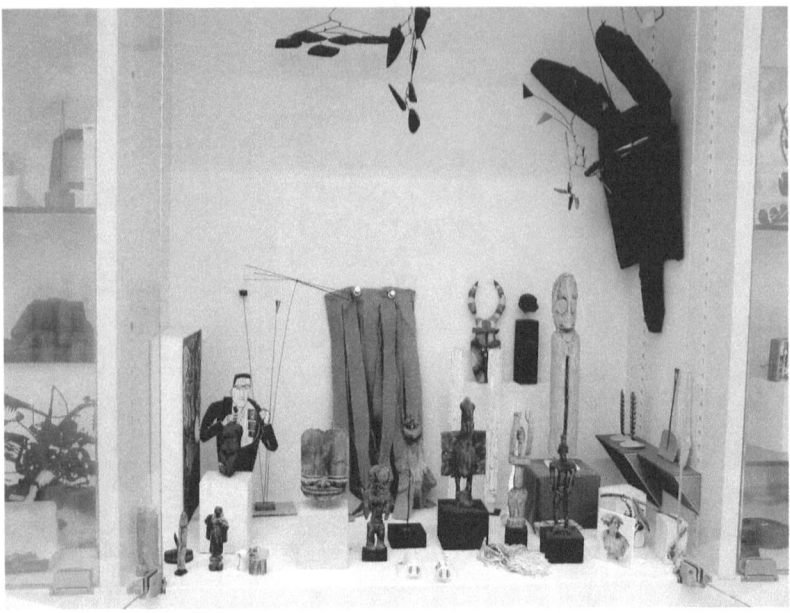

Miniatures shelved in the exhibitions department. The Menil Collection, Houston.

CONSERVATION

The conservation department is central in this economy of care; indeed, it seems central in a variety of ways. It has historically been the best staffed of the museum's departments.[2] The Menil Collection has an unusually strong commitment to conservation, particularly in contrast to many of the newer museums, especially those specializing in contemporary art, which do not have conservation departments and contract out what little work they consider necessary. Carol Mancusi-Ungaro, for twenty years the Menil Collection's chief conservator, identified a number of reasons for this high level of commitment. First, there was Dominique de Menil's training in science, which underpinned her special appreciation of the physical life of objects. Walter Hopps too had a particular concern for the object, which was born out of his involvement with artists and with the Ferus Gallery (which he and Ed Kienholz opened in Los Angeles in 1957); he had, as Mancusi-Ungaro put it, "a dealer's focus on the work itself." And Paul Winkler had a personal interest in conservation procedures.

But what solidified this base of interest was, Mancusi-Ungaro suggests, the Rothko project. It had begun in 1979 when she was called on to consult on problems with the Rothko paintings in the chapel, to determine what was causing the whitening of the triptychs. Advice had already been sought from a number of conservators, but Dominique de Menil had received inconclusive and often contradictory findings. Mancusi-Ungaro travelled to New York to get more specific information on Rothko's materials and practices, but found that no such resource was available. Dominique, Mancusi-Ungaro recounts, said, "You do it." So she brought Rothko's former assistant with her to Houston to identify materials and processes that had been used by the artist, and embarked on what was to become a ten-year project. They made simulations and artificially accelerated the aging process in order to discover the character of the specific interactions between materials, processes, and environmental conditions. It was not until these data were analyzed that a treatment program could be developed and carried out. Mancusi-Ungaro has become, in the process, the authority on the care of Rothko's work, publishing on the subject and consulting for other museums and collectors.

What is particularly notable for Mancusi-Ungaro is that Dominique and Hopps and Winkler were all willing to recognize that properly researched solutions to problems take time. Throughout the long Rothko project, Dominique never once pressured her to hurry, Mancusi-Ungaro pointed out with evident gratitude and respect. While conservators in some museums feel compelled to simply make things look better so that they can be rehung or loaned for an exhibition without delay, at the Menil Collection the approach is different. Works are looked at in terms of their present and future care, and in light of this, attention is focused on the condition of the work and not just its appearance, on a cure rather than merely symptomatic relief.

But attention to the long-term care of works, particularly contemporary ones, raises the question of precisely in what kind of condition works should be sustained.[3] While we accept cracks in the surface of a Rembrandt, there is no consensus as to what constitutes acceptable aging for post-1940s abstract painting. In the absence of any consensus, ad hoc decisions on treatment must continually be made. In response to this, Mancusi-Ungaro initiated an extensive project, funded by the Mellon Foundation, that documents on video conversations between Mancusi-Ungaro and contemporary artists regarding what they consider to be acceptable aging of their own work. Artists were invited to the Menil Collection to speak particularly of their work that is held by the Collection, providing a general resource for conservators, but also contributing to the collection's own very specific documentation of its objects.

Although artists' views on the disposition of their objects are not definitive, this kind of documentation offers conservators at least one basis on which treatment decisions might be made. But more importantly for Mancusi-Ungaro and for the Menil Collection, this project is primarily motivated by their commitment to artists, and ensures that the future care of their work can be informed by their own intentions and not by the abstract assumptions and conventions of the profession.

For Douglas Crimp, invoking this particular concern for the artist as a rationale for conservation practices should not be read as a mark of the Menil Collection's distinctive regard for the artist, since it is thoroughly consistent with the modernist cult of the artist. This is, according to Crimp, a common-place in museums. It is, he compellingly argues, a central means by which aura has been recuperated in the wake of the mechanical reproduction of art and the subsequent loss of authenticity, and this recuperation is a central task of museums, since "the museum is the institution that was founded on those values [that constitute the auratic], whose job it is to sustain those values" (Crimp 1993, 114). This advancement of the aura of objects, underpinned by the special subjectivity, the "unique vision," of the artist, the producer of objects, is, as Crimp notes, conventional in the key legitimizing practices of art history, connoisseurship, and, to some extent, museology. Museums have been central in this process, both in commissioning this connoisseurship and in promoting the "vision" of the artist; the latter is at its most powerful, perhaps, in the form of the retrospective exhibition (Crimp 1993).

Crimp's observations are apt, but his notion of aura, which serves first and foremost to establish the authenticity of objects, cannot encompass the kind of auratic seductions that the Menil Collection participates in. When Dominique de Menil wrote of Jerry MacAgy, "She was an alchemist. . . . The dullest abstract painting, the most musty object from a museum closet became extraordinary when seen through her magic lantern," she invoked a sense of the auratic that is not confined to the presence of the object but is extended to the possibility of transport (Menil 1968a, 10).

The Menil Collection's attention to artists, with regard to both the long-term disposition of their artworks and the manner in which they should be mounted, does not assert the authenticity of the object so much as its sovereignty. Artworks cease to be objects that can freely be acted upon, and this sense of the primacy of the object recurs throughout the discourse of the Menil Collection.

The recognized stature of the conservation department also serves to further the reputation of the Menil Collection. Pragmatically, it might make the difference between an anxious lender agreeing to loan a piece for exhibition or not. Indeed, it is not uncommon for the Collection to carry out valuable conservation work on artworks that have been lent to them for exhibition.

Conservation also operates, in symbolic terms, as the guarantor of art's enduring character, in contrast to the pervasive obsolescence of commodity capitalism. Philip Fisher argues that the museum operates most seductively in offering itself as a counterworld to the banality of mass-produced commodities. "As objects become more short-lived and geared to obsolescence, or rather to an ongoing series of inventions and adjustments that produced as one side effect obsolescence," Fisher writes, "the museum became more skilled at preservation, that is, at keeping things in a state that would never deteriorate or change" (Fisher 1991, 165). Fisher surely overstates his argument when he goes on to claim that in late capitalism the museum "is *simply* an institutional expression of the usefulness of art as a counterworld to the world of the factory with its mass produced objects" (166; emphasis added). But this idea that the intense singularity of "authentic" artworks, along with their permanence and sovereignty, serves to fulfill longings for an enchanted realm does resonate with the Menil Collection. The Menil has assiduously eschewed commerce within the museum—there is no café, no gift store, and not even the exchange of money for admission, which has always been free. (The Menil bookstore is across the street from the museum.) But I imagine that Dominique de Menil might have objected to this idea of a counterworld, with its intimations of a turn from the world rather than an engagement directed at its transformation. For those who follow, however, those who are now anxious for the Menil to continue to sustain aesthetic experience, it is by no means obvious that their own investment might not be of precisely the sort that Fisher characterizes. In any event, there can be no doubt that conservation contributes much to the economy of exemplary care and, thereby, to the crafting of careful dispositions.

Both Dominique de Menil and Renzo Piano were interested in the idea of the public being able to look into the museum and watch people work. They wanted the museum to have the air of a place of work, "a little bit like a shop or a light industry," as Walter Hopps suggests (quoted in Howard 1988, 65). A glimpse through the window into the conservation lab reveals a luminous and immaculate space that shimmers with authority.

The authority of conservation, however, does not extend to a rigorous adherence in the museum to standardized codes of conservation practice. This is not to suggest that Menil Collection personnel are anything less than scrupulous in their handling of objects, but that, on the contrary, there is a strong sense among staff members that professional codes are designed for other kinds of institutions. In museums where objects have become mere instruments of the institution, and where relations between the objects and the staff that manages them have become alienated, formalized regulations become necessary. By contrast, at the Menil Collection, the extraordinarily high level of staff identification with the Menil aesthetic has ensured such a personalized and more or less impassioned relationship with the objects that, it is imagined, one's judgment can be relied upon.

This is not simply a vanity. Rather, the Menil Collection's indifference to conventions of museum management, far from being cavalier, is an expression of the Menil's deep commitment to the care of the art object. The daily work of crafting the Menil aesthetic, of doing things in what is routinely referred to as "the Menil way," was not taken up as a set of techniques or procedures designed to achieve a specific outcome, but rather as a response to a series of ethical injunctions—not the empty proceduralism of merely following professional codes of practice, but the task of the exercise of judgment, of care, that ethical conduct calls for.

This practice of caring for the object through the exercise of careful ethical judgment generates effects that extend well beyond the disposition of the artworks. It is central to Dominique de Menil's project of crafting affecting relationships between artworks and the personnel who manage them as well as between artworks and those who enter into their milieu. Through this exercise of care, in concert with the operation of the artifice of intimacy, artworks are imbued with an affecting force that is, in Dominique de Menil's phenomenology, seldom experienced in art museums, where artworks are called upon primarily as instruments in the service of the institution. The density of the relationship between persons and artworks that is sought at the Menil Collection, and the notion of artworks acting upon the sensibilities of those who are drawn in to engage with them, is the kind of phenomenon that is elsewhere referred to in the language of aura.

AURA

Among the critics of modernity, it is not only the politically conservative "Romantic anticapitalists," as Lukács (1971) identifies them, who have regretted the loss of aura, but also the "progressive" advocates of the modern avant-garde's recuperation of authenticity.[4] It has, nevertheless, widely been taken as an article of faith among critics of the modernist autonomization of art that the decline of aura is inevitably liberatory insofar as the operation of aura is considered to be a central mechanism in the deeply obfuscatory practices by which art as a field of restricted production is sustained. The debate over aura has its intellectual roots in the struggle among Theodor Adorno, Walter Benjamin, and Bertolt Brecht over the meaning and political ramifications of aura, but while the debate is ongoing, its terms have been transformed. Robert Kaufman notes that the "most familiar representations of the aura-debate have tended to recast it as a drama between, on the one hand, an elite, embattled, and hermetic commitment to a high-modernist aesthetic that—for all its anti-romantic professions—stands as the inheritor of the transcendental impulse (this is frequently presented as the picture of the Adornian position); and, on the other hand, a popular or populist engagement with the more immediate, evidently technical-mechanical situation—the modern experiential reality—of social labor (this is the Brechtian-Benjaminian position)" (2002, 46–47). In this formulation, an investment in the maintenance of auratic experience can be seen only as politically objectionable and backward looking, while its counterpart enjoys the virtue of a fearless embrace of the contemporary rendered transparent.

But in Adorno, and at times in Benjamin as well, modern aura, far from being a rearguard, reactionary defense of the elite precincts of high art, is understood to be essentially critical and future oriented. It is this provocative, processual dimension of aura, the conjuring of aesthetic experience and not the "unreflective acquiescence" (R. Kaufman 2002, 48) familiar as "art appreciation" fostered by aestheticization, to use Adorno's distinction, which I draw on here. Benjamin, in "On Some Motifs in Baudelaire," draws attention to the interrogative potential of aura: "Experience of the aura thus rests on the transposition of a response common in human relationships to the relationship between the inanimate or natural object and man. The person we look at, or who feels he is being looked at, looks at us in turn. To perceive the aura of an object we look at means to invest it with the ability to look at us in return" (1982b, 190).[5]

The notion of art putting us on the spot is an idea to which Dominique de Menil returned often in her characterizations of what effects exhibitions ought to achieve. It is this, and the understanding that being put on the spot calls for a critical response rather than merely passive contemplation, that she is referring to when she explains that she installs art in such a way that one is "constantly encouraged to reassess what one sees and to explore it as a challenge rather than as a fait accompli" (quoted in A. Holmes 1968b, 13). Aura, in Dominique de Menil's aesthetic economy, does not emanate from the object or encase it, but instead is understood as a carefully rendered artifice designed to produce relationally the conditions of possibility for acutely aesthetic experiences and the sensibilities produced by them.

ISLANDS BEYOND

Jermayne MacAgy's first show at the University of St. Thomas, "Islands Beyond," was a moody, partially candlelit installation of modern paintings by Max Ernst, Paul Klee, Fernand Léger, René Magritte, Mark Rothko, Rufino Tamayo, and others, juxtaposed with medieval ecclesiastical sculptures, very much in the spirit of Couturier's reaching back to medieval forms as an antecedent to modern art.[6] In the foreword to the catalogue for the show, the Reverend G. B. Flahiff speaks of the invisible realms to which the show gave access:

> The significant word is "beyond," for the pieces have been selected with a view to manifesting the power of art to evoke what lies beyond the world of the senses. . . . The work itself is more than a material thing. It is a veritable "incarnation" of a glimpse of reality that the artist has caught and that he has to

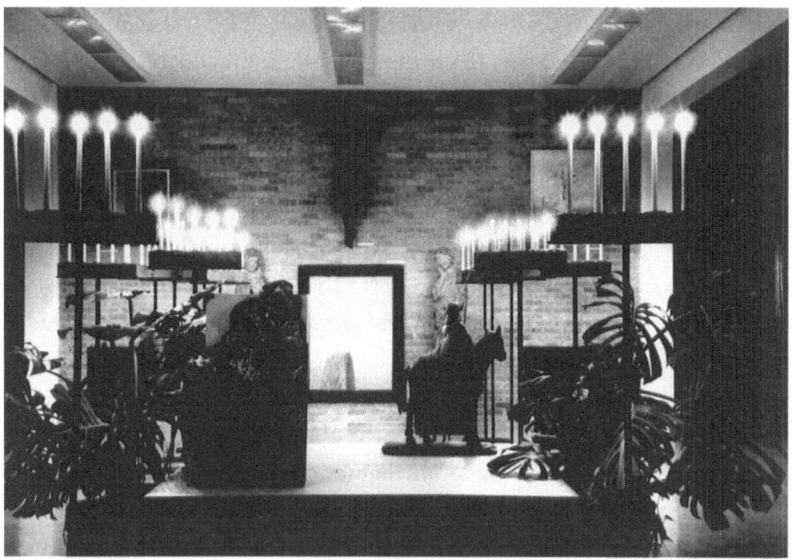

Installation view of "Islands Beyond," Jones Hall, University of St. Thomas, 1962. Photo: Eve Arnold. Courtesy Menil Archives, the Menil Collection, Houston.

express not in a logical statement but only in a work of art through a material medium like sound, lines, colors or masses. It is for this reason that the deepest joy attendant upon the experience of contact with a work of art is not that of the senses or the emotions, but that of the intelligence as it grasps intuitively rather than rationally realities beyond the senses and reacts to their beauty. For some, these realities float like distant islands on the horizon of another world: for others, they constitute but a single all-embracing realm: for all, they are, willy-nilly, a part of the Reality beyond, in leading us to which, art has intrinsically an affinity with religion. (1959, 5)[7]

Flahiff's characterization of the structuring principles of "Islands Beyond" speaks to the redemptive possibilities of art, an understanding that was central to the aesthetic projects of John and Dominique de Menil and that evokes fundamental Catholic preoccupations.

While still with the California Palace of the Legion of Honor, MacAgy wrote of her approach to installation: "To create an aura, an atmosphere belonging personally to the objects, rather than merely building an edifice against which the objects look well, is the purpose of the Museum's installation plans. And yet this is not to say that the settings should not look well . . . but [they should be] at all times subservient—acting with and always evoking the innateness of the things exhibited" (1953).

While this passage, which is concerned with the full presence of objects, may seem to be at odds with Flahiff's characterization of their referential force, the point of both comments is to stress that the exhibition itself is not the primary object, but serves instead as a means by which attention to its constituent objects (or to what might be glimpsed through them) might be focused and refined. MacAgy's close attention to exhibition design, then, was not in the interest of creating spectacle for its own sake, but of making the ineffable present. This point is worth noting because it reveals a very particular relation to art objects, one that resists their reduction to mere art historical artifacts or to spectacles of surplus value. It is a view that recurred among those whom the de Menils sought out to work with them on their various projects.

For many Menil staff, this particular regard for the object and for the sensibilities it might conjure not only has defined their practices within the museum but has also resided at the heart of their deep personal investment in the Menil Collection. What is expressed and reproduced through the alchemy of Menil Collection exhibitions is a longing that is not necessarily strictly religious (of the sort expressed by Flahiff and held dear by Couturier and by Dominique de Menil), but that takes a secular form in the desire to maintain the conditions of possibility for experience that is irreducibly aesthetic in character. This calls for the production of aesthetic experience not only through the crafting of exhibitions, but also through a constellation of details that underpin the exhibition—the architectural elaboration of luminous work spaces, attentive maintenance, intelligent and seductive exhibition design and installation, beautiful and scholarly publications, meticulous attention to conservation, and the storage of works in the treasure house. But most crucially it refers to the exercise of a careful disposition toward the Collection's objects. To treat artworks as ordinary things is to compromise their aura—to make them banal. The practice of care that has been cultivated at the Menil Collection is not just a set of injunctions to do things in a manner that is excellent—although the rhetoric of excellence was always something of a de Menil mantra—but amounts to the maintenance of an aesthetic disposition, a careful mode of engagement that sustains the affecting force of the artworks.

EXHIBITIONARY INTENT

Exhibition installation is the centerpiece of the Menil Collection's efforts to conjure the acutely aesthetic experience that Adorno characterizes as auratic. The arresting quality of Menil installations under the curation of Dominique de Menil, Hopps, and Winkler was frequently remarked upon by commentators, just as it had been for exhibitions mounted by MacAgy and Sweeney. Hopps and MacAgy are nothing short of legendary in art world circles for their facility for installation. This quality can't be explained in terms of a set of techniques or design principles, which makes it difficult to identify just what it is that makes their installations work so well. At the Menil Collection, one can point to the quality of the architectural space, the light (that afforded by Piano's "leaves" and by attentive use of artificial lighting), the absence of barriers and crowds, and the low hanging of the work. But rather than any particular characteristic, it is a constellation of approaches underpinning exhibition installation that critically shapes the affecting force of a show.

Dominique de Menil tried to account for what made an exhibition work: "The beauty of an exhibition is made of lots of little details. It is a *combination of a certain vision with the impeccable revealing.* Every detail has to be perfect. Mies used to say: GOD IS IN THE DETAIL. As to the planning it cannot be done with more than one or two or three people closely working together. *Exhibitions, like architecture,* are the most *undemocratic* activities—you can't do [them] by committee and vote" (quoted in Brennan 2007, 23). But there are some other elements that it is worth articulating.

First, there is a preoccupation with making the art look good. While such regard for the object might suffer from a supervening preoccupation with art historical narratives in many public museums, at the Menil Collection the sovereignty of the object has always been asserted. Further, despite a tendency among curators of modern art to create shows that treat art objects "as raw materials for exhibitions that are themselves mega–art works" (Tomkins 1991, 34), at the Menil Collection the very point of a show is to draw attention to the works, "to make each piece look good," as Dominique de Menil put it.

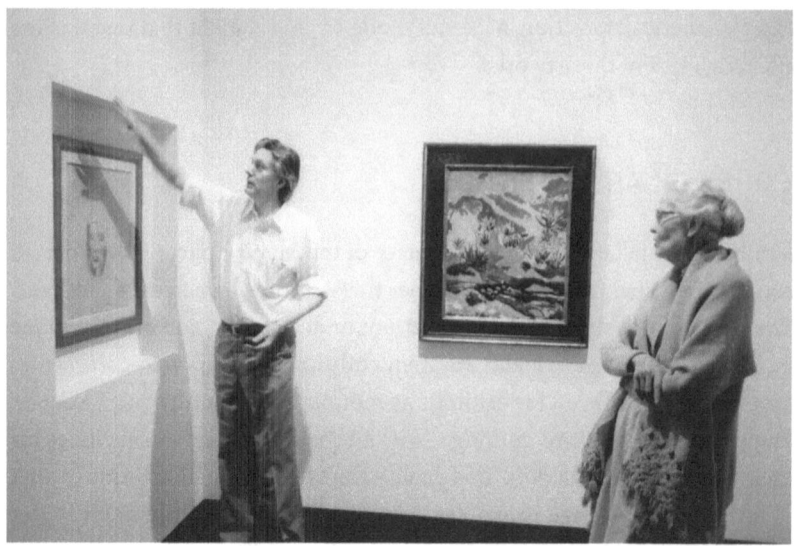

Walter Hopps and Dominique de Menil discussing the installation of Pablo Picasso's La porteuse de pain *(ca. 1906) and Henri Matisse's* Le ruisseau aux aloes *(1907), in preparation for the opening of the Menil Collection, 1987. Courtesy Menil Archives, the Menil Collection, Houston.*

This is not to say that any of the Menil curators have been uninterested in the history of art, but rather that art historical understanding should inform rather than govern how work is shown. "In a Hopps exhibition," Calvin Tomkins wrote in his *New Yorker* profile of the curator, "considerations of art history and scholarship are often present, along with ideas about style and influence and social issues, but the primary emphasis is always on how the art looks on the wall, and this, surprisingly, makes Walter Hopps something of a maverick in his profession" (34).

When Hopps was asked to name important predecessors, the first name he offered was Willem Mengelberg, the music director of the New York Philharmonic from 1922 to 1928, "not so much for his styles, but for his unrelenting rigor" (Hopps 1996, 101). "Fine curating of an artist's work," Hopps explains, "that is, presenting it in an exhibition—requires as broad and sensitive an understanding of an artist's work as a curator can possibly muster. This knowledge needs to go well beyond what is actually put in the exhibition. . . . To me, a body of work by a given artist has an inherent kind of score that you try to relate to and understand. It puts you in a certain psychological state" (101).[8] When Hopps worked on an installation, he attended to the rhythm, tempo, and volume of the show through the careful calibration of juxtaposed artworks.

Hopps's sense of the central importance of establishing the conditions for a dialogue between works is thoroughly consistent with the MacAgy legacy that informed the curation of shows at the University of St. Thomas and the Rice Museum and that continues to be expressed in Menil Collection exhibitions. Dominique de Menil drew an uncharacteristically folksy analogy between an installation of works and the dynamics among dinner guests: "Its just like with guests at a dinner party; the seating and the ambiance is so important. A guest may seem reticent, perhaps a little dull, in one setting, but seat him with the right person and he might really sing. Art objects too can be made to sing."[9]

Another hallmark of this legacy, and what made Hopps's orchestrations work so well, is a deep regard for the artist, a regard that is strangely muted in public museums (except, perhaps, in the hagiographic narration provided by acoustiguides). Robert Rauschenberg, whose work was the subject of several Hopps shows, had enormous admiration (and gratitude too, no doubt) for Hopps's work: "He uses intuitive logic to locate and solve the artistic mysteries that lie within a work, which is either forgotten or never realized. . . . This serious energy then is transformed into the most sensitive and intelligent presentation I have ever witnessed" (quoted in Gray 1993, 42–43).[10] Indeed, Paul Winkler pointed out that Hopps's Rauschenberg shows went a long way to win for the Menil Collection the trust and confidence of Cy Twombly, who agreed to donate a significant body of work to the museum's Twombly Gallery (Gray 1993). (Though, by all accounts, Dominique de Menil's reputation among artists was also decisive, as was Winkler's very strong feeling for Twombly's work.)

Although Hopps was by no means immune to the pleasure of a well-received show, like his colleagues he was free to work at the Menil Collection without the pressure of public success, since there was no admission income to be accounted for and, moreover, no conviction within the museum that the success of a show should be measured by the size of its audience. More highly valued than popularity was the willingness to take risks intellectually, aesthetically, and conceptually.

The conventional critical response to the unwillingness of the Menil Collection to produce exhibitions in response to some real or imagined public interest is to read it as indicative of a cavalier disregard for "the public." While it is true that the Collection does not seek to gratify "popular" taste, for Dominique de Menil this refusal was not an inadvertent expression of elitist sensibilities or an attempt to maintain high-cultural distinction. Rather, it marked Dominique's strong conviction that because contemporary taste has been dulled by aestheticization, in Adorno's usage, producing a kind of complacency, and by a more generalized malaise of the spirit, our judgment (that is, popular judgment) cannot be relied upon to serve us well. And this recalls the redemptive character of her project. When characterizing her project, Dominique invoked Couturier consistently. Responding to suggestions that his chapel projects might be informed by the vanity of progressivism, rather than serving the interests of their congregations, Couturier argued:

> [Since this is] precisely the time when the most confining, most crushing servitude weighs upon working people, would not the primary role of art be to create places of enchantment, poetry, deliverance? . . . But, the argument continues, why choose, for people who are totally unprepared for them, the most taxing and difficult "poetic" forms of our time?
>
> To that argument our answer is this: first of all these forms were not chosen because they were the most difficult (although in their difficulty and harshness there is an almost certain power of purification and discipline that is sorely lacking in contemporary "piety"). They were chosen because these difficult forms were also the most precious. . . . To give the best, even if it were not understood, not recognized—this . . . seemed to us to show more respect for those who put their confidence in us.
>
> Furthermore, obscurity and lack of comprehension are only temporary. Pure works have a kind of radioactivity. . . . In the semi-darkness where such things dwell, their energy builds up, and there comes a day when children and grandchildren draw life from the treasure that their fathers, to their credit, had accepted in faith. (1989, 105)

Art in contemporary circumstances, for Couturier as for Dominique de Menil, was not merely (nor necessarily) a source of pleasure, nor an instrument of instruction, but might best serve as a medium of spiritual remediation. While Hopps could hardly be said to have subscribed to this particularly Catholic preoccupation, he did share with his patron the conviction that nobody was well served by mounting shows that condescended to their audience.

But there is also the question of how Dominique conceived of the museum's audience. Insofar as scholarship on museums has addressed the museum's audience, it has overwhelmingly evoked a public, or perhaps publics (when "underrepresented" populations are addressed). But it is not to this liberal, undifferentiated public, or population group, that the Menil Collection addresses itself, but rather to a highly pluralist, "illiberal" community. The notion of the illiberal here is not meant to convey the character of an audience's politics, as conservative rather than progressive, say, but to draw attention to the understanding of the self that is operative here—to the "person" rather than to the autonomous "individual" on which the liberal notion of the public is predicated.

The conviction that the museum should address itself to persons who together might constitute pluralistic, internally differentiated communities rather than an abstract public has its roots in the "integral humanism" of Maritain, as discussed earlier. As a consequence, the Menil has shown no interest in producing shows with a mass appeal, nor exhibitions aimed at drawing in particular "niche" markets, since it has steadfastly held the view that people are best served by being shown exemplary work in a manner that establishes conditions for aesthetic experience.

In many public museums, the line between behind-the-scenes operations and public presentation draws a distinction between a culture of knowing cynicism among insiders and the naïve suggestibility of the public. Such a distinction does not seem to obtain at the Menil Collection. It is perhaps because the Collection has not felt bound to attract a mass public, as civic museums are under pressure to do, that it has not considered itself compromised by its audience. While civic museums have succumbed to a regime of crowd-pleasing blockbuster shows and corporate fund-raisers, the Menil Collection has avoided such expediencies. It has pursued its own projects, believing that the audience that it seeks to engage is one that will inevitably be well served so long as the Collection continues to pursue its commitments in an "exemplary" manner. And in the view of the Menil Collection, it is not only the audience but the objects as well that get their due in this context.

Menil Collection personnel often spoke to me of what they characterized as the museum's unusual respect for its audience, expressed principally by showing "difficult" work without any accompanying explanatory text that would intervene between the viewer and the work, defining the terms by which one might approach it. However, the spare aesthetic of Menil Collection installations, in addition to the refusal to offer interpretive texts, is often understood, and criticized, as exemplifying the elitist, high-modern orthodoxy that the work of art should properly stand on its own, its meaning contained within, unsullied by extraneous considerations (elitist, in this view, because in the absence of interpretive frames of reference, the works tend to baffle and intimidate those who are not already immersed in the art world).[11] Such a reading recognizes the operation of what Bourdieu calls a "restricted economy" (Bourdieu and Darbel 1991). In Dominique de Menil's characterization, however, signification is thoroughly relational, both by virtue of the juxtaposition of objects within a show as well as by the exchange between a viewer and the object. Far from expecting the object to "speak for itself," as Clement Greenberg insisted, it requires a viewer willing to give herself up to seeing or experiencing the object in a manner unmediated by conceptual preoccupations. This suspension of conceptual frames in the experience of art might be suggestive of Kant (as might be Couturier's comment that "what we see judges us"), but far from Kant's disinterested subject, Dominique de Menil sought a thoroughly impassioned engagement with works that might not be considered as "ends in and of themselves," but that instead might properly be understood as instruments of devotion and technologies of remediation.

Couturier devoted an issue of L'Art Sacré "exclusively to restoring the sensitivity of the eye, even if the exposition of ideas must be set aside" (1989, 14), presenting pictures "if possible without caption or explanation, so that no exercise of reason may intrude into what should always be a simple, direct sensory intuition" (16–17). It is the echo of Henri Bergson, not Clement Greenberg, that reverberates here in Couturier's words and resounds in the exhibitionary intent of the Menil Collection.

This principle of the Menil aesthetic could be seen at work in the terms of apprehension established in the installation of "African Zion: The Sacred Art of Ethiopia," a temporary exhibition that had been curated and designed by another institution.[12] As with any touring show, this exhibition of Ethiopian images and devotional objects arrived in crates, complete with very detailed handling and installation instructions, but unlike most shows that are accepted by the Menil, this one was accompanied by large textual panels and labels with lengthy descriptions of the objects. To the unconcealed chagrin of the registrar and conservator from the originating institution, who accompanied the show to watch over its installation, Menil personnel, under the curatorial oversight of Winkler and Davezac, set about the laborious tasks of concealing the text fixed in the interior of many of the vitrines and rewriting label copy for the walls. The information panels, along with the large color photographs meant to depict contemporary Ethiopian life, remained stored in their packaging. Both Winkler and Davezac worried that the selection of pieces and their ordering in the exhibition gave the impression of artistic decline in the more recent work represented. Anxious to avoid such a depiction, several works were rearranged to hide the offending pieces. Given that any change was considered insulting to the show's organizers, a fact that Menil personnel were sensitive to, at least in principle, the process of installing the show served as a vivid enactment of how things were done in "the Menil way."

The Menil Collection's refusal to offer interpretive signage that would define the terms in which one viewed artworks is not solely due to Dominique's Bergsonian valorization of intuition over information, a position that can all too easily be dismissed as simply thinly veiled elitism, no matter how heartfelt the conviction. Instead, it raises serious questions not only about how the museum communicates with its audience, and to what end, but also about how it conceptualizes its audience. In thinking about the Menil Collection's very specific preoccupations and practices, it becomes apparent that the familiar terms of reference do not serve us very well. It is taken as an article of faith in the literature on museums that those institutions that refrain from offering interpretive assistance are inevitably engaging in bad politics—by preserving the opacity of art, they secure its elite status. By contrast, it is considered equally self-evident that those museums that work to make art "accessible" through the provision of information and explanation thereby demystify art and as a consequence "democratize" it. But this kind of engagement, insofar as it renders the viewer a more or less passive recipient of received understandings, was precisely what Dominique wished to disrupt. By eschewing the popularizing practices that other museums have adopted under the rubric of "democratization"—practices that Couturier would surely have characterized as submission to mediocrity—the Menil Collection treats its public with respect. But more than respect is at stake. More important is the museum's crafting of circumstances that can foster and sustain resolutely aesthetic commitments that are not vested in a longing for an imagined past of authentic experience, but instead are oriented to the future.

This commitment to a poetic rather than a didactic experience of art, and the kind of subjectivity it is imagined to engender, is made very explicit in relation to the museum's sole institutionalized project of "outreach," albeit one initiated by another institution. The Writers in the Schools Program (WITS), developed by the University of Houston's prestigious Creative Writing Program, is the mechanism by which the museum hosts tours of schoolchildren. On Mondays and Tuesdays, when the museum is closed to the public, groups of children are introduced to the galleries not by art historians, but by writers. While the graduate creative-writing students report that they often have to actively resist the urge to explain the works, it is the explicit intent of the program to refrain from teaching art history or "art appreciation." Instead, far from being constrained to be passive recipients of instruction, the children are encouraged to be active interlocutors, experiencing the works they see as catalysts for their own creative imaginations. Conventional education programs in museums seek to "explain" the works that we are brought before so that we may experience the pleasure of mastery rather than the instability of confrontation or genuine dialogue.[13] What is sought in the WITS program and throughout the Menil Collection's relationship with its audience is a visceral engagement unmediated by conceptual frames, wherein a work of art "invades" one's territory so strongly that it "demands a response" (Menil 1968b).

What is at stake here is not the inculcation of young audiences with a taste for art, but fostering in them an orientation to art that Dominique wished to see generalized throughout other domains of life; an orientation that is active, critical, creative, and imbued with confidence in one's own judgment.

It has to be said that countervailing pressures are inevitably being exerted here. Notwithstanding the museum's conviction that art should be presented so that pedagogy does not displace poetry, and all its operational efforts to foster an interrogative engagement with artworks, some nevertheless experience the museum as overwhelmingly didactic. It is an effect of the museum's ambition to be exemplary. Anthony Vidler argues that museum objects, simply by virtue of being in a museum, inevitably are invested with an exemplary status, and so acquire a didactic character (1987, 165–167). At

the Menil Collection, this effect is intensified by the museum's thoroughgo-
ing program of exemplarity and by the charisma and moral authority of its
benefactor. I once asked Dominique de Menil about the effects she was trying
to achieve in relation to the museum's audience, and she tersely admonished
me—"I am not a missionary." However, ample evidence from the de Menils'
projects reveal their efforts to set an example: the architectural commissions
they pursued, the modeling of art-buying behavior through Art Associates,
their practices of patronage, and, not least, Dominique's practices of piety.

ETHICAL DISPOSITIONS

In the practice of exemplary care, the elements of which are not codified in the
form of institutionally mandated policy but the pursuit of which constitutes
what is referred to routinely among museum personnel as "the Menil way,"
what I observed was a set of practices that were essentially ethical in character. While these practices were addressed toward the care of the object, their
effects extended beyond the artworks to the sensibilities of those engaged in
these practices and, in a less intensified form, perhaps, to those experiencing
artworks within this milieu of care.

While these ethical imperatives were no doubt made more acute by the
charisma of Dominique de Menil, and by the privilege of working with such
a splendid collection, much of what has impelled Menil Collection staff has
been their own longing for an enchanted experience of art and their abiding anxiety that such an experience might not be sustainable in a public art
museum. This recognition that an aesthetic engagement calls not only for
evocative exhibitionary practices but also for an exercise of care toward artworks is taken up not only by many Menil staff, but also by certain members
of the public to which the Menil Collection presents itself.

In their ongoing production of the Menil aesthetic, museum personnel
have at the same time been engaged in the pursuit of a particular mode of
self-formation that has been extended to the Menil's audience too (in the
terms of apprehension that the museum establishes). These ethical practices
are directed toward the care not only of the objects and their institutional
circumstance but also of the self.

Among Menil staff and audience members, there are those who engage with the museum in a manner that is not a submission to the orthodoxies of museum conduct, but a self-conscious process of elective cultivation of an aesthetic disposition that takes the form of a sort of ethical pedagogy. As James Faubion points out, what distinguishes the ethical field, beyond mere obedience or mere transgression, is its reliance on "practical intuition," which equips one to do the right thing from one ethically sensitive moment to the next (2001, 85). Ethical practice, then, is always, as Michel Foucault put it, "'the considered practice of freedom,' a practice always analytically distant from the moral principles or codes to which it has reference" (85). Clearly, then, we are not talking here of scrupulous conformity to codes of professional practice, the sort of empty proceduralism that, once in place, demands adherence instead of ethical agency. Under such strictures, "practical wisdom" and "skill at deliberative choice," by which Aristotle characterized the ethical actor, must be suspended in favor of mere adherence (Faubion 2001, 85).

The kind of ethical engagement that I am invoking is, as Foucault argues in his essay "What Is Enlightenment?" a distinctive "attitude of modernity," notwithstanding its opposition to the proceduralism of modern bureaucratic organization. "And by this," he writes, "I mean a mode of relating to contemporary reality; a voluntary choice made by certain people; in the end, a way of thinking and feeling; a way, too, of acting and behaving that at one and the same time marks a relation of belonging and presents itself as a task" (Foucault 1994, 309). In this he draws on Baudelaire's defining characterization of modernity in which, to quote Foucault, "the high value of the present is indissociable from a desperate eagerness to imagine it, to imagine it otherwise than it is, and to transform it not by destroying it but by grasping it in what it is" (309). In this, Baudelaire offers an early formulation of the kind of attitude that is a central element of what Schloesser describes as the off-modern, the distinctive orientation to the present in relation to the past that Maritain was so central in elaborating, drawing heavily on Baudelaire, whose work he greatly admired. However, modernity for Baudelaire, as Foucault points out, is "not simply a form of relationship to the present; it is also a mode of relationship that has to be established with oneself. . . . To be modern is not to accept oneself as one is in the flux of the passing moments; it is to take oneself as object of a complex and difficult elaboration" (310)—an elaboration that is taken up at the Menil Collection as an ethical imperative.

Submission to the Menil aesthetic and to doing things in the Menil way is certainly called for at the Menil Collection, but since there is no program defining such conduct, it calls for constant calibration of one's sensibility and practice toward the realization of this end. Central to this is one's conduct in relation to the art object, both in one's actions and one's affect.

Doing things the Menil way requires learning about the collection, its constituent objects, and how they should be shown, handled, and regarded in order to give the objects their due, but also to conjure the desired affect. It also calls for a regard for the artist. So, while the Menil Collection has exerted, and continues to exert, considerable suasive force on its staff (and its audiences), what I am describing here are not simply what we might call processes of enculturation or inculcation, whereby normative behavior is taken up through unselfconscious repetition—whereby one develops a "feel for the game," as Bourdieu puts it in his formulation of "habitus," the theoretical construct he uses to explain how the structural and class positions of individual subjects come to be embodied as dispositions, largely through unconscious processes (Bourdieu 1977). Indeed, while Bourdieu's notion of habitus has much to recommend it in relation to many theorizations of enculturation, it falls seriously short when it comes to trying to account for the sort of self-conscious practices of cultivation undertaken at the Menil. For Bourdieu, such practices would come under the purview not of habitus so much as sheer instrumentalism. These are the actions of agents vying to "outflank" and "outmaneuver" others operating within their cultural field, no matter how much such acts are couched in legitimating terms that might veil their strategic character (82). Or, less aggressively, he would construe them as strategies of identity formation, since assertions of distinction are essentially claims to belonging. But the kind of activity that I wish to address is directed not so much toward recognition as toward a training of ethical sensibilities so as to foster the possibility of a new social and moral order.

I wish to draw on a longer and richer history of habitus—one that, as Saba Mahmood observes, "specifically addresses the centrality of gestural capacities in certain traditions of moral cultivation" (2005, 136). Writing of the notion of habitus in this older, Aristotelian sense, Mahmood notes that "*habitus* in this tradition of moral cultivation implies a quality that is acquired through human industry, assiduous practice, and discipline, such that it becomes a permanent feature of a person's character. In other words, 'a habitus can be said to exist only when someone has actively formed it'" (136). The appeal here is its emphasis on human activity and deliberation, rather than on claims either to inherent "taste" or "sensitivity" or to the inadvertent conformity to convention embodied in Bourdieu's habitus.

For Mahmood, who is addressing the veiling practices of Egyptian women who are adherents of the piety movement, attention to elective cultivation, which the Aristotelian formulation of habitus foregrounds, offers an approach that does not insist on rendering veiling as an expression or sign of modesty—whether out of mere submission or as a gesture of resistance to modernity—but as a means of becoming and being a modest person. Similarly, the cultivation of an aesthetic disposition may be understood not inevitably from the point of view of the expressive labor it may perform—in which an aesthetic disposition is understood, first and foremost, to operate as a sign (typically of taste and, thereby, of distinction)—but as a means by which one might *be* a person who experiences affecting engagements with artworks.

9

Institutionalization of an Aesthetic

Tradition is a fire to which each generation brings its own wood.
—DOMINIQUE DE MENIL (1977, 8)

When I met with Louisa Sarofim just a week after Dominique de Menil's death, she explained that as the new president of the Menil Foundation, she saw an urgent need to make the museum "more accessible," to foster a larger, broader audience. The Menil Collection, she averred, needed "to engage the public and educate the public." There are a number of questions raised by this perfectly orthodox expression of perhaps the defining contemporary imperative under which art museums operate: to increase audience size by "democratizing" the museum's programming and exhibitionary practices. But before I address these matters, I want first to respond to a question that many readers may be troubled by. I have said much about the Menil Collection's distinctive commitment to conjuring engagement rather than mere appreciation or admiration among those who are its audience. We observed these efforts particularly in the crafting of an artifice of intimacy, by which the experience of art might be enlivened by the vicarious possession of artworks, and in an economy of care that seeks to foster not only aesthetic effects but also an ethical disposition that would extend beyond the experience of art to a kind of ethical citizenship.

So how are we to understand Sarofim's intimation that the museum had been less than energetic in engaging its audience? In large measure, the problem lies in discrepant notions of the museum's public and of the form of engagement that is imagined. And there is another matter to address. Sarofim's concern about increasing the size of the museum's audience is an expression of her experience as a foundation steward steeped in the ethos of nonprofit development departments and in business models of growth more broadly.[1] According to this orientation, an organization that is not showing growth is essentially an operation in decay. In an art market in which acquisition budgets do not go very far at all, pursuing growth by making significant additions to the collection is a very expensive proposition. As a result, capital growth has been pursued with vigor by many museums, as evidenced by the extraordinary expansion of museum buildings. But the cost has been plain to see: boards locked in irresolvable conflicts in response to the demands of the benefactors of these architectural projects, staff members constrained and frustrated by the squeeze on operating funds occasioned by expansion, and often a need to search for a new director, since resignations tend to follow the completion of such a project, whether out of exhaustion or because the completion of a capital project puts a director in a uniquely favorable position to entertain competitive offers from other museums. There is no doubt that the least taxing means of generating a sense of institutional vitality and momentum is to increase museum attendance and membership. But the idea that museums should attract larger audiences—in the discourse of Sarofim, "to engage the public"—has motivations that are many and that extend far beyond the article of faith that a robust museum is a growing one.

PUBLICS

There is a deep conviction not only among critics of museums as bastions of privilege and exclusion but also among those who are the stewards of museums with a keen sense of responsibility for maximizing the potential of the assets that they manage, that there is virtue, for the public, in encouraging more people to avail themselves of the museum's resources. Indeed, Sarofim was clear about this. It is the duty of Menil Foundation trustees to ensure that the riches of the museum are not squandered by a failure to fully utilize the collection, she explained, adding that the provision of art education is a key means of extending the resource to a wider public. This view is taken up from a critical rather than a fiduciary perspective by Vera Zolberg (1994). Her essay remains a particularly concise articulation of an enduring view among many who worry about the politics of museums in relation to the public. Zolberg asserts that it is the duty of art museums to broaden their public, to "seek out those who would normally not enter" (49). Art museums, she argues, "appeal to artists, art historians, collectors, and a well-educated public" to the exclusion of a mass audience. This is because, she continues, they focus on the display of objects as "authentic" works (51). According to her account, museums of science, natural history, and history are, by contrast, "much more oriented to the general public than to professional scientists or historians. They devote a great deal of attention to educational programs and, until recently, less to collecting 'genuine' specimens" (51). This commitment to a broad dissemination of information is indicative of what Zolberg describes as the "democratizing" impulse of such museums, in contrast to the elitist tendencies of art museums, with their focus on auraticized objects.

Zolberg is right in her characterization of art museums as institutions that sustain the inequitable distribution of cultural capital. In their failure to mount significant education programs, she continues, they perpetuate a mystified understanding of art and taste that arrogates these domains to those already equipped with the appropriate cultural resources. Given the amount of public funding these institutions enjoy, Zolberg argues, it is incumbent upon them not to intensify but to disseminate this capital. This should be achieved through the provision of education.

But Zolberg does not adequately address the specific character of art museums. Art does not have the kind of empirical referent that is the underpinning, and perhaps the raison d'etre, of science and history. Museums of science, natural history, history, and ethnography can be seen as sites where information about the world is communicated. Notwithstanding the artifice of museum installations and the ideological character of knowledge production, such museums are supported and have legitimacy insofar as they are understood to provide access to empirical knowledge (Conn 2000; MacDonald 2002). Educational programs are meant to assist in this. But what does education amount to in the context of an art museum? To enable hitherto disenfranchised publics access to art, Zolberg calls for the provision of art historical education, since this, in her view, would facilitate the dispersion of cultural capital: "One way to do this is to revalorize the art museum's public mission by enhancing education as a legitimate function" (1994, 61). The Museum of Fine Arts, Houston has embraced this approach; indeed, its embrace is now widespread among public museums. The legitimacy of this function at the MFAH was surely enhanced when it became the recipient of a $1.5 million grant from the Lila Wallace–Reader's Digest Foundation in 1993 for "outreach" activities.[2] The funding, administered by personnel in the museum's education department, was to be devoted expressly to making the museum more accessible to a broader public. The standing of education programs in art museums is hardly unequivocal, however. Although the education department of the MFAH gained considerable stature institutionally—its staff increased to thirteen, and other departments had to defer to it, at least to some extent, on matters of programming and installation—within the hierarchy of reputation among museum professionals, education specialists seldom register.

Drawing on Bourdieu, Zolberg makes the now well-rehearsed argument that the mystification of art serves to maintain exclusionary structures of power. Moreover, she argues, "because art museums have come to stand for the idea of excellence in a highly valued form of culture, to the extent that they fail to distribute their cultural capital in an understandable way to visitors who lack the *habitus* of the [museum's] regular public, they help to perpetuate the status quo" (1994, 56). But one wonders how training in art history could really be either disruptive of the status quo or democratizing, since it is itself such a central mechanism in the constitution and concomitant mystification of art. Indeed, those art museums that are engaged in educational programs (and this is true of the vast majority of American art museums) tend to understand their educational mission to be one of socializing new audiences into the appreciation of art via the adjudications of art history, and thereby into the ongoing support of art museums. This is considered to be all the more urgent as funding is increasingly tied both to the number of visitors a museum can attract and to the breadth of that constituency.

Dominique de Menil, as we have seen, had no interest in developing a public that would engage with artworks as artifacts of art history—not because she wished to maintain art as a restricted field of production, but because she understood the suasive force of art to lie in its aesthetic effects, which tend to be displaced by pedagogic framing. Moreover, the kind of aesthetic experience that she wished to foster, and the conditions that she believed would support that experience, called not for laying art bare—demystifying it, as Zolberg wishes—but, on the contrary, for crafting terms of apprehension that conjure more intensified and seductive relations with art. It is through these dense, affective experiences, and not through the acquisition of art historical knowledge, that the sense of "being an intruder in the realm of art" (Maleuvre 1999, 99), which is characteristic of public museums, might be overcome.

This outsider position is made all the more acute at public museums with large audiences. En masse, visitors in a gallery are inclined to appear to museum professionals—at least to conservators and curators—as a hazard from which the art must be defended, with works hung higher, protected behind Perspex. By contrast, the intimate installations that are characteristic of the Menil Collection rely on the assumption that people won't need to look over the heads of others to see a work, and that the distractions of other people won't render visitors oblivious to the work and thereby at risk of brushing by it or leaning against it. The pressures of crowds on museums puts a strain on the relationship between the audience and museum staff members, who come to feel contempt toward visitors even as the museum actively courts them—all the more so, perhaps, *because* they have to be courted. The Menil, despite Sarofim's impulse to enlarge its audience, seems resolved to pursue its own projects, in accordance with Dominique de Menil's conviction that the public will inevitably be well served so long as the Collection continues to pursue its commitments in an "exemplary" manner.[3]

That people might find Menil exhibitions "difficult" is not only not meant to exclude or alienate, but, on the contrary, it is understood as a precondition for an active, critical engagement, as discussed in Chapter 8. Moreover, this difficulty has implications for the constitution of the kind of subject whose formation has been at the core of Menil projects. It is in the effort of exercising careful attention, which challenging exhibitions call for, that the labor of crafting an ethical disposition might be pursued.

All this can sound like just the sort of special pleading that has always served to cordon off privilege, but it is worth taking seriously the experiential flattening that tends to be the entailment of the appeal to a mass public. And although described by the language of "democratization" and supported by liberal political sensibilities, a mass public should hardly be assumed to be a politically felicitous entity. When a mass public is invoked by critics of museums, it is in relation to the supposed public obligation of the museum to promote civic virtues, most notably education, and the fulfillment of this duty has conferred upon museums benefits both financial and moral. However, we have seen already that education in art history can hardly be assumed to be liberatory in and of itself. But the greatest irony of this critical insistence on reaching a mass public is that it has been taken up so enthusiastically within museums, albeit with a radically different inflection. Over the last quarter of the twentieth century, there developed in museums an overwhelming tendency—under the exigencies of financing—to conceptualize their public as ideally constituting a mass market rather than imagining it in civic terms. The language of education and moral development still circulate, but the preoccupation with getting the greatest number through the door is seldom cloaked.

The problem with the museum's audience really lies not in the adjudication between a mass public and an exclusionary elite, but in the fact that these are the only two possibilities that are recognized critically. There is also the category, in the discourse of museology, of "underrepresented publics," as distinct from the mass public; this term is used to refer to population groups that have been disinclined to attend museums and that should be appealed to as special interest groups and, more often than not, as niche markets. These publics, however, don't help us much in terms of political virtue, since, like the mass public, they are conceived of essentially as consumers.

Moreover, how a museum addresses its public, whether conceptualized as singular or plural, calls for identification, "which entails the mimetic absorption of the individual into an ideal image of the group, the prototype, the ancestor, the father" (Maleuvre 1999, 109). As Maleuvre argues, the purported therapeutic or emancipatory virtue of recognizing and appealing to diverse identities has a darker aspect: it assumes, indeed it insists, that identification with a group is a "good" thing, placing "the group (and whatever profit might be derived from it) above the individual (less easily managed than crowds)" (109): "The empowerment that cultural identification promises is a generalization: it necessarily cuts across, perhaps even annuls, the manifold contingency of personal experience. Once made into a fetish, identity undermines the very individuality it purports to support. Celebration of identity becomes joyless and sinister when it insists that dignity exists only inside the law of identification" (110).

By contrast, the Menil Collection has always insisted on conceiving of its audience as pluralistic, differentiated not categorically but as self-individuated, active agents. Indeed, this ecumenical conceptualization of the museum's audience inevitably exceeds mere confessional or denominational differences, whether religious or secular.[4]

It is one thing to characterize the audience to which the Menil addresses itself, but it is quite another to ask just who does attend the museum. In truth, there is not much that can be said about the museum's actual audience beyond impressionistic accounts. Records kept by the museum indicate a remarkably steady total of around 120,000 visits to Menil facilities annually. Even this bland measure of the Menil's audience, reduced to a quantity, is neither very informative nor particularly reliable. It includes all visitors—those for events, school groups, and Da Camera concerts, as well as unprogrammed exhibition visitors—and since it is not unusual for people to move back and forth between the campus's buildings, there is inevitably some overcounting as they are recorded at each entry. But then, there may also be some undercounting: because admission to the museum is free, visitors are recorded not by ticket sales but simply by the click of counters used by security guards located more or less unobtrusively near the entrances. On quiet occasions, this is hardly a complicated task, but at times of higher traffic, which present a variety of distractions, it is easy to imagine that the recording might be somewhat less than exact.

What can be said about the museum's audience beyond a numerical tally? The Menil Collection has, since its opening, kept comment books on a diminutive table not far from the building's main entrance. For at least a decade, this was attended by Winfrey Purington, who had for years served Dominique de Menil as a shoe clerk at Foley's department store downtown. The table at which this kind, welcoming figure sat accommodated not only

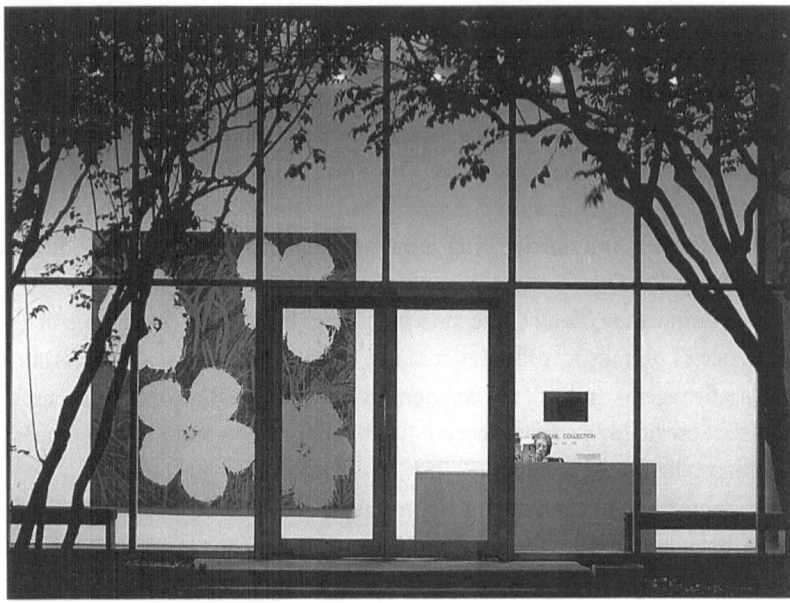

South entrance, Menil Collection, Houston. Photo: George Hixson. The Menil Collection, Houston.

the comment and visitor books but also a pamphlet showing the layout of the galleries and identifying what was currently on display in them. Often, there were also small, beautifully illustrated booklets, no more than two inches by four inches, inviting visitors to become members of the Menil Collection. When they were not available, it was likely because Dominique de Menil had secreted them discreetly in a drawer, as she often did, embarrassed, a regular attendant at the south entrance told me, at the idea of importuning visitors to make a contribution.

The comment books were of considerable interest to Dominique. She frequently looked at them when she came into the museum, routinely had completed books delivered to her, and, I was told, read their contents assiduously. While these books offer anecdotal evidence of how visitors responded to their experience, the impressions only of those sufficiently motivated and confident enough to write an entry hardly serve as reliable data on which to form an understanding of exactly who attends the museum or the character of their experience. In fact, garnering usable data on museum audiences is notoriously difficult. When admission is charged, it is typically pretty straightforward to record numbers, but demographic information is much more elusive. Many museums conduct exit surveys to gauge visitors' responses to an exhibition, and these sometimes include identifying questions concerning various demographic markers—age, ethnicity, gender, income level, highest education achieved, and so on.[5] But even were one not skeptical about the reliability of the measures, there is reason to worry about conducting such surveys, since many people take offense at being asked questions intended to fix them in some demographic category or another, and all the more within the precincts of high cultural institutions, where doubt about the legitimacy of one's presence might already be lurking. More significant, perhaps, is the fact that although the administration of surveys serves as a plausible measure of outputs in the service of bureaucratic accountability, it seldom allows researchers to get at what they really want to know, much of which is not susceptible to evaluation by questionnaire. This is certainly true of the Menil Collection, precisely because the kinds of experiences that it has sought to cultivate are resistant to reflexive articulation and are therefore inaccessible.

The following sketch of who actually visits the Menil Collection is informed by my own observations over the past two decades and by the Menil's membership department, the department that is perhaps the most acutely interested in knowing just who the museum's audience is. The most readily identifiable elements of the Menil's audience include school groups with the Writers in the Schools program, university students and faculty, "old-timers" who have been coming to events and exhibitions for years, artists (in whom the Menil recognizes a strong impulse to be connected to the museum—an impulse that the museum reciprocates), and national and international art world participants. Other visitors, and there are many of them, are more difficult to categorize. There are local residents with a real affinity for the Menil Collection, those simply seeking leisure activity or a place to proudly bring guests, and tourists doing the rounds of Houston's cultural institutions— the same kind of mix that might be observed in many art museums. But the public to which the Menil has primarily addressed itself distinguishes it from many other museums, and this is a matter both of luxury (of freedom from the burden of having to appeal to a large audience) and of intent.

At the Menil Collection, as was the case also at Rice University and at the University of St. Thomas, Menil personnel have continually experimented with and refined their communicative practices of exhibition, based not on what they imagine audiences might want or enjoy, but on what they themselves want to experience. On its face, this seems extraordinarily self-serving, and it may be, but it is also an entailment of the de Menils' conviction, drawn from the *renouveau catholique*, that their task was to rehabilitate sensibilities that had widely become compromised. Since Menil personnel were, until recently, selected on the basis of their identification with the Menil project, the working understanding has been that the public will be well served if the museum resolutely pursues its own program. In so doing, the museum hasn't produced exhibitions designed to attract the public, but rather it has worked to create a public for the museum—just as Couturier created places of worship that would draw people to faith rather than serve the already faithful. It is for this reason that the emerging routinization of Menil hiring practices, whereby professional qualifications might hold sway over sensibility, is of considerable concern to those who are invested in the maintenance of the Menil's distinctive aesthetic.

STEWARDS

In her discussion with me, Louisa Sarofim identified the formalization of the administrative structure of the museum, especially of the board, as a key imperative for the Menil. And to support the growth of its endowment, the museum needed, she argued, to strengthen its efforts in development and membership and increase the Houston presence on the board. She understood that there was considerable resistance to change, for fear that what made the Menil distinctive would be lost. But, Sarofim insisted, John and Dominique had been "progressive and visionary," so their legacy should not be locked, unchanging, into a past moment, but instead should remain vital and future oriented. We return then, to the question with which we opened this analysis: how can an off-modern, experimental legacy, oriented to the future and centrally pursued in an aesthetic idiom, be institutionalized?

This was not the first time that the Menil Foundation had felt compelled to seriously consider the legacy for which it is responsible. In August 1970, John de Menil was diagnosed with the cancer that would take his life in 1973. As he worked to put the foundation that he and Dominique had established in 1954 on a firmer financial footing and to clarify its objectives, he sought advice from the foundation's board members. His youngest daughter, Philippa, wrote to him: "I'm glad you leave flexibility—so it's not a tomb but a reincarnation. I would dislike being on the board of something which acts like an undertaker carrying out minutely the last wishes of you and mother."[6] He replied, "You're right … not sclerosis but continuity."[7] "The Foundation must be kept alive and non-conformist," he elaborated later, "taking risks on pioneering endeavors. The founders therefore prefer that loyalties to them be waived in order that the board members not be trammeled in tradition."[8] It is perhaps worth noting here that these aren't just the musings of a wealthy idealist, but rather the convictions of one of the most subtle industrial managers of the time, a man who played a major part in making Schlumberger such a successful and innovative global corporation.[9] It is clear from John's personal notes, correspondence, and public talks that he had taken a serious interest in the foundation as a distinctive institutional form, with its own managerial exigencies and accountabilities.

The legacy that Dominique de Menil would leave was, as we noted at the outset, not something that she failed to attend to but rather something that she decided to refrain from formalizing, entrusting the legatees with the charge to interpret her sacred modern vision anew. In other words, she created a context for ongoing experimentation. However, this is far from a straightforward proposition. Beyond the standard challenges of transforming an organization from one operating under the direct and highly personal auspices of the founder to a more rationalized managerial regime under the control of career professionals are the particular challenges posed by the character of the Menil project. The experimental ethos of the Menil Collection and the dispositional effects that it seeks to elicit obviously run counter to the formalization of mission and operations that would lend an institution momentum and stability in the absence of the charisma and moral authority of the founder. The alternative to bureaucratization as a response to the loss of the founder—an attempt to set "what Dominique would have done" in place operationally—would be to anoint another charismatic leader, but such figures tend to have their own ambitions, which are likely to put pressure on the confidence of those invested in sustaining things as they have been, or as they are imagined to have been.

"Any time you go through the death of a founder, it's not easy," Peter Marzio, the director of the MFAH, observed with considerable understatement. "Without Mrs. de Menil's presence, and her vision and her energy and compassion that she always conveyed, it would just be another place. Now the institution has to stand on its own, without that kind of magician" (quoted in Adams 2002). Since Dominique de Menil's death, the Menil Collection has experienced significant internal uncertainty and disruption. That this was to be expected is apparent from the literature on the problem of succession for charismatic projects (Weber 1947, 1958b), and this transition at the Menil has been all the more difficult given what is understood to be at stake in the maintenance of the Menil way—whether for Dominique's own project or for those people who are now anxious to sustain the possibility of aesthetic experience in a public museum.

My narration of institutional events as they unfolded over the course of the decade following Dominique de Menil's death not only makes these difficulties apparent, as we shall see, but also indicates that among museum personnel, responses to various changes were far from uniform, revealing a range of conflicting interests. My intent in what follows, then, is not to adjudicate virtue but to understand what has been at stake in each of these key moments of transition, especially from the perspective of what we have characterized as the Menil project, and for those invested in sustaining what they understand to be the Menil's defining difference from most other museums, but also too for those whose commitments are aligned first and foremost with contemporary professional museum structure and practice. We will also see, as the chapter unfolds, that there have always been struggles within the Menil Collection, not simply, as one might expect, between loyalists and those insufficiently incorporated into Menil orthodoxy, but for everyone. They are struggles that are inherent in trying to pursue a project like the de Menils' within the institutional form of a museum, a form that both by definition and convention is at odds with much that the de Menils were committed to pursuing.

When staff members have invoked the "time of crisis," it has never been immediately obvious just which crisis over the past decade is being referred to. It might be, and often is, the resignation of director Paul Winkler in February 1999. Despite the grief that many felt at the death of Dominique de Menil, institutionally the effect of her loss was muted, since Paul Winkler was understood to share her sensibilities, to understand and respect her wishes, and, by and large, to have had Dominique de Menil's moral authority conferred upon him. The presidency of the foundation was passed to Louisa Sarofim, whom Dominique de Menil had identified as her successor. In addition to this continuity of leadership, the Collection was understood to be in satisfactory financial shape. With the bulk of Dominique's estate to be transferred to the Menil Foundation, the Collection's endowment would stand at a respectable $240 million, affording it a modest but manageable operating budget of around $12 million.

The moment of rupture was occasioned by the board demanding the resignation of Miles Glaser, who for thirty years had served as the Menil Foundation's chief financial officer. The timing of this, just before the transfer of Dominique de Menil's estate to the foundation and only months before Glaser's eligibility for retirement, cast a cloud over Glaser's reputation. It was this implicit impugning of the character of someone who had served the foundation for so long, who had been a close friend and financial adviser to the Menil family, and yet who was punitively being denied retirement benefits, that, along with the manner in which the board took its action, prompted Paul Winkler to immediately submit his resignation from the board and from his position as director of the museum.

The Menil Collection was then without the compass that Winkler afforded, and many felt themselves to be subject to the whims of a hostile and untrustworthy board. Following Winkler's resignation, the museum endured a seven-month interval before Thomas Leavitt was appointed interim director. Leavitt had no particular connection to the Menil Collection, but had some experience of serving as an interim director, having worked in this capacity both at the Rhode Island School of Design and later at the Newport Art Museum in the years following his retirement from the directorship of Cornell University's Herbert F. Johnson Museum of Art in 1991. This "period of crisis," in which the Menil Collection staff operated essentially without leadership and with little faith in the board, drew to a close with the appointment of Ned Rifkin as director in February 2000.

However, Rifkin's directorship, far from calming the waters, was considered by many to be the time of most acute crisis. Although he resigned from the Menil Collection less than two years into his five-year contract, he made a number of key appointments and acted decisively to restructure the institution in an attempt to bring it into line with more conventional museum practices and priorities. Rifkin's ten-year tenure as director of Atlanta's High

Museum of Art had been particularly notable for his having increased the endowment from $15 million to $56 million and doubling the annual attendance with crowd-pleasing shows, including a Norman Rockwell retrospective, photographs from the collection of Elton John, and "Rings: Five Passions in the World of Art for the Atlanta Olympics."

His impact on the Menil Collection was most enduring in the personnel he hired, including an entire team of planning and advancement personnel, additional positions in the formerly lean business office, and, in the curatorial department, Matthew Drutt, who was hired from the Guggenheim to be chief curator. It is not clear whether the attrition of staff of long standing during this period was in response to the loss of Dominique de Menil and subsequently of Paul Winkler or to Rifkin's directorship and the ongoing effects of the structural and personnel changes that he made, but in any event, such losses intensified the sense among staff and associates that the Menil Collection was undergoing a radical transformation. Bertrand Davezac, the collection's senior curator since 1979, specializing in medieval and Byzantine art, announced his retirement in May 2000. Carol Mancusi-Ungaro, the chief conservator, resigned in January 2002 to take up a joint appointment as director of the Center for the Technical Study of Modern Art at Harvard University and director of conservation at the Whitney Museum. She had been with the collection for twenty-two years and, like Davezac, had enjoyed a close personal relationship with Dominique de Menil, and was considered to have an impeccable understanding of and sympathy for her project. Susan Davidson, who had worked as a curator at the Menil throughout the seventeen years of her career, left in May 2002 to take a curatorial position at the Guggenheim, where Walter Hopps, by whom she had been mentored at the Menil, took a position also, though a consulting one that enabled him to continue as a Menil board member and senior adjunct curator, a position he had held since he stepped down as inaugural director in 1989, until his death in March 2005. Julie Bakke, the longtime registrar, resigned in favor of a position at the MFAH, and William Steen, the long-standing framer for the collection, left to pursue his own art making.

To understand the profound significance of these departures, it is worth noting the already small staff numbers: Davezac's and Davidson's departures left only Hopps remaining in the curatorial department; Liz Lunning, who became chief conservator, was the only other conservator on staff; and Bakke's absence left only one other person in registration. It wasn't long before Deborah Velders, the head of exhibitions, who had been with the Menil since its opening, left to become director of the Cameron Art Museum, in Wilmington, North Carolina. At the time of her resignation, hers was the only full-time position in exhibitions. While these personnel did not go unreplaced in some form or another, the loss of these particular people, each with a deep history with the Collection, had profound effects on the fabric of the institution.

During Rifkin's tenure at the Menil, he divided the institution into three operational units—the business office, planning and advancement, and art services—each with its own divisional head, who was responsible for defining and managing budgets, setting priorities, and representing his or her unit at regular management meetings with the director. Within each division, departmental heads were charged with representing their constituency's interests in regularly scheduled divisional meetings. While this might seem unremarkable on its face, such formalized lines of communication and budgetary control were foreign to the Menil Collection. When Rifkin left the Menil in November 2001 to become director of the Hirshhorn Museum, and subsequently undersecretary for art at the Smithsonian Institution, this management structure remained in place, and the divisional heads, all Rifkin appointments, along with board president, Louisa Sarofim, constituted the interim management team. James Demetrion, whose position as director of the Hirshhorn Rifkin had recently filled, came out of retirement briefly in April 2002 to serve as the Menil Collection's second interim director. In his temporary capacity, he simply joined this interim management team, focusing his efforts on identifying a suitable replacement and regularizing the bylaws under which the board operated, a poisonous task ideally suited to someone with his years of dealing with the intricacies of board governance and, as an interim appointment, invulnerable to the distaste of board members.

There are some at the Menil Collection, though few will speak openly of this now, who consider not Rifkin's appointment but his resignation to constitute the moment of crisis. They are the ones who welcomed the procedural regularization that he instituted and were glad of the signs of institutional life that emerged under his directorship. The galleries that had housed works from the collection were not only rehung but also switched around; walls were moved; and temporary shows were installed in the galleries formerly dedicated to the permanent collection, new selections from which were now hung in spaces that had been used for temporary shows. And the number of temporary shows was increased from roughly six or seven a year to nine or ten. These exhibitionary changes were initiated by the new chief curator, but they found their support among those who inhabited offices "across the road," in the business office, in public relations, and in planning and advancement.

Among those who worked in art services, the response was much more equivocal. Whereas people across the road thought this activity enhanced the public perception of the Menil Collection, offering a much greater turnover of art for visitors to enjoy, thereby indicating institutional energy rather than the sense of stagnation that might be associated with less obvious activity, for people in art services, it meant a huge amount of work on top of their existing responsibilities. But what concerned many wasn't just the amount of work, but its character. The chief curator, many felt, was insufficiently socialized into the Menil way of doing things, and, moreover, his shows didn't look or feel like Menil shows. The disjuncture between his own sensibilities and those of the Menil was decisively expressed, many felt, in his rehanging of art in the de Menils' residence.

The house had undergone an eighteen-month restoration that was as rigorous as any de Menil project. In returning the house to its early condition, Stern & Bucek Architects, which led the project, produced fifty mechanical and architectural drawings, more than twice the number Johnson had drafted, and hired an architectural historian to interview friends and family members in order to inform the architects' understanding of the character of the home. The *New York Times* reported the degree of meticulousness observed: "To protect wall surfaces that still had original paint, wood or velvets, the rewiring was done through the ceilings. Conservators dared not repaint walls that were completely original; those surfaces, including the dressing room doors and the pale pink hallway, became known as 'sacred walls.' For those that had been repainted, conservators sent paint samples to a laboratory to help match the exact shades" (Middleton 2004, 2). The task of returning the house to its early condition presented significant technical challenges, but was more or less straightforward in its content, since nothing really had been changed throughout Dominique's almost half century of living there. It was more a matter of taking care of long-delayed maintenance and repair, some structural work to ensure the building's future well-being, and attention to wear and tear on the interior, which bore the marks of fifty years of use. The restoration team, however, had no wish to erase either the appearance of a home well lived in or the presence of its occupants. Bill Stern, the chief architect recounted, "Everyone has asked, 'You're going to do something about that scratched-up velvet aren't you?' . . . Well no! Those surfaces ensure a patina—the age of the house is written into the architecture" (quoted on 2).

In 2004, to complete the project and prepare the house for use as a venue for Menil Foundation events, the art, which had always been such a defining element of the home, was reinstalled. In the following summer, when I visited the Menil again for several weeks, people were still talking about the inappropriateness of hanging *Portrait of Dominique* over the fireplace in the living room, something that Dominique would never have countenanced. Dominique's daughter Christophe, everyone hoped, would, on her anticipated visit to Houston, rehang the house and restore her mother's sensibility. This kind of commentary is hardly a novel criticism of someone recently hired into an established organization, but at the Menil Collection, the commitment to the Menil way has particular resonance, as does maintenance of the Menil aesthetic.

Indeed, reference to the Menil way was an element of staff rhetoric long before the museum was opened, but its use intensified after Dominique de Menil's death. Invocation of this distinctive way of doing things often serves as an expression of nostalgia for a time when the Menil way was pursued in a more pure form; it also operates as a claim to authority, the privileged insight of those who get it, especially those who got it from Dominique de Menil herself or, indeed, from John de Menil. It is the people who knew and worked with both John and Dominique who claim the greatest privilege in this regard, since, they are careful to remind me, John's vision, sensibility, and energy has been defining in this, despite his death. The Menil way is also invoked as a heartfelt commitment to that which made the Menil Collection mercifully different from ordinary museums, both as a place to work and as a place for art and for its audience.

But just what the Menil way is has increasingly become a deeply fraught matter. While it has always eluded definitive identification—too ephemeral to pin down, and subject to varying interpretations—as long as its nominal author was alive, and even while Paul Winkler still operated as her proxy, differences in its interpretation could authoritatively be resolved, at least sufficiently for operational purposes. Over subsequent years, however, this has not been the case.

When Josef Helfenstein became director in January 2004, many hoped that he would be able to exercise the kind of moral authority that would enable him to generate a working consensus among the board and the staff, a set of understandings that would enable them to move forward without the bruising differences and anxieties that had made it so difficult to proceed under his predecessor. In his favor, people pointed out, he is first and foremost a scholar rather than a museum person, notwithstanding his significant museum experience. To be a "museum person," in this context, is to be someone whose priorities are institution building and the growth of audiences and endowments rather than creating favorable conditions for art and its audience. In contrast to Rifkin, known within the museum world as an entrepreneurial "agent of change," drawing funding and audiences to the High Museum after an extended period of neglect, Helfenstein was known for his intellectual preoccupations. He came to the Menil from the directorship of the Krannert Art Museum at the University of Illinois, having previously worked for seventeen years at the Kunstmuseum Bern, as chief curator of prints and drawings and later as associate director, while also heading the Paul Klee Foundation's nine-volume catalogue raisonné project. His sensibility, many felt, was well calibrated to the Menil, understated, seeing the art as primary rather than privileging the museum as an institution. Others, however, worried that under his leadership the museum would be hijacked by a preservationist impulse to restore things to the way it was imagined they had been before the intervening years of crisis. Growth, they feared, would not be fostered, and the gains made in refining the administrative procedures of the institution would be lost. It is true that Helfenstein's authority is the authority of the curator or teacher, authority of the sort that, as Georgina Born points out, tends toward the maintenance of tradition, in contrast to "the authority of the artist or creator with prophetic ambitions, which is personal and rests on flashes of originality" and is, therefore, engaged in production rather than the curator's tendency toward reproduction (Born 1995, 28).

After his appointment, Helfenstein spent a good deal of time talking with people who had had significant relationships with the Menil project historically, some of whom had come to feel distant from it over the years since Dominique's death. This process was looked upon very favorably by those invested in the maintenance of the Menil way. His hiring of a consultant to lead the museum through a process of strategic planning whereby the "core values" of the institution could be identified, the long-range goals of the museum could be formulated, and institutional structures and procedures could be developed and formalized to enable their realization—among them mechanisms for routinely assessing the fulfillment of its mission, or at least progress toward its goals—generated a much more equivocal response.[10] The Menil Collection underwent, over a period of a year or so, a process by which the de Menil legacy was defined and institutionalized through the instrument of the strategic plan. This kind of bureaucratic technique was considered foreign to the ethos of the Menil. But for Helfenstein, the process was intended primarily to be therapeutic, especially for staff members and Menil associates who had, in the years of crisis after Winkler's resignation, come to feel embattled in their relationship with the institution. It was meant to bring people back into conversation rather than to produce an authoritative organizational blueprint. It seems to be clear to Helfenstein that the distinctive project of the Menil Collection (if it is to be maintained) will always be in tension with the standards and accountabilities of any business model, and indeed with the conventional model of the museum. The navigation of this tension, if it is to gain any kind of traction, must inevitably be pursued with recourse to "what Dominique would have done."

THE ARCHIVE

Whatever the interests of board members, staffers, and various public constituencies, commentaries on what the Menil should or should not do—day to day as well as in its long-term planning for the future—are invariably couched in terms of what Dominique would have done. Indeed, the characterization of what the museum is about in relation to a supervening set of values and intentions that Dominique de Menil sought to further through the Menil Collection has become well rehearsed and increasingly nuanced throughout the years of my research. This reflexive thrust has emerged largely, perhaps, as a strategy for claiming authority and for underwriting extant procedures and proposals for the future. It is used as much to defend the way things have been as to promote change. And it has been given substance by the increasing access over the last few years to articulations of Dominique de Menil's project that had hitherto largely been seen piecemeal rather than as an integrated whole. Staff and researchers now have access to an archive, in which one can readily find authoritative renderings in the box titled "Dominique de Menil's Writings," which comes with a sheet of prepared quotations selected from her speeches, interviews, and catalogue essays and offered as handy crystallizations. There have been numerous journalistic accounts of the museum, a tribute (Shkapich and Menil 2004), some scholarly works (Brennan, Pacquement, and Temkin 2007; Van Dyke 2007), and, indeed, my own dissertation and published papers circulate through the institution and can be found in the offices of new personnel, sometimes unread, but at times, disconcertingly, it is my own analysis that forms the content of an interlocutor's account to me.

Among those Menil personnel who talked to me about my earlier characterizations of the Menil Collection, especially in my dissertation, it was the holism of that account that most animated them. It was interesting to them, in the late 1990s, to understand the Collection as an element of a broader coherent project. They now felt less inclined, they commented, to see the museum as engaged in a struggle with Dominique de Menil's other projects, interests that they had hitherto seen primarily as competing calls upon her resources. But the downside of a holistic portrayal is precisely its totalizing tendency—the effect is to read fulfillment and closure where experimentation and critical responsiveness to the contemporary should reside.

It is perhaps hardly surprising that in recognition of the twentieth anniversary of the opening of the Menil Collection, curatorial staff members, none of whom were with the museum when Dominique was alive, engaged in sustained archival research to guide them in the conceptualization and elaboration of exhibitions to mark the anniversary. "A Modern Patronage: De Menil Gifts to American and European Museums" (June 8–September 16, 2007) was thoroughly informed by the Menil archive (and by the archives of recipient institutions, especially the Pompidou, the MFAH, and the Museum of Modern Art), and "Andy Warhol: Three Houston Women" (March 16–July 8, 2007), which featured Warhol's portraits of Dominique de Menil, Jermayne MacAgy, and Caroline Wiess Law (a founding benefactor of the museum), also had recourse to the archive. Kristina Van Dyke's reinstallation of the African art galleries (on view beginning April 11, 2008) and her

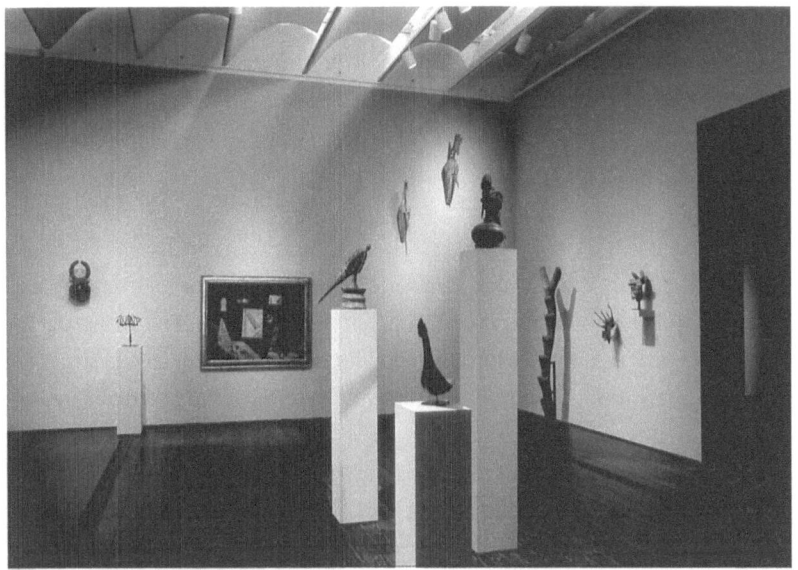

"Chance Encounters: The Formation of the de Menil's African Collection," installed by Kristina Van Dyke, May 26–September 10, 2006. The exhibition shows the continuity of Menil conventions of display—especially the juxtaposition of objects from different traditions, and the absence of barriers between viewers and objects—which was achieved largely through the curator's attention to the archive. Photo: Hester + Hardaway. Courtesy Menil Archives, the Menil Collection, Houston.

"Chance Encounters: The Formation of the de Menils' African Collection" (2005) took "the philosophy the de Menils developed about art through their wide-ranging projects as a starting point" (Van Dyke 2007, 49). While Van Dyke conducted new research to augment existing documentation and analysis, her curating was centrally informed by published and unpublished materials in the archive. Such material also was the catalyst for "Imaginary Spaces: Selections from The Menil Collection" (August 22, 2008–March 1, 2009), which was conceived in reference to the de Menils' sustained interest in the 1960s in shows about environmental and architectural space.[11]

There increasingly is a sense in which the institution is defined through its archive, since researchers and journalists use the archive as a point of entry, and museum staffers use it as a touchstone. Moreover, the archivist, Geri Aramanda, has institutionally one of the longest, and surely one of the richest, memories of the de Menil project, having been engaged in Menil activities since her student days at St. Thomas and on throughout her adult life in various capacities. When people call upon the archive to inform their understanding of the Menil Collection or of its benefactors, the archivist's sense of what to draw their attention to is, at least initially, defining.

ANXIETY

But it is not really Dominique de Menil's own project that is at stake, nor simply the professional ambitions of those who call upon that project strategically. There is a more profound anxiety that lurks here, a fundamental question about the contemporary plausibility of aesthetic projects generally and about the ability of this particular aesthetic to sustain its affective character. This anxiety is vested in the maintenance of the Menil Collection's distinctive aesthetic sensibility, along with the particular exhibitionary style and managerial form that produce it.

But the contradictions that underlie this deep concern that acutely aesthetic experience may not be sustainable in a public museum are not just a function of the shift from ownership to stewardship, with the increasingly perfunctory managerial mode that such a change entails, which Maleuvre characterized; the contradictions in fact preceded Dominique's death. Indeed, they have been evident ever since the museum's inauguration. In its transformation from a private collection to a public museum, the Menil Collection found itself subject to the imperatives of rationalization, to the very forces of modernity for which it had sought to serve as a countermodel. To manage a large, high-status public museum requires attention, even if not adherence, to codified procedures, professional specialization, the formalization of human relations, and the strictures of efficiency and accountancy. Insofar as contradictions were recognized at the Menil, they overwhelmingly provoked a redoubling of efforts to mitigate their effect, to ensure that the museum's economy of care was sustained. But these contradictions could never be resolved.

It was just three weeks before Christmas 1994 when the staff of the Menil Collection were called to a meeting at which it was announced that seventeen people would be laid off in order to contain the museum's operating costs. Among those whose positions were terminated were security guards and administrative and professional staff members. Many of them had worked for

Dominique de Menil for years before the opening of the Menil Collection, either at the Rice Museum or for the foundation. Some had formerly worked for Schlumberger. The personal impact for those who found themselves without work was of course devastating, but it seemed all the worse to them, and to those who remained, because it had never been anticipated. Indeed, such a rationalization was unthinkable. Menil operations had never followed such a model.

The de Menils employed two approaches to the hiring of staff for its various projects. The first was to hire the top people in the field—"remarkable" people—ensure they had whatever resources they needed, and take care of them very well. Their other method was to take on young people who had revealed a potential that would be tested and trained on the job. If they proved themselves suitable, they would be drawn into increasingly more central positions. Both models foregrounded the specific qualities of the person hired; neither was driven by an overriding imperative to fill abstractly formulated positions or to meet conventional measures of professional qualification. What was centrally important was identification with the Menil aesthetic, but crucial also, and by no means unrelated, was loyalty.

THE DIRECTORS

When Dominique de Menil hired Walter Hopps as a consultant to the Menil Foundation in 1980, he had already done some consulting work for her on the lighting problem at the Rothko Chapel and had served, at her request, on the board of the Georges Pompidou Art and Culture Foundation. This initial caution in hiring was characteristic, even though Hopps was already legendary in museum circles for his facility for installating exhibitions and for his prodigious knowledge of the art world. He was equally well known for his less than orthodox work habits. Nobody ever complained that Hopps was not adequately committed to his work, but his "imperial disregard for time" (Tomkins 1991, 35) infuriated even his most ardent advocates and had already cost him the support of trustees in several high-level museums jobs. "I had been forewarned that he [Hopps] was difficult—impossible, sometimes— but I also knew," Dominique told Calvin Tomkins, "that he had a very good eye and that he was extremely good at display, and I was sure that we could get along" (54). In Dominique's taxonomy, Hopps was one of the "remark-ables," and his idiosyncratic behavior, set against his virtuosity, only served to confirm this standing.

Hopps's reputation had been established through the Ferus Gallery, which he and artist Ed Kienholz opened in Los Angeles in 1957, and which served as the catalyst for modern art in Los Angeles, essentially creating a contempo-rary-art scene where there had been none.[12] His first museum position was an appointment as the first full-time curator at the Pasadena Art Museum in 1962, and he soon became its director, serving until his resignation in 1967, having lost the support of his board. He took a fellowship at the Institute for Policy Studies in Washington, D.C., "a liberal think tank whose founders, Marcus Raskin and Richard Barnet, were interested in having a resident fellow who could think (and write) about issues of art and public policy" (Tomkins 1991, 49). While at the institute, Hopps produced an analysis of the causes of the imminent demise of the young and adventurous Washington Gallery of Modern Art (WGMA). Tomkins recounts that that document came to the attention of members of the board of trustees of that institution, who asked Hopps to take over as director. Among the recommendations Hopps put forward for salvaging the gallery, whose collection had already been sold to pay off debts, was for it to merge with the Corcoran Gallery.

With the remnants of the WGMA folded into the Corcoran, Hopps became the director of special projects, and the old WGMA exhibition space became the Corcoran's experimental Dupont Center. But the Corcoran was itself in financial straits, rendered particularly vulnerable by its seriously inadequate endowment. "As several other troubled museum boards have done since," Tomkins recounts, "the Corcoran trustees sought financial stability by hir-ing a chief executive officer, whose main function would be fundraising, and whose authority would be superior to the director's" (1991, 50). This situa-tion became intolerable for the Corcoran's director, James Harithas, whose resignation left Hopps in the position of acting director. Soon confirmed as director, he pursued a variety of projects that were well suited to his interest in contemporary art making. "He had the courage to show whatever he thought was good, and he went out on a limb on so many things. His allegiances were always to the artists; he would always fight for them, against the bureaucracy" (Frances Fralin, Hopps's secretary at the Corcoran, quoted on 51). Indeed, his identification with artists and museum staff members (by no means discrete categories in such "alternative" art spaces) was to be his undoing at the Corcoran. He was dismissed for his failure to intervene against the unionization of staff, but was immediately offered a position as senior curator for twentieth-century art at the National Collection of Fine Arts (NCFA, now the National Museum of American Art), a branch of the Smithsonian Institution.

But for all his successes with exhibitions at the NCFA, his erratic habits and administrative failures were insupportable finally in such a bureaucratized institution. In the "alternative" context of the Corcoran, staff members had been willing to adjust to Hopps's working hours, which were reputed to begin at around 5 p.m. and to end some time after midnight. Frances Fralin commented, "Some people couldn't put up with it, but a lot of us just did, because it was so mesmerizing" (quoted in Tomkins 1991, 51). At the Smithsonian, his colleagues tended to be less willing to make concessions for his behavior. But it was not so much the demands he made on his staff, as it was his protracted absences and intolerance for bureaucratic obligations that brought Hopps under increasing pressure to find work elsewhere. He was passed up for several significant West Coast museum appointments, since he was, in his habits, too much like an artist and not enough like an administrator.

Hopps's old friend John Coplans identified his structural problem: "An artist has to engender his own work, and be his own man. Walter was incapable of doing that. He could not work without patronage, and institutions could not provide him with the right kind of patronage. Only the rich could do that" (quoted in Tomkins 1991, 53). Dominique de Menil was just the sort of patron Hopps required, and Hopps had just the authoritative talent and singularity of vision that Dominique de Menil admired and liked to support. While Hopps could hardly be said to have shared Dominique's sacred modern project—in response to an early conversation concerning his faith, Dominique asserted, "We'll just have to call you an honorable nonbeliever"[13]—his sense of how art should be engaged, the critical intelligence he brought to thinking about the collection and its exhibition, his deep regard for artists, and, most importantly perhaps, the serious pleasure he took in looking at art drew them into a very close and enduring collaboration.

In Houston, Hopps joined an established team of researchers, a registrar, and Carol Mancusi-Ungaro, the conservator, all working out of the Rice Museum and the Menil residence on San Felipe. He worked closely with Dominique de Menil on the conceptualization of the museum and got to know the collection while working on "La Rime et la Raison." With the opening of the Menil Collection in 1987, however, Hopps's role was transformed into that of museum director, with the attendant administrative functions he had always found burdensome. This was exacerbated by the fact that the Menil Collection opened during a period of plummeting oil prices, which seriously weakened the value of the Schlumberger stock with which the Menil Foundation and Collection were endowed. As a consequence, Hopps found himself again the director of an institution that was inadequately endowed and no longer able to make the kinds of acquisitions he had envisaged. In May 1989, Hopps stood down as director, and until his death in 2005, he worked out of an office at the Menil Collection under the title of consulting curator and continued to play a central role in the life of the museum.

Hopps publicly raised the seriousness of the Menil's financial circumstances while announcing his decision to step down, causing many to react with alarm, although the situation was by no means dire. It meant, however, that formerly rich resources for acquisitions were no longer available, and that staffing levels, always quite lean, would become even tighter with the loss, without replacement, of several staff members. And for Hopps, it had meant that as director he increasingly found himself preoccupied with fund-raising rather than curatorial matters.

In response to this announcement, Dominique de Menil demurred, "Its a new situation for me. I'm sort of shy about it. . . . Before, my husband and I assumed entirely whatever project we had" (quoted in Chadwick 1989, 1). This was not entirely accurate. They often gave seed money to projects, with the intention that others would do their part. And once the decision was made to build the museum, a $20 million endowment drive was also planned in order to secure sustainable operating funds. But before long, the collapse in oil prices seriously damaged Houston's economy, and it became apparent that fund-raising would be more successful if deferred until the economic climate improved. The Menil Foundation agreed to meet the operating costs of the museum in the interim, a commitment that ran to between $2.7 and $2.9 million a year (Glueck 1989). It also funded an annual acquisitions budget of more than $1 million. But the foundation had significant holdings of Schlumberger stock, the value of which dropped from a high of $87 in 1980–1981 to $38.25 at the close of the decade (Chadwick 1989, 6). In 1989, the Menil Collection launched a $35 million endowment campaign, to which

Dominique de Menil contributed $17.5 million. The Brown Foundation contributed $5 million in addition to the $5 million it had already contributed to the construction of the museum, and various other foundations, along with family members and corporate and private donors, contributed enough to achieve the endowment goal in 1992. By this time, however, annual operating expenses had increased significantly from the budgeted $3.4 million. And by 1994, when the layoffs were announced, annual spending had reached $7.9 million (Johnson 1995). The restructuring signaled by the layoffs was directed toward reducing that expenditure to $5.5 million annually and toward broadening the base of financial support for the Collection.

Paul Winkler was appointed acting director after Hopps's resignation, and then in October 1990 he was formally named director. In fact, until Dominique's death, the Menil Collection was managed jointly by Dominique, Winkler, and Hopps, with Dominique retaining central authority throughout. Winkler was hired on the second model, as someone whose sensibilities had been honed within the Menil milieu, whose loyalty was assured, and whose judgment could be relied upon. A graduate of the de Menil–driven art programs at the University of St. Thomas and later at Rice, Winkler worked on de Menil art projects in the early 1970s before taking up a position in Santa Fe as the assistant director of the Museum of International Folk Art. Among its various attractions, Dominique's job offer, which at the outset of the museum-construction process was primarily to coordinate that project, appealed not only to Winkler's feeling for the aesthetic sensibilities that were to be materialized in this project, but also to his abiding interest in architecture. It also presented an extraordinary opportunity for a young man with a bachelor's degree in art history.

Directors of public art museums are now increasingly called upon to be entrepreneurs or, at worst, mere bureaucrats. They are also the servants of highly contentious boards, whose agendas are often at odds with those of an equally rancorous professional staff. The primary duty of the director has increasingly become the management of budgets and the procurement of contributions to the collection, whether in the form of bequests or grants.

The directorship of the Menil Collection has not conformed to this model, though had Rifkin's tenure not been so brief, the sharp swerve toward this form would likely have become institutionalized. While Winkler and subsequent directors have of course had to attend to practical matters of administra tion, their activities have by no means been confined to the acquisition and dispersal of resources. Winkler, along with Dominique de Menil and Walter Hopps, formulated exhibition schedules, curated exhibitions, worked on the Cy Twombly Gallery project—securing a very significant gift of a body of work from the artist and working with Twombly and Renzo Piano on the design and realization of the gallery—and, like his two colleagues, took particular pleasure in the installation of shows.[14] Here the continuity with Helfenstein is clear. He too is a curator who has been active since becoming director of the museum in curating shows that, everyone agrees, are perfectly calibrated to the Menil aesthetic.

But for now, let us continue to understand the operation of the Menil Collection under the purview of Dominique de Menil, since it gives insight into the difficulties of institutionalizing a project such as hers, which are in some ways not unlike the challenges faced by start-up companies and nonprofit agencies that are defined by the charismatic figure of the founder and characterized, at least for start-ups, by the energetic commitment of staff members who participate in the creation of the project and not merely in its routine perpetuation. For the Menil, these challenges are more acute because of the particular character of the Menil project and the institutional and professional domains with which it is enmeshed.

PROFESSIONAL STAFF

In the first decade or so of the Menil Collection and in the years leading up to its opening, staff members tended not to be hired to fill positions that had established duties, as had been the case at St. Thomas and Rice too. They had the opportunity to carve out niches for themselves that would accommodate their idiosyncrasies and would enable them, in principle, to discover and focus on what they did best. But the absence of anything approaching a clear job description could be crippling. As one staff member put it when I was first conducting research there, "Ideally, you hire someone to do a job, give them the means to do the work, and then hold them accountable." But the informal structural character of the Menil Collection made it all but impossible, some complained, to do their work effectively. Worse, such informality could breed a great deal of insecurity; according to this same staff member, "You feel like hell, because finally you only have the status of a courtier." She had come to the Menil from a large, well-regarded museum and with professionally certified specialized expertise, a rare asset among the Menil staff. What she had sought at the Menil was some relief from what she had experienced as the brutalizing effects of cynicism and bureaucratization. And she did find relief from this, but only to suffer from the radical contingency of an organization in which favor was determinant. Access to financial resources, information, and procedural systems, under this model, became ultimately a matter of privilege.

There were those who sought a remedy in the formalization of organizational structures, whereby the vestiges of the old familial model of organization would be abandoned once and for all. Others, who opposed what they described as "the forces of normalization," considered the problem to lie not in the familial model itself but in its imperfect realization. They considered calls for routinization vulgar, a failure to recognize properly the practices and dispositions that underpinned the Menil aesthetic. Indeed, they feared the progressive erosion of that aesthetic under a bureaucratized regime. They spoke with nostalgia for the days when management was "really" familial.

Their accounts tell of staff members working out of the foundation offices in the Menil home in the 1960s and 1970s, enjoying a high degree of informality and collegiality, and working on projects that were not discretely bounded. The staff all sat down to lunch together, with John and Dominique de Menil if they were around, to eat a meal prepared by their resident cook.[15] They were insiders, part of a handpicked group of people working together on various projects. "It was like a family," according to many. At the Rice Museum too, people worked together in loosely defined spaces and with very fluid job descriptions. Enthusiasm about putting a show together was such that people were happy to work late into the night, figuring out idiosyncratic solutions to any technical problems that might arise.

These were, by and large, not trained professional staff members but a number of people who had developed their craft over the years by working with Dominique de Menil, and many of them were graduates of de Menil programs at Rice University and at the University of St. Thomas. The experience of working on very well-regarded exhibitions and with very well-connected personnel at the Rice Museum presented many with the chance for other art-world employment.

In the absence of departmental distinctions or architecturally defined divisions among the staff, there was no call for formal operational boundaries or hierarchies. But with the opening of the new museum, staff members found themselves working in particularly discrete spaces. For example, curators, immediately upon entering the building, take an elevator to their offices on the second floor, alongside the storage areas and boardrooms. To the left of the back entrance to the museum are the exhibitions department (where the head of exhibitions and public programming, glassed off in her mezzanine office, was kind enough to offer me desk space in the early period of my fieldwork), the staff room, and the library; to the right, across the entrance lobby, is shipping and receiving, and then registration, leading on through to the conservation department. In the shipping and receiving area are stairs down to the shop, where shipping crates and display hardware are fabricated, and up to a mezzanine office that for more than a decade was occupied by the building manager, until his relocation to more spacious accommodations while he oversaw the major maintenance project on the museum's exterior. Since only one or two people work in each area, the camaraderie of the Rice Museum was absent. Information did not circulate inevitably, and the informal sharing of tasks and responsibilities could not be sustained.

There is a sense in which the familial model seems natural for a small private institution like the Menil Foundation, and certainly its operation in the Menil Collection for a decade was understood as a continuation of the way in which the Collection had always been managed. But this management style is also self-consciously asserted in distinction to the bureaucratized structure of art museums like the Museum of Fine Arts, Houston. This assertion is driven by the sense that the corporate style of the MFAH overwhelmingly compromises the possibility of deriving an acutely aesthetic experience of the artworks shown therein. At the Menil Collection, the governing ethos is that work should be conducted as a vocation rather than merely as a job. One former senior staff member gave voice to this in her account of her decision to join the Menil staff in order to work again with Walter Hopps, with whom she had worked at the Smithsonian. She came to the Menil Collection from working in "alternative" art spaces, since after some years of working in more conventional art-world institutions, she had become dismayed by the cynicism that seemed to predominate in them. The Menil offered the opportunity to work with an extraordinary collection, to enjoy the stability of an institution that was not foundering, as alternative spaces so often are, and to participate in a project that appealed to her sensibilities.

While the standard characterization of alternative spaces depicts them as participating in a more or less radical critique of "high art," it is a critique that seeks not to demystify art (though it may engage in projects that seek to demystify the power relations of the art world), but to recuperate a more pure form of it. In the language of difficulty and commitment that typifies much "alternative" discourse can be read the desire for, and the claim to, a more virtuous, exemplary relation to art—indeed, a more seamlessly mystified relation than has been sustained in the conventional sphere of art world operations. The familial relations of the Menil Collection, along with its ethical commitments, rendered it very appealing to those who wished to recuperate an enchanted engagement with art. Yet the status of the Menil Collection is complicated for "alternative" agendas: on the one hand, it is, as we have seen, considered politically elitist in its refusal to accommodate itself to some imagined mass public, but, on the other, it exudes a depth of integrity that appeals powerfully to this recuperative sensibility. It is true, however, that in recent years people had felt a change in the institution, recognition of which was typically expressed in the form of nostalgic narratives of a more energetic and integrated organization.

This integrity is posed in opposition, as I argued in Chapter 7, to the more routinized managerial approach of those many art museums that attempt to align their operations with the codes of practice laid out by the American Association of Museums, codes that must be adhered to in order to achieve and sustain accreditation. Modeled on "best practices," these procedural models have done much to professionalize and regularize museum practice. They have done little, however, to sustain the affecting force of the artworks that museums house and display.

But even among staff members who are invested in the Menil way, their professional training and experience yield some quite profound tensions. These are acutely felt in conservation. As we have seen, Dominique de Menil placed much store on the accessibility of objects. When she and Jerry MacAgy established the teaching collection at the University of St. Thomas, it was, she often said, so that works of art could be touched and held. And her famous "For Children" show at the Rice Museum, which drew around 2,000 children on every exhausting day that it was open, allowed children

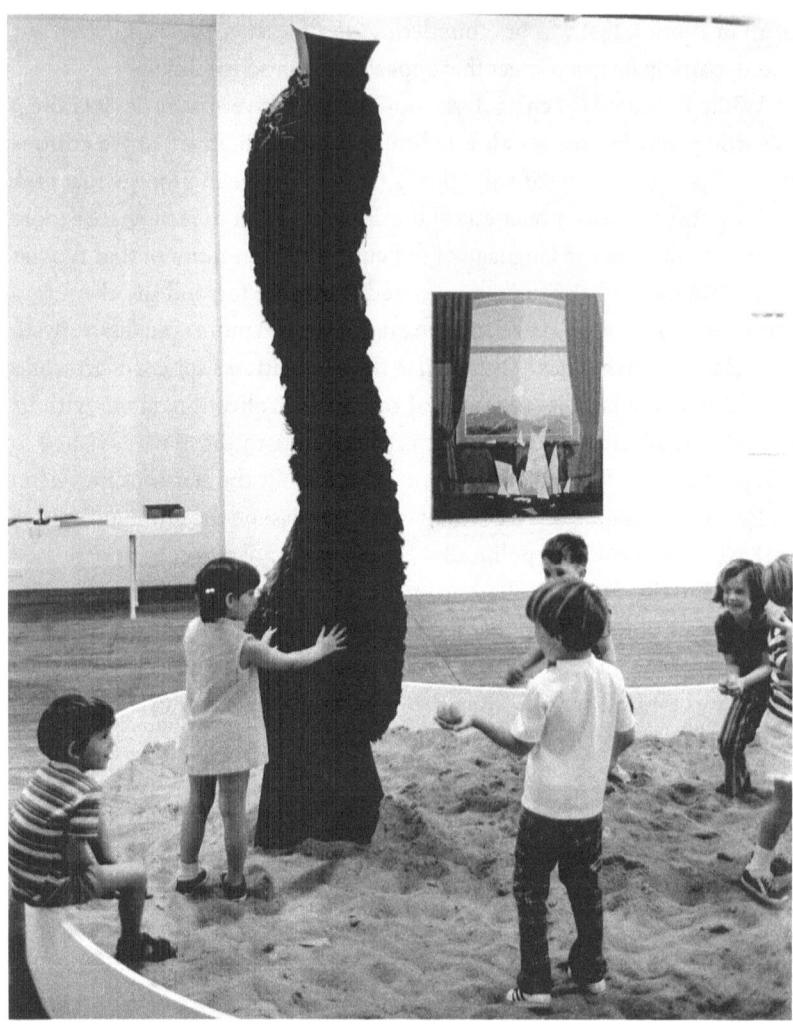

Children playing in free-form sandbox with a sculpture by Kurhajec, at "For Children," Rice Museum, 1971. On the wall: René Magritte, Le soir qui tombe (1964). Photo: Hickey-Robertson. Courtesy Menil Archives, the Menil Collection, Houston.

extraordinarily immediate access to all kinds of ingeniously installed objects, some banal, but others precious. I asked Carol Mancusi-Ungaro about the shift from the radical accessibility of objects in these earlier contexts to the more constrained, though still unusually unguarded, presentation of work in the museum: "At the time when the art was newer, and the artist was still

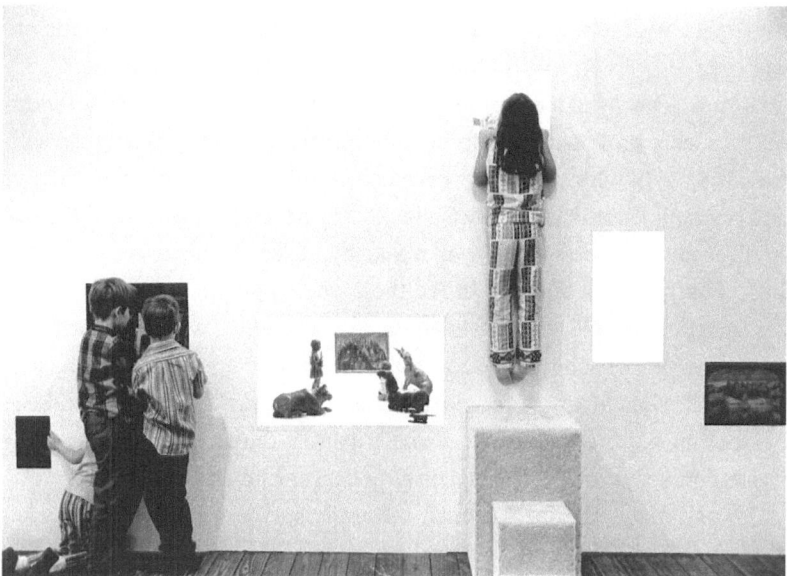

"For Children," Rice Museum, 1971. Photo: Hickey-Robertson. Courtesy Menil Archives, the Menil Collection, Houston.

alive, and the artist was not necessarily as famous as now, a playfulness towards the objects was possible. As an object becomes more a part of history, as it gets older and more fragile and in a *museum*, it has become necessary to harness the eagerness to allow children to handle the objects—a shift in Mrs. De Menil and in us all." But the Menil Collection remains notable for its absence of barriers and its sparing use of Plexiglas. While this does much to foster the kind of immediate engagement that Dominique de Menil seeks, it can give specialists with professional responsibilities pause.

A newer conservator spoke with dismay of three-dimensional objects being installed on plinths without the protection of Plexiglas "bonnets." Though she felt compelled to speak up "in defense" of conservation protocol, she also recognized how different the Menil is from her experiences in other museums. It was perfectly clear to her that people's dispositions toward the objects were, indeed, more careful than she had observed elsewhere, notwithstanding widespread divergence from what is professionally considered "best practice." She understood that there was a distinction that should be the subject of ongoing contestation as to whether the calculus of preservation or the longevity of artworks should inevitably outweigh the quality of intimate engagement with art that is typically the exclusive privilege of owners.

In 2005, Paul Winkler returned to assist with the installation of Cy Twombly's drawing show, which afforded him the opportunity to work again with the artist, with whom he had worked so closely on the conceptualization and realization of the Twombly Gallery.[16] His process of installing the show, by all accounts, sounded not at all unlike that used for the installations that I had observed a decade earlier. To the current staff, however, it appeared high-handed. People were offended that works might have been exposed to the off-gassing of paint, since, according to standard guidelines, insufficient time had been allowed to elapse between the painting of plinths and the positioning of objects; they were also irked that things had to be altered at the last minute, causing them inconvenience; and so on.

It was difficult for me to reconcile my understanding of Winkler's careful, deliberate disposition with this characterization of him as somewhat cavalier. The answer lies in part in the fact that this was a new generation of personnel, who had not been as thoroughly drawn into the Menil view that in the bureaucratization of conservation principles, "too much had been made of restrictions," as Winkler had told me long before. Of course, he had noted, ideal circumstances for the conservation of artworks would have them stored indefinitely in darkness in perfectly calibrated environmental conditions. While this might ensure the stable endurance of the work into the future, it would rob the work of vitality, the artist of the communicative opportunity of having the work seen, and audiences of the ability to engage with it—and it would further partition art from life. Conservation protocols designed for use by museum professionals are not based on absolute measures but are the result of adjudications concerning acceptable risk along a continuum of circumstances from ideal to awful. In the view of Winkler (and of his erstwhile colleagues), these determinations for the long-term disposition of artworks had come at the expense of their agency in the present. As a result, the Menil had not felt itself bound by those codes. Moreover, as discussed in the previous chapter, the Menil has sought to foster the cultivation of ethical actors, and if we are to follow Aristotle on this, the exercise of "practical wisdom" and "skill at deliberative choice" (Faubion 2001, 85) at any ethically sensitive moment should take precedence over mere adherence to routinized codes of practice, notwithstanding the fact that these codes go under the banner of "professional ethics."

But something else seems to be at work here too. Winkler and his cohort had very close relationships with artists and spent considerable time with them and their art in their studios. The radical transformation of the disposition of an artwork that is moved from a studio to a museum is plainly arbitrary. But what is more significant is that the Menil personnel's identification with artists and with the work that they do led them to see themselves not merely as museum professionals working to present the work of others, but also as cultural producers engaged, like artists, in exacting practices of creative experimentation. The implication that I wish to draw from this is that Winkler understood himself first and foremost to be responding to the creative exigencies of making an exhibition. If something didn't look just right—if a plinth wasn't of quite the right dimensions and needed to be rebuilt and painted at the last minute, then so be it—no effort would be spared. What to Winkler was coded as rigor was read by some, who, while invested in the idea of "the Menil way," had not been trained in it by its primary exponents, as arrogance.

It might be objected that the difference is essentially a temporal one— that Winkler's practice was derived from the curatorial approach honed by MacAgy and Dominique de Menil in the 1950s and 1960s, which had become, by the twenty-first century, simply old-fashioned, out of step with the contemporary professional protocols that lenders require to be followed before making their work available for exhibition. But it can hardly be said that Winkler and his colleagues at the Menil were simply out of touch, unaware of contemporary codes of practice, since they were continually working in collaboration with personnel from other major museums. So maybe they were simply overinvested in the idea of the exceptionalism of the Menil—an idea that certainly has had traction in the privileged milieu of the Menil— allowing them to feel somehow above the constraints that others were subject to. Such a view might be sustained by the fact that the Menil is able to secure difficult loans by virtue of the strength of its collection, given the importance of reciprocity in the practice of putting together major exhibitions. And it may well be true that this fact has allowed Menil personnel significant latitude on matters of protocol, but I remain unconvinced that distaste for professional codes of practice has simply been a matter of cavalier disregard. To take such a view would be to refuse to take seriously the commitments that I have been describing throughout, not necessarily for oneself, but for those who claim adherence to them.

Kristina Van Dyke, an associate curator of collections, was hired in 2005 to work with what had hitherto been described as the collection's "tribal art." Notwithstanding the de Menils' significant interest in this area, the collection had been without a specialist in this field since the premature death of Mino Badner in 1977. Over the intervening decades, nobody who had come into the Menil orbit had shown herself suitable, and it was not until after Winkler's departure that any serious consideration was given to advertising for personnel. The Menil legacy posed something of a dilemma for Van Dyke, as it had for new conservation staff, but for her the issue was one of significa-tion rather than the physical disposition of objects. For anyone academically trained in African or Oceanic art over the past couple of decades, Dominique de Menil's understanding of the significance of "primitive" or "tribal" art is discomfiting—naïve certainly, and imbued with the politically distasteful romanticism of the "primitive" as the bearer of childlike innocence and humanity. For a curator to do justice to what is recognized as a collection of remarkable quality, curating it in a manner that does not compromise her own intellectual sensibilities, but without impugning the collectors' own exegesis, is a far from straightforward proposition. In Dominique's expres-sions of the significance of these objects, her integral humanism is inclined to take on the appearance of an all too familiar, but no less uncomfortable, romantic exoticization.

There is another addition to the museum's professional staff whose ap-pointment, far from revealing tensions between the collection's legacy and its present circumstances, serves as some kind of resolution, partial no doubt, of a long-standing embarrassment within the Menil Collection. For all the de Menils' activist commitment to overcoming racial inequality, the Collection had never had a person of color on its professional staff. The appointment of Franklin Sirmans in 2006 as curator of modern and contemporary art was a belated, though welcome, corrective.[17]

For those staff members trained conventionally in art history, the kinds of thematic shows for which St. Thomas and later the Rice Museum were so well known posed difficulties, going against the priorities they were trained with. Indeed, since the opening of the Menil Collection, there had been a notable shift in the style of exhibitions it mounted. The de Menils had mounted many single-artist shows, as we have seen, but it was for their thematic shows that they were renowned. But with the opening of the Menil Collection, these increasingly gave way to exhibitions that focused on the work of a single artist. When I asked Dominique de Menil about this shift, she spoke first of the cost of the elaborate installations that both she and MacAgy had produced. "We were living in a fantasy," she explained. "We did not have to worry about the expense." But perhaps more to the point was her comment that with the opening of the museum, they felt compelled to do shows that were "more serious."

In this can be read a concession to changing fashions in the conceptualization of museum exhibitions generally, and a corollary to this is that museums seeking to mount high-status exhibitions were increasingly obliged to bring in as participants other major museums from which loans would be made and to which the show would travel. This practice of touring shows and thereby sharing their expense has long been pursued by museums, but the imperative for the Menil Collection has been as much a matter of the leverage that such collaboration affords as it has been a matter of economy. Private collectors might not be willing to lend a major work for a show that would be seen only in Houston, but one that would be hung at such high-profile venues as the Museum of Modern Art, the Whitney, the Guggenheim, or the Art Institute of Chicago afforded additional cachet.

The shift toward single-artist exhibitions, however, can also be understood as a concession to the curatorial style of Walter Hopps. He had a strong interest in paying very close attention to an artist's body of work rather than to single pieces, not as an art historical retrospective survey but as a focused deliberation on a particular aspect of the work. His approach revealed a deep concern for the relationships between objects, and his concern for the relation between the object and its viewer was demonstrated in his installations of exhibitions.

NOSTALGIA

In the context of the Menil Collection, we have seen the atomization of staff because of the architectural delimitation of interaction, information, and functions; a degree of formalization of roles that was due not only to spatial exigencies but also to the intensified demands of handling loans, security, shipping, and so on, in a much more substantial operation; and perhaps a less-exhilarating sense of innovation than had been enjoyed at Rice.

There was, on the other hand, in the elegant accommodations of Piano's building, a deepened sense of the prerogatives of wealth and art-world stature. In the early days of the museum, staff refrigerators were stocked not only with the endless supply of Perrier, as I found when I began research in 1994, but also with daily supplies of fresh food to sustain the professional and security staff alike. In those days, it seemed no expense was spared. Whether it was to care for staff members who were working through meal times on Hopps's idiosyncratic schedule, or to pursue a project for which no compromises had to be made, so long as the outcome was exemplary, the resources were available. And there was pride in the collection, in the extraordinary caliber of the exhibitions, and in having been chosen by Dominique or by Hopps. And central to this experience of privilege was the museum's commitment to care.

Much of this was recounted to me in the early to mid-1990s as an expression of regret, not for the passing of the Menil way of doing things, but for the mounting vulnerability that was made manifest by the layoffs. The layoffs effected a shift in sentiment insofar as they disrupted the reciprocal operation of trust and loyalty. The long and irregular work hours, the toleration of ambiguous status relations, and so on, which had been understood as acts of commitment, began to appear to the staff as questionable labor practices.[18] The nostalgia that this provoked was repeatedly articulated in wistful conjurings of the days when those who worked with the collection at St. Thomas, Rice, or the Menil residence felt themselves to be integral to a project that was being pursued with great energy and conviction, and in the context of which their loyalty and commitment, no less than their personal skills, were being rewarded by a reciprocal and highly personalized commitment to them. They were family.

Beyond the precincts of the Menil milieu, they had been recognized, in the parlance of the 1960s and 1970s, the period to which much of this nostalgia was directed, as cool people involved in the coolest projects—putting on shows the likes of which had never been seen in Houston, with patrons who repeatedly created ructions in Houston "society" by their active engagement in the civil rights movement and their hosting of artists and intellectuals who were considered audacious.

But it wasn't just the sense of insider status and privilege that was at stake. What people worried about also was whether the museum would be able to sustain the conditions that they understood its distinctive aesthetic to be predicated upon. In short, their anxiety was underpinned by the suspicion that the cultivation of an aesthetic disposition through the practices of care and attention, which the Menil Collection had afforded, would no longer be supported institutionally.

Among the current staff, very few remain who worked on Menil projects while Dominique was alive. The pervasive nostalgia that I had earlier observed is no longer palpable—at least not among the staff (though it still prevails among many other commentators). The anxiety that the museum may not be able to sustain its distinctive aesthetic and the dispositional effects that could be cultivated in relation to it is now expressed not so much in the deeply retrospective form that had emerged over the preceding decade, but in a notably more future-oriented cast, as we shall see.

ROUTINIZATION

The layoffs were announced just weeks after the appointment of Dominique de Menil's goddaughter, Susan Barnes, to a new position as chief operating officer of the Menil Foundation. Although her role was subject to a good deal of speculation, it became clear that her primary task was to secure the long-term disposition of the Menil Collection by increasing its endowment and rationalizing its practices in order to reduce operating costs. I had taken this to be an expression of the collector's anxiety about maintaining the integrity of her collection posthumously, the urgency of which was clear to see if one understood the collection under the generally persuasive rubric of the collection as a surrogate self. But what only subsequently became clear to me is the extent to which Dominique de Menil did not see the collection and the museum as the culmination of her life's work, the fulfillment of her commitments, or much less a proxy for her self. While her prior benefactions had been less substantial, they, like the Menil Collection, were all elements of a larger project, not of museum building, but of critique and experimentation. Increasingly, the size and complexity of the Menil Collection made it cumbersome. For Dominique the experimentalist, the constant demand that the museum made on her own financial resources and those of the foundation had become distasteful, preventing her from pursuing other projects and putting considerable pressure on her relationships with Winkler, Hopps, and others whose responsibility was toward sustaining the institution. Throughout her fifty years of patronage, begun in partnership with her husband, she had enjoyed being in a position to participate in projects that they had considered exciting and important. Now, with the museum open, her benefactions were tightly constrained, and her residence had ceased to serve as the base for the foundation. Her home was no longer abuzz with staff and activity, and she found herself unable to support new projects that came her way.

So Susan Barnes was brought in to free her godmother from some of the museum's claims upon her. In this endeavor, she joined Julie Gibbs, a development specialist hired just months before in conjunction with the launching of an endowment drive in 1994. Their task was an unenviable one (and, indeed, Barnes stayed for less than a year before returning to the Dallas Museum of Art). They had been called upon to overcome the widely held perception of wealth, which had mitigated against the recognition of need among potential donors, while, on the other hand, refraining from disrupting the museum's presentation of exemplarity, which remains a key element of its economy of care.[19] Moreover, they had to demonstrate to potential donors the museum's fiscal responsibility, read through the trope of efficiency. This too ran counter to the excessive economy of care that is central to the poetics of the Menil Collection. The scrupulous attention to presentation, the prestigious but expensive guest speakers, and the value placed on the slow, meticulous realization of ambitious projects all became luxuries that could no longer be sustained, despite their being cited over and over as integral aspects of the Menil aesthetic.

Georgina Born, writing about the Institut de Recherche et Coordination Acoustique/Musique (IRCAM), an institution with otherwise quite different commitments from the Menil Collection, notes the contradiction between

"IRCAM's aesthetic and its rationalized social form" (Born 1995, 29). Like the Menil Collection, "IRCAM operates primarily according to the 'laws' of avant-garde culture: aiming to maximize cultural capital, oriented to the future, and unconcerned with stimulating present demand" (29). But she also noted "fragmentary signs of a shift in the Institute's terms of legitimation influenced by its bureaucratization, a shift from the avant-garde discourse of the pursuit of future knowledge toward one of legitimation by efficiency or 'performativity'—in which the assessment and manipulation of demand are pivotal" (29).

This marking of the disjuncture between two radically different institutional forms, one defined by personal, flexible relationships imbued with a deep commitment to a shared project, the other formulated in terms of efficient, bureaucratic forms of management, at first glance seems to express an inevitable contradiction at the heart of the Menil Collection. As I have argued, the Menil, which was conceived of as the materialization of a critique of the imperatives of modernity and as a means by which those exigencies could be overcome, became subject to precisely those urgencies in the transformation of the collection into a public museum—subject to procedural requirements for the handling of loans, the maintenance of security, the management of staff, and so on. The Menil Collection, in this model, is a failed project, structurally unable to fully pursue its commitments, notwithstanding its local and international art-world stature. But such a characterization is surely too facile. To expect the Menil to resolve these contradictions is to insist on a kind of hygiene that refuses to acknowledge the complexities of ethical agency. The challenge that the legacy presents is to navigate these complexities.

10

For Aesthetics

In preparation for his death, John de Menil crafted his own memorialization in his closely detailed funeral arrangements.

To my Executor
c/o Pierre M. Schlumberger

I am a religious man deep at heart, in spite of appearances. I want to be buried as a catholic, with gaiety and seriousness.

I want the mass and last rites to be by Father Moubarac, because he is a highly spiritual man. Within what is permissible by catholic rules, and within the discretion of Moubarac, I want whoever feels so inclined to receive communion.

I want to be buried in wood, like the Jews. The cheapest wood will be good enough. Any wood will do. I want a green pall, as we had for Jerry MacAgy. I would prefer a pickup or a flat bed truck to the conventional hearse.

I want the service to be held at my parish, St. Anne's, not at The Rothko Chapel, because it would set a bad precedent.

I want music. I would like Bob Dylan to perform, and if it isn't possible, any two or three electric guitars playing softly. I want them to play tunes of Bob Dylan, and to avoid misunderstanding, I have recorded suggestions on the enclosed tape. The first one, Ballad of Hollis Brown is evocative of the knell (nostalgic bell tolling). Then at some point Blowin' In The Wind, The Times They Are A-Changin' and With God On Our Side, because all my life I've been, mind and marrow, on the side of the underdog. Then Girl From The North Country to the rhythm of which the pall bearers would strut out of the church. Father Duploye could also be asked to sing Veni Creator in Latin, to the soft accompaniment of a guitar.

I would like the funeral director to be Black.

I would like the pall bearers to be Ladislas Bugner, Francesco, Francois, Miles Glaser, Mickey Leland and Pete Schlumberger.

I would like George to stand with Dominique, Christophe, Adelaide, and Phil. Simone Swan, Helen Winkler, Jean Riboud, Ame Vennema, Rossellini and Howard Barnstone will be part of the family. Also Gladys Simmons and Emma Henderson.

I want no eulogy.

These details are not inspired by a pride, which would be rather vain, because I'll be a corpse for the meat wagon. I just want to show that faith can be alive.

Date: November December 13, 1972
[signed] John de Menil

In this event can be read the range and scope of John and Dominique de Menil's commitments. His body was prepared by Ross Mortuary, a black funeral home in the Fifth Ward, and he lay in state in his bedroom wrapped only in a white sheet, in traditional French peasant fashion. From there he was transported in a plain pine coffin with rope handles to an early evening mass at St. Anne's, where he and his wife regularly worshipped. The coffin, covered with the specified green velvet pall, on which was laid a single red rose and a seventeenth-century crucifix bearing the image of a black Christ, was carried to the church in the Volkswagen bus that had been used for years to carry Menil art from one venue to another around Houston. Driven by Sara Cannon, an associate of the Rice Institute for the Arts, the van and the procession took a circuitous route by the Rothko Chapel, in front of which they paused for a moment.

John de Menil had specified the pallbearers who were to carry his coffin into the church, and indeed every other detail, though in the event their number was increased to eight. State Representative Mickey Leland; Jim Love, a Houston sculptor who had long been a close associate of the family and worked with them and with Jerry MacAgy at the Contemporary Art Association and at St. Thomas before moving with them to Rice; Ladislas Bugner, the director of the Image of the Black in Western Art project in Paris; William Camfield, the art historian whom the de Menils hired at St. Thomas and took with them to Rice; Miles Glaser, the longtime friend of John de Menil who had served as a board member of the Menil Foundation since its inception and became its chief financial officer following John's death, in accordance with his wishes; Pierre-Marcel Schlumberger, a nephew; François de Menil, of New York, John and Dominique's second son, who had been selected to make the arrangements for the funeral; and Francesco Pelizzi, the collector, anthropologist, member of the board of the Rothko Chapel and later of the Menil Foundation, and former husband of their daughter Philippa.

Inside St. Anne's, as one reporter described it, the church was overflowing with mourners. "In the front pews sat the family and their closest friends. Behind them sat the rich and the powerful of Houston, New York, Los Angeles, and Paris. Behind them were ranked the local members of the Black Panthers, in full uniform, holding their berets, and behind them were hundreds of friends and admirers from all over the world" (Browning 1983, 202).

Quadraphonic speakers, specially installed for the occasion, blared out Bob Dylan's "Girl from the North Country" and "Blowin' in the Wind" before the rites began. The Reverend Youachim Moubarac, a Lebanese priest and Islamic scholar who was teaching at the Collège de Paris, crossed the Atlantic to celebrate the requiem Mass. But officiating also were the Reverend William Lawson, the Baptist preacher and civil rights leader; Rabbi Robert Kahn; and Dr. Thomas Shannon, the director of the Institute for Human Development, with whom the de Menils had collaborated on the Rothko Chapel project. Several lay readers also participated.

The theater of the funeral proceedings was heightened when the congregation, leaving the church at six thirty on a summer evening, found the sky black with dense cloud cover, lit suddenly by an awesome streak of lightning. Then the rain fell as heavy as anyone could remember. Roberto Rossellini, it is said, commented to his companion, "So speak the prophets. This funeral is attended by the gods" (Browning 1983, 202).[1]

In accordance with John de Menil's wishes, the Third Ward cemetery where he was buried was lit and kept open after hours so, it is said, that working-class people would not be excluded from the proceedings.

I recount this meticulously crafted event because it presents itself as a testament to John de Menil's understanding of the way in which an affecting aesthetic might be rendered through a highly refined and stylized performance, and to his unyielding commitment to the power of example. But most importantly, it serves as a compelling enactment of his commitment, above all, that life should be grasped and "that faith can be alive." Echoing her husband's opening comment, though (consistent with her less demonstrative disposition) refraining from any further elaboration, Dominique specified simply that she wished to be buried as a Catholic. But the conviction that faith could be made plausible—potent even—in the contemporary was no less energetically pursued by her than by her husband.

RELIGIOSITY

Pius IX's *Syllabus Errorum* (*Syllabus of Errors*) (1864) was a condemnation of modernity that explicitly defined the timeless, eternal values of Catholicism in opposition to modern temporality, rationalism, liberalism, and religious toleration. Later, Pius X, repositioning the papacy in the wake of Leo XIII's more conciliatory approach in the intervening years, required in 1910 that all priests having pastoral charge sign the "Oath Against Modernism" (Schloesser 2005, 56). These stark pronouncements remind us of the extent to which the Catholic Church identified itself with the premodern. But the notion that religion is concerned with the past, "doomed to lose all cultural plausibility in the modern world and only able to turn itself to account in instances of cultural regression" (Hervieu-Léger 2000, 84), is a commonly held view, particularly in the academic literature, and one that has inhibited serious analysis of contemporary religious faith. If contemporary religion is regarded as merely emotionally compensatory, its generative sociality is inevitably overlooked.

We have seen that the efforts of the *renouveau catholique* to reestablish the spirit in all domains of social life yielded not only a revised theology but also an all-encompassing political theory and a critical aesthetics, along with the injunction that contemplation is not the end but the predicate to action.

The conceptualization of engagements with art in religious terms is by no means novel. Museums are "temples" of art, spaces of reverent contemplation and transcendence, and the notion of modern art itself as redemptive is a familiar rendering. But these characterizations don't really go beyond asserting a religious analogy. I want to suggest a continuity that goes beyond mere analogy.

The idea of substitute religions or replacement religions, those taking the place of historic religions in a world where reference to the supernatural has increasingly lost credibility, can be observed in Max Weber, as Danièle Hervieu-Léger notes: "In modernity, it is towards art, politics, physical and sexual fulfillment or science itself, spheres through which the process of rationalization have been gradually weaned away from the hold of traditional religions ... that the thirst for meaning is turned" (2000, 27). These spheres, she explains, not unlike the practices of self-cultivation described in Chapter 8, "call forth endurance and asceticism, the exercise of ritual, devotion and ecstasy, just as does traditional belief. ... The disenchantment of the world does not signify the end of religion or even of traditional religious institutions; rather, just when these are contracting, new forms of religiosity make their appearance and take the place they occupied" (27).

Whether this should be considered a regressive impulse or, alternatively, an indication of an irreducible religious dimension of human life is beyond our purview here. But the notion of art as a medium of redemption has certainly been the subject of serious skepticism. Indeed, Michael Camille is scathing in his assertion of the inevitable bad faith that renders such notions rotten to the core. For Camille, the shimmer of the aesthetic only feigns freedom, anagogically "pretending to provide transcendence, all the while tightening the spectral fetters that bind the subject in subjugation to the terrible real" (Camille 1994, 74). This observation echoes Weber's argument that insofar as art "takes over the function of a this-worldly salvation," not only does it not offer a means of true redemption, much less a means of service to God, it instead "begins to compete directly with salvation religion" (Weber 1958a, 342). Since the domain of art is governed by aesthetic values that take precedence over moral adjudications, "art becomes an 'idolatry,' a competing power, and a deceptive bedazzlement" (343). Camille's mistrust of this anagogical operation expresses his view that the aesthetic functions preeminently in the service of power, "as tyrannous and tainted as any hegemonic practice" (1994, 74). Art objects cannot, in this view, provide access to transcendent realms, and to claim otherwise is at best false consciousness, at worst, bad faith.

This objection may well be a proper response to bourgeois aesthetics, which are defined by art's autonomy and by the mode of passive veneration. Such aesthetics are, however, very distant from the Menil Collection's project of critical aesthetics, as we have seen. While art has been at the heart of the project, or rather, what has been at the heart of the project has been the crafting of aesthetic dispositions, art, in this understanding, is far from the flight from the world that is often its telos in bourgeois aesthetics, but it is also distant from, or at least not reducible to, the rationalized instrumentalism or false consciousness ascribed to it by critics like Camille. To dismiss these convictions is to dismiss a worldview that has sought to systematically engage with the key questions of modernity and develop activist strategies of intervention that span the sacred and the profane.

One need not subscribe to the metaphysical foundational principles that animated the de Menils' project to recognize that its aesthetic practices were configured in an activist modality, directed toward fundamental political and sociological effects. Analytically, to understand the museum and its formation of aesthetic dispositions as a domain of contemporary religiosity is to see the practices of such an aesthetic disposition as efforts at good-faith meaning making rather than either bad-faith instrumentalism—as in the struggle for distinction—or, merely, the unreflexive practices of habitus, in Bourdieu's sense. Attention to aesthetic processes, as we have pursued them here, suggests the possibility of a museum that is not "a lesson in compliance to authority and conformity" (Maleuvre 1999, 4), but that seeks to engage its public in a manner that has alternative ethical and political entailments.

EXPERIENCE

When Carol Duncan describes museums as "powerful identity-defining machines" (1991, 101), what she is drawing attention to is the operation of museums since their emergence in the nineteenth century as central elements in the building of public solidarity in the service of the state. Much of the scholarship on museums has elaborated on precisely this aspect of their disconcerting (and mystified) authority as cultural institutions. In the Menil Collection, however, we see a shift away from a "metaphysics of solidarity" toward a privatized, diffuse moral order hinging on a seemingly unmediated, "intimate" "metaphysics of care" (Muehlebach 2007, xvii).

It is precisely the privatized character of these aesthetic dispositions, perhaps even more than the customary association of their cultivation with privilege, that renders them suspect as a modality of meaningful activism, of politics. Indeed, Martin Jay has recognized in the discourse of aesthetic experience, from its origins in the eighteenth century, the "gnawing doubt that [aesthetic experience] might be more a compensatory simulacrum of political activism than a stimulus to it . . . a displacement of 'real' politics, a way to gesture towards redemption without a means to realize it through what normally passes for political practice" (Jay 2005, 176).

We saw the de Menils' conventional political engagement in their early support of civil rights and in their later support for social justice activists internationally. Their investment in aesthetic experience was addressed to a more encompassing understanding of what might be understood as political effects achievable through the crafting of subjectivities imbued both with ethical sensibilities honed through the cultivation of an aesthetic disposition and with the interrogative spirit of ecumenicism. However, those who have fallen under the thrall of the Menil Collection's aesthetic project likely have done so not with politics in mind, nor solely because of the charisma of Dominique de Menil. Rather, their anxiety that aesthetically saturated experiences may not be sustainable in a public museum and their deep investment in maintaining the condition of possibility for such experience are, perhaps, no more than expressions of a longing for experiential intensity that we can observe in various contemporary domains.

Barbara Kirschenblatt-Gimblett quite rightly identifies the contemporary preoccupation in museums with crafting seductive responses to their public's appetite for "experiences" (1998). But the commodified form of experience she describes is distant from the modality of experience sought by the people I am characterizing. It is analogous perhaps to the distinction between the figures of the tourist and the traveler—the former is content with the consumption of "authentic" experiences, whereas the latter is intent on finding herself engulfed in authentic experiences, or so she imagines. But just as one suspects that the traveler is engaged in a no less bourgeois set of desires than the tourist, albeit in a distinguishing rarefied form, one feels bound to ask of these longings for consummatory aesthetic experience whether they are any less bourgeois than the more overtly commodified aesthetic experience that they shun.

For John and Dominique de Menil, having fully assimilated the sensibilities and activist commitments of the *renouveau catholique*, their entire project was directed against the complacency of bourgeois aesthetics, as we have seen. They were as troubled by the "contemplative and spectatorial impulse behind Kantian notions of aesthetic disinterestedness which denigrated the more active, engaged attempts to live life on the model of a work of art" (Jay 2005, 162) as by commoditized populism.[2] In both of these registers, the affective force of aesthetic experience was, in their view, seriously compromised—the peculiar density of the relationship that might be established with artworks in the labor of cultivating and exercising an aesthetic disposition yielded not merely the pleasure of intensified experience, or the chimera of wholeness that is the promise of reenchantment, but also the challenge of encounters that "open onto a future that is not fully contained in the past or present" (Jay 2005, 407). This is the kind of experience that Adorno elaborated in his defense of aesthetics, as Jay reminds us: "an openness to the unexpected with its dangers and obstacles, not a safe haven from history, but a reminder of the encounters with otherness and the new that await those who, despite everything, are willing and able to embark on the voyage" (360). But it is more than that, since it is experience that in its desired form crafts ethical citizenship while also making the ineffable present.

THE LEGACY

This discussion of the centrality of experience to the Menil project returns us to the problem that was the provocation for this analysis: how, more than a decade after the death of the founder, should the Menil Collection understand the legacy for which it must now serve as steward? It is a problem both of definition and of implementation.

To produce a strategic plan, its facilitator explained, an institution must identify those priorities that are more important than others, based on the "core values" of the organization. Having identified these core values, values "we need to take forward with us," people can "become confident about talking about the future," since basic operating assumptions will no longer need to be negotiated at every turn. But the identification and defense of "core values" pursued under the rubric of the strategic plan tends to reduce these commitments to articles of legitimation, since it is with recourse to these values that performance will be measured and institutional success defined. Insofar as core values cannot be expressed in a bureaucratized form or don't lend themselves to measurable evaluation, they are considered to have been poorly formulated. It is the task of the consultant to coax out of her clients a statement that can be translated into a set of managerial imperatives. We can see already that the kind of ethical practice that Dominique de Menil sought to foster, that calls for an ongoing and rigorous assessment and adjudication of conduct that might not conform to normative codes, is antithetical to this model. Furthermore, the kind of critical "grasping of the present" in order to remake it, which, I have argued, the de Menils took up from the *renouveau catholique*, seems unlikely to flourish under such a framework, which inevitably tends—to use the idiom of the day favored by John de Menil—to "sclerosis."

On the other hand, for anyone committed to sustaining the affecting character of the Menil, it is surely foolhardy and certainly too worrying (too contingent on the adjudications of people who are, after all, merely serving as stewards) to imagine proceeding into the future without some kind of expression of the principles that are at stake. As staff members now mine the archive, articulating the past and limning the spirit of the Menil historically, it is not so much to "recognize it the way it really was," as to address, as Ernst Bloch put it, "the problem of the present" (quoted in Miyazaki 2004, 18). In the archive, one finds not outcomes that should be pursued, that could be formulated as core values and written into the goal-oriented form of a strategic plan, but rather iteration after iteration of a method that is both prospective and open-ended. As in Hirokazu Miyazaki's characterization of what he calls the method of hope, this practice introduces "a prospective momentum to a present moment constantly invaded by retrospection" (27).

This experimental method, underpinned by an off-modern embrace of temporal ambiguity and instability, is not directed toward the fulfillment of an identifiable end, and thus there is no outcome against which performance might be measured, and no experts who can advise on how to achieve it. There is, of course, no shortage of people who claim an expertise that rests upon privileged knowledge of what Dominique would have done, but the retrospective and definitive cast of this is hardly in the spirit of the project. Indeed both the absence of an authoritative, tested model and the recognition of the possibility that the experiment can "fail" underwrite the experimental ethos (Miyazaki and Riles 2004). As Douglas Holmes observes in relation to the experimentalism of central bankers: "Experimentation here is not merely or necessarily about a formal testing of a particular proposition or hypothesis; rather, it is about the continuous evolution of a set of social practices and the critical labor by which the personnel of central banks bring to bear new insights and knowledge to modify and to refine the assumptions that inform their practices" (2009, 387). At the Menil Collection, those practices are directed fundamentally toward dispositional effects—the ongoing labor of ethical practice in the exercise of both the care of objects and the cultivation of the self pursued primarily in an aesthetic idiom.

So what is at stake is not a set of substantive outcomes but a mode of being that is not an end in and of itself. For Dominique and John de Menil, this subject formation was understood as a precondition for, or foundational element of, the social transformation they sought. For others who are now anxious to sustain the Menil aesthetic, the impulse is more diffuse, absent, perhaps, the political theory and religious metaphysics that animated the de Menils' projects. The investment in maintaining the conditions of possibility for experiential intensity and for the cultivation of an aesthetic disposition might best be understood as a method of hope—as a set of practices that while not directed toward a particular end, do serve to sustain a sense of possibility, conjuring hopefulness for the future while also offering a means to its fulfillment.

Notes

CHAPTER 1

1. From the leaflet accompanying the exhibition "A Piece of the Moon World: Paul Klee in Texas Collections," Menil Collection, March 9–June 5, 1994. It was not until 1995 that the exhibition catalogue, *A Piece of the Moon World: Paul Klee in Texas Collections*, was published.

2. Like the Byzantine Chapel, the Rothko Chapel operates as an independent entity; it is overseen by the Rothko Chapel Foundation.

3. My usage here is informed by Annette Weiner's (1994) characterization of the densities that are created in objects that are constituted as inalienable.

4. This view was resolutely articulated in Pope Pius IX's *Syllabus of Errors* (1864).

5. Schloesser adopts the term "off-modern" from Svetlana Boym's work (2001) on the aftermath of the Soviet collapse.

6. The other model pursued by some museums is to offer art as therapy, as an instrument of identification, and as a source of pride. This is particularly evident in museums seeking to attract what are referred to as "formerly underrepresented" audiences, typically conceived of according to cultural identifiers.

7. I should comment on my linguistic shift from "aesthetic" to "poetic" as if they were the same thing that, strictly speaking, of course they are not. However, it is my view that reference to poetics that has become increasingly common in cultural commentary over the past decade or so, is intended to draw attention to just the same representational and experiential modalities that aesthetics does, but without the taint of transcendentalism and privileged connoisseurship that aesthetics evokes. It tends to be used as both self-evident and innocent, and as a result has not been subject to theoretical elaboration in the context of this usage.

8. This is a phrase that Dominique de Menil quoted frequently, drawing on the words of her close friend and adviser Marie-Alain Couturier (Couturier 1989, 10–11).

9. Dominique de Menil, interview by the author, Houston, Texas, February 10, 1994.

10. An account of Schlumberger is given by Dominique de Menil's sister, Anne Gruner Schlumberger (1982). A more technical account may be found in the history by Louis Allaud and Maurice Martin (1977). But perhaps the richest narrative is to be found in Ken Auletta's two-part *New Yorker* profile of Jean Riboud, the former chairman and chief executive officer of Schlumberger (1983a and 1983b). See also Geoffrey Bowker's (1994) analysis of Schlumberger's institutional culture of innovation, focusing on the period between 1920 and 1940.

11. There is another element, internal to this text, that might further the impression of undue identification with the protagonists, in contrast to the more distanced stance

that typifies critical scholarship. I frequently refer to Dominique de Menil simply as "Dominique." This is not meant as a marker of intimacy, but simply makes clear exactly which de Menil I am referring to while avoiding the cumbersome repetition of the Menil name, already heavily used in relation to the museum and foundation, which a more formal locution would call for. Furthermore, the nomenclature I use serves to refer both to Dominique the person as well as to "Dominique," the figure who, particularly since her death, is regularly invoked in Menil circles, very often in the form of "what Dominique would have done."

CHAPTER 2

1. The force with which the Church pursued its opposition to the modern is indicated in the establishment of "a secret international anti-Modernist network. . . . During this epoch, later dubbed by one historian the 'Stalinist era of the Vatican,' Pius X both encouraged and subsidized the activities of this secret police" (Schloesser 2005, 56).

2. Congar (1939) provides an account of the schism between the Eastern Orthodox Church and Roman Catholicism.

3. Ultramontanists "looked 'beyond the mountains' of the Alps, beyond national churches, and most especially beyond Gallican Paris to the Pope in Rome for the center of a cosmopolitan 'Roman Catholicism'" (Schloesser 2005, 5).

4. Jean-Marie Domenach and Robert de Montvalon (1967) locate the conditions of possibility somewhat later, in the aftermath of the Second World War, though for similar, albeit much less thoroughly elaborated, reasons.

5. Jacques and Raïssa Maritain, raised Protestant and Jewish, respectively, were among the many French intellectuals to convert to Catholicism in the interwar period. Although they worked outside of official church institutions, their theological work positioned them as central figures in the Catholic revival of the interwar years and has given them enduring stature both in France and in the United States, where they were exiled during the Second World War. Jacques held teaching positions at Columbia and Princeton, and with the exception of a period in Rome when he served as French ambassador to the Vatican, they stayed at Princeton until 1960, when they again took up residence in France.

6. The provocation for this reorientation came in 1926 with the Vatican's condemnation of the integralist publication *Action Français*, edited by the non-Catholic Charles Maurras. Trenchantly antirepublican and antimodern, Maurras and his publication appealed to the conservative and reactionary elements of French Catholicism that had become impassioned not least by the republic's anticlerical legislation of 1905. According to Amato, "At one and the same time the Action Français was, as it remained until the Second World War, monarchist, decentralist, and traditionalist, as well as nationalist and statist" (1975, 72).

7. The Church was committed as well to a past in which it had enjoyed considerably more stature than it was able to sustain in republican France.

8. "In *Catholic Lives, Contemporary America* Thomas Ferraro has offered a cautionary note on the word '*cultural* as a qualifier to *Catholicism*': it 'does not necessarily mean dilution or dissolution—a draining of the religious imagination into banal secularity— but can in fact signal the opposite, a form of transfigurative reenvisioning that refuses to quarantine the sacred'" (Schloesser 2005, 17).

9. According to Schloesser:

> The philosophical doctrine of hylomorphism . . . holds that all real things are composed of two elements: material stuff that is pure potentiality, and the actuality of "form," an unseen causal force that gives order, unity, and identity to matter. The theological doctrine of sacramentalism holds that created things are a visible "sign" . . . which both bears within itself and simultaneously points beyond itself to an invisible "reality" . . . which is, in the final analysis, the Creator. This dialectical vision that sees created matter as the *visible sign* carrying an uncreated *invisible reality* underlies the fundamental Catholic practices of sacraments and sacramentals.
>
> Third, the substance-accident metaphysics inherited from Aristotle was most famously used by medieval scholastics to explain transubstantiation, that is, the divine presence of Christ effected at Mass in the bread and wine. "Substance" in this ontology, contrary to our modern notion of it as physical stuff, is rather the underlying deepest reality of a thing. Similarly, what we now think of as the contingent characteristics of a thing that are more or less "substantial" in their physical properties (e.g., size, quantity, weight, colour, odour) are the "accidents" that exist not in themselves but as the contingent and non-necessary . . . modifications of the substance. Thus . . . the the line of transubstantiation (which became an identity marker for Catholics after the Reformation) . . . holds out the promise of earthly reality's ability to transcend itself. (2005, 6)

10. As their religious longings developed, the Maritains moved away from Bergson to pursue, briefly though passionately, the austere Catholicism of Léon Bloy. Bloy was the catalyst for their conversion to Catholicism and, in the years preceding the First World War, for the conversion of a number of other young intellectuals who would become architects of the *renouveau catholique*.

11. Maritain's opposition to Bergson's "intuition" was due largely to Bergson's opposition of intuition to intellect, characterizing intellect as the means by which we might know the (merely) material world, and intuition as the faculty by which reality (the absolute) could be perceived. Maritain's objection was that in opposing these modes of apprehension, Bergson thereby denied the intellect the power to grasp spiritual reality (Kernan 1975).

12. Mounier's first publication on personalism, *Personalist Manifesto* (1936), reiterated in its central formulation the integral humanism of Maritain, whose ideas were most comprehensively worked out in his *Humanism intégral: Problèmes temporels et spirituals d'une nouvelle chrétienté* (1936). Mounier further elaborated his political theory in *Introduction*

to Existentialisms (1946), *Treatise on Character* (1946), *What is Personalism* (1947), *The Little Fear of the Twentieth Century* (1948), and *Personalism* (1949).

13. Information about the colloquium is at http://www.rothkochapel.org/colloquia .htm (accessed February 24, 2010).

14. In January 1991, to mark the twentieth anniversary of the Rothko Chapel, the Rothko Chapel Foundation, in collaboration with the Istituto per le Scienze Religiose of Bologna, organized and hosted the colloquium "Christian and Churches on the Eve of Vatican II."

15. "The renouveau catholique was not primarily an effort on the part of the Church's ecclesiastical institutions. Catholic revivalists created their own 'imagined community,' and this relocation from cultural margin to centre depended on the printed word. These shifts in Catholic identity and self-understanding were thus produced for the most part by laypersons. Even the clerics associated with the movement exerted their influence not through the pulpit but via the publishing house" (Schloesser 2005, 15).

16. This refers to the intensive building program launched by Cardinal Verdier, the archbishop of Paris (1929–1940). The churches built under this program in Greater Paris became known as "les Chantiers du cardinal."

17. See Rubin (1961); Matisse, Couturier, and Rayssiguier (1999); and Coombs (2000).

18. The crucifix that Couturier commissioned from Germaine Richier for the Assy church had no cross, but only an abstracted faceless figure, the embodiment of wrenching agony, cast roughly in the shape of a cross. It was removed by the bishop almost a year after he had consecrated the church. He acted in response to widespread complaints within the Church and from local parishioners. As *Time* (1951) reported it, "They had come to accept their church's Rouault windows, Lurçat tapestry, Léger mosaic and Matisse sketch, but never the Richier crucifix. 'It was evil,' a woodcutter ventured. A young girl agreed: 'The figure was thin and frightening. The colors of the other art in the church make me feel alive and strong, but this thing only scared me like a dark devil.'" In response, the influential Paris weekly *Arts* protested its removal as being "too categoric and too late; it justly provokes scandal and nothing can justify adhesion to the ideas defended by the partisans of mediocre art, by those who refuse the church the possibility of finding the means of expression our times demand." The crucifix was eventually restored to the church, purportedly at the request of the patients of the hospice that the church was meant to serve. It was never quite clear how much the intense rejection of the work was triggered by the image itself and how much by public knowledge of Richier's atheism (Rubin 1961).

19. See also Couturier (1989, 52), and for a discussion of the position of the sacred art movement on the issue of the faith of artists, see Rubin (1961, 64–73); for Maritain's position on this question, see Schloesser (2005, 141–172). Before agreeing to accept his commission for the church at Assy, Lipchitz insisted that his sculpture of the Madonna bear the inscription: "Jacob Lipchitz, Jew, faithful to the religion of his ancestors, has

made his Virgin to foster understanding between men on earth that the life of the spirit may prevail" (Rubin 1961, 126–127).

20. A *Time* story on Couturier's chapel projects presented the issue thus:

> Whatever the state of an artist's faith, Couturier welcomes them all: "We start," he explains, "with the assumption that artists are men and therefore sinners. If their sins are sometimes startling, it is because they are men of imagination, artists. But all spring from our culture and even our religion.... When some think themselves communist, it is as artists are communist, out of love for the poor. We must free them to work for us, give them the right to paint on our walls, and they will tell our great story as it has not been told in 500 years." To those who would draw the line at the abstractionists he says: "Abstract art has as much a place in church as the organ music of Bach." (Time 1949)

21. This view is posed in opposition to the teachings of the Ateliers d'Art Sacre, where Couturier trained as an artist priest. Drawing on Jacques Maritain's neo-Thomist *Art and Scholasticism* (1917), the atelier took the position that "the maker of sacred art must first live a sacred life before picking up a paintbrush" (J. Weber 1994, 2). This was a point that many readers of Couturier's *L'Art Sacré* were unwilling to concede (Rubin 1961, 64–73).

22. Whether authentic sacred art could be made only by pious artists was to remain an issue of contention between Couturier and Maritain (who insisted on the necessity of piety).

23. Dominique de Menil reported that Alfred Barr, the first director of the Museum of Modern Art, considered the Audincourt stained glass to be Léger's masterpiece (Menil 1989b, 158).

24. Couturier had earlier worked with Le Corbusier on what is described as the "underground" Basilique de la Sainte Baume project with Léger. This project was never realized, leaving Le Corbusier disinclined to take on another church project, but for the persuasive élan of Couturier.

25. Conversation between Dominique de Menil and Adelaide de Menil, Houston, July 16, 1989; transcript in the Menil Archives, Menil Collection, Houston (hereafter cited as Menil Archives). Earlier in this conversation, Dominique had been prompted by her daughter to recount a much earlier instance of architectural patronage: "Yes, that was just . . . very typical of our character and enthusiasm. . . . We were just married and went to ski at l'Alpe d'huez. And there was a charming little wooden chapel. At Mass the priest announced he needed to build, and we thought, how sad, he's going to build a big cement thing. Jean offered him architectural plans. We thought of Pierre Barbe [who had remodeled Dominique and John's Paris apartment] right away. The priest accepted."

26. John de Menil to the Reverend Father Cemon, April 4, 1952 (Menil Archives).

27. Conversation between Dominique de Menil and Adelaide de Menil, Houston, July 16, 1989 (Menil Archives).

28. Dominique de Menil, interview with the author, February 1996, Houston, Texas.

29. Rothko was particularly interested in creating works for a single environment and had already completed two such commissions.

30. They had earlier, at the urging of Rothko's friend Douglas MacAgy (to whom Jermayne MacAgy had formerly been married), visited the artist in 1960 to view the paintings—originally commissioned for the Four Seasons restaurant of the Seagram Building, though withdrawn by Rothko before completion—with the idea of possibly using them for a chapel project. While they determined finally that it would be less than ideal to use paintings made for a different space and purpose, their decision not to proceed was merely a postponement (Barnes 1989, 34–35).

31. An account of the Rothko Chapel written by Dominique de Menil's goddaughter gives an authoritative rendering of her conception of the project and of its development (Barnes 1989). Also useful is Saenz (1980).

32. Very early in the process, a full-scale mock-up of three of the chapel walls was built in Rothko's studio, since it was with the calibration of components that Rothko was particularly concerned. He also used a working scale model of the whole structure. The model was open at the bottom so that one could put one's head inside the space and approximate the experience of standing within the space (Barnes 1989, 63–65).

33. Rothko is renowned for the concern he showed over the future disposition of his paintings, sometimes insisting that his works, whether hung publicly or privately, be installed according to his directives, including, particularly, specifications regarding lighting. Indeed, he was often reluctant to give up his works, and on occasion refused to.

34. Accounts of the acquisition of Broken Obelisk are among the most often-repeated narratives told in an effort to characterize the presence of the de Menils in Houston. In 1969, Dominique and John went to the Houston Municipal Art Commission with an offer to match a grant from the National Foundation on the Arts and Humanities for the purchase of a work of contemporary sculpture. The commission agreed to their stipulation that the funds be spent on the acquisition of Broken Obelisk, but agreement could not be reached over the de Menils' subsequent insistence that the sculpture be dedicated to the memory of Martin Luther King, Jr. The matter was turned over to city council, which decided not to accept the sculpture with the dedication to King. In response, the de Menils withdrew their support, resolving to purchase Broken Obelisk themselves. They subsequently brought Barnett Newman to town to help select an appropriate site for the piece, and its present location as a complement to the Rothko Chapel was settled upon. In her foreword to the Menil Collection catalogue, Dominique de Menil, perhaps to demonstrate the uncompromising character of their enthusiasms, commented, "It went exactly where Barney thought it should go. A house happened to be at this location. It was bought and pulled down without a moment's hesitation" (Menil 1987, 8).

Some versions of this story tell of the courage and principle of the de Menils in the face of the ignorance and conservatism of city hall. This account is heightened by the claim that John de Menil very nearly added to the dedication to King this homily directed toward the city: "Forgive them, for they know not what they do." For others, the argument over the King dedication signified rather differently. They read it as a characteristically impetuous gesture (the dedication was apparently an afterthought in the proceedings), an act of willfulness converted into a claim for moral high ground. According to this version, the de Menils were made fully aware of the policy that prohibited city hall from sanctioning, in the interests of evenhandedness, explicitly political monuments.

35. These sermons formed the foundation for Congar (1939).

36. In this can be read an expression of one of the tenets of Catholic social doctrine, the principle of subsidiarity.

It is a fundamental principle of social philosophy, fixed and unchangeable, that one should not withdraw from individuals and commit to the community what they can accomplish by their own enterprise and industry. So, too, it is an injustice and at the same time a grave evil and a disturbance of right order, to transfer to the larger and higher collectivity functions that can be performed and provided for by lesser and subordinate bodies. Inasmuch as every social activity should, by its very nature, prove a help to members of the body social, it should never destroy or absorb them. (Pius XI, Quadragesimo anno, quoted in Miller 1964)

The development of subsidiarity rests on a delineation of the boundary between public authority and civil society and serves as a means for negotiating fundamental conditions for the maintenance of human rights and social justice in complex industrial societies. Further, in the broader context of transnationalism, it takes a position against cultural imperialism, particularly insofar as the principle operates to promote what is called "vertical pluralism."

"Vertical" [pluralism] refers to the way in which ideologies cut vertically through all the layers and groups of society. . . . Different "spiritual families," in a common French phrase—Catholics, Protestants, Marxists, "humanists," or whoever they may be—should on the principle of "vertical" pluralism be permitted and enabled to follow their own way of life. . . .

. . . It reduces conflicts, since it allows everyone, without discrimination . . . to build up a set of associations which fits his own ideals. Since, in an imperfect world, some conflicts of ideals and loyalties are inevitable, the essential thing is that they should be fought out in a way that lets the truth eventually emerge and form the basis for a settlement. But this is likely to happen only if the parties in conflict hold firm, clear, views which provide a solid basis for argument, and yet are open and sensitive to the views of others. . . . Everyone must sail "under his own flag" or "with banners unfurled" . . . . "Tolerance" is hardly the word for this attitude . . . There is in "vertical pluralism" a warmth of common humanity and common responsibility before God. (Fogarty 1957, 42–43)

For Dominique de Menil, the importance of subsidiarity lay in its promotion of a robust civil society, in which personal sovereignty is not assimilated by the state, and of a form of humanism in which cultural pluralism is actively engaged.

The modern application of subsidiarity dates from Leo XIII's famous encyclical *Rerum novarum* (1891; "Of New Things," also known as "The Condition of the Working Classes"), which drew on the writings of Thomas Aquinas to set out the tenets of Catholic social doctrine. The first explicit use of the term came in Pius IX's encyclical *Quadragesimo anno* (1931), and was later elaborated by John XXIII in *Mater et Magistra* (1961) and *Pacem in terris* (1963).

37. The phrase "new approaches for parishes" refers to initiatives like the worker-priest movement, which had been an officially sanctioned postwar Dominican initiative to ameliorate the alienation of the working class from the Church. France, in recognition of the sharp decline in its congregations, would be treated as a "missionary country." By 1951, when the Holy See ordered the suspension of recruiting for this program, around ninety young priests were working in factories and on docks. It was felt that these priests were rendered in this context unduly subject to the seductions of the flesh and of socialism. In 1953, all worker priests were recalled, though many refused to submit to this command, proving "by this resistance how urgently necessary Rome's intervention had been" (Blet 1981, 597).

38. There has been considerable debate concerning the authorship of the texts of Vatican II. The conventional role of the *periti* (of which Congar was one) was editorial, "to revise and then to harmonise drafts in the light of the comments (either written or verbal) from the Council fathers.... Some observers," however, "seem to indicate that the periti were the real authors of the texts with the bishops simply ratifying, or, in a more moderate view, tweaking the draft texts that had been written in the various commissions and sub commissions" (Barratt 2006, 83).

39. See the Rothko Chapel website, http://rothkochapel.org/colloquia.htm, for a full listing of Rothko Chapel colloquia.

40. In 1991, the chapel celebrated its twentieth anniversary with a worldwide convocation of Catholic theologians and scholars: "Their mission was to examine the ideas and lasting influence of the three years of work leading to Vatican II, that historic meeting of bishops called in 1965. The Houston event was part of a six-year study under the aegis of Bologna's Institute for Religious Sciences. In her opening remarks, de Menil called Vatican II a 'precious legacy' in its commitment to greater love and understanding in the world. To her, it was an opening up of the Roman Catholic Church to ecumenicism, which is precisely what the Rothko Chapel stands for" (A. Holmes 1991, 228).

CHAPTER 3

1. After the signing of the armistice in 1940, with Paris essentially cut off, all of Schlumberger's worldwide operations became dependent on Houston (Allaud and Martin 1977).

2. Marie-Alain Couturier to John and Dominique de Menil, January 19, 1948 (Menil Archives). I thank Ed Shephard for assistance in translation.

3. Undated handwritten notes for a talk to a group of architects' wives in Houston (Menil Archives). Dominique de Menil commented to her friend Rosamond Bernier on the early days of their activity in Houston: "People in Houston wouldn't dream of spending $5,000 on a painting. They'd put $30,000 into a bull, but into a painting? Never!" (quoted in Bernier 1987, 129–129).

4. Stephen Fox recounts that when John de Menil died, Howard Barnstone wrote of him: "I was challenged, influenced, torn down, hired, [and] fired. . . . I have lost my sharpest critic and my closest friend" (Fox 2005, 3).

5. Georges de Menil, draft of letter to Ken Auletta, May 1, 1982 (Menil Archives). The letter was for Auletta's *New Yorker* article on Jean Riboud.

6. Dominique de Menil studied physics and mathematics at the Sorbonne. There is no indication, however, that she was ever considered to have a future in the company as a scientist, though she did briefly work on the company's in-house newsletter.

7. Dominique and John had sufficient confidence in the importance of what they were doing that they didn't hesitate to call major museums and private collectors alike, seeking loans from their collections.

8. Strictly speaking, MacAgy had been appointed acting director of the Palace of the Legion of Honor in 1943, holding the position until director Thomas Howe returned from military service in 1946. She continued to work there as assistant director until 1955, when she accepted the position with the CAA.

9. These contemporary works were Constantin Brancusi's *Chimera*, 1918; Henri Lavers's *Caryatid*, 1930; Lipchitz's *Study for Figure*, 1926; Amedeo Modigliani's *Head*, 1912; and Picasso's *Femme Nue*, 1909.

10. The display of African expressive culture was hardly common in American art museums in the 1950s. However, there was significant precedent for an exhibition like "Totems Not Taboo." In the 1920s and 1930s, the Brooklyn Museum of Art (1923), the Cleveland Museum of Art (1929), and the Museum of Modern Art in New York (1935) all mounted significant African shows, as did the Museum of Fine Arts, Houston, in 1933. As Doran Ross observes, however, very little further attention was paid to African material in U.S. museums until the founding of the Museum of Primitive Art in 1957 (on whose board John de Menil served) and the emergence of an increasingly robust civil rights movement, which intensified interest in African traditions. At the close of the 1950s and through the 1960s, several major shows of "primitive" art established the now-familiar grouping of African art with Oceanic and Native American arts and laid the ground for the creation of curatorial positions responsible for this these widely divergent collections (D. Ross 2003).

11. This argument can be traced through the published exchanges between William Rubin (1984, 1985a, 1985b) and Kirk Varnedoe (1985a, 1985b), cocurators of "'Primitivism' in 20th Century Art," on the one hand, and critic Thomas McEvilley (1984, 1985a, 1985b) on the other. See also James Clifford (1985) and Arthur Danto (1984).

12. Through its first thirty years, the Museum of Fine Arts was under the part-time directorship of James Chillman, Jr., a professor of architecture at Rice University.

13. She dedicated her autobiographical *Out of This Century* to Sweeney, and in it described Pollock as the "spiritual offspring" of Sweeney and herself (Beauchamp 1983, 40). During the process of determining the long-term disposition of her collection, Peggy Guggenheim acceded to the urgings of the dealer Alexander Iolas to seriously consider the suitability of Houston as a home for the collection. The presence in Houston of the de Menils and Sweeney was crucial to her interest, though she finally elected to give it to the Solomon R. Guggenheim Museum.

14. Cullinan Hall doubled the exhibition space of the museum, but with its 30-foot ceilings, an open space 112 feet wide and 76 feet deep, and a curving glass-curtain wall 132 feet long, its vastness made it extremely difficult to show works there (Beauchamp 1983, 75).

15. When Mies van der Rohe was asked at the opening of Cullinan Hall whom he would recommend if he could have anyone to run the museum, his immediate response was James Johnson Sweeney (Beauchamp 1983, 86).

16. In 1961, more than 50 percent of the museum's budget was contributed by patrons; 30 percent was derived from memberships, special events, and sales; and less than 8 percent was allocated by the city of Houston. This was a testament less to the city's parsimony in relation to the museum than to the museum's unwillingness to accept public money that might compromise its autonomy (Beauchamp 1983, 87). Given the contentious relations among major donors on the board, however, the museum was by no means free from struggles over influence.

17. Sweeney's correspondence during his tenure as director of the Museum of Fine Arts is held as part of the Records of the Office of the Director, James Johnson Sweeney, Correspondence and Miscellaneous Subjects, 1961–1967 (Archives, Museum of Fine Arts, Houston, microfilmed by the Archives of American Art Texas project, Smithsonian Institution).

18. See Beauchamp (1983) for a full account of the unraveling of Sweeney's position.

19. These pieces were subsequently incorporated into the Menil Collection.

20. Browning recounts an insult to an important patron of the Museum of Fine Arts, Houston, in the name of maintaining quality: "[Dominique de Menil's] standards for [the teaching collection at St. Thomas] were so unbending that when Jane Blaffer Owen tried to donate a tapestry . . . Mrs. de Menil refused the gift on the grounds that it was not of high enough quality." Mrs. Owen wrote the following extraordinary response, "If a child brings a gutter flower to its mother, and tells her it is an orchid, should the mother throw the flower away because it isn't?" (Browning 1983, 200). It should be noted, however, that these two women were to become close friends and fellow travelers of sorts, insofar as Jane Blaffer Owen was to commission Philip Johnson to design what is now referred to as the "roofless church" for New Harmony, her utopian community in Indiana.

21. As a testament, perhaps, to the success of these efforts to develop a taste for modern art in Houston, Sophy Burnham recounts, in her evocation of the burgeoning U.S. market

in contemporary art, that in 1969, Sakowitz, a Houston department store, advertised in its Christmas catalogue a "Masterpiece of the Month" club; for one million dollars, it promised to deliver each month for a year a painting by a "twentieth-century master"— among them Picasso, Chagall, and Matisse (Burnham 1973, 31).

22. John de Menil to James Schramm, April 29, 1957, regarding the AFA Convention (Archives of American Art, roll 1780, fr. 148. Archives, Museum of Fine Arts, Houston).

23. Early in their residence in Houston, John and Dominique de Menil were quite active in the establishment of a professional theater company, underwriting the hiring of Nina Vance to direct the Alley Theatre.

CHAPTER 4

1. The story was recounted to me by Dominique de Menil herself, and by Menil Collection staff and associates, and can be found in various iterations in the Menil Archives. It has also appeared in numerous journalistic accounts (see, for example, Browning 1983).

2. Amato here is paraphrasing William James on the idea of conversion (Amato 1975, 52).

3. See Schwartzwald (1990, 2004) for an account of Couturier's work in Montreal during this period, when he elaborated his arguments on behalf of modern art in liturgical settings and mounted a searing critique of the Church's anti-Semitism while he worked assiduously to secure North American visas for Jewish artists and intellectuals in France.

4. In subsequent renderings, this is described as a Chinese head.

5. Written answers to questions posed by Julia Brown and Bridget Johnson for *The First Show: Painting and Sculpture from Eight Collections, 1940–1980* (1983); the original documents are in the Menil Archives.

6. This theme recurs throughout Couturier (1989).

7. While these friendships were enormously important in shaping the collection, artists were not invited to assist in formulating an acquisitions strategy for the collection as a whole, as Duchamp, for example, was for the Arensbergs. Speaking of her relationship with Ernst, Dominique de Menil commented, "We did not discuss other artists. We never tried to find out what artist we should acquire. We had no buying policy or counselor" (quoted in Brown and Johnson 1983, 38).

8. Dominique de Menil, interview by the author, February 10, 1994, Houston. The painting Dominique de Menil refers to—the "Metaphysical"—is presumably de Chirico's *Metaphysical Interior with Biscuits* (1916).

9. See Sylvester and Whitfield (1992, 1993), Whitfield and Raeburn (1993, 1994), and Sylvester, Whitfield, and Raeburn (1997).

10. See Spies and Leppien (2004) and Spies, Metken, and Metken (1975, 1976, 1979, 1987, 1988, 2007).

11. In deference to the sensibilities of current curatorial staff members, who are un-

comfortable with the politics of this nomenclature, the Menil Collection now refers to what had been characterized as "tribal" or "primitive" as "non-Western."

12. Dominique de Menil, "Welcoming Words" (handwritten), November 11, 1988 (Menil Archives).

13. Dominique de Menil gave poetic voice to her sense of a historical moment of unity in the first volume of *The Image of the Black in Western Art*:

> When Orient and Occident were swept by the high winds of Christianity and Islam, ideals of fraternity blossomed. There was a time when the West adopted a black knight as its patron saint, a time when artists did not neglect to include an African among the resurrected, a time when Solomon embraced a black Queen of Sheba. Reality might have followed in the footsteps of this dream: it was in the arms of the Pope that the first ambassador of the Congo died.... But the dream of an authentic cooperation between Europe and Africa, of a sharing of ideals and knowledge, was shattered by crimes so atrocious they left no images. (1976, xi)

14. Couturier articulated throughout *L'Art Sacré* this sense of degradation and disenchantment progressively infecting our sensibilities since the outset of the Renaissance, such that we could now barely recognize our malaise (see Couturier 1989). Dominique de Menil likewise spoke to the effects of disenchantment in her foreword to *The Menil Collection*: "Except for music, the natural longing for enchantment is discouraged in our culture. And what is art if it does not enchant? Like Jacob's ladder, it leads to higher realities, to timelessness, to paradise. It is the fusion of the tangible and the intangible; the old hierogamy myth—the marriage of heaven and earth" (1987, 8).

15. This view of the artist, characteristic of proponents of the *renouveau catholique*, is crystallized in this formulation given by James Schall: "Art, though a practical virtue, is primarily an intellectual virtue. It includes the idea or understanding of what is to be made, the intelligibility that goes into the work, including all the mystery and insight that the artist sees in his intuition of what he wants to bring forth into the world.... There is no formula for making a good and beautiful piece of art, but there is a knowledge at its very core, a knowledge or intuition that is first in the mind of the maker and from thence incorporated into the thing made (1998, 28).

16. Baudelaire's continuity with romanticism is, it should be noted, limited in scope: "In his rejection of nature, Baudelaire is anti-Romantic, and in his aristocraticism, he stands against the most famous poets of the Romantic era. But he is one with them in his hatred of commercial/instrumental civilization, and certainly follows them in seeking the antidote in art" (Taylor 1989, 436). Maritain, looking back on his youth, commented, as Joseph Amato notes: "'I was crazy with Baudelaire.' Baudelaire and the whole decadent and revolutionary tradition associated with him under the generic term symbolism, beckoned Jacques. As for the youth of his generation and the generations before, symbolism seemed to call them from the confines of bourgeois life to the music of the inner soul; to death, to fate, to loneliness, to destruction, to the point where the individual self becomes the

source of the universe and the universe but part of the poetry of the self—to the point where every feeling receives a form and every form evokes a feeling, where life and art become one" (Amato 1975, 45).

17. This critical, active (well-informed) agency also characterizes the kind of art historian that Dominique sought to produce at the University of St. Thomas.

CHAPTER 5

1. Dominique de Menil to Menil Foundation board members, memo, November 2, 1989 (originally circulated October 16, 1976); (Menil Archives).

2. Minutes of a meeting of the Grants Committee, October 6, 1972, 1–7 (Menil Archives). The quotation is from page 1.

3. See *The DeLuxe Show* (1971).

4. This was not without precedent. Black Panthers had started a free-breakfast program for children in Oakland, California, in 1969, and it quickly expanded across the United States, feeding thousands of grade-schoolers in inner cities and becoming a model for current school breakfast programs. The use of the Black Panthers for the provision of security services had been provoked in the summer of 1969 when the New York Police Department refused to provide security for what became known as Black Woodstock, the Harlem Cultural Festival, held at the northern end of Central Park. But above this precedent, perhaps, was the kind of risqué allure of the Black Panthers that Tom Wolfe (1970) observed in his astringent account of the Park Avenue party thrown in their honor by Leonard Bernstein and his wife, Felicia.

5. For responses to "The Deluxe Show," see Akston (1971), Berger (1990), G. Davis (1972), and Butterfield (1971).

6. Discussions recorded in Menil Foundation documents reveal the extent to which John de Menil wrestled with the nuanced politics of these kinds of interventions.

7. This impulse was not unlike that of Edward Steichen, who was motivated to mount the antiwar "Family of Man" exhibition of photographs (Museum of Modern Art, New York, 1955) by the idea that atomic war would not be pursued if the humanity of others was recognized (see Sandeen 1995).

8. For volumes in the series, see Vercutter et al. (1976), Devisse and Mollat (1979), and Honour (1989); the final volume to be published, volume three, is being prepared. For other books and catalogues resulting from the project, see Suckale-Redlefsen (1987), Karageorghis (1988), and Wood and Dalton (1988). In 1994, the archive was transferred to Harvard University, which assumed full responsibility for it in 2000, in accordance with a transfer deal worked out with the Menil Foundation.

9. The text drafted by Dominique is in the Menil Archives.

10. John de Menil to Philippa de Menil, August 28, 1970 (Menil Archives).

11. These scholarships were awarded anonymously so that students could experience them as something they had earned rather than as something for which they should feel

indebted to benefactors (Fox 1999). Henry Louis Gates, the W. E. B. Du Bois Professor of the Humanities at Harvard and director of the W. E. B. Du Bois Institute for Afro-American Research, was the recipient of de Menil educational support. The Menil Foundation Grants Committee files give evidence of the strength of this commitment to educational opportunities for African Americans. Weighing a request to support a white student, "one of our best graduates" from the media studies program the de Menils had established at Rice University, to attend graduate school at UCLA, against funding a student of color, Dominique emphatically explained: "If it came to a priority rating between one year at UCLA graduate school and sending a black one year to college, my vote would go to the second. True, the black is a four year commitment" (Advisory Committee on Grants, September 17, 1972, Menil Archives).

12. Warhol screened *Lonesome Cowboys* (1968), a film financed by the de Menils in a deal set up by Fred Hughes. The original commission had been for the film *Sunset* (1967), and some of the sunsets filmed for the commission were included in **** (*Four Stars aka The Twenty Five Hour Movie*, 1967). Leftover funds were used for *Lonesome Cowboys* (1968).

13. Kilian, now retired from his retail activity, is again tightly entwined with the Menil enterprise, serving as director of public programs for the Menil Collection.

14. John de Menil to unknown recipient, May 15, 1966 (Menil Archives).

15. The Sewall Art Gallery was at that time still in the planning phase.

CHAPTER 6

1. The initiative to retain Kahn for the Rice project was not John and Dominique's, though it has often been attributed to them. John identifies the architecture department as the source, though Henry Malcolm Lovett, the son of Rice's inaugural president and himself a Rice trustee at the time, insists that it was he who commissioned these plans (Fox 2005). As John describes it in a memo: "Kahn came to Houston a couple of times. None of the interested parties were shown his sketches. Dr. Simms, who's in charge of the campus, and who has the ear of the board, didn't like the idea. He put it to sleep" (John de Menil to the Grants Committee of the Menil Foundation, October 5, 1974, Menil Archives).

2. John and Dominique de Menil, "Purpose of the Menil Foundation," July 27, 1970 (Menil Archives). This document is one of many articulations of the foundation's mission produced in the process of clarifying the foundation's priorities in the early 1970s.

3. In 1962, their non-Western and Native American collection, or at least significant elements of it, were exhibited at the Museum of Primitive Art, New York, but it was not until "La Rime et la Raison" that the collection as a whole was shown.

4. John de Menil to the Grants Committee of the Menil Foundation, memorandum, October 5, 1972 (Menil Archives). The subject of the memo, "Rothko Chapel Plaza," was altered in Dominique's handwriting to "Rothko Chapel Neighborhood," consistent with

her repeated efforts to ensure that the project would not be allowed to become monumental in style.

5. Ibid. In 1972, the members of the Grants Committee were Miles Glaser, the foundation's financial officer; Simone Swan, whose company, Withers Swan in New York, was contracted to attend to public relations for the foundation; Helen Winkler, formerly a St. Thomas student and at this time described for official Rice purposes as executive assistant at the Institute for the Arts; and Dominique and John.

6. Ibid.

7. John de Menil to Menil Foundation board members, March 15, 1973, and notes from a telephone conversation with Louis Kahn, conveyed by Simone Swan to Dominique de Menil, June 7, 1973 (both in Menil Archives).

8. The phrase "this project needs... no monumentality" comes from the memo (dated February 26, 1974) of a meeting held January 31, 1974, with Louis Kahn, Dominique de Menil, and Simone Swan (Kahn file, Menil Archives). "Beautiful frugality" appears in the memo of a meeting held March 13, 1973, with Louis Kahn, Miles Glaser, and Simone Swan (Menil Archives).

9. Dominique de Menil commented on the difficulty of working with the famously erratic couturier, whose idiosyncrasies were not merely tolerated but embraced. His virtuosity and élan elevated him to the ranks of the "remarkables": "Charlie was impossible, as we soon found out. But all that mattered was that he was a genius" (Dominique de Menil, quoted in Bernier 1987, 129).

10. A comprehensive account of Johnson's projects that were derived in significant ways from his relationship with the de Menils can be found in Welch's study (2000).

11. Aubry, who went on to become partners with S. I. Morris in Morris Aubry Architects, was the architect of Houston's performing arts theater complex, the Wortham Center, which was under construction during the same period as the Menil Collection, and opened May 9, 1987, just a month before the Menil Collection.

12. They visited the Carnegie Museum of Art in Pittsburgh, Cleveland Museum of Art, Toledo Museum of Art, Detroit Museum of Art, Milwaukee Art Museum, Des Moines Art Center, Walker Art Center in Minneapolis, Minneapolis Institute of Arts, and Nelson-Atkins Museum of Art in Kansas City.

13. Piano characterized the contrast between the two buildings as a response to their radically different locations: "Whereas Centre Pompidou took a polemic attitude toward the unbearable weight of the past and the monuments of Paris, the Menil Collection was born out of a completely different need. In Houston, a city without memory, the problem was one of imparting a sacred character to the museum" (Piano 1997, 74).

14. The museum in Ein Harod, designed by the little-known architect Samuel (Shmuel) Bickels, was in fact built in stages between 1948 and 1958.

15. Dominique de Menil, interview with the author, February 10, 1994, Houston. This directive has been repeated many times, for example, in Walter Hopps's introduction (1987, 12) to the Menil Collection catalogue.

16. The Menil Foundation insisted that "valuable heart [cypress] milled from South

Carolina trees up to 2,000 years old" be used for exterior cladding, rather than the cedar that is more conventionally used (Davey 1987, 37). Heart cypress is known for its notable resistance to decay, even in humid climates. As a further precaution against the effects of Houston's punishing climate, screws rather than nails were used to install the cladding. In fact, however, the cypress warped because of the manner in which it was milled—"plane sawn," cut parallel to the heart of the tree, rather than "vertical sawn"—and in 2001, the entire cladding was replaced with vertical-sawn cypress in a manner that retains the original appearance.

17. The Twombly Gallery, opened in 1995, is another of Dominique de Menil's projects; it is operated under the auspices of the Menil Collection. In it are installed works from the Menil Collection, in addition to works on long-term loan from the Dia Foundation and a number from Twombly's own collection.

18. By the time the museum site was being cleared for construction, the Menil Foundation owned virtually all of the houses, apartments, and businesses in the twenty-two-acre, nine-block area surrounding it. Da Camera was established with considerable support from the Menil Foundation and from Dominique de Menil herself. Its mission is not unlike that of the Menil Collection, insofar as it seeks to generate new audiences for classical music not through performing a popular repertoire, but through carefully curated programming that makes unexpected and productive juxtapositions of genres and periods.

19. Tenants in the early 1990s were already seeing a softening of this initial attention to ensuring the desired kind of resident, with waiting lists for housing beginning to operate with some predictability. But the modesty of the interior finishes was meant, tenants understood, to mitigate against an intrusion of resolutely bourgeois residents, in favor of a mix of somewhat lower-income intellectuals and artists.

20. Had Rothko lived to see the completion of the chapel, he would no doubt have made last-minute alterations to its design. As it was, the building was completed strictly in accordance with his instructions, though without the benefit of his having anticipated the light conditions in Houston, which were notably more intense and changeable than those Rothko was used to in his Manhattan studio. Dealing with the effects of the Houston sunlight continued to be a source of difficulty, and various modifications were undertaken in the years following the chapel's opening. In 1976, an adequate solution was reached with the installation of a baffle made to deflect natural light and reduce its level (see Barnes 1989).

21. In response to this comment, David Ross observed: "For a contemporary museum, I'd take the Menil any day—talk about natural light, and beautiful, clean spaces—it's fantastic. And yet it's not flashy, it has no glitz whatsoever. All you have are simple rooms with great walls and fantastic light" (quoted in Fried 2003, 133).

22. Stephen Fox pointed out to me that in the various presentations Piano has made on the Menil Collection project, he speaks almost exclusively on the ferro-cement leaves designed to filter light. Additionally, he might comment on the clapboard exterior, but it is as if all other aspects of the building took care of themselves.

23. Philip Fisher (1991) offers a provocative discussion of the relationship between contemporary art production and the practices of museum installation.

24. The air-conditioning plant is housed in a separate building some distance from the museum, but connected to it by an underground tunnel. All the building technology that might be considered a fire risk is located here, away from stored and displayed artworks. A quiet environment is achieved further through the absence of docents, audio-guides, and cash registers.

25. Steve McConathy, like Larry Young, the technical specialist, came to his position at the Menil Collection through his work with one of the contractors on the construction of the building. At a time when buildings were being knocked together at an extraordinary pace to meet the demand of the boom years in Houston, many contractors appreciated the opportunity to do a job well, without feeling pressured to cut corners, McConathy told me. As he describes it, the concealed aspects of the building, like the administrative and work areas, indicate the same level of care that is apparent in the public spaces; the wiring, he pointed out with evident pleasure, is laid in unusually straight lines.

CHAPTER 7

1. Hazlitt goes further, arguing that this kind of vicarious possession is to be desired in preference to mere ownership, since ownership confines one to a limited array of objects, whereas possession carries no such limitation: "It is not we who should envy them … but they who should envy us the true and exclusive enjoyment of it" (Hazlitt 1991, 194).

2. Jeremy Braddock, "Neurotic Cities: Barnes in Philadelphia," Art Journal 63, no. 4: 46–61.

3. I quote here from Davezac's unpublished translation of his essay (Menil Archives).

4. This idea of museums representing art history is somewhat spurious, since museums are key participants in the definition and constitution of art history itself.

5. See, for example, the articles and books by Clifford (1988), Donato (1979), Duncan and Wallach (1980), Pomian (1990), and Stewart (1993).

6. This imperative to defer completion is not just to ensure that the collector has a passion that will impel her through each day; it rests on the more existential rendering of the collection as a surrogate self. This formulation has become basic to contemporary theorization of collecting.

7. In discussions concerning the gendered character of processes of self-constitution, a unified self is typically characterized as the prize of male privilege. It is clear, however, that such easy dichotomies do not stand up in the face of the crosscutting privilege of class. The resources that Dominique de Menil was able to bring to bear on her projects of self-fashioning rendered her gender more or less inconsequential in this regard. But this privilege is suppressed in the Menil Collection, since, as Julie Taylor told me, "Art is incandescent, and when the flame burns, it burns away difference."

8. While Bourdieu attributes the term "stylization of life" to Max Weber, Bourdieu's formulation of it owes considerably more to his own project than to Weber's. The stylization of life is richly illustrated in an account by Dominique de Menil's granddaughter, Taya Allison, of how the sensibilities of her aunt and uncle, Lois and Georges de Menil, differ from those of other family members: "When Georges and Lois moved to Paris, they started using the de Menil family house in the country on weekends, and Lois redecorated it, in *her* style, which was *not* everyone else's style. What's the difference? Well, when my grandfather was near the end of his life, he gave Georges and Lois a Matisse cutout, and she went to Pierre Deux and found this print fabric in the same colors and had their whole living room in New York done in it. That's not something my mother or Aunt Adelaide or Uncle François would do" (quoted in Colacello 1996, 199).

9. Dominique de Menil continued to make acquisitions, but in 1985 she was carrying the financial burden of the museum's construction in the midst of the collapse of the price of oil, an economic shock that reverberated throughout Houston's philanthropic community and brought about a precipitous fall in the value of the Menil Foundation's Schlumberger holdings and of her personal stock. It was hardly a felicitous moment for a major acquisition.

10. These comments were made by Dominique de Menil in her speech at the opening of the Byzantine Fresco Chapel in 1997.

11. The Menil Foundation is reported to have spent $900,000 to purchase and restore the frescoes (Johnson 1988b).

12. This loan period has since been extended, and is now often described as indefinite. Certainly it was recognized that fund-raising for the chapel project could not proceed successfully unless a favorable loan agreement was worked out. Whatever the formal terms of the agreement, the consensus among Menil personnel is that repatriation would be inappropriate before political stability is restored to the region.

13. It should be noted, however, that reaching a huge number of viewers has never been a priority at the Menil Collection, though making works available to the public rather than having them sequestered in a private collection was, of course, a key concern.

14. For many at the symposium, Michener's rational approach rendered him ineligible as a collector. For them, passion—the passion to possess—was what distinguished their practice and, moreover, was its central source of virtue. Commonly, among collectors, this desire is articulated as the degree to which one is willing, or driven, to sacrifice in order to assuage it. And herein lies its virtue: it demands that one relinquish more than can be given up without regret, thereby becoming a sign of transcendence over mere practicality. This is suggestive of Georg Simmel's characterization of value, wherein value expresses both the distance between desire and its object, and the level of sacrifice undertaken in order to bridge it (Simmel 1978). Dominique de Menil commented, "Everything is always too expensive. Even in those days when great paintings cost a hundredth of what they do now, it seemed especially expensive. You have to be spellbound. It has to mean so much that you are unreasonable" (quoted in Johnston 1971, 6).

15. He assembled 163 books and articles about American art, cataloguing and cross-

referencing the material therein, thereby gaining a fully documented sense of what every major art writer and critic had to say about all the major American artworks. He then prepared lists of what, in light of his research, he had come to consider the top six representational painters, the top six abstractionists, and so on, with all others ranked in relation to these. He established an annual budget that constrained him from paying more than $5,000 for any individual piece. He would not, he made clear, be driven by passion. Within a decade, he had assembled a 300-piece survey of American painting, with a concentration on New York School abstract painters, who were still working at the time he was collecting (and whose work was still modestly priced). Less than ten years after beginning the process, he had identified the University of Texas at Austin as a culturally impoverished and therefore suitable recipient. In Michener's residences there was no art.

Ironically, given the general outrage at his being described as a collector, the symposium at which this material was presented was "The Art of Collecting Art: A Symposium in Honor of James A. Michener," sponsored by the Art Department of Swarthmore College and the William J. Cooper Foundation in collaboration with the James A. Michener Art Museum, in Doylestown, Pennsylvania (a museum not of his collection, but of his personal effects and the local art of Pennsylvania). Bruce Katsiff (1993) presented material on Michener.

16. As Philip Fisher has pointed out, a very powerful formulation of art as history was established by Clement Greenberg, though Greenberg was no doubt an unlikely ally of Michener. In Greenberg's *Art and Culture* (1961), the history of art takes precedence over the individual object: "What Greenberg provides is a way of immediately valuing an art object in terms of its potential future as part of a museum collection. The goal of the artist is to design a work that is inevitable to what the future will see as the order of the past" (Fisher 1991, 170). Dominique de Menil's approach had much more in common with that of Greenberg's contemporary, Meyer Schapiro, who, in posing modern art in opposition to mass production, sought to valorize its authentic singularity (see the works by Fisher [1991] and Schapiro [1978]). While Greenberg, like the de Menils, was engaged in the intellectual labor of making contemporary art arresting, it is not only his transposition of the contemporary as history but also the naked instrumentalism of his formulation that makes it so antagonistic to the experimental enthusiasms of the de Menils.

17. To maintain this commitment, Hopps pointed out, and in keeping with the Menil's characteristically fastidious attention to the maintenance of moral authority through symbolic details of this sort, the lettering naming the Menil Collection was applied to the outside of the glass and not the inside.

18. The galleries, the largest of which is eighty by eighty feet, are designed on a twenty-by-forty-foot module that echoes, Stephen Fox observed, the dimensions of Dominique de Menil's living room in her Philip Johnson–designed home. Another echo of Johnson can be identified, perhaps, in the expression of the steel frame on the exterior of the building, in a manner similar to that followed by Johnson at the University of St. Thomas. Some of the galleries have conventional ceilings to accommodate exhibitions requiring artificial lighting or significantly reduced light levels. Menil Collection personnel justify

the higher than recommended light levels throughout the museum on the grounds that since only about 5 percent of the collection is on display at any time, works will be routinely rotated into dark storage conditions, thus limiting their exposure.

19. Here, Fisher refers to the classicist Johann Winckelmann, who, in the mid-eighteenth century, developed a linear history of Greek art, on the basis of which he systematically arranged the antiquities in the Villa Albani by subject, "placing goddesses, emperors, and tragic reliefs together" (Fisher 1991, 8).

20. The Guggenheim Museum begins to take on the features of the art book that Malraux proposes, though the book goes one step further than the museum because it dematerializes the object: "In our museum without walls, picture, fresco, miniature, and stained glass window seem of one and the same family. For all alike . . . have become 'colorplates.' In the process they have lost their properties as *objects*, but, by the same token, they have gained something: the utmost significance as to style that they can possibly acquire" (Malraux 1967, 44). But as Fisher points out, no matter how important the art book has been, it has not been nearly so decisive as museums themselves in informing what artworks look like. Indeed, "in terms of the art book, modern works are naïve objects, unconscious of the fact that they will be produced in roughly 8" by 10" format" (Fisher 1991, 24). Certainly modern art works do not seem as preoccupied with their future as color plates as they do with their candidacy as museum objects, scaled as they are to commandeer the vast spaces of the museum.

21. The "MacAgy rule" is "fifty-six inches from the floor to the center of the painting, for works of moderate size" (Tomkins 1991, 37).

22. Dominique de Menil, handwritten notes for a talk to a group of Bill Jordon's students at Rice University, October 15, 1976 (Menil Archives).

23. Ibid.

24. Memo (dated February 26, 1974) of a meeting held January 31, 1974, with Louis Kahn, Dominique de Menil, and Simone Swan (Kahn file, Menil Archives).

CHAPTER 8

The epigraph to this chapter is taken from Dominique de Menil's address at the opening of "Spirituality in the Christian East: Greek, Slavic, and Russian Icons from the Menil Collection," an exhibition that ran November 12, 1988–June 4, 1989.

1. The need to make the treasure house visible was noted by the designers as one of the earliest specifications for the museum. See the article by members of the design team (Barker, Guthrie, Noble, and Rice [1983]).

2. At the time of my early research, conservation was staffed by two professional conservators, both of whom have excellent reputations in their areas of expertise (painting and works on paper), as well as by a third conservator (a different Mellon Fellow annually), a framer, and one person providing secretarial support.

3. See the study by Altshuler (2005).

4. Peter Burger (1984) identifies avant-garde tendencies with anti-aesthetic ones. But the avant-garde impulses that I am thinking of here are those that, for all their more or less radical critique of "high art," seek not to demystify art (though they may seek to demystify the power relations of the art world), but to recuperate a more pure form of it, liberated from a perceived cynicism born out of art's entanglements with commodity culture. In the language of difficulty and commitment that typifies much avant-garde discourse can be read the desire for, and the claim to, a more virtuous, exemplary relation to art—indeed, a more seamlessly mystified relation than has been sustained in the conventional sphere of art world operations.

5. See the studies by McCole (1993) and Wolin (1994) for rich exegeses of Benjamin's various invocations of the term, and the one by Foster (1993) for a characterization that has particularly strong resonances here. Robert's Kaufman's work (2002) on the critical dimension of aura has been central here.

6. "Islands Beyond" was installed at the University of St. Thomas from October 2 through October 19, 1958.

7. Flahiff's privileging of "intuitive" intellect over other modes of experience expresses St. Thomas's articulation of the hierarchy of faculties, wherein intellect (not to be confused with learning or reason) reigns supreme. Dominique de Menil also subscribed to this Catholic valorization of the intellect. But the notion of intellect has significance also in terms of French class distinctions. It brackets off judgment as a facility with which one is blessed by birth. Judgment is thereby rendered beyond contention and beyond acquisition by education. Whether intellect is rendered as a faculty of the spirit or as a natural endowment, structural differences are effaced and personal distinction is foregrounded.

8. Hopps also identified Katherine Dreier, Alfred Barr, James Johnson Sweeney, René d'Harnoncourt, and Jermayne MacAgy as his other key predecessors in exhibition making.

9. Dominique de Menil, interview with the author, February 10, 1994, Houston.

10. Hopps curated "Robert Rauschenberg: A Retrospective," February 13–May 17, 1998; "Robert Rauschenberg: The Early 1950s," September 27, 1991–January 5, 1992; "Works on Paper by Jasper Johns, Robert Rauschenberg, and Larry Rivers," April 14, 1989–February 4, 1990.

11. It is perhaps noteworthy that I heard this objection expressed most often by personnel working in other museums. This is, no doubt, a function of the extent to which museum professionals are attuned to the politics of audience, but in some articulations, it seemed to betray resentment toward the Menil for its freedom from the kind of strictures under which their own institutions are obliged to operate.

12. It was organized by Intercultura, Fort Worth, and the Walters Art Gallery, Baltimore, in association with the Institute of Ethiopian Studies, Addis Ababa University, in 1993, and was shown at the Menil Collection from April 28 to July 31, 1994. The Menil Collection produced a brochure, "Guide to Galleries," as its own supplement to the official exhibition catalogue by Marilyn Heldman (1993).

13. WITS writers have settled on a policy of resisting the impulse to seek art historical

background on the objects, for fear that this mode of understanding would inevitably seep into the way in which they would frame the objects for the children. Like Couturier and Dominique de Menil, they suspect that given half a chance, pedagogy will overwhelm poetry, and they are earnest in their efforts to avoid abetting this.

CHAPTER 9

1. At the time of her appointment as Menil Foundation president, Sarofim already had considerable experience in the governance of foundations. She is a past president and current board member of her family's Brown Foundation, which has long been a significant contributor to numerous Houston arts organizations. A past president and lifetime board member of the Houston Ballet Foundation, she has served on the boards of Da Camera and the Cullen Trust for the Performing Arts also.

2. This five-year grant was followed in 1999 by another five-year grant of $1.25 million from the renamed Wallace–Reader's Digest Funds.

3. Under the more entrepreneurial directorship of Ned Rifkin, some movement toward audience enlargement might have been evident, but it was muted by the brevity of his tenure and the continued authority of longtime Menil loyalists Walter Hopps, Bertrand Davezac, and Deborah Velders, the director of exhibitions.

4. As discussed earlier, this view is consistent with Maritain's integral humanism and Mounier's personalism.

5. The Metropolitan Museum of Art, for example, has operated its own Office of Research and Evaluation since 1988, and sociologists, following Pierre Bourdieu and Alain Darbel (1991), have conducted extensive demographic studies of museum audiences.

6. Philippa de Menil to John de Menil, n.d. (Menil Archives).

7. John de Menil to Philippa de Menil, August 10, 1970 (Menil Archives).

8. John de Menil, draft of a statement of purpose, July 27, 1970 (Menil Archives).

9. See the works by Bowker (1994) and Auletta (1983a).

10. For nonprofits and start-up businesses, the process of strategic planning and the practice of hiring a consultant to steer that process is prescribed as a key remedy for what is referred to as "founder's syndrome."

11. These include, as the news release for the exhibition notes, "1964's *Out of This World: An Exhibition of Fantastic Landscapes from the Renaissance to the Present*, and its thematic predecessor, *Visionary Architects: Boullée, Ledoux, Lequeu* (which explored drawings of unrealized structures from three of 18th-century France's notable architects whose careers all but vanished after the Revolution). It was during this period that Dominique de Menil was preparing an unrealized exhibition, *Dream Monuments*, a cross-cultural examination of monuments, ranging from the impossible and absurd to iconic landmarks such as the Eiffel Tower" (*Fall 2007–2008 Exhibition Schedule 2007*). The de Menil's research for these shows extended also into the work of contemporary artists "who were creating

large-scale works that would later be seen as part of the nascent 'Earth Art' or 'Land Art' movements." The news release continues: "They invited to Houston central figures such as Claes Oldenburg, Dennis Oppenheim, Michael Heizer, and Christo to imagine site-specific projects for Texas. As a result of these relationships, The Menil Collection is today rich in works that deal with the creation of hypothetical environmental projects, some of which will be on display in *Imaginary Spaces*."

12. Ferus is the focus of *The Cool School*, a documentary made by Morgan Neville for PBS's *Independent Lens* (2008). "Operating out of a small storefront, the gallery hosted debut exhibitions and served as a general launching point for Ed Kienholz, Ed Ruscha, Craig Kauffman, Wallace Berman, Ed Moses, and Robert Irwin, among many other artists. By the time it closed in 1966, the gallery had also played a role in solidifying the careers of many of New York's brightest talents, including Roy Lichtenstein, Andy Warhol, Donald Judd, Frank Stella, Robert Rauschenberg, and Jasper Johns" (http://www.pbs .org/independentlens/coolschool/film.html; accessed August 4, 2008).

13. Walter Hopps recounted this while explaining to me that it was not people's religious beliefs but their sensibilities that were of particular interest to Dominique.

14. Piano identifies Twombly rather than the Menil Foundation as the real client for this project, in recognition of the extent to which the Menil was willing to allow Twombly's wishes to prevail, much as it had done with Rothko and the chapel. It is this serious respect for the artist and the disposition of his work that enabled the Menil to become the recipient of such a significant gift from an artist, as Winkler told me.

15. This model did not suit all employees, however. One staff member of long standing who did not care to blur the boundaries between work and personal time felt John de Menil's disapproval as he watched her drive off to lunch each day.

16. "50 Years of Works on Paper," a major Twombly show that originated at the State Hermitage Museum in St. Petersburg, Russia, traveled to the Whitney Museum of American Art in New York and then to the Menil Collection.

17. Sirmans's resignation from the Menil Collection was announced in September 2009. He left the Menil to become department head and curator of contemporary art at the Los Angeles County Museum of Art.

18. This disquiet was intensified for some as a consequence of the incidental fact of their changed personal circumstances. Staff members who had been in their twenties when they worked at the Rice Museum had relished the excitement and camaraderie of working together through the night. By the time they were in their thirties and forties, the appeal of these eccentricities waned. They now resented being made to feel disloyal for wanting to get home to eat dinner with their children and help with their homework.

19. This problem of the public perception of wealth was exemplified for me by the recently appointed chief financial officer of the Menil Collection, who told me, with perhaps a little admiration, that more than one major museum had announced a reduction in hours of operation in order to generate the appearance of financial crisis and lay the groundwork for a successful endowment drive.

CHAPTER 10

1. This recounting of the event is a distillation of many versions, including those given in the media and those that circulate in the popular memory of Houstonians.

2. This is an understanding that Jay attributes to John Dewey, some of whose commitments to aesthetic experience bear a marked similarity to those of John and Dominique de Menil, though without the religious convictions that so powerfully animated their analysis.

Reference List

Adams, Lorraine. 2002. "Frame and Fortune." *Washington City Paper*, October 11–17. http://www.washingtoncitypaper.com/display.php?id=24747&utm_source=inform&utm_medium=lobox&utm_campaign=InformBox (accessed September 22, 2009).

Adorno, Theodor W. 1967. "Valéry Proust Museum." In *Prisms*, trans. Samuel and Shierry Weber, 173–186. Cambridge, Mass.: MIT Press.

Akston, Joseph James. 1971. Editorial. *Arts* 45 (May): 3.

Alberigo, Guiseppe, and Joseph A. Komonchak, eds. 1995–2006. *History of Vatican II.* Vols. 1–5. Trans. Matthew J. O'Connell. Maryknoll, N.Y.: Orbis.

Alexander, E. P. 1983. *Museum Masters: Their Museums and Their Influence.* Nashville, Tenn.: American Association for State and Local History.

Allaud, Louis, and Maurice Martin. 1977. *Schlumberger: The History of a Technique.* New York: Wiley.

Alsop, Joseph. 1982. *The Rare Art Traditions: The History of Art Collecting and Its Linked Phenomena Wherever These Have Appeared.* New York: Harper and Row.

Altshuler, Bruce, ed. 2005. *Collecting the New.* Princeton, N.J.: Princeton Univ. Press.

Amato, Joseph. 1975. *Mounier and Maritain: A French Catholic Understanding of the Modern World.* Tuscaloosa: Univ. of Alabama Press.

Asad, Talal. 2003. *Formations of the Secular: Christianity, Islam, Modernity.* Stanford, Calif.: Stanford Univ. Press.

Auletta, Ken. 1983a. "Profiles: A Certain Poetry—1," *New Yorker*, June 6. 46–49, 102–109.

———. 1983b. "Profiles: A Certain Poetry—2," *New Yorker*, June 12, 50–91.

Bal, Mieke. 1996. *Double Exposures: The Practice of Cultural Analysis.* New York: Routledge.

Barker, Tom, Alistair Guthrie, Neil Noble, and Peter Rice. 1983. "The Menil Collection, Texas," *Arup Journal* 18 (April): 2–7.

Barnes, Susan J. 1989. *The Rothko Chapel: An Act of Faith.* Houston: The Rothko Chapel.

Barratt, Anthony. 2006. "Interpreting Vatican II Forty Years On: A Case Of Caveat Lector." *Heythrop Journal* 47, no. 1: 75–96.

Battaglia, Debbora. 1995. "Problematizing the Self: A Thematic Introduction." In *Rhetorics of Self-Making*, ed. Battaglia, 1–15. Berkeley and Los Angeles: Univ. of California Press.

Baudrillard, Jean. 1972. *For a Political Economy of the Sign.* Trans. Charles Levin. St. Louis: Telos.

———. 1996. *The System of Objects.* Trans. James Benedict. New York: Verso.

Bazin, Germain. 1967. *The Museum Age.* Trans. Jane van Nuis Cahill. New York: Universal.

Beauchamp, Toni. 1983. *James Johnson Sweeney and the Museum of Fine Arts, Houston: 1961–1967.* Master's thesis, Univ. of Texas at Austin.

Bellah, R. N., R. Madsen, W. M. Sullivan, A. Swidler, and S. M. Tipton. 1985. *Habits of the Heart: Individualism and Commitment in American Life*. Berkeley and Los Angeles: Univ. of California Press.

Benjamin, Walter. 1973. *Charles Baudelaire: A Lyric Poet in the Era of High Capitalism*. Trans. Harry Zohn. Cambridge, Mass.: Harvard Univ. Press.

———. 1979. "Eduard Fuchs, Collector and Historian." In *One-Way Street and Other Writings*, trans. Kingsley Shorter. London: New Left Books.

———. 1982a. "The Work of Art in the Age of Mechanical Reproduction." In *Illuminations*, trans. Harry Zohn, 219–253. Suffolk, UK: Fontana.

———. 1982b. "On Some Motifs in Baudelaire." In *Illuminations*, trans. Harry Zohn, 157–202. Suffolk, UK: Fontana.

———. 1982c. "Unpacking My Library." In *Illuminations*, trans. Harry Zohn, 59–67. Suffolk, UK: Fontana.

Bennett, Tony. 1995. *The Birth of the Museum: History, Theory, Politics*. New York: Routledge.

Berger, Maurice. 1990. "Are Art Museums Racist?" *Art in America* 78 (September), 68–78.

Berman, Russell. 1989. *Modern Culture and Critical Theory: Art, Politics, and the Legacy of the Frankfurt School*. Madison: Univ. of Wisconsin Press.

Bernier, Rosamond. 1987. "A Gift of Vision." *House and Garden*, July, 121–129.

"Best Foot Forward." 1952. Exhibition curated by Jermayne MacAgy. California Palace of the Legion of Honor, July–September.

Billot, Marcel, ed. 1993. *La Chapelle de Vence: Journal d'une creation / Henri Matisse, M.-A. Couturier, L.-B. Rayssiguier: textes établis et présentés par Marcel Billot: avant-propos de Dominique de Menil*. Paris: Cerf.

Blet, Pierre. 1981. "The Catholic Church of France." In *History of the Church*, volume 10: *The Church in the Modern Age*, ed. Hubert Jedin, 583–599. London: Burns and Oates.

Bois, Yve-Alain. 1985. "La Pensée Sauvage." *Art in America*, April, 178–189.

Born, Georgina. 1995. *Rationalizing Culture: IRCAM, Boulez, and the Institutionalization of the Musical Avant-Garde*. Berkeley and Los Angeles: Univ. of California Press.

Bourdieu, Pierre. 1968. "Outline of a Sociological Theory of Art Perception." *International Social Science Journal* 20: 589–612.

———. 1977. *Outline of a Theory of Practice*. Trans. Richard Nice. Cambridge: Cambridge Univ. Press.

———. 1984. *Distinction: A Social Critique of the Judgement of Taste*. Trans. Richard Nice. Cambridge, Mass.: Harvard Univ. Press.

———. 1987. "The Historical Genesis of a Pure Aesthetic." *Journal of Aesthetics and Art Criticism* 46: 201–210.

Bourdieu, Pierre, and Alain Darbel. 1991. *The Love of Art: European Art Museums and Their Public*. Cambridge: Polity Press.

Bowker, Geoffrey. 1994. *Science on the Run: Information Management and Industrial Geophysics at Schlumberger, 1920–1940*. Cambridge, Mass.: MIT Press.

Boym, Svetlana. 2001. *The Future of Nostalgia*. New York: Basic Books.

Braddock, Jeremy. 2004. "Neurotic Cities: Barnes in Philadelphia." *Art Journal* 63, no. 4: 46–61.

Brennan, Marcia, Alfred Pacquement, and Ann Temkin. 2007. *A Modern Patronage: De Menil Gifts to American and European Museums.* New Haven, Conn.: Yale Univ. Press / Menil Collection.

Brown, Julia, and Bridget Johnson, eds. 1983. *The First Show: Painting and Sculpture from Eight Collections, 1940–1980.* Los Angeles: Museum of Contemporary Art, Los Angeles, in association with Arts Publisher, Inc., New York.

Browning, Dominique. 1983. "What I Admire I Must Possess." *Texas Monthly,* April, 141–147, 192–209.

Buck-Morss, Susan. 1991. *The Dialectics of Seeing: Walter Benjamin and the Arcades Project.* Cambridge, Mass.: MIT Press.

Burger, Peter. 1984. *Theory of the Avant-Garde.* Minneapolis: Univ. of Minnesota Press.

Burnham, Sophy. 1973. *The Art Crowd.* New York: McKay.

Business Week. 1964. "Art Gets Its Own 'Mutual Fund.'" October 31, 30–31.

Butterfield, Jan. 1971. "The DeLuxe Show." *Texas Observer,* September 24.

Camille, Michael. 1994. "How New York Stole the Idea of Romanesque Art: Medieval, Modern, and Postmodern in Meyer Schapiro." *Oxford Art Journal* 17, no. 1: 65–74.

Carr, Annemarie Weyl, and Laurence J. Morrocco. 1991. *A Byzantine Masterpiece Recovered: The Thirteenth-Century Murals of Lysi, Cyprus.* Austin: Univ. of Texas Press / Menil Foundation.

Castenada, Terri. 1987. "Families and Foundations: Explorations in Philanthropy and Patronage as Dynastic Phenomena." Unpublished paper, Department of Anthropology, Rice University.

Chadwick, Susan. 1989. "Image, Finances Haunt Menil." *Houston Post,* May 11.

Clifford, James. 1985. "Histories of the Tribal and the Modern." *Art in America* 73 (April), 165–177, 215.

———. 1988. *The Predicament of Culture: Twentieth-Century Ethnography, Literature, and Art.* Cambridge, Mass.: Harvard Univ. Press.

———. 1997. *Routes: Travel and Translation in the Late Twentieth Century.* Cambridge, Mass.: Harvard Univ. Press.

Colacello, Bob. 1996. "Remains of the DIA." *Vanity Fair,* September, 173–174, 181–186, 191, 198–204.

Comenas, Gary. n.d. "Sunset (1967)." Warhol Filmography, http://www.warholstars.org/warhol/warhol1/warhol1f/sunset.html (accessed December 31, 2009).

Congar, Yves Marie Joseph. 1939. *Divided Christendom: Principles of a Catholic "Ecumenism."* London: Bles.

———. 1953. *The Catholic Church and the Race Question.* Paris: UNESCO.

———. 1988. *Fifty Years of Catholic Theology: Conversations with Yves Congar.* Trans. Bernard Lauret. London: SCM Press.

Conn, Steven. 2000. *Museums and American Intellectual Life, 1872–1926.* Chicago: Univ. of Chicago Press.

Coombs, Robert. 2000. *Mystical Themes in Le Corbusier's Architecture in the Chapel Notre-Dame-Du-Haut at Ronchamp: The Ronchamp Riddle.* Mellen Studies in Architecture, vol. 2. Lewistown, N.Y.: Mellen.

Couturier, Marie-Alain. 1951a. "Religious Art and the Modern Artist." *Magazine of Art* 45, no. 7 (November): 268–272.

———. 1951b. " A Note by Father Couturier." *Liturgical Arts,* February, 30–31.

———. 1984. *La Vérité Blessée.* Paris: Plon / Menil Foundation.

———. 1989. *Sacred Art.* Ed. Dominique de Menil and Pie Duployé. Trans. Granger Ryan. Austin: Univ. of Texas Press.

Crane, Diana. 1987. *The Transformation of the Avant-Garde: The New York Art World, 1940–1985.* Chicago: Univ. of Chicago Press.

Crimp, Douglas. 1993. *On the Museum's Ruins.* Cambridge, Mass.: MIT Press.

Cuno, James, ed. 2006. *Whose Muse? Art Museums and the Public Trust.* Princeton, N.J.: Princeton Univ. Press.

Danto, Arthur. 1984. "Defective Affinities: 'Primitivism' in 20th Century Art." *Nation,* December 1, 590–592.

Davey, Peter. 1987. "Menil Museum." *Architectural Review* 181, no. 1081 (March): 36–42.

Davezac, Bertrand. 1984. "La transparence de l'Histoire." In *La Rime et la Raison: Les Collections Ménil,* 18–21. Catalogue for the exhibition organized by the Menil Foundation at Galeries nationales du Grand Palais, Paris, April 17–July 30, 1984. Paris: Éditions de la Réunion des museés nationaux.

Davis, Douglas. 1990. *The Museum Transformed: Design and Culture in the Post-Pompidou Age.* New York: Abbeville.

Davis, George. 1972. "The DeLuxe Show." *Art and Artists* 6 (February): 14.

Debord, Guy. 1994. *The Society of the Spectacle.* Trans. Donald Nicholson-Smith. New York: Zone.

The DeLuxe Show. 1971. Published in conjunction with the exhibition "The DeLuxe Show," organized by the Menil Foundation and shown at the De Luxe Theater, Houston, August 15–September 12. Houston: Menil Foundation.

Devisse, Jean, and M. Mollat. 1979. *The Image of the Black in Western Art,* vol. 2: *From the Early Christian Era to the "Age of Discovery."* Houston: Menil Foundation.

DiMaggio, Paul. 1982. "Cultural Entrepreneurship in Nineteenth-Century Boston: The Creation of an Organizational Base for High Culture in America." *Media, Culture, and Society* 4: 33–50.

Doering, Bernard. 1983. *Jacques Maritain and the French Catholic Intellectuals.* Notre Dame, Ind.: Univ. of Notre Dame Press.

Domenach, Jean-Marie, and Robert de Montvalon. 1967. *The Catholic Avant-Garde: French Catholicism since World War II.* New York: Holt, Rinehart and Winston.

Donato, Eugenio. 1979. "The Museum's Furnace: Notes Toward a Contextual Reading of *Bouvard and Pécuchet.*" In *Textual Strategies: Perspectives in Post-Structuralist Criticism,* ed. Josué V. Harari, 213–238. Ithaca, N.Y.: Cornell Univ. Press.

Douaire, J. R. 1951. "Pilgrimage to Assy: An Appraisal." *Liturgical Arts,* February, 28–30.

Dubin, Steven. 2006. Transforming Museums: Mounting Queen Victoria in a Democratic South Africa. New York: Palgrave Macmillan.

Duncan, Carol. 1991. "Art Museums and the Ritual of Citizenship." In *Exhibiting Cultures: The Poetics and Politics of Museum Display*, ed. Ivan Karp and Steven D. Levine, 88–102. Washington, D.C.: Smithsonian Institution Press.

Duncan, Carol, and Alan Wallach. 1980. "The Universal Survey Museum." *Art History* 3, no. 4: 447–469.

Fall 2007–2008 Exhibition Schedule. 2007. http://www.menil.org/exhibitions/past.php (accessed February 28, 2010).

Farelly, E. M. 1987. "Piano Practice." *Architectural Review* 181, no. 1081 (March): 32–35.

Faubion, James D. 1993. *Modern Greek Lessons: A Primer in Historical Constructivism*. Princeton, N.J.: Princeton Univ. Press.

———. 2001. "Toward an Anthropology of Ethics: Foucault and the Pedagogies of Autopoiesis." *Representations* 74 (Spring): 83–104.

———. n.d. "An Ethics of Composure." In *What Becomes a Subject: An Anthropology of Ethics*, 123–213. Forthcoming.

Feldman, Morton. 1973. "Obituary for John de Menil." *Art in America*, November–December, 19.

Feldstein, Martin, ed. 1991. *The Economics of Art Museums*. Chicago: Univ. of Chicago Press.

Ferraro, Thomas, ed. 1997. *Catholic Lives, Contemporary America*. Durham, N.C.: Duke Univ. Press.

Fisher, Phillip. 1991. *Making and Effacing Art: Modern American Art in a Culture of Museums*. New York: Oxford Univ. Press.

Flahiff, G. B. 1959. Foreword to *Islands Beyond*. Catalogue of an exhibition at the University of St. Thomas, Houston, October 2–19, 1958. Houston: University of St. Thomas.

Fogarty, Michael F. 1957. *Christian Democracy in Western Europe, 1820–1953*. Notre Dame, Ind.: Univ. of Notre Dame Press.

Foster, Hal. 1985. *Recodings: Art, Spectacle, Cultural Politics*. Port Townsend, Wash.: Bay Press.

———. 1993. *Compulsive Beauty*. Cambridge, Mass.: MIT Press.

Foucault, Michel. 1994. "What Is Enlightenment?" In *Essential Works of Michel Foucault*, vol. 1: *Ethics: Subjectivity and Truth*, trans. Robert Hurley, 303–319. New York: New Press.

Fox, Stephen. 1999. "Unpublished Report to the National Historic Places Trust in support of the Inclusion of the Rothko Chapel on the National Register."

———. 2005. "Visionary Builders: Dominique and John de Menil as Architectural Patrons." Lecture presented as part of the Rothko Chapel's Art Series "Images of the Seen and Not-Seen: Search for Understanding," Rothko Chapel, May 10.

Francis, Richard, ed. 1996. *Negotiating Rapture: The Power of Art to Transform Lives*. Chicago: Museum of Contemporary Art.

Freedberg, David. 1989. *The Power of Images: Studies in the History and Theory of Response.* Chicago: Univ. of Chicago Press.

Fried, Michael. 1965. *Three American Painters: Kenneth Noland, Jules Olitski, Frank Stella.* Cambridge, Mass.: Fogg Art Museum.

———. 2003. "Is This an Age of Museums? Session 1: Panel Discussion." *Salmagundi* 139–140 (Summer–Fall): 112–139.

Geeslin, Campbell. 1965. "Museum Buys 12 Sculptures by Swiss Artist." *Houston Post,* February 25.

Gell, Alfred. 1992. "The Technology of Enchantment and the Enchantment of Technology." In *Anthropology, Art, Aesthetics,* ed. Jeremy Coote and Anthony Shelton, 40–66. Oxford: Oxford Univ. Press.

Glueck, Grace. 1986. "The de Menil Family: The Medici of Modern Art." *New York Times Magazine,* May 18, 28–46, 66, 106, 113.

———. 1989. "Menil Collection Seeks $35 Million," *New York Times,* May 29.

Goffman, Erving. 1959. *The Presentation of Self in Everyday Life.* Garden City, New York: Doubleday.

Gray, Lisa. 1993. "Bad Walter, Good Walter." *Houston Metropolitan,* October, 42–45, 105–107.

Greenberg, Clement. 1967. *Art and Culture.* New York: Beacon.

Greenberg, Reesa, Bruce W. Ferguson, and Sandy Nairne, eds. 1996. *Thinking about Exhibitions.* New York: Routledge.

Greenblatt, Steven. 1980. *Renaissance Self-Fashioning: From Moore to Shakespeare.* Chicago: Univ. of Chicago Press.

———. 1991. "Resonance and Wonder." In *Exhibiting Culture: The Poetics and Politics of Museum Display,* ed. Ivan Karp and Steven D. Lavine, 42–56. Washington, D.C.: Smithsonian Institution Press.

Greenfeld, Liah. 1992. *Nationalism: Five Roads to Modernity.* Cambridge, Mass.: Harvard Univ. Press.

Guilbaut, Serge. 1983. *How New York Stole the Idea of Modern Art.* Trans. Arthur Goldhammer. Chicago: Univ. of Chicago Press.

Handler, Richard. 1987. *Nationalism and the Politics of Culture in Quebec.* Madison: Univ. of Wisconsin Press.

Harris, Neil. 1962. "The Gilded Age Revisited: Boston and the Museum Movement." *American Quarterly* 14: 545–566.

———. 1978. "Museums, Merchandising and Popular Taste: The Struggle for Influence." In *Material Culture and the Study of American Life,* ed. I. M. G. Quimby, 160–178. New York: Norton.

———. 1990. *Cultural Excursions: Marketing Appetites and Cultural Tastes in Modern America.* Chicago: Univ. of Chicago Press.

Hazlitt, William. 1991. "On Personal Identity." In *Selected Writings,* 190–201. New York: Oxford Univ. Press. (Orig. pub. 1828.)

Heinich, N. 1988. "The Pompidou Center and its Public: The Limits of a Utopian Style."

In *The Museum Time-Machine: Putting Cultures on Display*, ed. Robert Lumley, 197–210. London: Routledge.

Heldman, Marilyn. 1993. *African Zion: The Sacred Art of Ethiopia*. Ed. Roderick Grierson. New Haven, Conn.: Yale Univ. Press.

Hervieu-Léger, Danièle. 2000. *Religion as a Chain of Memory*. New Brunswick, N.J.: Rutgers Univ. Press.

Holdengräber, Paul. 1992. "Between the Profane and the Redemptive: The Collector as Possessor in Walter Benjamin's *Passagen-Werk*." *History and Memory* 4, no. 2 (Fall–Winter): 96–128.

———. 1995. "Portrait of the Artist as Collector: Walter Benjamin and the Collector's Struggle against Dispersion." PhD diss., Princeton Univ.

Holmes, Ann. 1959a. "Speculation in Art Circles." *Houston Chronicle*, January 23.

———. 1959b. "Primitive Art on Show." *Houston Chronicle*, February 27.

———. 1965. "Museum Buys Mechanical Sculpture." *Houston Chronicle*, February 5.

———. 1968a. "Dominique de Menil: A New Kind of Patroness in a Changing Art Scene." *Houston Chronicle*, May 26.

———. 1968b. "One to Grow On: St. Thomas' Art, a Collection with a Difference." *Houston Chronicle*, November 10, *Zest*, 12–14.

———. 1970. "A Law unto Themselves: John and Dominique de Menil." *ARTgallery Magazine* 13, no. 8 (May): 35.

———. 1972. "Decisions and Art Specialists." *Houston Chronicle*, November 9.

———. 1991. "Dominique." *Town and Country*, September, 197, 228–230.

Holmes, Douglas. 2009. "Economy of Words." *Cultural Anthropology* 24, no. 3: 381–419.

Honour, Hugh. 1989. *The Image of the Black in Western Art*, vol. 4: *From the American Revolution to World War I*. Cambridge, Mass.: Harvard Univ. Press.

Hooper-Greenhill, Eilean. 1992. *Museums and the Shaping of Knowledge*. New York: Routledge.

Hopps, Walter. 1984. "Les Collections Ménil et la Présent Exposition." In *La Rime et La Raison*, ed. Walter Hopps, 13–17. Paris: Édition de la Réunion des Musées Nationaux.

———. 1987. Introduction to *The Menil Collection: A Selection from the Paleolithic to the Modern Era*, 9–13. New York: Abrams.

———. 1996. "Walter Hopps Hopps Hopps." Interview by Hans-Ulrich Obrist. *Artforum International* 34, no. 6: 60–63, 98, 101, 104, 106.

Houston Post. 1968. "Modern Art Collectors." November 3.

Houston Press. 1961. "New Director for Fine Arts Museum." January 10.

Howard, M. 1988. "The Menil Collection." *Gettysburg Review* 1, no. 1 (Winter): 64–68.

Hughes, Robert. 1987. "How to Start a Museum: Three U.S. Collections Go Public, With Mixed Results." *Time*, August 10, 46–48.

Hulten, K. G. Pontus. 1968. *The Machine as Seen at the End of the Mechanical Age*. New York: Museum of Modern Art.

Huyssen, Andreas. 1986. *After the Great Divide: Modernism, Mass Culture, Postmodernism*. Bloomington: Indiana Univ. Press.

Ibish, Yusuf, and Ileana Marculescu, eds. 1978. *Contemplation and Action in World Religions.* Seattle: Univ. of Washington Press.

Ingersoll, Richard. 1987. "Pianissimo: The Very Quiet Collection." *Texas Architect,* May–June, 40–46.

———. 1989. "New Texas Art Museums and Sectional Space." Paper presented at the College Art Association Annual Meeting, San Francisco, February 18.

Jay, Martin. 2003. "Drifting into Dangerous Waters." In *Aesthetic Subjects,* ed. Pamela Matthews and David McWhirter, 3–27. Minneapolis: Univ. of Minnesota Press.

———. 2005. *Songs of Experience: Modern American and European Variations on a Universal Theme.* Berkeley and Los Angeles: Univ. of California Press.

Jermayne MacAgy: A Life Illustrated by an Exhibition. 1968. Catalogue for an exhibition at the University of St. Thomas, Houston, November 1968–January 1969. Houston: University of St. Thomas.

Johnson, Patricia. 1988a. "Byzantine Icons at Menil Colorful Collection of Celestial Images." *Houston Chronicle.* November 13, Zest, 16–17, 29.

———. 1988b. "Two Byzantine Frescoes Safe and Sound in Houston." *Houston Chronicle,* December 22.

———. 1990. "Dominique De Menil's Passion for Art: Menil Collection the Fruit of a Lifetime of Learning, Collecting, Caring." *Houston Chronicle,* July 29, Zest, 8.

———. 1992. "Great Art, No Hype: The Menil Moves at Its Own Pace." *Houston Chronicle,* June 7, Zest, 12–13.

———. 1993. "Designs on the Future." *Houston Chronicle,* October 7.

———. 1995. "Menil's Barnes Resigns Post After 10-Month Association." *Houston Chronicle,* August 18.

Johnston, Marguerite. 1971. "The Institute for the Arts Comes to Rice." *Rice University Review* 6 (Summer): 6–11.

———. 1977. "The de Menils," *Houston Post,* January 9.

John XXIII. 1961. *Mater et Magistra.* Rome: Acta Apostolicae Sedis.

———. 1963. *Pacem in terris.* Rome: Acta Apostolicae Sedis.

Kalil, Susie. 1993. "The Quiet Eye." *Houston Press,* September 2.

———. 1995. "Cooperate—or Die?" *Houston Press,* February 9.

Kant, Immanuel. 1951. *Critique of Judgment.* Trans. J. H. Bernard. New York: Hafner. (Orig. pub. 1790.)

Karageorghis, Vassos. 1988. *Blacks in Ancient Cypriot Art.* Houston: Menil Foundation.

Karp, Ivan. 1992. "On Civil Society and Social Identity." In *Museums and Communities: The Politics of Public Culture,* ed. Ivan Karp, Christine Mullen Kreamer, and Steven D. Lavine, 19–33. Washington, D.C.: Smithsonian Institution Press.

Karp, Ivan, Corinne Kratz, Lynn Szwaja, and Tomás Ybarra-Fausto, eds. 2006. *Museum Frictions: Public Cultures/Global Transformations.* Durham, N.C.: Duke Univ. Press.

Karp, Ivan, and Stephen Lavine, eds. 1991. *Exhibiting Cultures: The Poetics and Politics of Museum Display.* Washington, D.C.: Smithsonian Institution Press.

Katsiff, Bruce. 1993. "James A. Michener as a Collector." Paper presented at "The Art of

Collecting Art: A Symposium in Honor of James A. Michener," sponsored by the Art Department of Swarthmore College and the William J. Cooper Foundation, Swarthmore, Pennsylvania.

Kaufman, Jason Edward. 2002. "Renzo Piano: The World's Leading Builder of Museums." *Art Newspaper*. Available at http://mail.architexturez.net/+/Design-L.V1/archive/msg21617.shtml (accessed February 28, 2010).

Kaufman, Robert. 2002. "Aura, Still." *October* 99 (Winter): 45–80.

Kernan, Julie. 1975. *Our Friend, Jacques Maritain: A Personal Memoir*. New York: Doubleday.

Kirshenblatt-Gimblett, Barbara. 1998. *Destination Culture: Tourism, Museums, Heritage*. Berkeley and Los Angeles: Univ. of California Press.

Krauss, Rosalind E. 1994. *The Optical Unconscious*. Cambridge, Mass.: MIT Press.

Kuh, Katherine, and Daniel Catton Rich. 1949. *Twentieth Century Art: From the Louise and Walter Arensberg Collection*. Chicago: Art Institute of Chicago.

Langdon, Gabrielle. 1988. "'A Spiritual Space': Matisse's Chapel of the Dominicans at Vence." *Zeitschrift für Kunstgeschichte* 51, no. 4: 542–573.

Lauret, Bernard, ed. 1988. *Fifty Years of Catholic Theology: Conversations with Yves Congar*. Trans. John Bowden. London: SCM Press.

Lavine, Steven. 1992. "Audience, Ownership, and Authority: Designing Relationships Between Museums and Communities." In *Museums and Communities: The Politics of Public Culture*, ed. Ivan Karp, Christine Mullen Kreamer, and Steven D. Lavine, 137–157. Washington, D.C.: Smithsonian Institution Press.

Léger, Fernand. 1950. "Entre Giotto et nous, je ne vois rien." *L'Art Sacré*, July–August: 25.

Léger, Our Contemporary. 1978. Catalogue of the exhibition, organized by the Rice University Institute for the Arts, Rice Museum, Houston, April 14–June 11.

Leo XIII. 1891. *Rerum novarum*. Rome: Acta Apotolicae Sedis.

Le Thierry d'Ennequin, Benoît. 2001. "La machine à lumière d'Ein Harod." *AMC: Le Moniteur Architecture*, October, 106–113. English translation as "Sophisticated Lighting at the Museum of Art, Ein Harod." http://www.museumeinharod.org.il/english/about/articles/sophisticated_lighting.html (accessed July 9, 2008).

Lévi-Strauss, Claude. 1985. "New York in 1941." In *The View From Afar*, 258–267. New York: Basic Books.

Levi Strauss, David. 2007. "The Bias of the World: Curating after Szeemann and Hopps." In *Cautionary Tales: Critical Curating*, ed. Steven Rand and Heather Kouris, 15–25. New York: Apexart.

Louchheim, Aline. 1953. "Diverse Museums." *New York Times*, December 27.

Loud, Patricia Cummings. 1989. *The Art Museums of Louis I. Kahn*. Durham, N.C.: Duke Univ. Press.

Lukács, Georg. 1971. *The Theory of the Novel*. Trans. A. Bostock. Cambridge, Mass.: MIT Press.

Luke, Timothy W. 1992. *Shows of Force: Power, Politics, and Ideology in Art Exhibitions*. Durham, N.C.: Duke Univ. Press.

MacAgy, Jermayne. 1953. *Bulletin of the California Palace of the Legion of Honor* 2, nos. 1–2 (May–June).

MacDonald, Sharon. 2002. *Behind the Scenes at the Science Museum.* New York: Berg.

The Machine as Seen at the End of the Mechanical Age. 1968. Catalogue of the exhibition mounted by the Museum of Modern Art, shown at the Museum of Modern Art, November 1968–February 1969; Rice Art Museum, March–May, 1969; and San Francisco Museum of Art, June–August, 1969. New York: Museum of Modern Art.

MacPherson, C. B. 1962. *The Political Theory of Possessive Individualism.* Oxford: Oxford Univ. Press.

Mahmood, Saba. 2005. *Politics of Piety: The Islamic Revival and the Feminist Subject.* Princeton, N.J.: Princeton Univ. Press.

Maleuvre, Didier. 1999. *Museum Memories: History, Technology, Art.* Stanford, Calif.: Stanford Univ. Press.

Malraux, André. 1967. "A Museum Without Walls." In *Voices of Silence,* 13–129. Trans. Stuart Gilbert. Garden City, N.Y.: Doubleday.

Marcus, George E. 1983. "The Fiduciary Role in American Family Dynasties and Their Institutional Legacy." In *Elites: Ethnographic Issues,* ed. George E. Marcus, 221–256. Albuquerque: Univ. of New Mexico Press.

———. 1992. *Lives in Trust: The Fortunes of Dynastic Families in Late Twentieth-Century America.* Boulder, Colo.: Westview.

Matisse, Henri, M.-A. Couturier, and L.-B. Rayssiguier. 1999. *The Vence Chapel: The Archive of a Creation.* Houston: Menil Foundation, Skira.

McAuliffe, Mary. 1987. "The Erasure of Canopy: Spatial Definition at the Menil Museum." *Crit* 19 (Winter): 32–37.

McClellan, Andrew. 1994. *Inventing the Louvre: Art, Politics, and the Origins of the Modern Museum in Eighteenth-Century Paris.* Cambridge: Cambridge Univ. Press.

———. 2008. *The Art Museum: From Boullee to Bilbao.* Berkeley: University of California Press.

———, ed. 2003. *Art and Its Publics: Museum Studies at the Millennium.* Malden, Mass.: Blackwell.

McCole, John. 1993. *Walter Benjamin and the Antinomies of Tradition.* Ithaca, N.Y.: Cornell Univ. Press.

McEvilley, Thomas. 1984. "Doctor Lawyer Indian Chief: Primitivism in Twentieth-Century Art at the Museum of Modern Art." *Artforum* 23, no. 3 (November): 54–61.

———. 1985a. Letter to the editor. *Artforum* 23, no. 6 (February): 46–51.

———. 1985b. Letter to the editor. *Artforum* 23, no. 9 (May): 65–71.

Menil, Dominique de. 1959. Foreword to *Totems Not Taboo.* Houston: Univ. of St. Thomas.

———. 1962. Introduction to *The John and Dominique de Menil Collection.* New York: Museum of Primitive Art.

———. 1968a. Foreword to *A Young Teaching Collection.* Houston: Univ. of St. Thomas.

———. 1968b. Introduction to *Jermayne MacAgy: A Life Illustrated by an Exhibition*. Houston: Univ. of St. Thomas.

———. 1971. Address in the Rothko Chapel. February 26. Menil Collection Archives.

———. 1974. Unpublished "'Interview' by Myself." Addressed to Les Levine. Menil Collection Archives.

———. 1976. "Acknowledgements and Perspectives." In *The Image of the Black in Western Art*, vol. 1: *From the Pharaohs to the Fall of the Roman Empire*, ed. Ladislas Bugner, xi. Cambridge, Mass.: Harvard Univ. Press.

———. 1977. Foreword to *Contemplation and Action in World Religions*, ed. Yusuf Ibish and Ileana Marculescu, 7–8. Seattle: Univ. of Washington Press.

———. 1978. "Léger, Our Contemporary," in *Léger: Our Contemporary*. Pp. 6–7. Houston: Institute for the Arts, Rice Univ.

———. 1983. Interview in *The First Show: Painting and Sculpture from Eight Collections, 1940–1980*, ed. Julia Brown and Bridget Johnson, 35–50. Los Angeles: Museum of Contemporary Art; New York: Arts Publisher.

———. 1987. Foreword to *The Menil Collection: A Selection from the Paleolithic to the Modern Era*. New York: Abrams.

———. 1989a. "To Recapture the Voice of Père Couturier." In *Sacred Art*, ed. Dominique de Menil and Pie Duployé, trans. Granger Ryan, 9. Austin: Univ. of Texas Press.

———. 1989b. Biographical note in *Sacred Art*, ed. Dominique de Menil and Pie Duployé, trans. Granger Ryan, 157–159. Austin: Univ. of Texas Press.

Menil, John de, and Dominique de Menil. 1964. "Delight and Dilemma of Collecting." Typed notes for a talk given at the University of St. Thomas, Houston, April 9 (Menil Archives).

Menil Collection. 1987. *The Menil Collection: A Selection from the Paleolithic to the Modern Era*. New York: Abrams.

Message. Kylie. 2007. *New Museums and the Making of a Culture*. New York: Berg.

Meyer, K. E. 1979. *The Art Museum: Power, Money, Ethics*. New York: Morrow.

Middleton, William. 2004. "The House That Rattled Texas Windows." *New York Times*. June 3. http://www.nytimes.com/2004/06/03/garden/03DEME.html?ex=140159 5200&en=0104dbcef9e42997&ei=5007&partner=USERLAND (accessed August 1, 2008).

Miller, R. J. 1964. "Quadragesimo Anno." In *The Catholic Encyclopedia*, 9. New York: McGraw-Hill.

Miyazaki, Hirokazu. 2004. *The Method of Hope: Anthropology, Philosophy, and Fijian Knowledge*. Stanford, Calif.: Stanford Univ. Press.

Miyazaki, Hirokazu, and Annelise Riles. 2004. "Failure as an Endpoint." In *Global Assemblages*, ed. Aihwa Ong and Stephen Collie, 320–331. Oxford: Blackwell.

Modern Textiles and Ornamental Arts of India. 1956. Catalogue of the exhibition, curated by Jermayne MacAgy, August–September. Houston: Contemporary Art Association.

Mounier, Emmanuel. 1951. *Be Not Afraid*. Trans. Cynthia Rowland. London: Rockliff.

Muehlebach, Andrea. 2007. "'The Moral Neoliberal': Welfare State and Ethical Citizenship in Contemporary Italy." PhD diss., Univ. of Chicago.

Musil, Robert. 1955. *Young Törless*. New York: Pantheon.

Myers, Fred. 2004. "Social Agency and the Cultural Value(s) of the Art Object." *Journal of Material Culture* 9, no. 2: 203–211.

Nadelman, Cynthia. 1985. "Broken Premises: 'Primitivism' at MoMA." *ARTnews*, February, 88–95.

Nelson, Laurie. 1994. "'This Kind Of Circus, All In Cordiality': Marcel Duchamp's Speech 'The Creative Act.'" Master's thesis, Rice Univ.

New York Times. 1987. "Alexander Iolas, Ex-Dancer and Surrealist Art Champion." June 12.

Nichols, Aidan. 1990. *From Newman to Congar*. Edinburgh: Clark.

Nord, Philip. 2003. "Catholic Culture in Interwar France." *French Politics, Culture, and Society* 21, no. 3: 1–20.

O'Doherty, Brian. 1986. *Inside the White Cube: The Ideology of Gallery Space*. Santa Monica, Calif.: Lapis.

O'Meara, Thomas. 1997. *Thomas Aquinas, Theologian*. Notre Dame, Ind.: Univ. of Notre Dame Press.

Panofsky, Erwin, ed. 1979. *Abbot Suger: On the Abbey Church of St.-Denis and its Art Treasures*. Princeton, N.J.: Princeton Univ. Press.

Papanikolas, Theresa. 2006a. "Alexander Iolas: The Influence of Magritte's American Dealer." In *Magritte and Contemporary Art: The Treachery of Images*, ed. Stephanie Barron and Michel Draguet, 67–73. Los Angeles: Los Angeles County Museum of Art / Ludion.

———. 2006b. "A Deliberate Accident: Magritte in the Collection of John and Dominique de Menil." In *Magritte and Contemporary Art: The Treachery of Images*, ed. Stephanie Barron and Michel Draguet, 87–93. Los Angeles: Los Angeles County Museum of Art / Ludion.

Pearce, Susan. 1995. *On Collecting: An Investigation into Collecting in the European Tradition*. New York: Routledge.

A Piece of the Moon World: Paul Klee in Texas Collections. 1995. Catalogue for the exhibition, curated by Susan Davidson, Menil Collection, Houston, March 9–June 5.

Piano, Renzo. 1997. *Renzo Piano Logbook*. New York: Monacelli.

Pietz, William. 1985. "The Problem of the Fetish." *RES* 9 (Spring): 5–17.

Pius XI. 1931. *Quadragesimo anno*. Rome: Acta Apostolicae Sedis.

Pomian, Krzysztof. 1990. *Collectors and Curiosities. Paris and Venice, 1500–1800*. Cambridge: Polity Press.

Printz, Neil. 1988. "Machinery of the Menil Collection: Interview with Neil Printz." By Patti Candelari. *Houston Public News*, January 13, 12.

Rabinow, Paul. 1989. *French Modern: Norms and Forms of the Social Environment*. Cambridge, Mass.: MIT Press.

Régamey, Pie-Raymond. 1963. *Religious Art in the Twentieth Century*. New York: Herder and Herder.

Rello, Franco. 1982. "The Vertigo of the Mélange: The Collector's Fight Against Time." *Lotus International* 35: 22–25.

Reynolds, Sarah. 2008. *Houston Reflections: Art in the City, 1950s, '60s, and '70s*. Houston: Rice Univ. Press.

Ricoeur, Paul. 1970. *Freud and Philosophy: An Essay on Interpretation*. New Haven, Conn.: Yale Univ. Press.

Riles, Annelise 2000 *The Network Inside Out*. Ann Arbor: Univ. of Michigan Press.

———. 2006. Introduction to *Documents: Artifacts of Modern Knowledge*, 1–38. Ann Arbor: Univ. of Michigan Press.

La Rime et la Raison: Les Collections Ménil. 1984. Catalogue for the exhibition organized by the Menil Foundation, at the Galeries nationales du Grand Palais, Paris, April 17–July 30.

Ross, Anne. 1987. "A Celtic Head from Roscrea." In *The Menil Collection: A Selection from the Paleolithic to the Modern Era*, 50–59. New York: Abrams.

Ross, Doran. 2003. "African Art at the Museum of Fine Arts, Houston." *African Arts* 36, no. 3 (Autumn): 34–55.

Rothko Chapel. 1979. *Toward a New Strategy for Development*. New York: Pergamon.

Rubin, William S. 1961. *Modern Art and the Church of Assy*. New York: Columbia Univ. Press.

———. 1984. *"Primitivism" in 20th-Century Art: Affinity of the Tribal and the Modern*. New York: Museum of Modern Art.

———. 1985a. Letter to the editor. *Artforum* 23, no. 6 (February): 42–45.

———. 1985b. Letter to the editor. *Artforum* 23, no. 9 (May): 63–65.

Saarinen, Aline B. 1959. *The Proud Possessors*. London: Weidenfeld and Nicolson.

Saenz, Kelly. 1980. *The Rothko Chapel: The Slow Arrow of Beauty*. Master's thesis, Univ. of Texas at Austin.

Salomone, A. William. 1975. Preface to *Mounier and Maritain: A French Catholic Understanding of the Modern World*, by Joseph Amato, viii–xxiii. University: Univ. of Alabama Press.

Sandeen, Eric. 1995. *Picturing an Exhibition: The Family of Man and 1950s America*. Albuquerque: Univ. of New Mexico Press.

Sawin, Martica. 1995. *Surrealism in Exile and the Beginning of the New York School*. Cambridge, Mass.: MIT Press.

Schall, James. 1998. *Jacques Maritain: The Philosopher In Society*. Lanham, Md.: Rowman and Littlefield.

Schapiro, Meyer. 1978. *Modern Art: 19th and 20th Centuries*. New York: Braziller.

Schloesser, Stephen. 2005. *Jazz Age Catholicism: Mystical Modernism in Postwar Paris, 1919–1933*. Toronto: Univ. of Toronto Press.

Schlumberger, Ann Gruner. 1982. *The Schlumberger Adventure*. New York: Arco.

Schmied, Wieland. 1973. "Learning to Rid Oneself of One's Blindness: Max Ernst and Giorgio de Chirico." In *Max Ernst: Inside the Sight*, 19–26. Houston: Rice Univ., Institute for the Arts.

Schwartzwald, Robert. n.d. Introduction to the unpublished English translation of *La Vérité Blessée*, by Marie-Alain Couturier, xxiv. Menil Archives.

———. 1990. "The 'Civic Presence' of Father Marie-Alain Couturier, O.P., in Québec." *Québec Studies* 10 (Spring–Summer): 133–152.

———. 2004. "Father Marie-Alain Couturier, O.P., and the Refutation of Anti-Semitism in Vichy France." In *Textures and Meaning: Thirty Years of Judaic Studies at the University of Massachusetts Amherst*, ed. Leonard Ehrlich, Shmuel Bolozky, Robert Rothstein, Murray Schwartz, Jay Berkovitz, James Young. Published electronically, http://www.umass.edu/judaic/anniversaryvolume/index.html (accessed September 25, 2006).

Sherman, Daniel J. 1989. *Worthy Monuments: Art Museums and the Politics of Culture in Nineteenth-Century France*. Cambridge, Mass.: Harvard Univ. Press.

———, ed. 2007. *Museums and Difference*. Bloomington: Indiana Univ. Press.

Sherman, Daniel J., and Irit Rogoff, eds. 1994. *Museum Culture: Histories, Discourses, Spectacles*. Minneapolis: Univ. of Minnesota Press.

Shkapich, Kim, and Susan de Menil, eds. 2004. *Sanctuary: The Spirit In/Of Architecture*. Houston: Byzantine Fresco Foundation.

Simmel, Georg. 1978. *The Philosophy of Money*. London: Routledge.

Simone, Nina. 2009. "Remembering Harlem's 'Black Woodstock.'" Interview by Guy Raz. *All Things Considered*, National Public Radio. August 15. http://www.npr.org/templates/story/story.php?storyId=111922784 (accessed August 26, 2009).

Smart, Pamela. 1997. "Sacred Modern: An Ethnography of an Art Museum." PhD diss., Rice Univ.

———. 2000. "Art of Transport." *Southern Review* 33, no. 3: 292–307.

———. 2001. "Crafting Aura: Art Museums, Audiences, and Engagement." *Visual Anthropology Review* 16, no. 2 (Fall–Winter): 2–24.

———. 2006. "Possession: Intimate Artifice at the Menil Collection." *Modernism/Modernity* 13, no. 1 (Spring): 19–39.

———. 2010. "Aesthetics as a Vocation." In *Art and Activism: Projects of John and Dominique de Menil*, ed. Laureen Schipsi and Josef Helfenstein, 18–37. New Haven, Conn.: Yale Univ. Press / Menil Collection.

Smith, Jeffrey K., and Lisa F. Wolf. 1996. "Museum Visitor Preferences and Intentions in Constructing Aesthetic Experience." *Poetics* 24:219–238.

Spies, Werner, and Helmut R. Leppien, eds. 2004. *Max Ernst: Oeuvre-Katalog*, vol. 1: *Das graphische Werk*. Houston: Menil Foundation; Cologne: DuMont Schauberg. (Orig. pub. 1975.)

Spies, Werner, Sigrid Metken, and Günter Metken, eds. 1975. *Max Ernst: Oeuvre-Katalog*, vol. 2: *Werke, 1906–1925*. Houston: Menil Foundation; Cologne: DuMont Schauberg.

———. 1976. *Max Ernst: Oeuvre-Katalog*, vol. 3: *Werke, 1925–1929*. Houston: Menil Foundation; Cologne: DuMont Schauberg.

———. 1979. *Max Ernst: Oeuvre-Katalog*, vol. 4: *Werke, 1929–1938*. Houston: Menil Foundation; Cologne: DuMont Schauberg.

———. 1987. *Max Ernst: Oeuvre-Katalog*, vol. 5: *Werke, 1939–1953*. Houston: Menil Foundation; Cologne: DuMont Schauberg.

———. 1998. *Max Ernst: Oeuvre-Katalog*, vol. 6: *Werke, 1954–1963*. Houston: Menil Foundation; Cologne: DuMont Schauberg.

———. 2007. *Max Ernst: Oeuvre-Katalog*, vol. 7: *Werke, 1964–1969*. Houston: Menil Foundation; Cologne: DuMont Schauberg.

Stewart, Susan. 1993. *On Longing: Narratives of the Miniature, the Gigantic, the Souvenir, the Collection*. Durham, N.C.: Duke Univ. Press.

Stocking, George, ed. 1986. *Objects and Others: Essays on Museums and Material Culture*. Madison: Univ. of Wisconsin Press.

Suckale-Redlefsen, Gude. 1987. *The Black Saint Maurice*. Trans. Genoveva Nitz. Houston: Menil Foundation.

Suger. 1979. "The Book of Suger, Abbot of St.-Denis." In *Abbot Suger: On the Abbey Church of St.-Denis and Its Art Treasures*, ed. and trans. Erwin Panofsky, 41–137. Princeton, N.J.: Princeton Univ. Press.

Swan, Simone. 1985. "The Menil Collection." *Ultra*, February, 64–67, 93–94.

Sweeney, James Johnson. 1962a. Records of the Office of the Director, James Johnson Sweeney, Correspondence and Miscellaneous Subjects, 1961–1967. Archives, Museum of Fine Arts, Houston, microfilmed by the Archives of American Art Texas project, Smithsonian Institution. Reel 1580, October 24.

———. 1962b. Records of the Office of the Director, James Johnson Sweeney, Correspondence and Miscellaneous Subjects, 1961–1967. Archives, Museum of Fine Arts, Houston, microfilmed by the Archives of American Art Texas project, Smithsonian Institution. Reel 1580, November 6.

Sylvester, David, and Sarah Whitfield. 1992. *René Magritte: Catalogue Raisonné*, vol. 1: *Oil Paintings, 1916–1930*. Houston: Menil Foundation.

———. 1993. *René Magritte: Catalogue Raisonné*, vol. 2: *Oil Paintings and Objects, 1931–1948*. Houston: Menil Foundation.

Sylvester, David, Sarah Whitfield, and Michael Raeburn. 1997. *René Magritte: Catalogue Raisonné*, vol. 5: *Supplement, Exhibitions Lists, Bibliography, Cumulative Index*. Bibliography by Lynette Cawthra. Houston: Menil Foundation.

Taylor, Charles. 1989. *Sources of the Self: The Making of the Modern Identity*. Cambridge: Cambridge Univ. Press.

Texas Catholic Herald. 1968. November 1.

Thomas, Nicholas. 2001. Introduction to *Beyond Aesthetics: Art and the Technologies of Enchantment*, ed. Christopher Pinney and Nicholas Thomas, 1–12. New York: Berg.

Time. 1949. "Religion: Art for God's Sake." June 20. http://www.time.com/time/printout/0,8816,800402,00.html (accessed July 28, 2007).

———. 1951. "Art: Removal at Assy." April 23. http://www.time.com/time/magazine/article/0,9171,821553,00.html (accessed August 17, 2008).

Tomkins, Calvin. 1980. *Off the Wall: Robert Rauschenberg and the Art World of Our Time*. Garden City, N.Y.: Doubleday.

————. 1991. "A Touch for the Now." *New Yorker*, July 26, 33–57.

————. 1998. "The Benefactor." *New Yorker*, June 8, 52-67.

Touraine, Alain. 1995. *Critique of Modernity*. Cambridge, Mass.: Blackwell.

"The Trojan Horse." 1958. Exhibition curated by Jermayne MacAgy at the Contemporary Art Association, Houston, September–November.

Turner, Gerard. 1985. "The Cabinet of Experimental Philosophy." In *The Origins of Museums: The Cabinet of Curiosities in Sixteenth and Seventeenth Century Europe*, ed. Oliver Impey and Arthur MacGregor, 295–307. Oxford: Clarendon.

Van Dyke, Kristina. 2007. "The Menil Collection: Houston, Texas." *African Arts*, Autumn, 36–49.

Varnedoe, Kirk. 1985a. Letter to the editor. *Artforum* 23, no. 6 (February): 45–46.

————. 1985b. "On the Claims and Critics of the 'Primitivism' Show." *Art in America*, May, 13–21.

Vercoutter, Jean, et al. 1976. *The Image of the Black in Western Art*, vol. 1: *From the Pharaohs to the Fall of the Roman Empire*. Houston: Menil Foundation.

Verhovek, Sam Howe. 1988. "How Houston's Adopted Daughter Said Thank You." *New York Times*, January 20.

Vidler, Anthony. 1987. *The Architectural Uncanny: Essays in the Modern Unhomely*. Cambridge, Mass.: MIT Press.

Weber, Joanna. 1994. Archival register of the Couturier Collection at Yale University.

Weber, Max. 1947. *The Theory of Social and Economic Organization*. Trans. A. M. Henderson and Talcott Parsons. Glencoe, Ill.: Free Press.

————. 1958a. "Religious Rejections of the World and Their Directions." In *From Max Weber: Essays in Sociology*, trans. and ed. Hans Gerth and C. Wright Mills, 323–359. New York: Oxford Univ. Press.

————. 1958b. "The Sociology of Charismatic Authority." In *From Max Weber: Essays in Sociology*, trans. and ed. Hans Gerth and C. Wright Mills, 245–252. New York: Oxford Univ. Press.

Weiner, Annette. 1994. "Cultural Difference and the Density of Objects." *American Ethnologist* 21, no. 2: 391–403.

Welch, Frank. 2000. *Philip Johnson and Texas*. Austin: Univ. of Texas Press.

Welchman, John, ed. 2006. *Institutional Critique and After*. New York: JRP / Ringier.

Werkmeister, Otto Karl. 1991. *Citadel Culture*. Chicago: Univ. of Chicago Press.

Whitfield, Sarah, and Michael Raeburn. 1993. *René Magritte: Catalogue Raisonné*, vol. 3: *Oil Paintings and Objects, 1949–1967*. Houston: Menil Foundation.

————. 1994. *René Magritte: Catalogue Raisonné*, vol. 4: *Gouaches, Temperas, Watercolours, and Papiers Colles, 1918–1967*. Houston: Menil Foundation.

Witcomb, Andrea. 2003. *Re-Imaging the Museum: Beyond the Mausoleum*. New York: Routledge.

Wolfe, Tom. 1970. *Radical Chic and Mau-Mauing the Flak Catchers*. New York: Farrar, Straus and Giroux.

Wolin, Richard. 1994. *Walter Benjamin: An Aesthetic of Redemption*. Berkeley and Los Angeles: Univ. of California Press.

Wood, Peter H., and Karen C. C. Dalton. 1988. *Winslow Homer's Images of Blacks: The Civil War and Reconstruction Years*. Austin: Univ. of Texas Press / Menil Collection.

A Young Teaching Collection. 1968. Catalogue of an exhibition shown at the Museum of Fine Arts, Houston, November 7, 1968–January 12, 1969.

Zolberg, Vera. 1994. "'An Elite Experience for Everyone': Art Museums, the Public, and Cultural Literacy." In *Museum Culture: Histories, Discourses, Spectacles*, ed. Daniel Sherman and Irit Rogoff, 49–65. Minneapolis: Univ. of Minnesota Press.

Index

activism, 7, 63, 221, 222; John and Dominique de Menil's method of, 89,
224–225. *See also* politics
Adorno, Theodor, 159–160, 163, 166, 223
aesthetic disposition, 134, 163, 221; elective cultivation of, 172, 174, 222, 223,
225; privatized character of, 222
aesthetic experience: affective force of,
223, 225; analytic attention to, 12;
anxiety over, 157, 222; and aura, 159;
commodified, 222; conditions of possibility for, 126, 160, 162, 170, 176, 196;
and ethics, 79; longing for, 223; at the
Menil Collection, 13, 163, 196; opposed
to aestheticization, 160, 166; production of, 162; as simulacrum of political
activism, 222; and social reform, 86
aesthetics: anthropology and, 7; bourgeois, 221, 223; critical, 221
African art: collected by the de Menils,
77–78; exhibition of, 235n10
"African Zion: The Sacred Art of Ethiopia" (Intercultura and Walters Art
Gallery), 168–169
Alberigo, Guiseppe, 29
Allaud, Louis, 227n10
Amato, Joseph, 27, 67, 237n2, 238n16
American Association of Museums
(AAM): and accreditation, 10; and bu-
reaucratization of museums, 205; and
codification of "best practices," 13
"Andy Warhol: Three Houston Women"
(The Menil Collection), 194
Aquinas, Thomas, 25, 41
Aramanda, Geri, 195–196
architecture. *See* de Menil, John and Do-
minique: architectural commissions;
museum architecture

Arensberg, Louise and Walter, 74, 237n7
Aristotle, 172, 208
Armstrong, Cameron, 114
art: aesthetic effects of, 179; anthropology
of, 7; demystification of, 169; "difficult," 166–167, 168, 179–180; efficacy
of, 7; and engagement, 7, 13, 158, 168,
170 (*see also* intuition); as history, 12,
13, 78, 140, 144, 245n16; mystification
of, 178; and naturalism, 81–84; ownership of, 141–143; and power, 7; and reality, 81; as redemptive, 67, 92, 128, 161,
166, 220–221; and religion, 220–221; as
restricted field, 168, 179
Art Associates, 64
Art Investments Ltd., 64
artists: African American, 92; Menil Collection regard for, 156, 209; as risk
takers, 85; special qualities of, 83–84,
84–86, 238n15. *See also* faith: of church
artists
art museums, 177–178; and audience,
167, 169, 175 (*see also* publics); "best
practices" of, 13, 205; bureaucratization of, 10, 158, 196, 205; conservatism
of, 18; "democratization" of, 169, 175,
177; directors of, 201; and education,
178–179, 180; elitism of, 169, 177; and
estrangement, 14, 143, 179; and funding, 178; and history of art, 12, 129,
144–145, 243n4, 163, 178; as places of
respite, 18; scholarly attention to, 12
l'Art Sacré, 26, 29, 31–32, 33, 63, 168
artworks: affecting force of, 163; disposition toward, 173, 207; as sovereign, 73,
135, 157, 163; as traces of humanity, 83
Aubry, Eugene, 39, 104, 113, 114–115, 241n11
Auletta, Ken, 227n10

aura, 59, 132, 163; and cult of the artist, 156; debate over, 159–160

Badner, Mino, 98, 210
Bakke, Julie, 188
Barker, Tom, 117
Barnes, Alfred, 127
Barnes, Marguerite, 111
Barnes, Susan, 29, 213, 214
Barnes Foundation, 13, 133
Barnstone, Howard, 39, 52, 104, 113–115, 120, 235n4
Battaglia, Debbora, 131, 133
Baudelaire, Charles, 85, 238n16, 172
Baudrillard, Jean, 127, 129
Bazaine, Jean, 35
Benjamin, Walter, 135, 138, 139, 140, 159–160
Bergson, Henri: Maritain influenced by, 25; Maritain's opposition to, 229n11. *See also* intuition
Black Arts Center, 93
Black Panthers, 91, 239n4, 218
Bloch, Ernst, 224
Blue, James, 106
Bonnard, Pierre, 33, 34
Born, Georgina, 192, 214–215
Bourdieu, Pierre, 133–134, 244n8, 168, 173, 178, 221
Bowker, Geoffrey, 227n10
Boym, Svetlana, 227n5
Braddock, Jeremy, 127
Braden, Father Patrick, 100
Bradley, Eric, 135
Bradley, Peter, 92–93
Brauner, Victor, 74, 75, 76
Brecht, Bertold, 159
Brown Foundation, 201, 248n1
Bugner, Ladislas, 95, 218
bureaucratization: of museums, 10, 13, 158, 196, 205; and professionalization, 59; and strategic plans, 193, 224

Byzantine Fresco Chapel, 6, 119; acquisition of frescoes by, 135–138; Foundation, 227n2

Callery, Mary, 111
Camfield, Ginny, 64
Camfield, William, 64, 98, 218
Camille, Michael, 220, 221
care: and careful disposition, 151, 157, 207; exemplary, 124, 126; metaphysics of, 221; of objects, 79, 138, 151; practice of, 157, 162, 214
Carlebach, Julius, 77
Carpenter, Edmund, 95, 106
Catholic avant-garde. See *renouveau catholique*
Catholicism: as against modernity, 9, 22, 219; conversion to, 24, 228n5, 228–229n8, 229n10; cultural, 24–26; French, 22, 23, 228n6, 82; and rapprochement with contemporary life, 23; Ultramontanist, 23, 228n3; World War I and, 23, 24. See also *renouveau catholique*
Catholic revivalism. See *renouveau catholique*
Catholic Social Doctrine, 233–234n36
Centre Pompidou, 116, 241n13, 194
Centro Intercultural de Documentación, 96
Cézanne, Paul, 82; *Montagne*, 70
Chagall, Marc, 33, 35
"Chance Encounters: The Formation of the de Menils' African Collection" (The Menil Collection), 195
Chapelle de Notre-Dame-du-Haut, in Ronchamp (Ronchamp Chapel). *See* Le Corbusier
Chapelle du Rosaire, in Vence (Vence Chapel or Matisse Chapel), 33, 35, 38
Children's Storefront, 96
de Chirico, Giorgio, 75, 76; *Hector and*

Andromache, 75; *Metaphysical Interior With Biscuits*, 75, 237n8
Clifford, James, 17, 76, 128
collecting: and agency, 130; as conservative, 130; counter-model of, 130; for exhibitions, 61; as flight from world, 130; as interior process, 127; John and Dominique de Menil's method of, 73–74, 128; orthodoxy on, 128, 130; and passion, 244n14; personal, 19–20, 126, 127; and redemption of objects, 134; scholarship on, 69; and self-formation, 19–20, 127, 128
collections: and agency, 131; eclectic, 128–129; encyclopedic, 129; integrity of, 127, 213; orthodox rendering of, 129–130; personal, 140; public, 140; and self-constitution, 133; as surrogates, 130, 243n6, 213–214
collectors: counter-model of, 134–138; in struggle against dispersion, 135–136
commodification: of aesthetic experience, 222; of relationships, 138
Congar, Yves: contemporary orientation of, 22, 42; ecumenicism of, 29, 40, 41, 42; and history, 21, 41–42; influence of, on John and Dominique de Menil, 21–23, 40; and rebuke from Vatican, 41, 42; and Thomas Aquinas, 41–42; and Vatican II, 42, 234n38
conservation: authority of, 158; and economy of care, 154, 157; Mellon Foundation project, 155–156; Menil collection commitment to, 154–156, 246n2; and permanence, 157; and professional codes of practice, 158, 207–208; and Rothko project, 155; in tension with accessibility of objects, 205–208
contemplation, linked to action, 28, 40, 130, 220
Contemporary Art Association (CAA) (now Contemporary Art Museum):

local commitments of, 59; and de Menil involvement, 51, 54, 56; schism within, 50–51, 54
Council of Trent, 31, 82
Couturier, Marie-Alain, 101, 160; church and chapel commissions, 21, 33–35, 36, 110, 166; critique of Catholic art and architecture, 30–35, 82; on Houston, 46–47; influence of, on John and Dominique de Menil, 21–23, 70–72; and intimacy with art, 62–63; and malaise of Catholic sensibility, 32, 238n14; on "native arts," 83–85; in New York, 70; and non-figurative art, 35; position of, on faith of artists, 33–35, 230–231n19, 231nn20–22; privileging of poetry over pedagogy by, 227n8, 63, 168; and relationships with artists, 34; on Renaissance, 84–85, 238n14; and *Sacred Art*, 25–26; and "universal humanism," 84. *See also* l'Art Sacré
Crimp, Douglas, 144, 156
Cuno, James, 17

Da Camara, 120, 242n18
Dalton, Karen, 95
Davezac, Bertrand, 114, 129, 135–136, 188, 248n3
Davidson, Chandler, 97
Davidson, Susan, 1, 2, 188
"The DeLuxe Show," 90–93, 110
Dia Foundation, 99, 242n17
Dimetrion, James, 189
distinction: aesthetic disposition as sign of, 221; art and, 7; of Dominique de Menil, 132; museums and, 12, 16; Pierre Bourdieu on, 133–134, 173, 221
Domenach, Jean-Marie, 228n4
Dominican Order: and church and chapel commissions, 33–35; Vatican objections to, 33–34; and worker-priest movement, 234n37. *See also* Congar,

Yves; Couturier, Marie-Alain; sacred art movement
Drutt, Matthew, 188, 190
Dubin, Steven, 17–18
Duchamp, Marcel, 74, 75, 76, 98
Duncan, Carol, 221–222

education: art historical, 178–179, 180; museum, 170; and school board politics, 96; and social reform, 100; and student scholarships, 96, 239–240n11. *See also* Rice University; University of St. Thomas
Ein Harod Museum, 122, 241n14
Ernst, Max, 67, 68–69, 74, 77, 160; in the Menil Collection, 69, 76; *Portrait of Dominique*, 67, 191; on surrealism, 76
ethical citizenship, 89, 176, 223
ethics: and ethical disposition, 180, 222; as exercise of judgment, 158, 208; as opposed to proceduralism, 172, 208–209, 224; of practice, 118, 172, 224
exhibition: communicative practices of, 183–184; and curation and installation, 1–5, 51, 56, 59–61, 142, 145, 151, 160–166, 169, 247n8, 208–210, 211; interpretive text for, 168, 169; and juxtaposition, 165, 168; labeling, 4; mass appeal of, 167; niche markets for, 167; object of, 163, 184; as seduction, 61, 156; single-artist, 211; and task of viewer, 61, 160; visceral response to, 63
experience: affective, 179, 223; commodified, 222–223; and experiential intensity, 222, 223; flattening of, 13–14, 30, 86, 180

faith: and church architecture and art, 30–35; of church artists, 33–35, 230–231nn19–22; contemporary plausibility of, 219; relevance of, in modern life, 22–23, 26

Faubion, James: and ethics, 172, 208; on hermeneutics of suspicion, 16–17; and the signature, 133
Ferraro, Thomas, 9, 228n8
Ferus Gallery, 198, 249n12
Fisher, Philip, 243n23, 144, 245n16, 246nn19–20, 157
Fitzgerald, Richard, 117
Flahiff, Reverend George Bernard, 160–161, 162, 247n7
Flavin, Dan, 6, 119–120
"For Children" (Rice Museum), 205–207
Foster, Hal, 76
Foucault, Michel, 172
Fox, Stephen, 235n4, 97, 111, 117, 118, 120, 242n22, 245n18, 151
Freedberg, David, 82
Frick Collection, 133
Fried, Michael, 122
Friedrich, Heiner, 99
"From Gauguin to Gorky" (MFAH), 52

Gehry, Frank, 116
Gell, Alfred, 7
Gibbs, Julie, 214
Glaser, Miles, 241n5, 187, 218
Grand Palais, Paris, 108
"Gray Is the Color" (Rice Museum), 120
Greenberg, Clement, 92, 245n16, 168
Greenblatt, Steven, 12
Guggenheim, Peggy, 54, 236n13, 74

habitus: Aristotelian, 173–174; Bourdieu on, 173, 174, 221
d'Harconcourt, René, 53
Haxthausen, Mark, 99
Hazlitt, William, 126–127, 243n1
Heizer, Michael, 141
Helfenstein, Josef, 192, 202; and Menil Collection legacy, 9–12, 192–193. *See also* legacy
hermeneutics of suspicion, 16–17, 18, 19, 89

Hervieu-Léger, Daniele, 220
High Museum of Art, 187–188, 192
Hines, Gerald, 113
Hogg, Ima, 2
Holdengräber, Paul, 135, 138
Holmes, Ann, 51, 54, 90, 131
Holmes, Douglas, 225
hope, as method, 88, 224, 225
Hopps, Walter, 6, 9, 114, 141, 245n17, 155, 188, 202, 204, 212, 214, 248n3, 249n13; and artists, 154, 165, 247n10, 199; audience and, 167; and care of the object, 154, 155, 245n17; and Corcoran Gallery, 198–199; as director of the Menil Collection, 116, 197–198, 199–201; and exhibition curation and installation, 56, 142, 145, 146, 151, 163, 164–165, 247n8, 211; and the Ferus Gallery, 198; and labeling, 5; and museum design, 6, 117, 241n15, 122, 158; and Washington Gallery of Modern Art (WGMA), 198
Houston, 58; American Federation of the Arts convention in, 65, 96–97; contemporary art in, 63, 236–237n21; as cultural desert, 47, 49; early institutional landscape of, 50–59; International Style architecture in, 111; John and Dominique de Menil's public profile in, 48; de Menil cultivation of, 49–50, 64–65, 66; de Menil promotion of, 65–66; Philip Johnson's impact on, 113; race politics in, 90–91, 93
Hughes, Fred, 99, 240n12
Hughes, Robert, 6, 118
Hulten, Pontus, 103, 108, 116, 122
Hunter, Fredericka, 114

Illich, Ivan, 96
Image of the Black in Western Art, 94–95
"Imaginary Spaces: Selections from the Menil Collection" (Menil Collection), 195

Ingersoll, Richard, 120–121, 149
integral humanism, 8, 41, 43–44, 167. See also integral humanism; Maritain, Jacques
intimacy: afforded by teaching collections, 62–63, 143, 205; artifice of, 126, 143, 147; crafting of, 145; of possession, 126
intuition: Bergsonian, 25, 168, 169; for Couturier, 26, 168; for Dominique de Menil, 25, 26, 79, 135, 169; Maritain on, 25, 229n11; as opposed to intellect, 229n10; "practical," 172
Iolas, Alexander, 57, 236n13, 75–76, 77, 99; and Alexander Iolas Gallery, 57; and Hugo Gallery, 77; and surrealism, 75
Isabella Stewart Gardner Museum, 13, 133
"Islands Beyond" (University of St. Thomas), 160–161

James, Charles, 112, 241n9
Jay, Martin, 222, 223
"The John and Dominique de Menil Collection" (Museum of Primitive Art, NY), 79–80
John XXIII, Pope: and Congar, 42; de Menil support of, 23; principle of subsidiarity, 233–234n36; Rothko Chapel as tribute to, 28–29
Johnson, Philip, 65; and Amon Carter Museum of Western Art, 113; and Art Museum of South Texas, 113; echo of, in the Menil Collection, 245n18; and Jane Blaffer Owen commission, 236n20; and de Menil residence, 111–112, 190; parish church proposal of, 36, 110–111; and Rothko Chapel, 38–40, 111, 122; and Schlumberger-Doll Research Center, 112–113; and Seagram building, 38; and University of St. Thomas commission, 37, 111, 113

Kadish, Mary, 138

Kahn, Louis, 107–110, 147, 148
Kant, Emmanuel, 168, 223
Karp, Ivan, 12, 18
Katsiff, Bruce, 245n15
Kaufman, Jason Edward, 117
Kaufman, Robert, 159
Kilian, Karl, 99, 240n13
Kimbell Art Museum, Fort Worth, 122
Kirschenblatt-Gimblett, Barbara, 222
Klee, Paul, 1; collected by John and
    Dominique de Menil, 2; exhibitions
    of, 1–4, 227n1, 66, 124, 160; in Menil
    Collection, 2; and Paul Klee Founda-
    tion, 192
Klejman, John J., 77–78
Kratz, Corinne, 18

Lavine, Steven, 12
Law, Caroline Wiess, 194
Leavitt, Thomas, 187
Le Corbusier, 21, 34, 231n24; and
    Chapelle de Notre-Dame-du-Haut, in
    Ronchamp, 21, 33, 35; and Sainte Ma-
    rie de la Tourette, 35
legacy: definition of, as problematic,
    9–12, 192–193, 223–225; experimental
    character of, 14, 184, 185; future-ori-
    ented, 9, 12, 14, 184; institutionaliza-
    tion of, 184–186, 193, 202; museum as,
    89–90; unrestricted by Dominique de
    Menil, 13, 14, 185
Léger, Fernand, 21, 160; church commis-
    sions of, 33, 34, 35, 231n24
Leland, Mickey, 90, 96, 218
Leo XIII, Pope, 22, 233–234n36
Levi-Strauss, Claude, 46
Lila Wallace-Reader's Digest Foundation,
    178
Lipchitz, Jacob, church commissions of,
    33, 35, 230–231n19
Lomax, Alan, 95
Louchheim, Aline, 50–51

Loud, Patricia, 109
Love, Jim, 74, 118, 218
Lowry, Glenn, 18
Lukács, Georg, 8, 159
Lunning, Liz, 188
Lurçat, Jean, 34

MacAgy, Jermayne, 4, 99, 194; affinity of,
    with Dominique de Menil, 59; exhibi-
    tions for MFAH by, 52; facility of, for
    exhibition, 51, 59–61, 145, 156, 161–162,
    163, 165; at University of St. Thomas,
    4, 5, 37, 38, 59, 97, 104, 160
MacDonald, Sharon, 17
MacDougall, David, 106
MacGregor, Neil, 18
"The Machine as Seen at the End of the
    Mechanical Age" (MOMA), 103–104
Magritte, René, 64, 74, 75, 76, 77, 99, 120,
    160
Mahler, Margaret, 95
Mahmood, Saba, 173, 174
Maleuvre, Didier, 139, 141–143
Malone, Lee, 53
Malraux, André, 246n20
Mancusi-Ungaro, Carol, 154–157, 188, 199,
    206–207
Marandel, Patrice, 120
Maritain, Jacques: against realism, 82–83;
    on Charles Baudelaire, 238n16; con-
    version of, to Catholicism, 228n5,
    229n10, 67; doctrinal problem of,
    24–25; on efficacy of modern art, 82;
    on faith of artists, 231nn21–22; integral
    humanism of, 8, 27–28, 229n12, 84,
    167; political philosophy of, 86; and
    reworking of Thomas Aquinas, 25, 41;
    temporal orientation of, 24
Maritain, Raïssa, 24, 228n5, 70
Martin, Maurice, 227n10
Marzio, Peter, 185
Masters Children's Center, 95

Matisse, Henri, 21, 34, 35, 83
"Matisse chapel," 33. *See also* Chapelle du
    Rosaire, in Vence
Maurras, Charles, 228n6
"Max Ernst: Inside the Sight" (Rice Mu-
    seum), 109
McCarty, Mark, 106
McClellan, Andrew, 116
McConathy, Steve, 124, 243n25
McEvilley, Thomas, 98
Mengelberg, Willem, 164
de Menil, Adelaide, 15, 36, 95
de Menil, Christophe, 15, 191
de Menil, Dominique: charismatic
    authority of, 14, 97, 115, 202, 222; as
    collector, 134–138; conversion of, to
    Catholicism, 68; disposition of, 101;
    and exhibition installation, 1–5, 61–63,
    160, 163; as experimentalist, 16; as
    figure, 227–228n11; integral humanism
    of, 210; and intuition, 25, 26, 79, 135,
    169; loyalty to, 10; as pious, 132, 171;
    on possession, 125, 126; on "primitive"
    art, 79–80, 210; Protestant upbringing
    of, 72; significance of Byzantine art to,
    80; writings of, 194
de Menil, François, 115, 119, 136–137, 218
de Menil, Georges, 15
de Menil, John: background of, 48–49;
    death of, 110, 184, 216; disposition of,
    47, 101; as exemplar, 101, 217; funeral
    arrangements for, 216–219; on Hous-
    ton, 47; Howard Barnstone on, 235n4;
    Morton Feldman on, 47; position of,
    on church architecture, 36–37; re-
    search of, on acquisitions, 78, 138; and
    Schlumberger, 14–15, 185; tribute to, 28
de Menil, John and Dominique: activist
    agendas of, 19, 221; aesthetic conver-
    sion of, 67–68; architectural com-
    missions of, 36, 37–38, 97, 103–104,
    107, 108–110, 111–112, 231n25 (*see also*

Menil Collection: architecture; Renzo
    Piano; Rothko Chapel: design of);
    civic commitments of, 49–50, 65–66;
    collection of, 69, 73, 76, 79, 108; as col-
    lectors, 70–81; ecumenicism of, 41; as
    exemplars, 110, 171; and experts, 76–
    77, 78–79; as future-oriented experi-
    mentalists, 14–16, 19, 26, 45; influence
    of Congar on, 21–22, 41; influence of
    Couturier on, 21–22, 70–72; and Max
    Ernst commission, 67, 68–69; method
    of, 26, 45, 89, 224–225; as off-modern,
    69; as overbearing, 59, 100; as patrons,
    50, 66, 88, 102–103, 214; personalist
    approach of, 88; public profile of, 48;
    relationships of, with artists, 34, 74;
    as "remarkables," 76–77, 85, 101, 115,
    241n9, 198; representations of, 131–132;
    and social justice projects, 41, 44–45,
    89, 90, 94; and University of St.
    Thomas, 4, 37–38. *See also* University
    of St. Thomas
de Menil, Philippa, 99, 185, 218
"Menil aesthetic": analysis of, 11–12; con-
    formity to, 172–173; crafting of, 14, 118,
    143, 158; and exemplary care, 124 (*see
    also* care); maintenance of, 196, 213,
    214, 224, 225; principle of, 168
Menil Collection, 5–6, 76, 79, 129, 130–131;
    and architecture, 116–124, 143–144;
    and archive, 10, 193–196, 224; and
    audience, 167–168, 175–176, 181–184;
    as avant-garde, 247n4, 215; Byzantine
    and medieval art in, 79–80, 135–136; as
    counter-model to museum orthodoxy,
    19–20, 193, 221; crafting of intimacy
    in, 126, 176 (*see also* intimacy); as
    didactic, 170–171; Dominique de
    Menil's motivation for, 13; donors to,
    141, 245n17; as elitist, 168, 205; ethic
    of practice in, 118, 158, 205, 208–209;
    exceptionalism of, 209; as exemplary,

167, 170–171, 212, 214; and experimentation, 14, 81, 116, 224–225; information within, 10–12, 204; institutional
crisis at, 186–190, 191–193; and light,
122–123, 242nn21–22, 245–246n18;
management of, 99, 189, 197–202, 204,
215; membership to, 182, 183; and "the
Menil way," 158, 169, 172–173, 191–192,
209, 212; neighborhood of, 118–121,
242n18; as off-modern, 9, 80–81,
184, 224–225; as place of work, 158;
preliminary research and planning
for, 115–116; "primitive" art in, 77–78,
79–80; procedural regularization of,
184, 189, 203, 213–215; as project of remediation, 8, 127, 166, 184; relationship
of, with public, 118, 165, 169, 170; and
Richmond Hall, 119–120; and self-formation, 20; singular vision of, 140, 141;
spatial organization of, 143–144, 145,
245n18, 204, 212; surrealism in, 76; and
"treasure house," 149–151, 152, 246n1;
and Twombly Gallery, 6, 118–119, 165,
242n17. See also exhibition; legacy;
"Menil aesthetic"
Menil Collection personnel: atomization
of, 204, 212; attrition among, 188–190;
hiring practices for, 184, 196–197,
202–203; investment of, in Menil Collection, 162; layoffs of, 196–197, 212,
213–214; and privilege, 212–213; and
work as vocation, 204–205, 249n18
Menil Foundation, 14, 45, 140; commitments of, 87–89; Dominique de Menil
on, 87–88; duty of, 177; endowment
of, 184, 187, 200–201, 213–214; formalization of, 184, 189; John de Menil
on, 88; objectives of, 240n2, 184–185;
projects of, 88–89
Menil residence, 97, 111–112, 190–191, 214
Menil signature. See "Menil aesthetic"
Message, Kylie, 17–18

Michener, James A., 139–140, 244–
245nn14–15
Mies van der Rohe, Ludwig, 38, 54, 55, 65,
236n15, 111
Miyazaki, Hirokazu, 88, 224–225
modern art: and the Church, 82; cultivation of, 63; and the ineffable, 25, 81, 82
modernity: attitude of, 172; Catholic
condemnation of, 9, 22, 228n1, 219;
Charles Baudelaire on, 172; critical
tradition within, 19; critique of, 8; and
European social and political crisis,
26–28; experiential impoverishment
of, 13–14; and faith, 9, 24–25; rehabilitation of, 8. See also off-modern
"A Modern Patronage: De Menil Gifts to
American and European Museums"
(Menil Collection), 194
de Montebello, Philippe, 18, 58–59, 100,
101
Montvalon, Robert de, 228n4
Mounier, Emmanuel, 8; personalism,
27–28, 229–230n12
Murphy, Father John, 104
Murray, Richard, 90
Museum: consultants, 10, 12, 193; early de
Menil conceptualization of, 107–110,
148; and fatigue, 143; storage at, 109,
148–149. See also Menil Collection:
and "treasure house"
museum architecture: "conservative" opposed to "expressive," 116; monumentality of, 120–121; and the problem of
light, 122–123
Museum of Fine Arts, Houston (MFAH),
2, 51–59, 61, 65; bureaucratic structure
of, 204; crowds at, 179; and Cullinan Hall, 52, 54, 236nn14–15; James
Johnson Sweeney's ambition for, 56;
and Jean Tinguely's acquisitions, 57;
local commitments of, 59; de Menil
involvement in, 2, 53, 54–59, 100, 194;

and modern art, 53, 58; and Modern Art Committee, 51–52; and outreach, 178; professionalization of, 53–54, 58–59

Museum of Modern Art, 111, 194

museums: authority of, 222; "best practices" in, 13; bureaucratization of, 10, 158; critical attention to, 12, 16–19, 222; cynicism of, 167; "democratization" of, 169, 177; as didactic, 170; donor-built, 6, 127, 130–131, 133, 140; and hermeneutics of suspicion, 16–17, 18, 19, 89; house, 147; and identification, 180–181, 221–222; institutional vitality of, 176; interpretive assistance in, 169; and self-constitution, 131; as sites of critical experimentation, 17–18; as therapeutic, 227n6. *See also* art museums

Musil, Robert, 138

Myers, Fred, 7

Newman, Barnett, *Broken Obelisk*, 40, 232–233n34, 108, 118

Nord, Philip, 33, 85

nostalgia, 19, 22, 80, 191, 203, 205, 212–213

Notre-Dame de Toute Grâce of Assy, 33; and contemporary artists, 34–35; Richier crucifix for, 230n18

off-modern: defined, 9, 227n5; Jacques Maritain as, 24; de Menil collecting as, 80–81; *renouveau catholique* as, 23; surrealism as, 80–81; temporal ambivalence of, 23; theological argument for, 25

O'Gorman, Neal, 95–96

O'Grady, Gerald, 106

oil industry, 14, 15. *See also* Schlumberger

Oliver-Smith, Philip, 98

Ove Arup and Partners, 117

Panofsky, Erwin, 102–103

patronage, 89, 102–103

"Paul Gauguin: His Place in the Meeting of East and West" (MFAH), 53

"Paul Klee" (MFAH), 52

Pellizi, Francesco, 108, 218

personalism, 8, 27–28, 88. *See also* Mounier, Emmanuel

Piano, Renzo, 5, 116, 124, 158; and Centre Pompidou, 116, 241n13; and collaboration, 117; experimental practice of, 117, 123; selection of, for the Menil Collection, 117. *See also* Menil Collection: and architecture; Menil Collection: and light

"A Piece of the Moon World: Paul Klee in Texas Collections" (Menil Collection), 2

Pius IX, Pope, 9, 227n4, 233–234n36; "Syllabus of Errors," 22, 219

Pius X, Pope, 228n1; "Oath Against Modernism," 22, 219

politics: aesthetics as simulacrum of, 222; of identification, 180–181; of practice, 89; of privatized dispositions, 222; of publics, 180–181; real, 89, 222; school board, 90, 96; symbolic, 97. *See also* race

possession: density of, 139; intimacy of, 143; and personhood, 128–129; reenchantment through, 139; vicarious, 126–127, 147

"primitive" art: in art museums, 52–53, 235n10; Dominique de Menil on, 79–80; in Menil Collection, 77–78, 79–80; in "Totems not Taboo," 52

"'Primitivism' in 20th Century Art: Affinity of the Tribal and the Modern" (MOMA), 53, 235n11

Print Club, 64

publics, 176, 177; as markets, 167, 180;

mass, 167, 180; pluralistic, 181; "under-represented," 180
Purington, Winfrey, 181–182

race, 90–93, 94–95, 96–97, 210
"Raid the Icebox with Andy Warhol" (RISD), 105
Rauschenberg, Robert, 74, 165
Rayssiguier, Louis-Bertrand, 35
reality, access to, 81–83
Régamey, Pie-Raymond, 26, 31, 63
religion: art and, 220, 221; as compensatory, 219; and contemporary religiosity, 221; as oriented to the past, 219
renouveau catholique, 8–9; and artists, 85, 238n15; conditions of possibility for, 23, 228n4; and French intellectuals, 24; influence of, on John and Dominique de Menil, 37, 45, 223, 224; as lay movement, 230n15; and modern art, 25; as off-modern, 23; as project of desecularization, 29; and rapprochement between eternal and contemporary, 81–83; social and political theory of, 27–28, 220. See also Congar, Yves; Couturier, Marie-Alain; sacred art movement
Rice, Peter, 117
Rice University, 102–106, 110; Institute for the Arts at, 103, 106, 108, 114; and Louis Kahn commission, 107–108; Rice Media Center at, 104, 106, 114; Rice Museum (Art Barn) at, 103–104, 109, 203–204; Sewall Art Gallery at, 104, 240n15, 107
Ricier, Germaine, 230n18
Ricoeur, Paul, 16
Rifkin, Ned, 187–188, 189, 192, 201, 248n3
"La Rime et la Raison" (Grand Palais, Paris), 108, 116, 240n3, 149, 200
Rogers, Richard, 116
Ross, David, 242n21

Ross, Doran, 54
Rossellini, Roberto, 106, 218
Rothko, Mark, 160; and chapel commission, 38–40, 45; and design of Rothko Chapel, 39–40, 122, 242n20; and Seagram Building commission, 232n30. See also conservation: Rothko project
Rothko Chapel, 6, 38–45; aesthetic effects of, 110; Award, 44; and Carter-Menil Human Rights Peace Prize, 44–45; and "Christianity and Churches on the Eve of Vatican II," 44, 230n14, 234n40; colloquia and symposia at, 43–44; dedication of, 21; design of, 38–40, 232n32; ecumenicism of, 29, 40, 42–44; influence of Vatican II on, 29, 40; and Institute for Religion and Human Development, Houston, 40; Mark Rothko commission for, 6, 38–40; mission of, 29; and Oscar Romero Award, 44; Philip Johnson's withdrawal from, 39, 114; problem of light in, 39, 114, 116, 122, 242n20, 197; shaped by renouveau catholique, 29, 43–44; as site of spiritual and political activism, 29; social justice projects of, 29, 44–45; and social reform, 44–45; "Traditional Modes of Contemplation and Action," 28–29, 44
Rouault, Georges, church commissions, 33, 34
Rubin, William, 31

Sacré Couer of Audincourt, 33; non-naturalist iconography for, 35
sacred art and architecture: and bourgeois taste, 83; contemporary, 36; decadence of, 82–83; and faith of artists, 33–35; John de Menil's position on, 36–37; non-naturalist, 35; and Renaissance, 82–83, 84; and Tridentine proscriptions, 82

sacred art movement: and church art and architecture, 33–35; and Council of Trent, 31; and critique of academicism, 31, 82; intent of founders of, 33; and Maritain, 31; on modernity, 82–83. *See also* l'Art Sacré; Couturier, Marie-Alain; Régamey, Pie-Raymond

Sarofim, Louisa, 175, 176, 177, 184, 187, 189, 248n1

Schall, James, 238n15

Schapiro, Meyer, 245n16

Schloesser, Stephen, 8–9, 227n5; on Maritain, 24, 82, 83; and *renouveau catholique*, 23, 24, 229n9

Schlumberger, 14–15, 46, 234n1, 111, 112, 185, 200; commitment to experimentation of, 15–16

Schlumberger, Ann Gruner, 227n10, 101

Schlumberger, Conrad, 14–15, 48

Schlumberger, Marcel, 14–15, 48

Schlumberger, Pierre-Marcel, 218

Schwartzwald, Robert, 32, 237n3, 101

"Seventy-five Years of Sculpture" (MFAH), 53

SHAPE, Inc. (Self Help to African People Through Education), 96

Sherman, Daniel, 17

Simmel, Georg, 244n14

Sirmans, Franklin, 210

social reform: collection as agent of, 128; and education, 100; through reform of sensibilities, 86, 88, 225

Solomon R. Guggenheim Museum, 144, 246n20, 188

"Some American History" (Rice Museum), 92

Southwest Alternate Media Project (SWAMP), 106, 120

Spies, Werner, 77

Steen, William, 3–4, 188

Steichen, Edward, 239n7

Stern & Bucek Architects, 190–191

stewardship, 139

Stirling, James, 144

Suger of St. Denis, Abbot, 102–103

surrealism, 75–76

Swan, Simone, 114, 241n5

Sweeney, James Johnson, 65, 236n13, 100, 101; as director of MFAH, 55–59; and exhibition design, 56, 163; de Menil support of, 55; at Solomon R. Guggenheim Museum, 54

Sylvester, David, 76–77

Szwaja, Lynn, 18

Taylor, Charles, 85–86, 138

Taylor, Julie, 243n7

Texas Southern University, 96

Thomas, Nicholas, 7

Tinguely, Jean, 57–58

Todd, Anderson, 48

Tomkins, Calvin, 164

"Totems Not Taboo" (MFAH), 52

Twombly, Cy, 74, 118–119, 165. *See also* Menil Collection: Twombly Gallery

University of St. Thomas, 65, 108; architectural plans for, 37; art and art history program at, 4, 37–38; de Menil patronage of, 4, 37–38, 59, 97–100, 103, 104; public programs of, 64; teaching collection of, 59, 61–62, 205

Van Dyke, Kristina, 194–195, 210

Vatican II: and Congar, 42, 234n38; and Instituto per le Scienze Religiose of Bologna, 29; de Menil support for, 29; tribute to, 28–29

Velders, Deborah, 189, 248n3

Veneziano, Domenico, *St. John in the Desert*, 125

Vidler, Anthony, 170

Walsh, John, 18

Warhol, Andy, 98, 99, 105, 240n12

Weber, Max, 8, 244n8, 220–221

Weiner, Annette, 227n3, 79

Welch, Frank, 47, 111

Welchman, John, 17

White, Michelle, 149

Widrig, Walter, 98

Winckelmann, Johann, 246n19

Winkler, Helen, 99, 241n5

Winkler, Paul, 1, 2, 99, 117, 141, 210, 214; and conservation, 154, 155, 208; and continuity with Dominique de Menil, 186, 188, 191; and director as curator, 201–202; and exhibition installation, 163, 169, 208–210; resignation of, from the Menil Collection, 186–187, 188, 193; and Twombly Gallery, 165, 249n14, 202

Witcomb, Andrea, 17–18

Wood, James, 18

Writers in the Schools, Program (WITS), 170, 247–248n13, 183

Ybarra-Fausto, Tomás, 18

Young, Colin, 106

Young, Larry, 1, 243n25

Young Teaching Collection, 59, 61

"A Young Teaching Collection" (MFAH), 61–62

Zolberg, Vera, 177–178, 179

www.ingramcontent.com/pod-product-compliance
Lightning Source LLC
Chambersburg PA
CBHW061338280526
45784CB00001B/52